Further Praise for *A Religious History of America:*

A Religious History of America

A RELIGIOUS HISTORY OF AMERICA
New Revised Edition

EDWIN SCOTT GAUSTAD

1817

Harper & Row, Publishers, San Francisco
New York, Grand Rapids, Philadelphia, St. Louis
London, Singapore, Sydney, Tokyo, Toronto

Library of Congress Cataloging-in-Publication Data

Gaustad, Edwin Scott.
    A religious history of America / Edwin Scott Gaustad. —
New rev. ed.
        p.   cm.
    Includes bibliographical references.
    ISBN 0-06-063092-2. — ISBN 0-06-063094-9 (pbk.)
    1. United States—Church history.   I. Title.
BR515.G3   1990
291'.0973—dc20   89-45746
                                                         CIP

90 91 92 93 94 HAD 10 9 8 7 6 5 4 3 2 1

This edition is printed on acid-free paper which meets the
American National Standards Institute Z39.48 Standard.

For Susan, Scott, and Peggy — as before.
But now also, for Mimi, Layna, and Evan;
for Stuart and Liliana.

Contents

Preface

The first version of this book was published almost a quarter of a century ago. So much has happened to American religion (and to the historiography of American religion) since that time that it was more appropriate to thoroughly rework the book than merely to revise it. Accordingly, a great deal of new material has been incorporated, and not just in connection with events of the last twenty-five years.

Other significant changes have likewise been introduced. Instead of setting block quotations off by themselves, the words of the actual participants in the making of America's religious history have been woven into the text. Less interrupting to the eye, this helps the story itself to unfold more smoothly. Furthermore, a chronological frame is pursued throughout, rather than resorting in Parts Four and Five to a largely topical principle of organization. While a history is never without its themes, those themes now move in step with calendar and clock.

The basic purpose of the book, however, remains the same: namely, to portray the role of religion in all stages of this country's development—from the moment that America was only a gleam in the eye of an Italian sailor to the full-blown and often bewildering present. Religion was a powerful motive in exploration, a significant causal factor in much colonization, a partner in territorial expansion and national cohesion, both a critic and an ally in the transition to "empire," and, finally, a veritable whirlwind of energies and contrary forces in the latter half of the twentieth century. What religion will offer and what new forms it will take as the United States enters a new millennium is, of course, impossible to say. A careful study of the past will, however, make the novelties of the year 2000—whatever they may be—less intimidating, less confounding. As Mark Twain observed, even though history doesn't repeat itself, it does rhyme.

Edwin Scott Gaustad

Riverside, California
Winter, 1989–90

Illustration List

Chapter 1
1. Early English settler, John White, portrayed the manner in which the East Coast Indians hollowed out a tree trunk in making a boat.

Chapter 2
2. The maker of this fifteenth-century globe (Martin Behaim, 1492) clearly understood the world to be round; just as clearly, he understood Spain and India to be separated by only a few small islands.

Chapter 3
3. The early French penetrations into North America left a lasting imprint up and down the Mississippi River; here Father Jacques Marquette and Explorer Louis Joliet sail down that river in 1673.

Chapter 4
4. In the 1580s John White sketched both the terrors of the sea and the promises of the land.

Chapter 5
5. This famous painting that hangs in the U. S. Capitol portrays the marriage between John Rolfe and Pocahantas in 1614.
6. When the capital of Virginia moved from Jamestown to Williamsburg at the end of the seventeenth century, the Bruton Parish Church took on greater importance; this building reached its present form with the addition of the tower in 1769.

Chapter 6
7. The artist imaginatively presents the departure of the Pilgrims from Holland—bound first for England, then for North America.
8. The early donor, John Harvard, watches over "his" college, the first founded in North America.

Chapter 7
9. Intimately connected to Brown University, the First Baptist Church in America honors Roger Williams as one of its founders; this structure was built in 1775.
10. The interior of Touro Synagogue in Newport, Rhode Island: designed by Peter Harrison and erected in 1763. This is the oldest synagogue building in North America.

Chapter 8

11. The first bishop of the Roman Catholic church in the United States, John Carroll built upon the earlier labors of Father Andrew White and the large hopes of Cecil Calvert.

12. Designed by the influential Benjamin Latrobe, the Baltimore Cathedral drew its inspiration in part from the Pantheon in Rome.

Chapter 9

13. This Dutch Reformed Church, erected in Albany, New York, in 1715, no longer survives.

14. The Swedish venture up the Delaware River in 1638 has a continuing witness in this "Old Swede's Church" located in Wilmington, Delaware.

Chapter 10

15. Benjamin West's famous painting portrays William Penn making a treaty with the Indians in 1701.

16. Pacifism received artistic expression here in Edward Hick's painting where the lion rests beside the lamb, as the Bible predicted.

Chapter 11

17. A restored "Old Salem" in North Carolina reminds the visitor of the Moravian eighteenth-century settlement; the Salem Community Store illustrated here was owned and operated by the church.

18. Throughout the South and all up and down the East Coast, the "awakener" George Whitefield attracted enormous crowds; his statue stands on the campus of the University of Pennsylvania.

Chapter 12

19. The Liberty Bell in Philadelphia's Independence Mall carries this inscription from the Book of Leviticus: "Proclaim liberty through all the land."

20. The Jefferson Memorial in Washington, D. C., recognizes the contribution of the third president to *all* liberty, civil, and ecclesiastical causes.

Chapter 13

21. Native American Samson Occom, ordained into the Congregational ministry in 1759, had great success in England raising money for the missionary efforts among the Indians back in America.

22. Richard Allen, distinguished leader of Black Methodists, served as bishop of the African Methodist Episcopal Church from 1816 to 1831.

23. Absalom Jones, ordained into the ministry of the Protestant Episcopal Church in 1796, led a black congregation in Philadelphia.

Chapter 14

24. Spokesman and apologist for the West, Lyman Beecher exercised his prodigious energies on behalf of Christianizing and taming the frontier.

25. Narcissa Whitman met her death in the Oregon Territory in 1847.

26. Methodist successes on the frontier owed much to the tireless labors of the circuit rider who gained near-mythological status.

27. Missionary to the western Indians and member of the Society of Jesus, Pierre Jean DeSmet served as intermediary between retreating tribes and advancing settlers from the East.

28. San Xavier del Bac Mission, located near Tucson, Arizona, is associated with the labors of Jesuit Eusebio Kino.

29. Martyred founder of the Church of Jesus Christ of Latter-Day Saints, Joseph Smith fell before a "gentile" mob in 1844.

30. Beginning as a religion of the American East, Mormonism ended up as emphatically a religion of the American West.

31. Sequoyah developed an alphabet for his own tribes of Cherokees; neither their literacy nor their Christianity, however, helped to spare their homeland in Georgia.

Chapter 15

32. Presbyterian clergyman Elijah P. Lovejoy died for both the freedom of the press and the freedom of the slave.

33. Author of *Uncle Tom's Cabin*, Harriet Beecher Stowe hoped for a great religious and moral revival that would forestall the Civil War; none came.

34. Julia Ward Howe memorialized that bloody war in her "Battle Hymn of the Republic": "Mine eyes have seen the glory of the coming of the Lord."

Chapter 16

35. The Jewish Market on the East Side of New York City found new immigrant buyers and sellers in 1900.

36. Solomon Schechter arrived in America early in the twentieth century to lead the forces of Conservative Judaism.

37. Kosher wine is produced and inspected in New York City in 1942.

38. Russian Orthodoxy found its way first into Alaska, then moved slowly down the Pacific Coast; this church in Sitka was photographed around 1900.

39. Lucretia Mott served as a Quaker minister from 1821 to 1880 in which capacity she fought for the rights of both slaves and women.

40. Dwight L. Moody dominated revivalism in the second half of the nineteenth century, as Charles G. Finney had in the first half.

41. Mary Baker Eddy, founder of Christian Science, is shown here in a photograph taken in 1910.

Chapter 17

42. Congregationalist Washington Gladden fought urban corruption and moral indifference close to home in Columbus, Ohio.

43. Roman Catholic James Cardinal Gibbons defended labor's right to organize and to receive fair compensation for fair productivity.

44. In the period of World War I, the Salvation Army in the United States was directed by Evangeline Booth.

45. An 1874 Currier & Ives engraving emphasized the prominent role that women played in moral reform, especially with respect to alcohol.

Chapter 18

46. Key figures in the Spanish-American War of 1898 gathered in Washington, D. C., soon after the war ended: President William McKinley, James Cardinal Gibbons, Admiral George Dewey.

47. Archbishop John Ireland of Minneapolis defended the right of Philippine Catholics to continue undisturbed in the practice of their religion.

48. World War I ambulance donated to the allied forces by American members of B'nai B'rith.

49. This medical mission, on the Amazon River, was a Seventh-Day Adventist enterprise that well represents Protestant missions.

50. Maryknoll Fathers constituted the front line of Roman Catholic missionary effort in South America, in this case in the Andes Mountains.

51. Ku Klux Klan members march in St. Petersburg, Florida, in 1926.

52. Roman Catholic Dorothy Day was an activist and humanitarian. This photo was taken in 1974.

Chapter 19

53. The National Shrine of the Immaculate Conception in Washington, D. C., is honored by all the nation's Roman Catholics, America's largest denomination.

54. Mainstream Protestantism enjoyed much popularity in the 1940s and 1950s, as here at the New York Avenue Presbyterian Church in Washington, D. C.

55. Mormonism went west to the Salt Lake Basin—and forgot to stop. Here is the prominent temple in Hawaii, on Oahu.

56. The rapid growth of Holiness and Pentecostal groups was due in part to a willingness to gather in crude and unpretentious structures such as this one near the New York-Pennsylvania border.

57. A modern synagogue in Jamaica, New York, has the Star of David built into the ceiling design.

58. Russian Orthodoxy had its impact in the East as well as the West, as seen here in Pittsburgh, Pennsylvania, in 1938.

59. A Zen Buddhist monitor here encourages proper posture and concentration.

60. William Jennings Bryan, three-time candidate for the U. S. presidency, won another kind of fame as the leading force against the teaching of evolution.

Chapter 20

61. Lyman Abbott, Congregationalist minister and influential editor, argued in behalf of evolution; he is shown here in a 1905 photograph.

62. Dr. Samuel McCrea Cavert, general secretary of the National Council of Churches, reads proof for the Revised Standard Version of the Bible that appeared in 1952.

63. By 1974, Catholics, Protestants, and Greek Orthodox agreed on and approved a single translation of the Bible.

64. Reinhold Niebuhr, shown here in 1963, had by that time retired from the Union Theological Seminary but not from the theological fray.

65. Rabbi Abraham J. Heschel addressed the problems of modern Judaism in particular and of modern civilization in general.

Chapter 21

66. Pictured here is an army chaplain serving at Fort Bragg, North Carolina, during World War II.

67. A Roman Catholic chaplain in Korea in 1951 ministers to a wounded soldier.

68. U. S. Army chaplain leads in the observance of a Passover seder in Korea in 1953.

69. Dr. Billy Graham joined with presidential candidate Richard M. Nixon in Pittsburgh, Pennsylvania, in the summer of 1968.

70. Monsignor Fulton J. Sheen speaking in White Plains, New York in 1948; Francis Cardinal Spellman, archbishop of New York, is at the left.

71. G. Bromley Oxnam, Methodist churchman of considerable note, took on the House Un-American Activities Committee in 1953.

72. Architectural renewal is evident in the Priory Church of St. Mary and St. Louis, in Creve Coeur, Missouri.

73. Pictured here is the chapel at Concordia Senior College in Fort Wayne, Indiana.

74. Shown here is the modern interior of the chapel, Concordia Senior College.

75. Chief Justice Earl Warren administered the oath of office to the nation's first Roman Catholic president, John F. Kennedy, in 1961.

76. John Courtney Murray, S. J., was the architect of the Declaration on Religious Liberty adopted by Vatican II in 1965.

Chapter 22

77. Shown here is the United States Supreme Court in the foreground, with the Library of Congress in the background.

78. Church of the Brethren conscientious objectors render alternative civilian service during World War II at Camp Stronach in Michigan.

79. Passions ran high in the Supreme Court rulings on prayer, as this 1963 cartoon by Herbert Block suggests.

80. Passions continued to run high for years after the United States Supreme Court heard its first "prayer case"; this Paul Conrad cartoon appeared in 1971.

81. Sixth graders in a Roman Catholic parochial school on Staten Island, New York, in the early 1960s.

82. A program of religious instruction was offered just off the campus of the public schools in Fort Wayne, Indiana, in 1964.

Chapter 23

83. With respect to civil rights, both the nation and its churches turned a corner in the 1960s. This march on Selma, Alabama, in 1965 brought together priests, rabbis, nuns, and ministers in their support of Martin Luther King, Jr.

84. In a unique meeting Martin Luther King, Jr. and Malcolm X greeted each other in Washington, D. C., in 1964. A potential coalition became impossible when Malcolm X was assassinated a year later, with King's assassination following three years after that.

85. Father Ksistaki-Poka, the first Blackfoot Indian to be ordained as a Roman Catholic priest, blesses his fellow tribesmen.

86. Amid much controversy and some schism, the Episcopal church in the 1970s began ordaining women to the priesthood; here three such recently ordained priests join in celebrating the Lord's Supper (or Eucharist) in New York City in 1974.

87. In 1972 Reform Judaism ordained its first female rabbi: Sally Priesand, standing in the center.

88. The official emblem of the National Council of Churches was adopted five years after the creation of this ecumenical body.

89. One symbol of ecumenicity, the annual Alfred E. Smith Dinner in New York City, brought these diverse figures together in 1968: Vice-President Hubert H. Humphrey (Congregationalist), Archbishop Terence J. Cooke (Roman Catholic), President Lyndon B. Johnson (Disciples of Christ), and Richard M. Nixon (Quaker).

Chapter 24

90. Father Charles Curran in a 1986 press conference defended his position as a professor of Moral Theology at Catholic University of America.

91. The Southern Baptist Convention gathered in Las Vegas in 1989 where, once again, the fundamentalist faction prevailed over the moderate group.

92. The Reverend Jerry Falwell addressed huge congregations in his Baptist Church in Lynchburg, Virginia; his television audience was estimated to be as high as four million at the peak of popularity.

93. Pope John Paul II, the first Roman Catholic pontiff to visit the U. S. Capitol, is shown here with President Jimmy Carter in 1979.

94. The Reverend Pat Robertson filed his candidacy for the presidency in Columbia, South Carolina, in 1988.

95. The Reverend Jesse Jackson campaigned for the presidency, often from church pulpits, in 1988.

96. California's newest Buddhist temple, Hsi Lai Temple in Hacienda Heights, was formally inaugurated in November, 1988, with the hosting of the first World Fellowship of Buddhists to be held in the West.

97. This lovely mosque in Plainfield, Indiana, serves as host to the Muslim Student Association of the United States and Canada.

A Religious History of America

Part 1

AGE OF EXPLORATION

CHAPTER 1

New Worlds and Ancient Peoples

The "New World" was of course not new to those peoples who had inhabited it for tens of thousands of years before any Europeans arrived. Having crossed a no longer visible land or ice bridge from Asia to the Aleutian Islands, migrants settled in Alaska or, over a period of centuries, slowly spread to the east and south all across North America, then even farther south into Central and South America. Completing this slow but steady dispersal of population may have taken as long as twenty-five thousand years. Evidence for such an expansive migration comes through archaeological discoveries and surviving, widely scattered microcultures, these revealing that lands unknown to medieval Europeans already enjoyed much human habitation and high civilization.

Long before pharaohs sat on ancient Egyptian thrones, long before Moses led his people out of that Egypt, and long before Homer wrote *The Iliad* or Rome rose to mighty power, inhabitants of the Americas had hunted and fished, planted and reaped, loved and married, given birth and buried their dead. These inhabitants also ordered their lives in accordance with certain patterns of behavior and explained their existence and their universe in accordance with certain principles of understanding. They had, in other words, become religious.

The religion of these earliest Americans was as diverse as the times of their settlement, as varied as the tribal organizations themselves. If one is inclined to think of pluralism as a phenomenon of the twentieth century, it is important to recognize that the American continents were never so pluralistic as in the centuries before European discovery and exploration. Pluralism was reduced, not enhanced, by the "invasion of America." No single religious institution, no single sacred book, no unified priesthood or common creed can be found in the multicolored patterns of the lives of these ancient peoples. Yet, the effort should be made to understand something of their religious aspirations and activities.

Understanding does not come easily, since we do not have the kind of rich literary documentation upon which historians traditionally

3

depend. We must draw upon oral traditions and the archaeologist's trowel, upon the geologist's data for the Ice Age and the chemist's methods of dating, upon reading from the present back into the past, upon informed guesses and presumed universalities, and in later centuries upon the reports of missionaries and other observers. We cannot draw upon a common history, for no recorded history is shared between European Americans or Afro-Americans and these wanderers of old. We can, however, draw upon a common nature shared with these as with all peoples: common needs, common anxieties, common questions if not-quite-common answers. What is most required in our search of the past is the desire to understand.

Misunderstanding came early in the application of the name *Indian*, since Christopher Columbus thought he had reached the outermost islands of India. Yet, in giving to these people an Asian origin, Columbus's misnomer was not hopelessly wrong. And some shorthand term is useful, just so long as it is not offensive and so long as it does not lull us into assuming a false unity. For never will we find that convenient construct called "the Indian," much less that abstraction designated as "Indian religion." When we use the shorthand, we are really referring to the Abnaki, Blackfeet, Crow, Delaware, Eskimo, Flathead, Ghost Dancers, Hopi, Iroquois—and so on through the rest of the alphabet. Each tribe had to come to terms with its own environment, whether of woodlands or plains, seashores or deserts. And each tribe had to find some terms to explain to themselves who and why they were.

Religious practices and religious stories played major roles in these accommodations and understandings. If rains were scarce and crucial to survival, then much religious ritual centered on urging or sacrificing or praying that rains might come. If the success of the hunt or the fertility of the soil were central to tribal life, then religion (along with sharp arrows and good seeds) was called upon to do its part. Just as environment dictated some of the differences, so the search for one's place in the universe could take many paths. The questions tended to be the same: Where did I (we) come from? Why must I (we) die? What is permitted (or forbidden) for me (us) to do? What separates us from, or unites us with, other peoples of other tribes or totems or lineages? What rules the sun, or the seasons, or even the affairs of the heart? And while the questions are widely shared, it is in the answers that one finds a rich diversity, a lively pluralism.

Cherokees of the Southeast regarded the earth as "a great island floating in a sea of water" and suspended at its four extremities "by a cord hanging down from the sky vault, which is of solid rock." Pimas in the Southwest saw the "Earth Magician" as the creative agent who shaped the world, "Round and smooth he molds it."

Earth Magician makes the mountains.
Heed what he has to say!
He it is that makes the mesas.
Heed what he has to say.

Tsimshians in the Northwest explained the light of the sun with a story of The One Who Walks All Over the Sky. This One wears a mask of burning pitch which warms and illumines as he makes his way from east to west. Sparks flying out of his mouth at night account for the stars, while the moon receives its light from the face of the sleeping sun. When the sun paints his face with red ocher, that redness visible in the evening tells the people that the weather will be good the next day. And in the Northeast the Iroquois elaborated their account of Sky World, Earth, and Underworld with stories that explained not only where people came from but where, after death, they would go.

All of these cosmologies or world views move beyond the restricted domains of human experience or empirical evidence. For who has witnessed the creation of the universe? And what laboratory is capable of duplicating the experiment? The questions which these cosmologies are intended to answer do, on the other hand, arise from the deepest and most pervasive of human experiences: the experience of limits, of unknowns, of finiteness, of that far beyond our poor powers to control or even comprehend. We begin to understand our ancient ancestors when we acknowledge that we too have limits to which answers may be sought in religion, or philosophy, or magic, or astrology, or tarot cards or in crystal balls, or in any number of nonempirical approaches. Even with all our astronomical sophistication and with all the creative genius of theoretical physics, we continue to debate the origins of the universe (as well as its size) and our place in it (as well as our responsibility toward it).

Another commonality which we share with the earliest Americans is the tendency, even in a secularized society, to call upon religious institutions or authority at critical junctures of life: christenings or circumcisions at birth, a confirmation or a *bar mistvah* at puberty, marriage as a sacred no less than a civil ceremony, and the company and comfort of the faithful at death. Activities marking these major transitions, or "rites of passage" to use the anthropologists' phrase, appear in virtually every society about which much is known. So also, in the many Indians tribes, countless ceremonies helped to usher the vulnerable individual from the womb to the world, from childhood to maturity, from a single to a conjugal state, and from life into and beyond death. Although what is happening to the individual may be thought of in the modern world as intensely private, in tribal societies the community as a whole was involved.

Pregnancy and childbirth are difficult times for the mother no less than for the fetus and child. In some folk societies, the father also is regarded as peculiarly vulnerable at the time of birth. All the empirical evidence one might require demonstrates the dangers and difficulties, the pain and the anxieties, and the not infrequent death of child or mother or both. It is not a time to spurn the help of the community nor the favor of the gods. Zunis of the Southwest present the eight-day old infant to the sun after a ceremonial washing by the women of the father's clan. With cornmeal as a sacrificial offering, the elders dedicate the child, praying to "our sun father" that his blessing might rest upon the infant and indeed upon the whole community: "May you help us all to finish our roads." Among the Chinook of the Northwest, one sees the concern directed toward the pregnant mother who is forbidden to wear certain jewelry or eat certain food or do anything that might endanger her life or the life she bears within. "She does not look at a corpse . . . [or] at anything that is dead." "She does not look at anything that is rotten." And the husband too is placed under restrictions or taboos, being also forbidden to look at a corpse, to kill animals related to the clan, or "to eat anything that has been found." Every precaution must be taken, every spirit appeased, every assistance—natural or supernatural—rendered.

The tribal community supervises and sanctions the transition of boys and girls from their status as children to the more responsible role of adults. Puberty ceremonies may be drawn out over a period of weeks, but even so the troubled period of "adolescence" is far briefer than in

1. Early English settler, John White, portrayed the manner in which the East Coast Indians hollowed out a tree trunk in making a boat. *Library of Congress*

modern society. Separate rites of passage for boys and girls generally include the revelation of sacred tribal truths, the inculcation of tribal duties, and training in the skills appropriate to the gender division within that tribe. For females, the ceremony may be related to the first menstruation, a time when special care must be exercised — as indeed in all successive menstrual periods. In ancient Israel, for example, a menstruating woman was deemed "unclean" for seven days, after which ritual purification was required, just as after the birth of a child (see Leviticus, chapter 12). In the Chinook puberty ceremony for the girls, several days of fasting were required and the girl "remains hidden for five days." And for a period of one hundred days, she must wear a specified garment, refrain from picking fresh fruit, and bathe only at night.

For the boys, puberty ceremonies might require arduous or even painful initiations that would become the mark of manhood. Among the Delawares, the young man's first successful hunt signalled the moment when he should be ceremonially accepted into the tribe and instructed in his proper duties. Moravian missionary to the tribe, David Zeisberger (1721–1808), reported that the felling of the first deer "proves the occasion of a great solemnity." First the deer, if a buck, is given to one of the male elders in the tribe; if a doe, to an older woman. The animal is then skinned and brought back to the village by the whole hunting party. As the group nears the village, one hears "a prolonged call, which is the old man's or old woman's prayer to the deity in behalf of the boy, that he may always be a fortunate hunter." A meal follows, in which the boy is instructed "regarding the chase and all the circumstances of his future life." Afterward, alone in the forest, boy-turning-man may have a spiritual vision of an "old man in a gray beard" who will assert his power over all things upon the earth and will promise the neophyte that he too shall have much power: "No one shall do thee harm and thou needest not to fear any man."

Marriage required more than the approval of the young couple or their respective parents. Since one had to marry outside of his or her own clan (exogamy), the union of two clans was once again a communal affair. A private ceremony might precede the public one, but only the blessing of the whole village and its sacred officers could make the marriage complete. In fact, the marriage might not be truly "complete" until many months or a year had passed during which time the groom must prove to his father-in-law his worthiness as hunter or food gatherer. Christian missionaries often deplored the sexual practices that differed so markedly from those of Europe (in some tribes polygamy was practiced, in others divorce was routine, and in others premarital sex was common), but just as often commented on the sexual modesty of the young ladies, the lack of public displays of affection, the monogamous fidelity encountered—especially after the birth of children, and the custom of punishing the adulterous lover more harshly than the adulterous wife.

Finally, the grim fact of death once more marshalled all the resources of the community, both sacred and secular, in affirming that the unfriendly forces responsible for this individual death would not destroy the community nor would hostile spirits trouble the family of the departed. However varied the rituals and the explanations which accompanied them, the message in one way or another was that death had lost its sting and the grave its victory. This world and the world beyond were not all that separate or independent: an aged Pueblo Indian might leave this world only to return in another form, as a cloud or as a kachina doll. The death of a young person or a child, on the other hand, could be much more ominous, implying on imbalance between the forces of good or evil. Among the Kwakiutl, when a child died, the greatest concern was to see that the spirit did not return to haunt or to hurt. The purpose of the ceremony was to insulate and protect the living. On the other hand, among the Hurons when an infant died, the child was buried near the road so that the young spirit might enter the womb of some passing wife, thus to be born again.

When an Ottawa warrior was on his death bed, the family dressed him in as fine a garment as could be procured; they then painted his face and dressed his hair "with red paint mixed with grease." The priestly shamans or medicine men gathered round him as his weapons were brought in and laid at his feet. And when the moment of death seemed near, the person was helped to a sitting position that he might look alive and thus defy death a little longer. When death finally conquered, however, the burial was public, the period of mourning carefully stipulated, and the feasts of reaffirmation and remembrance held. In tribal societies, funerals were never private, no more than were birth and puberty, betrothal and marriage. Life was social and the line between sacred and secular often impossible to draw.

While we can draw a line between antiquity and modernity, that demarcation is rarely as sharp as we like to believe. In the last ten thousand years or so, certainly much has happened that deserves the name of progress: in medicine, technology, longevity, communication, transportation, music, the arts, literature, education, and religion. So much has happened that we fear that the "generation gap" has grown too wide to permit any common parlance, any genuine understanding of the ancient past. The gap, moreover, is more than one just of time, for the cultural chasm is enormous and not readily crossed. Before Europeans learned much about the inhabitants of the New World, they tended to romanticize and idealize them as symbols of innocence, as the true inheritors of the Garden of Eden before the Fall. Even in the eighteenth century, the aboriginal Indian maiden was the preferred artistic symbol of America: richly endowed by nature, unsullied by civilization.

Yet this idealization did not fare well in toe-to-toe combat, in hostilities provoked by relentless European advancement, in misunderstandings (sometimes honest and sometimes otherwise) on both sides of that cultural chasm. Gradually, the tendency to sentimentalize the earliest Americans gave way to a tendency to brutalize them. In the nineteenth century, the period of most rapid sweep across the North American continent, racial stereotypes of white man versus red man developed as the Indian was thought of chiefly in terms of a problem which required solution. To some the solution was assimilation and intermarriage; to others the solution was removal and reservation; to still others the only enduring solution was warfare and extermination.

With some deliberation and some wisdom born of bitter experience, we move now toward a recognition of our common humanity, Indian and non-Indian. We need not regard the ancient peoples as something more than human; we must not regard them as something less. The movement toward a full humanity is uneven and often painfully slow: one step forward and two backward seems too often to be the pattern. Neither in diplomacy nor in legislation has the progress been steady; neither in social acceptance nor in empathetic understanding can the record be pointed to with pride. And constitutional guarantees have been tardy to arrive: citizenship not bestowed until 1924, religious freedom not recognized until 1978.

Long before any constitutional guarantees existed, the native population was dealt with largely in terms of its potential for trade, for labor or land, for military attack or alliance, and for conversion. These were the chief points of contact between the old inhabitants and the new arrivals. Trade was the least disruptive form of contact, for its success generally depended upon leaving Indian cultures intact. This was true all through the eastern half of North America: from the French along the St. Lawrence River to the Dutch along the Hudson River, from the English in the Carolinas to the Spanish in Florida and along the Gulf Coast. But as European settlement swelled, successful trading alliances gave way to contests over personal liberty and private property.

The Spanish spoke of the Indians' liberty, but it was a peasant's liberty: the liberty to do the labor assigned at the place designated. The English, gradually developing a system of black slavery in Virginia, experimented with making the Indians into slaves but without success. Indians, unlike blacks uprooted from Africa, still had cultural support, still had a nearby refuge to which they could flee. But land, even more than labor, became the sticking point in relationships between Europeans who on the one hand wanted to settle and possess, and Indians on the other hand who wanted to wander freely and hold all in common. In general, the two sides in their dispute talked past each other, since traditional patterns of behavior were so different and basic assumptions so far apart. The English could never make the Indian understand, and even had some difficulty explaining to themselves why they had a perfect right to take over whatever Indian land they happened to occupy. Did they have a title from King James or King Charles? And, if so, who had given the Indians' land to those English sovereigns? Did the Indians forfeit their land by being "uncivilized" or by merely passing over it rather than surveying, marking, and fencing it? Or was it simply true then, as now, that "possession is nine-tenths of the law"?

John Winthrop (1588–1649), founder of the Massachusetts Bay Colony, argued that land "which is common to all is proper to none. This savage people ruleth over many lands without title or property; for they enclose no ground, neither have they cattle to maintain it, but remove their dwellings as they have occasion." In other words, since Massachusetts woodlands did not look like English villages, all that territory was theirs for the taking. Besides, Abraham was called forth by God to leave his own homeland to "go and take possession" of the land of others. So may we, with similar justification, possess this land to which we have been called. "Why may not Christians," Winthrop asked, "have liberty to go and dwell amongst [the Indians] in their wastelands and woods?" The Indians, of course, had their own answers to that question, should anyone care to listen. But few cared to do so, with the consequence that advancing Europeans and long-settled Americans found themselves frequently at war.

Wars in Virginia, in New England, in Canada and elsewhere set the tone of "Indian-white" relationships through most of the colonial period of American history and well beyond. Adversaries in war rarely try to understand each other, but only to misrepresent and caricature each other. Indian land claims are meaningless and absurd, argued a Pittsburg resident in the 1780s: "I would think the man a fool and unjust," Hugh Henry Brackenridge wrote, "who would exclude me from drinking the waters of the Mississippi River because he had first seen it. He would be equally so who would exclude me from settling in the country west of the Ohio, because in chasing a buffalo he had been first over it." In fact, Brackenridge added, the Indian and the buffalo have about the same claim to all this vast continent. "To see how far the folly of some would go, I had once thought of supplicating some of the great elks or buffaloes that run through the woods, to make me a grant of a hundred thousand acres of land and prove he had brushed the weeds with his tail, and run fifty miles." Indian as noble savage had become Indian as enemy and exponent of outrageous claims. Such an Indian, if he cannot be silenced or moved, must be slain.

Religion endeavored to moderate the severity with which the Indian was treated, the hostility with which he was regarded. It has become the fashion to dismiss and denigrate the missionary as one who showed no sensitivity to tribal tradition, who regularly violated and probably destroyed all tribal integrity. First, it was not the missionary who initiated the trade in alcohol or guns, nor was it the missionary who was chiefly responsible for the imperialism and conquest. Second, missionaries did understand and sensitively report on tribal tradition; much of our modern knowledge comes from these sources, both Catholic and Protestant. Third, though the missionary did regard the Indians as "heathen" and therefore fit subjects for conversion, this represented a clear advance over the alternative of regarding the Indians as animals and therefore fit subjects for extermination. As an early clergyman declared, "The Israelites had a commandment from God to dwell in Canaan; we have leave to dwell in Virginia. They were commanded to kill the heathen, we are forbidden to kill them, but are commanded to convert them." Some clergy even accounted for the Indian presence on the North American continent in terms of their being the "ten lost tribes of Israel," lost, that is, to the later history of the Jewish people after the fifth century before the Christian Era. Finally, in weighing motivations, it is important to recognize that missionaries, in transmitting Christianity to the "heathen," believed that they were bestowing a great gift: a blessing, not a curse, a safe haven in this life and eternal happiness in the life beyond. Modern scales of value may put more emphasis on tribal integrity than on eternal felicity, but these value priorities ought not to be superimposed upon an earlier time.

This is not to argue that missionaries were or are beyond criticism, or that they escaped their own cultural bondage, sometimes being more concerned to transform Indians into good Englishmen or women than into good Christians. Nor is it to argue that Christianity was markedly superior, more "civilized," more ennobling than the many religions of the many different tribes. It is to argue that the thoughtless stereotype of "cowboys and Indians" as seen in the old Hollywood movies should not now be replaced with a "missionaries and Indians" stereotype that uniformly makes villains of the former and heroes of the latter. The fateful clash between Europeans and native Americans has all the elements of tragedy, but out of genuine tragedy should emerge reconciliation, along with a renewed sense of the dignity and significance of human life—of all human life.

CHAPTER 2

Spain's Vision and Spain's Mission

When one crosses a horizon never before traversed, that person not only sees a new world but helps to create one. This was the incomparable achievement of those who sailed west from Palos and Bristol, St. Malo and Amsterdam; of those who waded onto Florida's sands or paddled through the Mississippi's mud; of those who coursed the waters of the St. Lawrence or the Hudson; of those who confronted the Algonquian or the Iroquois; of those whose first steps onto American soil were often all too quickly their last journey. Among those nations who led in this sixteenth-century adventure, Spain stands tallest, and among those whom Spain sent forth Christopher Columbus achieved the most enduring fame.

Columbus (1451–1506), native of Genoa, wanted to go east by sailing west. He wished to find a new route to India, one that did not follow the medieval pattern of hugging a coastline, never allowing land to drop from sight, until one's proximate goal was reached. His vision was to strike out daringly across an uncharted ocean, a sea of unknown and therefore potentially infinite breadth, until at last India came into view. Portugal having declined to sponsor him (the Portuguese seamen much preferring to hug the African coastline until they came to its end, if it had an end), Columbus left Lisbon in 1485 for the port of Palos in the southwestern corner of Spain. By May of the next year, he was granted an audience with Catholic Queen Isabella. He made his plea, and Isabella made her move: she chose to refer the whole complex matter to a committee. And in the whole history of Western civilization, referring bold plans to a committee has been the surest way to maintain a dreary status quo. So it nearly proved to be in the case of the red-haired, blue-eyed Italian dreamer.

The committee to which Columbus's proposal was sent consisted of churchmen, for in the sixteenth century most educated persons—be they doctors or lawyers or astronomers or cartographers—also held ecclesiastical titles. And churchmen had for centuries carried on endless debate about other lands beyond the "known world," known to Europeans, that is. Did lands exist on the other side of the earth? And if so, were such lands inhabited? And if inhabited, did Christ appear to them sometime after he had appeared to people on "this side," to people who dwelled in the middle of the earth: that is, the Mediterranean world? But if Christ had not appeared to such people, were they then without hope of salvation until somehow European Christians could carry the gospel to them? Or perhaps God in his wisdom had so ordered the world that lands on the other side of the earth (if such really existed) would not be populated until the means for reaching those lands, called the Antipodes, had been developed or revealed. For a thousand years or more the discussion, entirely theoretical, raged back and forth until that day when it would no longer be a proposition for debate but an event for discovery.

In all of the centuries-long argumentation, the question of the earth's being round or flat was never the major issue. The myth persists that Columbus had to convince everyone, especially churchmen, that the earth was round. This is not the case. The question in the fifteenth century was not whether or not the earth was round, but how big around was it? Was its circumference some 20,000 miles as Columbus believed, or 180,000 as the ancient astronomer and mathematician Ptolemy believed, or 400,000 as the even more ancient philosopher Aristotle believed? Obviously, this question deserved debate, demanded debate, since its answer determined the likelihood of success or failure for any voyage setting out to cross a trackless ocean. But the earth a sphere? Yes, of course. Cartographers drew it so, astronomers reckoned it so, mariners intended to prove it so.

In order to prove it so, however, mariners needed help. What they needed most was the financial backing which would enable them to outfit a fleet of ships, complete with crew and ample provisions. Columbus, therefore, waited anxiously for the committee to issue its report. The wait was long, and the results were bad. After a leisurely four of five years in studying the problem, the committee concluded that the proposal to reach the East by sailing west was vain, impossible, and deserving of rejection. The reasons for so negative a reaction were these: (1) such a voyage would take at least three years; (2) the western ocean might be without limit; (3) even if Columbus were lucky enough to reach the Antipodes, he could never get back; (4) it was quite possible that there was no land to be found anyway on the other side of the earth; and, (5) because such presumed islands had not been known before, it is most unlikely—this long after Creation—that they could be discovered now. This last reason is, of course, always the perfect argument against ever doing anything for the first time.

Deeply discouraged, Columbus waited another half-year to see if the queen would summon him into her presence. No summons came. Shaking the Spanish dust from his boots, Columbus determined to set out for France in order to give King Charles VIII the opportunity to support what Queen Isabella had turned down. At this juncture, two persons intervened on Columbus's behalf. The first, Franciscan Friar Juan Pérez, persuaded Isabella to meet with Columbus one more time and appoint one more committee. Although this committee also reported negatively, it concluded that such a voyage might indeed be possible were not the cost too high. At that point, the General Treasurer Sanchez entered the debate on the side of Columbus. True, one took risks in backing such a novel venture, but on the other hand, Sanchez argued, the potential rewards were great. This daring expedition, Sanchez told the Queen, "could prove of so great service to God and the exaltation of his Church" that to decline the option would be "a grave reproach to her."

If such a voyage were truly possible and if the risks were truly acceptable, then nothing remained but for Queen Isabella to give reality to the dream. On April 30, 1492, she commissioned her "Admiral of the Ocean Sea": "Whereas you, Christóbal Colón, are setting forth by our command . . . to discover and acquire certain islands and mainlands in the ocean sea . . . it is our will and pleasure that you" shall discover and acquire same for the glory of God and the wealth of his nation, Spain. After three more months of careful preparation, Columbus, with ninety men aboard the *Nina*, *Pinta*, and *Santa Maria*, turned from the known waters of Palos to the unknown waters of the ocean sea. Sev-

2. The maker of this fifteenth-century globe (Martin Behaim, 1492) clearly understood the world to be round; just as clearly, he understood Spain and India to be separated by only a few small islands. *Library of Congress*

enty days later, Columbus and his men knelt on an island of the Bahamas. To that island they gave the name Holy Savior: San Salvador.

This expedition was an affair of state, but clearly also of church. The most loyal Roman Catholic nation in Europe at this time, Spain took seriously its responsibility to the Vatican and to maintaining the purity of its faith. For eight hundred years, Catholics in Spain had warred against Moslems, finally driving them back across the Strait of Gibraltar to Africa. For centuries Spain had sought to convert or isolate the Jews; now in the very year that Columbus sailed for parts unknown more than one hundred thousand Jews were exiled from their homeland. The Spanish Inquisition, known for its rigor in seeking out all heretics, had performed its task with cruel efficiency, purifying the national faith by fire. Spain's discovery of and adventures in the New World were but an extension of the Crusades that took place centuries before: claiming land and riches in the name of God and of his Church.

Columbus shared the religious vision even as he shared the conviction that God ruled human history. A regular communicant, given to daily prayer as well as to the study of the Bible and other religious writings, Columbus interpreted his expedition in scriptural terms. "God made me the messenger of the new heaven and the new earth of which he spoke in the Apocalypse of St. John, after having spoken of it through the mouth of Isaiah; and he showed me the spot where to find it." And to the general treasurer who had rendered such timely help, Columbus wrote in 1493 that his success was not due to his own merit "but to the holy Christian faith, and to the piety and religion of our Sovereigns." Our response to such great discoveries should not be prideful boasting but humble thanksgiving. Let us all "give thanks to our Lord and Savior Jesus Christ, who has granted us so great a victory and such prosperity. Let processions be made and sacred feasts be held, and the temples be adorned with festive boughs." Then, striking a note which was to be heard again and again as European nations justified their occupation of already occupied lands, Columbus added: "Let Christ rejoice on earth, as he rejoices in heaven in the prospect of the salvation of the souls of so many nations hitherto lost." The discovery of America was, above all else, the climax of a great pilgrimage, the end of a noble spiritual quest.

Spain moved quickly to secure her position, discovering more islands that turned out not to be islands at all but peninsulas of enormous land masses almost beyond comprehension. Spain discovered so much so fast that her next-door neighbor, Portugal, felt that she was being bypassed in this greatest land rush of all time. After all, Portugal was a Roman Catholic country too, and a faithful one as well; after all, Portugal had already explored a good portion of that ocean sea, having appropriated the Azores, the Canaries, and the Cape Verde islands. Should Spain have it all? Portugal appealed to the Holy See, the papacy in Rome, to settle the competitive tension between the two Catholic nations so busy in exploring and claiming new lands. The pope (Alexander VI) responded by drawing a north-south line west of which all lands "discovered or to be discovered" would belong to Spain, east of which all such lands would belong to Portugal. This "papal line of demarcation" first drawn in 1493 was, by the terms of the Treaty of Tordesillas (July 7, 1494), moved farther to the west, thus favoring Portugal and thus intersecting the "hump" of Brazil, giving Portugal thereby an important foothold in South America.

The Spanish, who benefitted most from this papal division of the spoils, proceeded rapidly with their exploration, planting on each new bit of soil both flag and cross. By 1511 a twenty-six-year-old Hernando Cortes (1485–1547) was in Cuba, making preparations for his legendary conquests of Mexico and Peru. In 1513 Ponce de León (1527–1591), sailing out of Puerto Rico through the Bahamas, made his way to a peninsula to the north and west. Making landfall on Easter Sunday (in Spanish, *Pascua Florida*), he gave the name *Florida* to what he believed at the time was another large island—perhaps about the size of Cuba. The following year Spain's King Ferdinand appointed de León governor of the "island," urging him to lead the native population "by all the means you may be able to devise . . . into the knowledge of Our Catholic Faith." Another Spanish explorer, Vásquez de Ayllón (1475?–1526), in 1521 ventured into northern Florida (naming the St. Johns River) and far beyond to the Chesapeake Bay. He too received imperial encouragement to bring the Indians "to understand the truths of our holy Catholic faith, that they may come to a knowledge thereof and become Christians and be saved."

Once Mexico City (the former capital of the Aztecs) was transformed into the major center of Spanish power and population, land expeditions from that point northward penetrated the vast continent into what would later become the states of Texas, New Mexico, Arizona, and California. In 1539 Brother Marcos of Nice (d. 1558), a Franciscan friar, walked over three thousand miles on such a journey, erecting a small cross near the Zuni pueblo at Cibola and claiming all in the name of Spain. To the Indians that he met he promised humane treatment, not enslavement, not slaughter. Such a promise represented not a report of how Spain had treated the Indians, but a commitment on the part of some churchmen to tolerate barbaric treatment no longer. In 1516 a Dominican missionary, Bartholomew Las Casas (1474–1566), received the title of "Defender of the Indians" for having vented his fury against fellow countrymen because of their cruel treatment of the native population. "In God's name," he cried, consider whether our tortures and murders of Indians "do not surpass every imaginable cruelty and injustice!" We must ask ourselves, however painful the question, "whether it could be worse to give the Indians into the charge of the devils of hell than to the Christians of the Indies." Keeping up a steady campaign for a recognition of the common humanity binding European and Indian, Las Casas finally found his position validated in a papal bull, *Sublimis Deus* ("The Sublime God"), issued in 1537. There Pope Paul III declared that the Indians were, in fact, human beings, not beasts of the field to be driven and whipped like oxen. Indians must not be deprived of their liberty or their property, "nor should they in any way be enslaved" whether they choose to become Christians or not.

While even this minimal ideal was not always observed, it could not be violated with utter impunity by those who saw themselves, in some way or another, as emissaries of the Catholic faith. Tensions between conquistadores and missionaries were constant at this point, these strains only aggravating the inevitable clashes between all Spanish intruders on the one hand and all native Americans on the other. Sometimes Indians converted to Catholicism, thinking that it was but another option to append to their already crowded ceremonial life. In 1597 Indians on St. Catherine's Island, off the coast of Georgia, justified their rebellion against Spanish overlords by explaining that their whole culture was being condemned: the friars "obstruct our dances, banquets, feasts, celebrations, fires, and wars, so that by failing to use them we lose the ancient valor and dexterity inherited from our ancestors; they persecute our old people, calling them witches. . . . ; they always reprimand us, injure us, oppress us, preach to us, call us bad Christians, and deprive us of all happiness." Christianity, it turned out, was not an additional layer atop the cultural cake, but a repudiation of all ancestral ways, a radical abandonment that pushed these and many other Indians much farther than they were prepared to go.

The southeastern corner of the North American continent proved generally inhospitable to both Spanish missions and Spanish settlements. Louis Cancer (1500–1549), a Dominican father (Order of Preachers) who came fresh from missionary successes in Central America, was determined to win equal victories in Florida. Sailing into Tampa Bay in 1549, he and several companions debarked, only to be slain the moment that they reached shore. In 1565 Pedro Menéndez de Avilés (1519–1574) managed to retake north Florida settlements from French Protestants (Huguenots) and to establish the oldest permanent settlement on North America soil: St. Augustine. But in his efforts to conquer territory to the north, the Carolinas and Virginia, Menéndez met with great resistance from the Indians and repeated defeat. Accompanying him were members of the Society of Jesus, the Jesuits, who shared in the defeat and discouragement. By 1571 the General of the Jesuit order, Francis Borgia (1510–1572), decided that the cost was too high, and the number of lives lost too great, to justify continuing efforts even in Florida, much less beyond. We can count on the fingers of one hand, said Borgia, the number of our converts, and even some of them have relapsed into their former ways. Since the Society has too much to do elsewhere and too few missionaries for the task, "not only is it not fitting to keep the Society in that land, but it must not be done."

Spain's ecclesiastical forces left a much more enduring imprint on the American Southwest. Franciscans (the Order of Friars Minor), building upon the earlier travels of Brother Marcos and others, entered New Mexico as well as Texas and Arizona quite early. The royal city of Santa Fe (Holy Faith), established in 1610 (three years after Jamestown, Virginia) developed into the political and religious capital for all the surrounding region. Such development, however, came at high cost. The initial governor, Don Juan de Oñate (1549?–1624?), leading his first expedition in 1595 visited great cruelty upon the New Mexico pueblo dwellers. A Franciscan friar in 1601 wrote to the Spanish viceroy to protest Oñate's totally unjustified behavior as he robbed and plundered, burned villages, killed men, women, and children. What Oñate has managed to do, the friar reported, is alienate an entire population, when it would have been possible for a more intelligent and compassionate commander to control this whole territory with fifty men, if only the conquest had been effected "in a Christian manner without outraging and killing these poor Indians, who think that we are all evil and [that] the king who sent us out here is ineffective and a tyrant."

Such undeserved treatment also played havoc with the missionaries' whole reason for being in the New World. Because of Oñate and his like, the Franciscan acknowledged, "We cannot preach the gospel now, for it is despised by these people on account of the great offences and the harm we have done them." That was the short-term effect of the brutality. The long-term effect was an Indian revolt in 1680 led by the Indian shaman, Popé. Santa Fe was virtually destroyed, with over four hundred lives lost, many of those lives being of Franciscans. Spain prevailed, however, with Diego José de Vargas leading a powerful military force into the region a dozen years later. The capital city was rebuilt, even as missions arose once more on the desert landscape. Here as elsewhere, however, the cost of early European cruelties was high in all future contacts between conquerors and conquered.

New Mexico, though a conspicuous center of Spanish missionary activity in North America, did not stand alone. On both sides of that territory, Franciscans and others labored to preach that gospel. In Texas, mission efforts began along the Neches River, with the creation of the San Francisco de los Texas mission in 1690. Father Damien Massanet reported that in the eastern woods of Texas he found "a delightful spot close to the brook" and within three days enough ground had been cleared and enough of a "roomy dwelling" had been built to permit Mass to be said "with all propriety." One mission, San Antonio de

Valero founded in 1744, achieved lasting fame a century later as the Alamo where Texans died in their struggle against Mexico for independence. In Arizona, it was the Jesuit Eusebio Kino (1645?–1711) who above all others left a palpable Spanish mark upon that land. Almost as much geographer as preacher, Kino travelled through northern Mexico (Sonora) as well as southern Arizona, mapping as he went, learning Indian languages, building chapels, and instructing the natives in the techniques of farming. In 1697 he founded his largest and best known mission, San Xavier del Bac, famed today for its restored beauty. When Kino died in 1711, much of the Christianizing effort in Arizona slowly withered away. A half-century later, however, Spanish Catholicism made a powerful comeback in California.

Under the direction of Franciscan Junípero Serra (1713–1784), a remarkable chain of missions stretched from San Diego (1769) in the South to San Francisco (1776) in the North. Serra's last mission was founded at Ventura in 1782, two years before his death. Serra and his companions, walking from Lower or Baja California into what is now American territory, spent many days crossing plains and gullies to get to that port of which they had heard. On the first of July, 1769, he recorded in his diary as follows: "We started early in the morning on our last day's journey. Already the beginnings of the port we were seeking are partly visible . . . we therefore continued on and finally arrived at said camp . . . a little before noon. . . . Thus was our arrival, with all in good health, happy and content, thanks be to God, at the famous and wished for Port of San Diego." All of this ecclesiastical activity on the Pacific Coast in the 1770s and beyond took place without reference to the excitement on the Atlantic Coast as thirteen colonies entered the struggle for their own independence from England.

Spain's presence in North America never equalled that so firmly fixed in Central and South America. In the latter territories, Catholic sisters no less than Catholic brothers and fathers contributed much to the transferring of Spanish civilization and Spanish religion to the New World. Despite the clear gender inequity that gave men the more active role of explorers and missionaries, women took charge of much education and social service; they also, like Saint Teresa of Avila back in Europe, often led in spiritual sensitivity and mystical discipline. One sister of some literary achievement, Juana Inés de la Cruz, argued in Mexico City for the right of women to learn and to apply that learning on behalf of the Church. When the Apostle Paul commanded women to keep silent, that counsel "was directed solely to the public office of the pulpit." Men simply by being men believe they are wise and have all authority to interpret Scripture, whether or not they are "learned and virtuous and of gentle and well-inclined natures." The proper distinction in the study and interpretation of Scripture, Sister de la Cruz noted, is not between male and female but between competent and incompetent.

On the whole, Spain found North America something of a disappointment: no great treasures of gold as they had found farther to the south, no great centers of civilization as among the Aztecs and the Incas, no great commercial or trading opportunities that could fill the coffers of merchants and princes back home. When Spain lost her North American lands to Mexico in 1821, it seemed that she had not lost all that much to an already advancing Anglo-American civilization. Yet, from the perspective of the late twentieth century, one recognizes that neither Spanish culture nor Spanish language ever really departed from those northern lands. While the Hispanic presence was never wholly negligible north of the Rio Grande or the Gulf of California, that presence was to assert itself far more visibly and powerfully in the twentieth century, both in society and in that Catholic church planted so tentatively in Florida long before.

CHAPTER 3

French Fur and French Faith

Newfoundland's fishing banks first drew France's attention to the New World. Breton fisherman crossed the northern Atlantic to net as great a catch as their tiny vessels could safely carry back. Then in 1534 Jacques Cartier (1491–1557) sailed from St. Malo with sixty men and two small ships past those fishing banks into the strait located between Newfoundland and Labrador. He explored inlets and small bays, made contact with natives of the Algonquian linguistic family, and took two Indians back home with him to learn French. The next year Cartier returned with three ships, over one hundred men, and his two "interpreters" to carry on even more serious exploration.

Like other Europeans, the French were charmed by the idea of a Northwest Passage, a waterway shortcut from Europe to Asia. Every bay or gulf or broad river raised hopes that it would prove to be this much-sought-after passage. On his 1535 voyage Cartier can be forgiven for believing that he had in fact found it. What he did find was the Gulf of St. Lawrence and then the St. Lawrence River which led in a southwesterly direction into the interior of this vast continent. Discovery of the St. Lawrence River, while it did not lead to Asia, did lead to exciting possibilities of a profitable fur trade and of significant French settlement far within North America. What other Frenchmen would later learn is that this major river would bring them within easy reach of the Great Lakes and even the headwaters of the Mississippi River. With access to waterways such as these, France could draw a cordon around the entire eastern half of the continent. Catholic France to the north and Catholic Spain to the south could divide the New World between them.

The promise far outran the reality. A settlement effort in the early 1540s proved disastrous as relations with the Iroquois turned sour, as supplies ran short, and as the cost of this entire venture proved exorbitant. All the money was going out and none was coming back in. France, moreover, found herself seriously distracted at home as the Reformation which permanently divided Germany between Protestant and Catholic segments threatened to do the same in France. Ultimately, France was not so divided but for most of the second half of the sixteenth century that nation teetered on the edge of a full-scale religious war. The Edict of Nantes, issued in 1598, brought a measure of peace to that troubled land, even as it enabled France once more to turn its attention to that great contest among the European nations for control of the New World.

The seventeenth century opened with commercial and colonizing ventures directed by Samuel de Champlain (1567?–1635). While the earliest efforts at settlement turned out as unhappily as those some sixty years earlier, a fort built at the first narrowing of the St. Lawrence River evolved into the town of Quebec and soon a bit farther up the river the village of Montreal had its beginnings. Political control was unsure, however, and population growth was insignificant in the first half of the seventeenth century. By the 1660s, only about three thousand French colonists dwelled in Canada, this at a time when about forty thousand English colonists inhabited New England alone, and French affairs in the New World were directed much more by the Society of Jesus than by the government itself.

Jesuits moving out from their base at Quebec explored, mapped, translated, and reported on the Indian tribes at great length, their seventy-three volumes of *Relationes* constituting still the major record of Algonquian and Iroquois tribal life. Of course, above all else, the Jesuit missionaries sought to win converts from among the Indians to their own Christian faith. That proved as frustrating for them among the northern tribes as it had for their Spanish brothers laboring among the Seminoles in Florida. Jean de Brébeuf (1593–1649), arriving in 1625, lived and worked with the Hurons (in the general neighborhood of the lake which bears their name) for two years without winning a single convert. Brébeuf had few illusions about the difficulty of the task before him, nor did he wish other missionaries to arrive unaware of the enormity of the challenge that confronted them.

After having worked with the Hurons for more than a decade, Father Brébeuf in 1636 advised potential missionaries to dispense with all illusions about the beauties and bounties of a wilderness life among the Indians. You will have, he wrote, no bed but the earth, no roof but the stars, and for dinner "a little corn crushed between two stones and cooked in fine clear water." By day the sun burns you and by night the mosquitoes torment you. If you fall sick, expect no help, for from what source could it be obtained? And if your illness is such as to make it impossible for you to keep up with the Indians in their journeys, "I would not like to guarantee that they would not abandon you." Then you confront the horrendous task of learning a totally distinct language in this wilderness. "The Huron language will be your Saint Thomas and your Aristotle," and despite the fact that you are likely a most clever person, you will do well to remain silent for weeks if not months. "You will have accomplished much if, at the end of a considerable time, you begin to stammer a little." In short, Brébeuf concluded, do not come to New France unless your soul burns with such a fire that no other vocation will satisfy you.

If all these hardships were not enough, still greater suffering lay ahead. In 1649 war broke out between the Hurons and the Iroquois, with the latter being victorious. Hundreds of Hurons were slain, with Brébeuf himself captured. And the Iroquois grievances against the Jesuit were several: he was an intruder, a Frenchman; he was an enemy to the Iroquois god, Areskoui; and he was a friend to the Iroquois enemy, the Hurons. On him, therefore, their full fury could and did fall. He suffered slow and agonizing torture which after some four hours brought a death that could only have been merciful. Father Brébeuf who had counseled his fellow Jesuits to have "sincere affection for the Savages" had surely demonstrated the sincerity of his own.

One of those fellow Jesuits, Isaac Jogues (1607–1646), had arrived in Quebec in the 1630s determined to assist in that missionary venture among the Hurons. In his soul that fire burned which could not otherwise be quenched. No sooner had his work begun, however, than an epidemic broke out, striking both Indian and French alike. For weeks Jogues himself hovered between life and death. By a primitive logic (not altogether outgrown in the modern world), the Hurons reasoned that since the plague arrived soon after the priests had come, the latter were responsible for this most unwelcome disease. As Huron chiefs deliberated the proper time and the proper means for putting the missionaries to death, the Jesuits (fully aware of these discussions) continued their ministry to the sick and dying. The threat of reprisal passed, the fevers subsided, and Jogues himself recovered.

In 1641 the Chippewas invited Jogues to establish a mission in their midst. In the peninsula between Lake Michigan and Lake Superior, the Jesuit father established Sault Sainte Marie, ultimately to become a major settlement. Though eager to press westward where no European had yet been, to preach to the Illinois, the Sioux, and other western tribes, Jogues remained near Georgian Bay and the mission at Sault Sainte Marie. Here for a time his work progressed without serious incident and with modest success. But the next year, 1642, Jogues accompanied some Indians back to Quebec for supplies. The journey, after portage, up the St. Lawrence was hazardous enough with rapids, waterfalls, hunger, and exhaustion. To these normal hazards, however, was added the menace of Iroquois warring parties along the banks of the river. Jogues and his party managed to make it to Quebec safely, but on their return he and several others fell into Iroquois hands. As prisoners of war, they received much abuse and repeated threat of execution. "Amid these dread and alarms," Jogues later wrote, he died many a death or ended up living "a life harder to bear than death." During his several months of captivity, "I made no effort to study the

Iroquois tongue, for why should I learn it, since I believed I was about to die at any moment?"

A year later, under heavy Mohawk guard, Jogues visited the Dutch trading post at the juncture of the Mohawk River with the Hudson, the site of present-day Albany, New York. There fellow Europeans tried to secure his release, but at the same time not alienate those Indians upon whom the Dutch depended for their fur trade. The Dutch Reformed pastor, Johannes Megapolensis (1603–1670), granted Jogues a rare moment of joy by returning to him his lost service book (or breviary) which the Dutch rescued from a Mohawk trying to use it in barter. Father Jogues, however, was obliged to return with the Mohawks to their village, though the Dutch continued to explore the possibility of arranging for his release or escape. Months later, the Dutch assisted him in getting aboard a ship bound for Europe, Jogues setting sail down the Hudson for Manhattan (being the first Catholic priest to visit that Dutch settlement), and then home.

But his story does not end there. Back in France, Jogues made plans to return once more to that mission field where he had labored for nearly a decade. By June of 1644 he was back in Quebec, ready to do whatever needed to be done. What needed doing most just then was to figure out a way to encourage the Indian groups to make peace with each other. The Iroquois, especially the Mohawks, carried on almost ceaseless war against the Hurons. At the request of the latter, the Jesuit agreed to be an emissary for peace to the Mohawks. Unhappily, a band of young Mohawks in a belligerent mood and ever ready to blame the French for all their troubles, captured Jogues and a companion. This time, in October of 1646, the torture and abuse did result in death, a martydom that later (1930) led to the canonization of Saint Isaac, Brébeuf being elevated to sainthood at the same time.

Probably in the very village where Jogues met his death, the daughter of an Iroquois chief and an Algonquian Christian mother converted to Christianity in 1676 when she was twenty years of age. So rigid was her discipline and so extreme her asceticism that she died before she was twenty-five, but her tomb soon became an object of pilgrimage with many stories of miraculous cures being widely circulated. Kateri (or Katherine) Tekakwitha (1656?–1680), though born in New York State, lived her few Christian years near Montreal. But that status as a native of American soil seemed even more important when in 1985 she was elevated to the status of a saint, the first American to be so honored.

French labors in the Mississippi Valley left a significant imprint on the interior of the North American continent. In 1669 a Jesuit named Jacques Marquette arrived as a missionary in Wisconsin; from that base he assisted in the explorations of the upper Mississippi River. His 1673 journey with Louis Jolliet gave Marquette such fame as virtually to obscure his long labors among several Indian tribes in Wisconsin and Illinois. Speaking at least six Indian languages and eager to reach new tribes to the south, Marquette proved the ideal traveling companion for Jolliet. The two men together hoped to find that ever-elusive route to the great western sea and thence to Asia; what they found instead was a silt-laden, widening river that flowed not to the Pacific but to the Gulf of Mexico. France now laid claim to the very heartland of America, from the mouth of the St. Lawrence River in the North to the mouth of the Mississippi in the South. And France's church now had before it a mission field of staggering dimension.

In 1682 Sieur de La Salle (1643–1687) completed the exploration of the Mississippi River south to the broad delta, proving its navigability all the way from the Illinois River to the Gulf of Mexico. For two decades, however, no French settled along the lower Mississippi. One reason for the delay was somewhat embarrassing: the French had difficulty finding the River when coming by way of the Gulf. La Salle tried in 1684, but ended up in Matagorda Bay off the coast of Texas. In another attempt three years later, La Salle was murdered by his own mutinous men. By 1700, however, Jesuits arrived in what is now Biloxi, Mississippi. Father Paul Du Ru (1666–1741) saw before him a missionary challenge that daunted even the bravest. Confronted by the vast diversity in languages and the difficulties of learning even one, Du Ru exclaimed, "If one would want to ask God for a miracle in their favor, it would be the gift of tongues."

In 1702 Mobile (Alabama) was founded, this becoming the oldest French town on the Gulf Coast—since Biloxi was only a fort. And in 1718 the settlement called New Orleans came into being, this destined to become the major center for French missionary activity and the po-

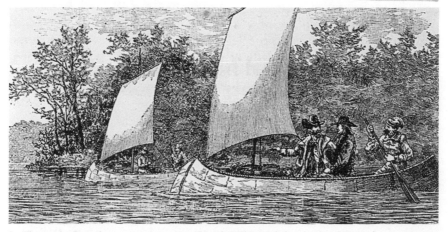

3. The early French penetrations into North America left a lasting imprint up and down the Mississippi River; here Father Jacques Marquette and Explorer Louis Joliet sail down that river in 1673. *Library of Congress*

litical capital for all the Louisiana Territory. Like the Spanish, the French quarreled among themselves over economic and religious priorities, these disputes frustrating the mission effort. The superior of the Jesuit mission, Father de Beaubois, in 1726 concluded an agreement with the responsible French company that made possible a more effective effort among the Indians. Jesuits were joined by other Catholic clergy—Capuchins, Carmelites, Récollets—and even an order of nuns, the Ursulines, in their labors in and beyond New Orleans. For nearly a half-century, however, Jesuits took the lead—reaching out to the Yazoos by 1726, and to the Arkansas, the Choctaws, and the Alibamons in successive years.

Yet two major events, unrelated except in time, brought an end to the extensive Jesuit effort and to much French dominance of interior America. The first event of 1763 was the French suppression of the Society of Jesus. The order had become so powerful and wealthy as to arouse jealousies and fears within both the church and the Royal Family. With a shattering suddenness Jesuit property was sold, seized, or transferred to the Capuchins. Jesuits themselves sought the first available passage back to France, there to be reassigned or pensioned off. Whatever the justifications for this French action (a decade later the pope abolished the Society of Jesus everywhere, though restoration came in 1814), the effects on New France were devastating and never really overcome, especially in the Mississippi Valley.

The same ship that arrived in New Orleans to bring news of the Jesuit suppression brought word of the end of the Seven Years' War between England and France. By the terms of the 1763 Peace of Paris, France ceded to England all territory east of the Mississippi River (except New Orleans) and to Spain all territory west of that great river. After 1763, the French religious presence in the entire interior valley could only be described as ghostly, a presence that lingered on largely in place names and missionary memoirs. Nonetheless, even in the late twentieth century a largely Protestant southeastern United States revealed a powerful Roman Catholic presence in Biloxi, Mobile, and southern Louisiana, these strongholds still offering bold testimony to those modest beginnings hundreds of years earlier.

CHAPTER 4

English Liturgy and English Lethargy

While England hesitated, Spain conquered and France explored. To many an impatient Englishman of the sixteenth century, it appeared that England's sun was being eclipsed by the brilliant daring and early adventuring of other European nations. This might mean that England's gospel, a Protestant gospel, would fall far behind the advances being made by Portugal, Spain, and France—Catholic nations all. What would it take to get England up and moving?

To be fair, England had not been sound asleep. John Cabot (1450–1498) sailed for King Henry VII at the close of the fifteenth century and later John together with his son Sebastian (1476?–1557) moved in for a closer look at Newfoundland and the Atlantic coastline. Like other explorers, they hoped that this closer look would reveal an opening to the Orient and all the riches thereof. The voyages of the Cabots did give England something of a claim to North American lands, but they did not result in any steady development of colonies or forts, conquest or trade.

The notorious Francis Drake (1540?–1596), knighted by Queen Elizabeth in 1581, also indulged in some exploration of the continent, just so long as "scientific observing" did not interfere with the more profitable enterprise of piracy. As English and Spanish hostility increased in the 1580s, Drake became a major maritime nuisance to the ships from the Spanish Main. He wrecked many a Spaniard's fortune, lined many an Englishman's pocket, and took the view—with surprising seriousness—that all his efforts constituted a kind of Protestant crusade. Like Columbus before him, Drake enforced regular religious services aboard his ships, ships that carried Bibles, prayer books, and that most Protestant of all English books, John Foxe's *Book of Martyrs* that offered blood-chilling accounts of the Protestant sufferings under the Catholic Queen Mary I (reign, 1553–1558). Drake believed that any blow against Spain was a blow on behalf of England and of England's own Protestant church. In 1588 came the most disastrous blow of all as the English (with God's help, they so believed) defeated the Spanish

Armada, thereby destroying Spanish naval supremacy and crippling the largely unchallenged ventures into the New World.

A little more than a decade before that defeat, Sir Humphrey Gilbert (1539?–1583) had argued for even more of the Drake type of activity; his argument was made to the Protestant Queen Elizabeth I whose long reign of nearly a half-century (1558–1603) set the course of England's church as well as of England's state. Gilbert contended in effect that heaven helps only those who help themselves, and that England should seize every opportunity to get ahead of her enemies or, as he put it, to "annoy the King of Spain." "The safety of States, Monarchies, and Commonwealths," Gilbert stated, "rests chiefly in making their enemies weak and poor, and themselves strong and rich." He added that God had placed opportunities for strength and wealth in Elizabeth's hands "if your highness shall not overpass good opportunities for the same." Put not your trust in foreign treaties, Gilbert advised, but only in God. And Christian princes can never be justified in making league "with such as are at open and professed war with God himself": that is, Catholic Spain itself. What Gilbert chiefly proposed was an attack upon Spanish shipping anywhere and everywhere, and by every means legal or otherwise. It is as lawful a Christian policy, he concluded, to prevent a mischief ahead of time as to revenge one too late.

Even more important than stopping Spanish trade and plundering her gold, other Englishmen argued, was planting an English foothold firmly in the New World itself. All that territory does not by some natural right belong to Spain or France: England had explored that land too! To establish colonies in North America would advance the national interest just as surely as it would advance the Protestant cause. And two Protestant clergymen, Richard Hakluyt the Younger (1552?–1616) and Samuel Purchas (1575?–1626), made that argument with force and effect.

A graduate of Christ Church, Oxford, Hakluyt maintained a dual loyalty to religion and geography. This was not an unreasonable combination when accurate cartography and improved navigation were so necessary to the spread of the gospel. And if it were to be the right gospel, "true and sincere religion" in Hakluyt's words, then it must be Protestant England and not Catholic Spain who bore the Christian message to North America. Working closely with Walter Raleigh in 1584, Hakluyt presented to Queen Elizabeth *A Discourse on Western Planting.* Here he pleaded for what was to become England's distinctive approach to the New World: settlements and towns rather than trading posts and forts. If the nation's energies be devoted to genuine colonization, he argued, then conversion of the Indian could go forward more surely and at less tragic cost than had been suffered by both Spanish and French. Missionaries would have the opportunity first to learn the language and the customs of the natives, then they could proceed diplomatically and discreetly to "distill into their purged minds the lively liquor of the gospel." Otherwise, the Oxford graduate noted, "for preachers to come unto them rashly without some such preparation for their safety, it were nothing else but to run to their apparent and certain destruction." Such had happened in Florida, such had happened in Canada; now, it was time to do things in a more deliberate and rational fashion.

England was called by God to this task, Hakluyt assured Elizabeth, just as surely as "the blessed Apostle Paul" had been called to be an apostle to the Gentiles. In his letter to the Christians in Rome, Paul asked: "How shall they believe in Him of whom they have not heard? And how shall they hear without a preacher? And how shall they preach except they be sent?" The parallel was exact. The Indians will remain heathen as long as they do not hear the (true) gospel; they cannot hear unless missionaries come to them; and missionaries cannot reach them unless the larger community sends them. Kings and queens of England have been called "Defenders of the Faith," Hakluyt noted, and by this "title I think they are not only charged to maintain and patronize the faith of Christ, but also to enlarge and advance the same." The time for such enlargement, moreover, is now. Spain and France are already well ahead of us; we must delay no longer.

To the argument that the pope had by his line of demarcation already divided the New World between Catholic nations, Hakluyt responded with scorn and utter indignation. The pope had no "lawful authority to give any such dominion at all." To establish this point, the Protestant preacher appealed to the Bible, to history, to the voyages of the Cabots, and to common sense. Besides which, in that century as in later centuries, possession made all the difference. Let's not waste time arguing about who has a right to what: let us go out and possess the land. "This enterprise may stay the Spanish King from flowing over all the face of that vast [land] of America, if we seat and plant there in time, in time I say."

To overcome all the inertia and timidity, Hakluyt mounted a publicity or promotion campaign rarely matched in Western history. He goaded his people by reminding them of the great daring exhibited by Englishmen in the past, of heroic adventures at home and abroad, of long forgotten feats of courage and lionhearted conquest. Hakluyt searched, probed, and pushed in order to gather all such records that "lay so dispersed, scattered, and hidden in several hucksters hands that I now wonder at myself to see how I was able to endure the delays, curiosity, and backwardness of many from whom I was to receive my originals." But he did not stop until he had enough to fill one volume, then three, with wondrous stories of *The Principall Navigations, Voiages,*

Traffics, and Discoveries of the English Nation, Made by Sea or Over Land.*
First published in 1589, this widely read, widely cherished book became England's epic for the Age of Exploration and Discovery. It inspired the country, it warmed the heart, it stirred the blood. Consider, Hakluyt argued, if so much had been so grandly done by so few in the centuries past, how could contemporary Englishmen and women continue to rest in "sluggish security"? In his dedicatory letter that preceded the work, Hakluyt confessed to his sorrow and shame that he heard other nations "miraculously extolled for their discoveries and noble enterprises" while England was at the same time either "ignominiously reported or exceedingly condemned." Many of his readers agreed: sluggish security was unbecoming to so proud a nation with so rich a past. Those who did not read could simply watch the indefatigable Richard Hakluyt as he told of Protestants entering Florida, as he encouraged the voyages of Martin Pring to New England, or urged the formation of the Virginia Company of London, or enlisted as a charter member of the Northwest Passage Company. As author, editor, joiner, geographer, and preacher, Hakluyt gave his whole being to that "most godly and Christian work . . . of enlarging the glorious gospel of Christ."

When he died in 1616, his successor was already hard at work. Fellow clergyman Samuel Purchas eventually in 1625 published *Purchas His Pilgrimes*, a large and untidy work that mixed geography and theology, anthropology and economics, piety and politics. But all these forces were in fact mixed in the minds and motives of those who sailed and those who planted and those who preached. As Walter Raleigh (1552?–1618) so aptly put it, "Men have traveled, as they have lived, for religion, for wealth, for knowledge, for pleasure, for power and the overthrow of rivals." Purchas intended his book to be a history of the known and the about-to-be-known world, with good chronology and accurate geography but with full recognition that the soul of that world was religion. Thus he would write of heathen lands, but with the comforting hope that their "worn-out rites or present irreligious religions" would all be washed in "the purer stream of sacred baptism."

From the vantage point of universal history, Purchas noted that so little of the world was Christian. Moreover, even that small part which was Christian was divided into "sects and superstitions," the Reformation being only a century old when he composed his opus. And when Purchas looked at Protestant England itself, he found little to encourage him. Mostly what he saw was ingratitude and sedition, "the beastly sin of drunkenness, that biting sin of usury, that devilish sin of swaggering. . . . These are payments we return unto the Lord, instead

---

* The archaic spellings here (and elsewhere in the text) are those of the time period under discussion.

of prayers for and loyalty to his majesty; peaceableness and charity to each other; modesty and sobriety in ourselves." His book of universal history contained these sermonic sentiments because the fate of the world depended upon such truths being heard and heeded. In his note to the reader, Purchas dedicated his book "to the glory of God and the good of my country." In order for that glory to be reached and that good attained, England now, Purchas said, must exchange her lethargy for her liturgy. She must rise up, answer the call, sail the seas, preach the gospel.

The promotional efforts of Hakluyt and Purchas did pay off, though the early English attempts at colonization gave little encouragement to either investor or preacher. Hakluyt's contemporaries, the half-brothers Gilbert and Raleigh, not only joined him in the promotion but took steps toward execution. After many delays, Gilbert set sail for New-foundland in 1583, boldly claiming all that he saw on behalf of England. His venture, unfortunately, displayed more vision than careful preparation; only one of the five ships completed the voyage as planned, and Gilbert himself was not among those who returned. His expiring patent or governmental grant was transferred to Raleigh who immediately backed an expedition to the North Carolina and Virginia coasts. Raleigh's two ships returned late in 1584 to report that they had seen a land full of deer, rabbits, and fowl; waters alive with fish; soil "the most plentiful, sweet, fruitful and wholesome of the whole world"; and Indians who were "a kind and loving people." This extravagant report, written by Arthur Barlowe, was only the first of a series of inflated advertisements of the delights of America, reports that regularly and sometimes tragically misled prospective settlers. Some who came to the New World expected not to work but only to reap the natural bounty all around them.

Actual settlement efforts got underway in 1585. Seven ships, commanded by Sir Richard Grenville and Sir Ralph Lane, left 108 settlers on Roanoke Island (off the North Carolina coast) in August of that year. But when Francis Drake (now Sir Francis) drifted by the following June, he found the weary colonists ready to accept passage home. Among other difficulties, the relationships with the Indians had deteriorated rapidly, without much love and kindness evident on either side. Two of the settlers, Thomas Hariot and John White, carried back detailed reports: Hariot in prose and White in drawings. These men believed that, even though their first effort had collapsed, a more carefully planned, a better supplied, and a more advantageously situated colony could actually succeed.

Thus encouraged, Raleigh sent three small ships from Plymouth, England, for the North Carolina coast once more, the party setting sail on May 8, 1587. The settlers, numbering 150 and this time including women and children, made landfall in early August, with the first recorded Protestant service of the New World being held on Roanoke Island that month. August saw another New World "first," as John White's wife gave birth to the first English baby born in North America: Virginia Dare. Shortly after this domestic event, John White (who had been named governor of the colony) found it necessary to return to England to insure that urgently needed supplies reached the struggling settlers. Incredibly, it took him four years to get back, the chief cause of delay being the outbreak of war between Spain and England. When at last White did secure passage back to the Carolina coast, he searched and searched but found no trace of family or friends. And the "lost colony of Roanoke" has still, some four centuries later, not yielded up all its secrets. As one authority noted, the Roanoke adventure began with a birth and ended with a mystery.

In all probability most of the colony, after waiting in vain for White's return, left the island for the region around present-day Norfolk to live near, perhaps eventually with, the Chesapeake Indians residing there. For as long as two decades these survivors may have maintained their English colony and their Protestant worship more or less intact, though with growing assimilation into the culture of the native Americans. Shortly before the settlement in Jamestown in 1607, these colonists fell victim to the fears of the powerful chief, Powhatan, leader of the Virginia Algonquians. No contact between the newly arriving English and the Sir Walter Raleigh colonists was ever made, leading historians to assume that the slaughter was complete. These early colonizing efforts,

4. In the 1580s John White sketched both the terrors of the sea and the promises of the land. *Library of Congress*

however, inspired Hakluyt and Purchas to redouble their zeal and their fellow citizens to reclaim their vision. If not in the reign of Queen Elizabeth, then perhaps in the years of her successor, England would at last leave her own mark upon the still beckoning land.

Suggested Reading for Part One

For documentary readings that expand upon points made in Part One, see Edwin S. Gaustad, *Documentary History of Religion in America* (Grand Rapids, 1982), Vol. 1, 1–92.

On the native American, newer historiography has radically revised most earlier perspectives, with every effort being made to see the history of North America more from the perspective of those present prior to the European "invaders." See, for example, James Axtell, *The European and the Indian* (New York, 1981); and, by the same author, *The Invasion Within: The Contest of Cultures in Colonial North America* (New York, 1985). On the religious life more specifically, one may consult Sam D. Gill, *Native American Religions* (Belmont, Calif., 1982); Walter H. Capps, ed., *Seeing with a Native Eye: Essays on Native American Religion* (New York, 1976); and, Ruth M. Underhill, *Red Man's Religion* (Chicago, 1965). The work of the missionaries, from earliest contact to the twentieth century, is carefully explicated in Henry W. Bowden, *American Indians and Christian Missions* (Chicago, 1981).

The classic biography of Columbus, Samuel Eliot Morison's *Admiral of the Ocean Sea* (Boston, 1942) is supplemented so far as the admiral's religious views are concerned by Pauline M. Watts' article in the *American Historical Review* 90:1 (Feb., 1985), "Prophecy and Discovery: On the Spiritual Origins of Christopher Columbus's 'Enterprise of the Indies' "; and by Leonard I. Sweet's essay in *The Catholic Historical Review* (July, 1986)72:3, "Christopher Columbus and the Millennial Vision of the New World." Morison's *The European Discovery of America: The Northern Voyages* (New York, 1971) offers an excellent introduction to the Age of Exploration and Discovery. The Roman Catholic enterprise in New Spain (and in New France as well) is authoritatively described in John Tracy Ellis, *Catholics in Colonial America* (Baltimore, 1963). On Bartholomew Las Casas, see Lewis Hanke, *All Mankind is One* (DeKalb, Ill., 1974); as well as Henry R. Wagner, *The Life and Writings of Bartholomew Las Casas* (Albuquerque, 1967). On the ventures into Florida, one may turn to Michael V. Gannon, *The Cross in the Sand* (Gainesville, Fla., 1965); and, for New Mexico, to G. P. Hammond and Agapito Rey, *Don*

Juan de Oñate, Colonizer of New Mexico (Albuquerque, 1953). For the story of Junípero Serra, see the biography by W. E. Wise, *Fray Junípero Serra and the California Conquest* (New York, 1967) as well as the splashy book on *The California Missions* published by Sunset Books in Menlo Park, California, in 1964.

Cornelius J. Jaenen's *Role of the Church in New France* (Toronto, 1976) examines both the "missionary church" and France's own "colonial church"; broader context for this religious development is provided in Marcel Trudel's *The Beginnings of New France* (Toronto, 1973) as well as in S. E. Morison's biography of *Samuel de Champlain: Father of New France* (Boston, 1972). For the lives and tragic deaths of France's most famous missionaries to the New World, see Jogues' own *Narrative of a Captivity Among the Mohawk Indians* (New York, 1977) and Joseph P. Donnely, *Jean de Brébeuf, 1593–1649* (Chicago, 1975). The story of the Jesuits in the interior of what became the United States is presented in great detail in G. J. Garraghan, *The Jesuits in the Middle United States,* 3 vols. (New York, 1938).

Louis B. Wright gave full attention to England's religious motivations in his *Religion and Empire: The Alliance between Piety and Commerce in English Expansion* (Chapel Hill, N.C., 1943). England's earliest attempts at colonization receive the most detailed treatment ever granted them in David Beers Quinn, *Set Fair for Roanoke: Voyages and Colonies, 1584–1606* (Chapel Hill, N.C., 1985); the two Richard Hakluyts are placed in context here along with Samuel Purchas, though the latter is treated only briefly. Quinn's "Bibliographical Note" is an extraordinarily reliable guide by the master of England's sixteenth century activity. John White's unique and often reproduced drawings have their most impressive presentation in Paul Hulton, *America at 1585* (Chapel Hill, N.C., 1984). And at last an authoritative edition of the writings of John Smith is available: *The Complete Works of Captain John Smith, 1580–1631,* 3 vols. (Chapel Hill, N.C., 1986). Volume 2 of *Women and Religion in America* (edited by Rosemary Radford Ruether and Rosemary Skinner Keller; San Francisco, 1983) contains excellent chapters, with supporting documents, on religious women in Spanish, French, and English America.

Part 2

AGE OF COLONIZATION

CHAPTER 5

"Almighty God Hath Opened the Gate": VIRGINIA

For England, as for so much of continental Europe, the Reformation began in politics and ended in blood. An affair of state and international diplomacy soon became a matter of life—and of death—for the ordinary citizen, the humble family, the local parish. In England, King Henry VIII took those first political steps in the 1530s, with Parliament at his bidding passing a series of measures that accomplished the separation of the Church in England from the papal authority in Rome. Henry would henceforth be the earthly head of England's national church: that much was clear. Less clear was how Protestant or how Catholic that English church should be.

While some blood was shed during Henry's reign (1509–1547), the nation as a whole escaped widespread persecution and recrimination. During the brief reign of the "Boy King," Edward VI (1547–53), England shifted sharply in the direction of Protestantism; then in the equally brief reign of Mary I (1553–1558), the shift turned sharply back toward Roman Catholicism. These turbulent, unsteadying, and often brutal years made the nation yearn for religious peace, if such could be found in the sixteenth century. A new and youthful queen came to the throne in 1558; fortunately her years of rule were long (1558–1603) and her policies judicious. Queen Elizabeth I also had the good fortune to see her nation emerge victorious over its bitter rival, Spain's defeat being dramatically symbolized in the defeat of its Armada in 1588.

Elizabeth did not have the good fortune of seeing colonies successfully launched in the New World. That outcome would await her successor, the first of the Stuart line of monarchs, James I, who reigned from 1603 to 1625. On April 10, 1606, James chartered two companies to support settlements somewhere in North America. One, the London Company, was granted exclusive right to settle in (and, everyone hoped, make a profit from) land between the thirty-fourth and forty-first degrees of latitude, with the company's authority extended westward over land one hundred miles and eastward over the ocean for the same distance. The other company, named Plymouth, received a similar grant farther to the north. On the first of January, 1607, the London

Company sent forth its first expedition, the group of three small ships sighting the Virginia coast near the end of April. The first permanent settlement, Jamestown, bore the name of England's monarch, but the colony as a whole took its name from the Virgin Queen (Elizabeth) who had so markedly advanced the nation's fortunes. Likewise, with an appropriate sense of history as well as of gratitude, the title of honorary rector of the first parish formed at Jamestown was given to Richard Hakluyt.

As one would expect in a visibly religious age, with the Reformation itself not yet a century old, religious motivations received explicit acknowledgment in the Royal Charter of Virginia. So daring an adventure was to be carried on only "by the providence of God," and the propagation of the Christian religion to those who "as yet live in darkness and miserable ignorance of the true knowledge and worship of God" remained a prime motivation. Also as John Rolfe observed on behalf of the settlers, the group saw themselves as "a peculiar people, marked and chosen by the finger of God, to possess [the land], for undoubtedly He is with us."

For many years, however, these colonists might well be forgiven for questioning whether God indeed was with them. Jamestown came perilously close to meeting a fate similar to that which befell the earlier efforts of Sir Walter Raleigh. The total number of settlers, a little more than one hundred in May of 1607, had by the following September been reduced by half. Indians attacked even before the first fort could be finished. And when it was completed, fire broke out, destroying that fort along with several houses, the church, and Chaplain Robert Hunt's entire library. Food rotted, rats invaded, supplies disappeared, and mutiny threatened. Sickness, always on the heels of famine, spread in the "malarial swamp" that the settlers had, through no great luck, settled upon. More settlers arrived along with more supplies, but these augmentations were themselves to be followed by more tribulations. An especially severe "starving time" in the winter of 1609 to 1610 so decimated the young colony that it seemed doomed to failure. But, asserted the explorer, governor, and historian, Captain John Smith, God "would not that it should be unplanted."

Whatever the motivations of the Englishmen who came to Virginia, the expectations were out of all proportion to the reality. The Spanish had found gold and silver in their colonies; these first Virginians found none. Neither did they find other natural resources to exploit nor profitable crops to raise for export. The Indians, not surprisingly, declined to become a docile labor force, and English gentlemen, all too surprisingly, declined to assume the necessary and obvious burdens of subsistence farming. The population of the struggling colony had reached about two thousand in 1622 when an Indian counteroffensive resulted in the deaths of about one-fifth of the settlement. Profits were nonexistent and the potential even for survival was not promising. In 1624 the king took over control of the colony to improve its direction and to prevent its demise. Virginia was saved, however, not so much by its new status as a royal colony as by its cultivation of a crop that promised to make the economy work at last: tobacco. Although James I vehemently condemned the vile weed and its corrupting effect in English society, Virginians found in its exportation the nearest equivalent to the Spaniards' gold.

Religious progress was no speedier than the economic improvement. After Jamestown, a second parish was organized in 1611 in Henrico where the rector, Alexander Whitaker (1587–1617), proved himself an able propagandist in the tradition of Hakluyt and Purchas. His sermon, "Good News from Virginia," found an eager audience in England, especially among the parish poor who were ready to believe that some better lot could be theirs in a new and promising land. The Reverend Alexander Whitaker also won a place in Virginia's early history by performing the celebrated marriage in 1614 between John Rolfe (1585–1622) and Pocahantas (1595?–1617). Rolfe took pains to emphasize that his courtship came not from "carnal affection" but from his concern "for the good of this plantation, for the honor of our country, for the glory of God, for my own salvation, and for converting to the true knowledge of God and Jesus Christ an unbelieving creature: namely Pocahantas." Rolfe did confess, however, that he—like any man in love—found his thoughts and emotions so tangled up, caught "in so intricate a labyrinth that I was even awearied to unwind myself thereout." Rolfe nonetheless, in words that many of his fellow colonists would also affirm, declared that "Almighty God . . . hath opened the gate and led me by the hand that I might plainly see and discern the safe paths wherein to tread." While the marriage did promise for a time to improve relationships between the English and the Indians, Pocahantas herself died in 1617, still in her early twenties, while Rolfe was killed five years later in the Indian uprising.

Before Rolfe's death in 1622, the Virginia legislature took its first steps in 1619 toward making the Church of England the officially established and publicly supported sole church in Virginia. Parishes were laid out, glebe lands (acreage that could be used to raise crops for the support of the church) were set aside, and support for the clergy was promised. Again in 1642 and 1662, in language ever more explicit and prescriptive, the legislature provided for a re-creation in Virginia of the familiar National Church at home. Only one doctrinal standard would be tolerated: namely, the Thirty-Nine Articles of the Church of England; only one ministry would be accepted: namely, that sent out by some bishop back in England. Any clergyman arriving in Virginia was obliged to present his credentials to the royal governor sitting in Jamestown. The governor would then induct the properly ordained and properly commissioned minister into his parish, "and if any other person pretending himself a minister shall, contrary to this Act, presume to teach or preach publicly or privately, the Governor & Council are hereby desired and impowered to suspend & silence the person so offending." The state, however weak, would protect and defend the church, however tentative its development.

In addition to laying out the geographical boundaries of the parishes, assuring the purity of doctrine, and guaranteeing a ministerial monopoly in Virginia, the legislature in 1662 provided for the governance of each local parish through the creation of a vestry of twelve "of the most able men of each parish." This board would be responsible not only for the ecclesiastical affairs as such, but would also have much broader community responsibility. The vestry would be specially responsible for the administration of charity in the area and the men were generally directed to conduct the "orderly managing of all parochial affairs." Such persons must, of course, pledge their loyalty not alone to the King of England but to the King's church, pledging their conformity "to the Doctrine & Discipline of the Church of England."

One-half century after the Jamestown settlement, the legal structure for a truly official church had been set into place. One might expect to see in the Virginia of the 1660s, therefore, the typical English church presiding over the typical English village in such serenity as to convince the English emigrant that he or she had never left home. That, however, is not the way that it worked out. First of all, no typical English towns arose along the banks of Virginia's broad and navigable rivers.

5. This famous painting that hangs in the U. S. Capitol portrays the marriage between John Rolfe and Pocahantas in 1614. *Library of Congress*

Parishes were measured not in blocks, but in miles, as they stretched in narrow bands along the James, or the York, or the Rappahannock rivers. Potential congregations were so widely scattered as to make gathering of a significant number difficult and, in bad weather, impossible. Covering even a single parish of such imposing breadth proved a formidable task, but because of scant population, a harried minister might find himself assigned to two or more of these sprawling and expansive parishes. A minister could hardly offer regular services in each parish, nor could he always be on hand for the christenings, weddings, and funerals where his presence was expected. In the absence of the minister and sometimes in the absence of a church building, the plantation home and the plantation cemetery could become more the center of sacred life, as they already were in secular life.

The parish church, therefore, was often both literally and figuratively at the edge rather than at the center of community life in the seventeenth century. The church's marginality was aggravated by a shortage of clergy, especially of well-qualified and well-motivated clergy. Virginia in its early years offered little to potential ministers but personal hardship and a meagre livelihood. Aware of this problem, the legislature tried from time to time to strengthen the position of the clergy and to assure their income, but salaries paid in tobacco and corn could never be stable since the market price of these products fluctuated so widely. Some parishes failed to provide even a modest dwelling for their ministers, so that Governor William Berkeley found it necessary at midcentury to instruct each congregation that had installed a minister to "build for him a convenient Parsonage House." The glebe lands should be cultivated for the benefit of the clergyman and his family as well as for the support and upkeep of the parish. But a dozen years later, an English observer in Virginia reported that the ministers there were condemned to "see their families disordered, their children untaught, the public worship and service of the great God they own neglected."

For their part, the parishes could complain that some of the clergy received better support than they deserved. Ministerial quality throughout the seventeenth century proved a problem virtually beyond solution. For a time, it seemed that only those clergy left England who wished to escape bad debts, unhappy marriages, unsavory reputations. In 1632 the Virginia House of Burgesses felt obliged to decree as follows: "Ministers shall not give themselve to excess in drinking, or riot, spending their time idly by day or night playing at dice, cards, or any other unlawful game; but they shall . . . occupy themselves with some honest study or exercise, always doing the things which shall appertain to honesty, and endeavor to profit the Church of God." They should, furthermore, keep in mind their solemn obligation to be a model, "to excel all others in purity of life and . . . be an example to the people to

live well and Christianly." A visitor two decades later concluded that
the legislation had not had much effect: "Virginia savoring not hand-
somely in England," John Hammond wrote in 1656. The young colony
managed to get only those who could dress themselves up in black
coats, who could "babble in a pulpit, roar in a tavern, exact from their
parishioners, and . . . by their dissoluteness destroy [rather] than feed
their flocks."

This dreary picture, overdrawn even for its own time, gradually improved over the second half of the seventeenth century and sharply
improved in the eighteenth. Yet, it could not be denied that the Church
of England in early Virginia did not enjoy anything like the good health
that its legislative favor would seem to ensure. A pamphlet appearing
in 1662, perhaps by Roger Green, carrying the title, "Virginia's Cure,"
pointed the sickly patient toward a path of renewed health: If Virginia
had no towns, if her population was widely scattered and without
education, if her clergy were few in number and deficient in quality,
obviously some heroic measures must be taken. Towns must be created, artificially if necessary, where the women and children at least

6. When the capital of Virginia moved from Jamestown to Williamsburg at the end of
the seventeenth century, the Bruton Parish Church took on greater importance; this
building reached its present form with the addition of the tower in 1769. *Library of
Congress*

may live while the plantation master and his laborers work the land. (The latter can come into town on weekends.) With such towns, schools can be supported and attended; parish churches can be, as they must, the true center of religious life. With respect to the clergy, "Virginia Fellowships" must be offered in England that will pay for the education of worthy young men who, in exchange for their education of seven years, will agree to spend a minimum of seven years in Virginia, elevating the morals of the people and giving real substance to the Anglican church in that wilderness. The advice, while it had much merit, was not followed until some forty years later when Thomas Bray (1656–1730) marshalled the forces of private philanthropy in England to create societies that would send both literature (Society for Promoting Christian Knowledge, 1699) and clergy (Society for the Propagation of the Gospel, 1701) to all of the English colonies in North America.

By mid-seventeenth century about thirty Anglican parishes had been created in Virginia, that number doubling by the end of the century, with the greatest number being created in the period from 1640 to 1660. Parishes in the most settled portions of the Tidewater region ranged from twenty to forty miles long, and five to ten miles in width. Though this was enough of a challenge to a single clergyman, parishes farther to the west or south of the James River might be a hundred miles or more in length. Just as the territory varied widely from parish to parish, so did the population and the ability, therefore, of any given parish to employ a minister, build a church, maintain a regular schedule of services, and care for the widows, the orphans, and the poor. Whatever the difficulties that Anglicanism faced in Virginia, the church steadily improved its position so that by the middle of the eighteenth century parishes numbered more than one hundred and Anglicanism was stronger in Virginia than anywhere else in North America.

Alone among the southern colonies, Virginia even had its own college, founded in the final decade of the seventeenth century. Under the prompting and coaxing of a commissary (a bishop's representative), James Blair, the audacious idea for a college became a positive movement. Blair petitioned the Virginia legislature for approval of the idea, raised money in support of the notion, sailed to England to win royal sanction and an official charter. In 1693 the College of William and Mary received its charter, so that Virginia youth might "be piously educated in good letters and manners," so that the Church in Virginia might be provided "with a seminary of ministers of the gospel," and so that "the Christian religion may be propagated amongst the Western Indians, to the glory of Almighty God." The college never managed to attract the Indians, nor did it prove an effective training ground for clergy since all young men still had to journey to England for ordination. But the school did, particularly in the eighteenth century, educate many who would play significant roles in the formative years of the new nation.

Just as the strength of Anglicanism in Virginia seemed assured, two challenges (one religious and one political) confronted this legally sanctioned, state-protected church. The religious challenge came in the form of dissenting (that is, non-Anglican) churches that, despite the legal prohibitions, began to infiltrate the colony of Virginia. Early penetrations in the seventeenth century by Puritans and Quakers met with such stern resistance and open hostility that these challengers did not grow from strength to strength. In the eighteenth century, however, Presbyterians, Baptists, and Methodists repeatedly battered against the wall of Anglican establishment. In general these dissenters settled not in the eastern Tidewater where Anglicanism dominated, but in the foothills and the backcountry of more western, more mountainous Virginia. Also, these dissenters in general shared a fondness for evangelical religion, for religion more passionate and personal than that often found in the formal liturgy and printed prayers of Anglicanism. A wave of religious excitement and revivalism known as the Great Awakening swept across much of North America in the 1740s and beyond; evangelical religion rode that wave into the hinterlands of Virginia, sweeping across the land with such force that it could be neither ejected nor defeated. Indeed, by the end of that century the evangelicals had totally transformed the society no less than the religion of colonial Virginia.

The Presbyterian preacher Samuel Davies (1723–1761) came into the colony from Pennsylvania in 1747. Finding himself outside the law, unable to perform marriages, unauthorized to travel from community to community, unwelcome by all authorities, civil or ecclesiastic, Davies protested again and again that Virginia was exceeding the prohibitions even of England. More than a half-century before when the cosovereigns, William and Mary, came to England's throne in 1689, they had issued a Declaration of Religious Toleration that granted some measure of recognition to Protestant dissenters. Now Virginia, even though it boasted a college that bore these monarchs' names, resisted the implementation of their liberality. As Davies evangelized widely, among both blacks and whites, political authorities grew fearful, resentful, and finally determined to stamp out dissent on their own home ground. Back in England, however, the authorities were not nearly so alarmed by this influx of dissent. Concerned about the economic growth of the colony, the London-based Board of Trade advised that "a toleration and free exercise of religion is so valuable a branch of true liberty and so essential to the improving and enriching [of] a trading nation, it should ever be held sacred to His Majesty's Colonies." The Board advised Virginia, therefore, to do nothing that would "in the least affect that great point."

So forceful a policy declaration did not immediately wipe away all impediments of law and custom, but it did make the colonial authorities somewhat more circumspect in their harassment and persecution. Many more years would pass, however, before "free exercise" would become a meaningful and effective phrase throughout Virginia. Meanwhile, Davies continued to preach, continued to push, continued to win converts to evangelical religion in general and to Presbyterianism in particular. Davies took seriously the obligation to see that the gospel reached Virginia's blacks who in 1750 numbered over one hundred thousand. In that year, Davies reported that he had personally baptized "about forty of them in a year and a half, seven or eight of whom are admitted into full communion and partake of the Lord's Supper."

Blacks had first come to Virginia more or less by accident in 1619, but once they proved to be an effective labor force, blacks were brought in ever-increasing numbers to Virginia's shores. Soon *blackness* and *slavery* became interchangeable terms, even though a few free blacks managed to maintain their own farms on Virginia's Eastern Shore. Religious instruction among this large proportion of the population (about forty percent by 1750) was impeded by several factors: resistance of the plantation owners to giving their workers sufficient time off for religious education; fear that a Christian baptism might change their civil status from that of slave to a free person; widespread illiteracy in the black population; and even, at the lowest level of rationalization, the baleful argument that blacks had no souls. With some exceptions, Anglicanism had not made significant, certainly not commendable, progress in converting the slave population to Christianity. A 1730 report from London deplored the lack of progress, even on the part of missionaries dispatched for that very purpose. Evangelical religion, on the other hand, made the gospel appear more accessible, more comprehensible, more emotionally satisfying. Davies had found blacks ready to hear, ready to sing, ready to learn; other evangelical leaders found the same to be true and, before many years had passed, blacks found leaders within their own ranks to preach, organize, and inspire.

A second evangelical group, the Baptists, succeeded in becoming a prominent force in Virginia during the second half of the eighteenth century. From New England, Shubal Stearns (1706–1771) arrived in 1754 to spread the notion of a free church, without a confining or authoritarian hierarchy, of a ministry that depended upon no credential or ceremony other than the call of God, of a baptism by immersion not of infants but of adult believers who heard a gospel that they were ready to accept and profess. Though Stearns himself soon left for North Carolina, he left behind many to continue the evangelical conquest. So many continued in such force that one Anglican leader in Lunenburg County warned in 1759: This "shocking Delusion . . . threatens the entire subversion of *true Religion* in these parts, unless the principal persons concerned in that delusion are apprehended or otherwise re-strained." Some forty to fifty Baptist preachers were jailed or "other-wise restrained" over the next fifteen years or so, usually the charge being one of disturbing the peace. One such arrest in 1774 of a half-dozen "well-meaning men" near the home of James Madison (1751–1836) in Orange County set the future president on a career dedicated to religious liberty. At the age of only twenty-two, Madison wrote to condemn that "diabolical, hell-conceived principle of persecution." No Baptist, Madison was ready to make common cause with them and other dissenters who found themselves arrested and jailed for no rea-son other than the assertion of their religious opinions.

John Leland (1754–1841), another New Englander come south, was for his part ready to make common cause with Madison if the latter promised to help make religious liberty a reality not alone in Virginia but throughout all the colonies now become states in the process of forming a new nation. Arriving in Virginia in 1776, Leland quickly identified himself with the cause of evangelical religion and with the cause of religious liberty. Baptists joined with Presbyterians in peti-tioning the Virginia legislature for relief from oppressive laws that fa-vored Anglicanism and discouraged all dissent. Baptists joined with Jeffersonians in urging that the best thing which government can do for religion is simply leave it alone. As Leland observed, state establish-ment of religion has done more harm to the cause of Christ "than all the persecutions ever did." Official government support of religion, like a bear, "hugs the saints but corrupts Christianity," while persecution, like a lion, "tears the saints to death, but leaves Christianity pure."

In his traveling all across Virginia, Leland led in the creation of many new churches and in the rapid development of the Baptist denomina-tion. Women as well as men assumed prominent roles in church wor-ship, this also alienating and horrifying the Anglican establishment which denounced a sect so disorderly as to allow women to pray in public, as to permit "every ignorant man to preach who chose," and as to encourage "noise and confusion in their meetings." Shubal Sterns' sister, Martha, even took to the pulpit and on "countless occasions melted a whole concourse into tears, by prayers and exhortations." Blacks turned to the Baptists in greater numbers than to any other religious body, in part because they were free to create their own fel-lowships, ordain their own clergy, improvise their own modes of wor-ship. Leland, who welcomed their conversion, grew ever more anxious about their condition. In 1790 he presented to Virginia Baptists a res-olution that condemned slavery as "a violent deprivation of the rights of nature" and as an institution wholly "inconsistent with a republican government." Although his resolution was adopted, the fate of slavery in Virginia (and elsewhere) was not to be so swiftly nor so peacefully settled.

Methodists achieved independent denominational status in America only after the nation itself had won its independence from England. Well before that denominational "Declaration of Independence" in 1784, Methodism as a movement within the Church of England made itself felt in Virginia. Launched by the brothers John and Charles Wesley, Methodism in England began as an effort to revive the languishing Church of England, to improve personal piety, and to reach the working classes who seemed to be abandoning the National Church in ever larger numbers. Methodism was, in other words, initially a little church within a larger church, not a separate ecclesiastical entity. As such, it drew upon laypeople to a great degree to spread its message both in England and in America. In Virginia, Methodism used some of the Anglican churches as a natural base of operations and at least one Anglican clergyman, Deveraux Jarrett (1733–1801) of New Kent County, found himself caught up in the fervor of this evangelical force. Anglicanism found Methodism even more disturbing than the other dissenting forces, since these Wesleyans were boring from within. They threatened, or at least many Anglicans believed, to turn the whole Church of England upside down, to alter its liturgy, dismiss its bishops, and totally refashion its mode of Christian living. Despite harsh condemnations and even passionate pleas from the Bishop of London to stop this virulent plague from spreading, Methodism continued to make rapid progress in Virginia—and elsewhere. And, after its formal break with the Church of England in the 1780s, the Methodist denomination grew even more swiftly.

So Presbyterians, Baptists, and Methodists all beat against that stout civil wall which surrounded and protected the Anglican church. It is doubtful, however, if that wall would have fallen if major political forces had not added their force and their voice. First among these was, of course, the American Revolution itself. In fighting a war against England, most Americans were disinclined to seek or preserve any special favor for the church of that England. The Revolution threw Anglicanism on the defensive not so much because Anglicans opposed the Revolution, though outside of Virginia large numbers did oppose it. While most Virginia churchmen and women supported the Revolution, nonetheless the very nature and government of their church was intimately joined with England: England's civil authority as well as her sacred authority. In 1776 when so much was happening in America on the political front, many Virginians began to take steps to sever those bonds which had identified the colony all too closely with her "Mother Church."

Thomas Jefferson (1743–1826), though nominally an Anglican himself, led in the battle for a full and free exercise of religion in Virginia. Proposing a "Bill for Establishing Religious Freedom" as early as 1779, Jefferson had to wait for many forces to coalesce before some seven years later his bill finally became law. One hundred and fifty years or more of an establishment tradition was not readily overturned. Virginia's legislature tended to be dominated still by the Tidewater region where Anglicanism was so strong and a pattern of church-state connection so fixed. Indeed, that long-standing pattern led some patriots to argue that if the Church of England were no longer officially supported, then at the very least Christianity must be declared the state religion.

Patrick Henry (1736–1799) took the lead in trying to get such a bill passed in the 1780s, a bill that would affirm that "the Christian Religion shall in all times coming be deemed and held to be the established Religion of this Commonwealth." James Madison on the other hand took the lead in seeing that such a bill never became law. In 1785 he presented his famous Memorial and Remonstrance against the Henry proposal, arguing (like Leland) that the effect of a government establishment of religion had always, since the days of Constantine, been bad for religion. Such special favor created "pride and indolence in the Clergy; ignorance and servility in the laity; in both, superstition, bigotry, and persecution." Christianity, Madison declared, was not created by human power nor did it depend upon human power for its survival; those who profess this religion deny its "innate excellence and the patronage of its Author" when they plead for the support and sanction of the state. As Patrick Henry lost and James Madison won, as a Revolution was concluded and a new frame of government adopted, the Anglican walls in Virginia came tumbling down.

Henceforth, the Church of England (renamed the Protestant Episcopal Church after the Revolution) would become only one among many denominations in that state where it had, for so long, played so dominant a role. Evangelical religion would prevail, reaching powerfully into the black population, offering leadership opportunities to the female population, and finding its first political cause in the common struggle for that "free exercise" which the Board of Trade had commended to its colony decades earlier. The most populous of the colonies by the 1760s, Virginia took bold steps in the 1780s toward religious liberty, steps that would light pathways for other states and for the nation.

CHAPTER 6

"One Small Candle May Light a Thousand": PURITAN NEW ENGLAND

While some Englishmen and women labored to transplant England's National Church to Virginia, others labored to transform that church into a more thoroughly Protestant institution, an institution closer to that which John Calvin had brought into being in Geneva. Still others, despairing of any genuine reformation of the state church, resolved to separate themselves from it in order to create a true and pure Christian church according to their understanding of what the New Testament required. The Puritans hoped to change the character, the liturgy, the theology, and the governance of the whole Church of England. The Pilgrims hoped to create a new church model, starting all over again, separate from politics, separate from royal control, separate from the pretensions of Parliament and of lordly bishops.

Those who in American history have won the name of "Pilgrims" and who are forever associated with the crossing of the Mayflower determined, while still in England, to go their own ecclesiastical way. In the early seventeenth century this was both illegal and dangerous. To be identified as a "nonconformist," that is as one who did not conform to the National Church and its Book of Common Prayer, was to fall not only into social disgrace but into the hands of the nearest sheriff. A small congregation of Separatists (or Pilgrims) in Nottingham, north of London, met secretly in the early years of the seventeenth century, trying to hide from the eyes of the law, trying to decide what was right in the eyes of God. If they stayed in England, they must either compromise their consciences or lose their estates and possibly their lives. If they left England, where could they go?

Holland presented the likeliest option, being only a few miles distant across the English channel. Also Holland provided a greater measure of religious toleration in the early 1600s than did any other European country. So around 1607 this congregation which had been meeting weekly in the home of William Brewster (always with a lookout posted

51

to warn of the sheriff's approach) determined to migrate, as a church, to a land "they knew not but by hearsay, where they must learn a new language, and get their livings they knew not how." But for freedom of worship, they would pay the price, take the risk, leave their farms and homes.

Amsterdam, a major commercial port, was their first new residence. The city proved too full of temptations and seductions, however, so that the group, under the leadership of John Robinson, removed to the smaller town of Leyden, "a fair and beautiful city, and of a sweet situation, but made more famous by the university with which it is adorned." This voluntary exile was assumed to be a temporary one: they would remain in Holland only until England came to its senses, until demands for religious conformity would become less stringent, until England like Holland would grant some measure of toleration to the nonconformist. The Pilgrims waited, then waited some more.

The hoped for changes did not come. Meanwhile, all was not going well for this congregation in Holland. Finding jobs and making a living had not proved easy. Families saw their children growing up not as English boys and girls, but as Dutch lads and lasses; some were even "drawn away by evil examples into extravagant and dangerous courses." The sabbath was not honored on the continent any better than it was being honored in England under James I. And surrounded by so strong a foreign culture, the unity and purity of their own fellowship seemed threatened. It was time to go home.

But how could they go home? As Separatists, they would be fined or whipped or jailed or forced to conform. As Englishmen and women, however, what other choice did they have? To stay in Holland was to lose their national identity; to return to England was to lose their religious integrity. Neither alternative had any appeal, and yet the hard dilemma offered no other way out. Unless. Unless they could return to English soil, but not in England itself where sheriffs were so near, and bishops so powerful. Unless they could cross a furious ocean far from the immediate force of intolerable law, yet not so far from England's flag or language or broad blessing. Could it work? Was it possible? How great would be the cost? What chance of royal permission did they, nonconformists still, possibly have?

Answering those tough questions took many years. Complex negotiations were required to gain the approval of the Virginia Company and of the king. The latter proved more difficult than the former, since the notion of religious liberty was no more acceptable to James I thousands of miles away than it was close to home. These Separatists had to prove that they were God-fearing Englishmen, not radicals, not hostile to the nation's interests, not likely to subvert the whole colonial enterprise. The Pilgrims came as close as they could to asserting their orthodoxy and loyalty; the king came as close as he could to recognizing their liberty; the Virginia Company came as close as it could to underwriting the costs of the voyage. Thus in July of 1620, not the whole Leyden church but a portion thereof left Holland for England where two ships would be readied for the Atlantic crossing. Two ships left Southampton in August, but one proved unseaworthy; the remaining ship, the *Mayflower*, put in at Plymouth to try again, now with more supplies and more passengers. On September 6, the single ship set out for "northern Virginia" with 102 passengers aboard. Sixty-six days and four deaths later, the ship sighted land off Cape Cod, far north of where they had planned to land. But weary Pilgrims had no intention of sailing any more: if this was where God wanted them to be, here they would settle, here they would farm, here they would worship, here they would establish another Plymouth in the New World.

7. The artist imaginatively presents the departure of the Pilgrims from Holland—bound first for England, then for North America. *Library of Congress*

William Bradford (1590–1657), governor of this small colony for thirty years, recorded the bleakness of that November arrival. We had, he wrote, "no friends to welcome [us], no inns to entertain or refresh [our] weatherbeaten bodies." No houses awaited them, and the wilderness that did await them seemed filled only with "wild beasts and wild men." What could sustain us in this winter season, Bradford asked, "but the Spirit of God and His grace?" He dared to hope that future generations would be willing to say, "Our fathers were Englishmen which came over this great ocean, and were ready to perish in this wilderness, but they cried unto the Lord, and He heard their voice and looked on their adversity."

The Plymouth Colony began to plant, to fish, to hunt, to cut and saw. The Indian Squanto, "a special instrument of God for [our] good," taught them how to cultivate and fertilize the corn. Like Jamestown, Plymouth found that first year almost too much to bear. Of the twenty-six heads of families, only twelve survived into the spring. Of eighteen married women, only three lived through the winter. But by the fall of 1621, with the first harvest in, Pilgrims and Indians could share in a thanksgiving meal, not an orgy of indulgence, but a grateful recognition that they had, somehow, survived.

The Plymouth colony never grew by great leaps. In 1630, the population was only a few hundred and a decade later barely a thousand. In 1660 only two thousand inhabited the colony which, a generation later, was absorbed into the much larger Massachusetts Bay Colony, located a few miles farther north. This latter settlement, which began in the 1630s with massive migration from England to the bay around Boston, reached a population of twenty thousand by 1660 and nearly three times that number by the end of the seventeenth century.

These Puritans who came in such strength regarded themselves as still very much part of the Church of England, the purer part that in a *new* England would be able to demonstrate what a truly revitalized Church of England ought to be. They had hoped, while still in England, to move the entire state establishment in a more Calvinist, less Catholic, direction. But like the Pilgrims, they found the bishops too strong, the inertia too great, the penalties of law too heavy. Unlike the Pilgrims, however, they did not take the dreaded step of schism from their dear mother church; rather, they took the bold step of emigration, carrying with them their own charter for the Massachusetts Bay Company, and carrying with them their firm conviction that to this land they were called by God and in this land they would be sustained by him.

John Winthrop, many times governor of the Bay Colony (as Bradford was of Plymouth) outlined the motives and the vision of these Puritans as in 1630 they sailed into what would become "their" bay. We come as a dedicated community, Winthrop declared, as a true and pure church, as members of a covenant one with another and with God. "We must love one another with a pure heart fervently; we must bear one another's burdens"; and above all we must keep faith with our God, for "we are a Company professing ourselves fellow members of Christ." We have made a contract, pledged ourselves to an agreement; "we have taken out a Commission." And we must not fail. God has promised to do certain things for us; in turn, we have promised to do certain things for Him. "Now if the Lord shall please to hear us, and brings us in peace to the place we desire, then hath he ratified this Covenant and sealed our Commission." Our duty is set before us, Winthrop noted, and if we neglect it, "the Lord will surely break out in wrath against us [and] be avenged of such a perjured people and make us know the price of the breach of such a Covenant."

That stern warning was to be repeated over and over during the course of the next several generations, as these Puritans built their city upon a hill, conducted their errand into the wilderness, sought "a due form of Government both civil and ecclesiastical," and labored to "work out our Salvation under the power and purity of his holy Ordinances." And though the Puritans initially thought of themselves as still part of the Church of England, that part gradually became so distinctive as ultimately to acquire an independent life and new name: Congregationalism. An early and prominent Boston clergyman, John Cotton (1584–1652), set down what he regarded as the major Puritan complaints against the National Church, and in these complaints one can see the beginnings of the Congregational or the New England Way.

In the National Church, Cotton noted, the rule exercised by the bishops and the rigid conformity demanded by the law had become burdens too onerous to bear. The use of the Book of Common Prayer, moreover, violated the Second Commandment which forbade men to bow down before the work of their own hands. Third, Cotton declared that the authority of the church should be congregational, not national; the highest human authority is neither king nor archbishop, but the members themselves. If that gave great power to the members, they for their part must prove themselves worthy of such power by giving evidence in their lives of their genuine conversion, of their having been chosen by God for eternal felicity with him. Finally, the church (said Cotton) is created not by legislative action from above, but by contractual agreement from below. Church members must covenant together to create a fellowship of the redeemed. The church is not a building (that's called a meeting house), but a gathering of the faithful who, in the words of the Salem group, "covenant with the Lord and with another; and do bind ourselves in the presence of God to walk together in all his ways, according as he is pleased to reveal himself unto us in his blessed word of truth."

In the colony of Massachusetts, then of Connecticut, and later of New Hampshire, the New England Way took shape, molding itself with such firmness and care as to stamp upon that region a way of thinking and living that would endure far beyond the colonial period and far beyond the reaches of the northeast corner of America. Congregationalism or Puritanism, unlike Virginia's Anglicanism, was built into the fabric of their lives by the immigrants themselves. London did not direct the enterprise or approve the clergy or enforce the doctrine. While the Virginia Company hoped for profits in Plymouth and the

Massachusetts Company shared similar dreams for Boston, the citizens themselves came to the New World primarily for reasons of faith, not to serve the commercial or mercantile interests above all else. Puritans came for freedom of religion, but only for their freedom of religion.

It is important to understand that they never intended to launch a colony which would be open to all persons of all religious persuasions—or of none. The Puritans and Pilgrims came to create a pure church, conduct a holy experiment in a wilderness where none would interfere, none would oppose or even distract. They were not hypocrites who came to America for freedom of religion, then would allow a similar freedom to no one else. That was never the plan, never the errand. They came to prove that one could form a society so faithful, a church so cleansed, that even old England itself would be transformed by witnessing what determined believers had managed to achieve many thousands of miles away. That was the vision to be steadily pursued, without weakening or wavering, without transgressing or backsliding, without forgetting that it is God who has made us and not we ourselves. We are his people, bound together with him in a solemn covenant.

THEOLOGY

Within the context of the Protestant Reformation, Puritanism identified itself with that broad tradition known as Calvinism. John Calvin and those who followed after him emphasized above all else the absolute sovereignty of God. God, not man, was in charge of the universe, and from that fundamental proposition all other theology must flow. As the Puritan poet Edward Taylor (1645?–1729) inquired:

> Lord, Can a Crumb of Dust the Earth outweigh
> Outmatch all mountains, nay the Chrystall Sky?

Humankind is that dust, more the folly than the glory of the universe, and the Lord of all the heavens above or below exercises a dominion, a power, that mere dust and pathetic worms cannot contend against. God rules, man obeys.

In the all important matter of salvation, therefore, one would expect the Puritan to hold that this is an affair wholly within the power and purview of God. And so it is. Men and women do not choose God; he chooses them. But he does so in accordance with the terms of that covenant agreed to by both parties. Samuel Willard (1640–1707), Harvard class of 1659 and Massachusetts clergyman, wrote glowingly of the covenant of grace and its inestimable benefit. God and mankind "strike hands in an everlasting covenant" by the terms of which "God bindeth himself in a promise that eternity, which should have been spent in executing his wrath upon them, shall be employed with the

entertainment of them with the highest expressions of an infinite love."
Once one enters into this saving covenant with God, "nothing shall
ever make a separation between them." Since salvation is given by
God, not earned by women or men, it is safe, secured, assured forever.
Once within the covenant, once of the chosen or the "elect," there is no
falling away. "God hath cast all their sins behind his back, blotted them
out as a cloud." Thus is the divine side of the agreement fulfilled. On
the human side, all redeemed persons find "their hearts are engaged to
him, devoted to his praise, and so fixed in their love to him, that all
waters of affliction cannot extinguish it."

If salvation of the individual is thus set and certain, the Puritan
society was not necessarily similarly set and stable. Both political and
religious leaders of the second and third generations grew anxious
about the declining faith, the cooling zeal. Would the children and
grandchildren of the original settlers prove worthy of their noble in-
heritance? Or would they fall into a kind of indifference, taking for
granted that for which parents and grandparents had been prepared to
die? Churches began to relax their requirements for membership, no
longer insisting that all newcomers tell the whole congregation of their
own personal, intense experience of conversion. Economic concerns
loomed large over religious ones, as the earlier piety no longer dominated the life of the whole society.

From this apparent decline, New England was recalled in the 1740s
by a wave of religious excitement and revivalism known as the Great
Awakening. Among the many significant consequences of this movement was its bringing to the fore New England's most brilliant theologian: Jonathan Edwards. Born in Connecticut in 1703, Edwards entered Yale College at a very young age, concluding his work there in
1720. After a brief pastoral charge in New York City, Edwards returned
to Yale as a tutor, then assumed the leadership of the Congregational
church in Northampton, Massachusetts. While here he not only took
an active role in the Awakening, but reflected deeply on its meaning.
After a painful dismissal from his Northampton charge, Edwards and
his large family moved to Stockbridge, about forty miles west of
Northampton, to minister to the Indians and others in the area. In
Stockbridge he wrote the major philosophical and theological treatises
that won for him so wide a reputation. In 1757 he was invited to become president of the College of New Jersey (later Princeton) and took
over the duties of his office early the next year. Unhappily, he died
soon thereafter as a result of complications from the still-new technique
of smallpox inoculation.

The passions aroused in the course of the Great Awakening—and
passions were aroused both for and against the revival—stimulated
Edwards to reflect on the essential character of religion itself. "There is
no question whatsoever that is of greater importance to mankind," Ed-

wards wrote, "than this: What is the nature of true religion?" In a *Treatise Concerning Religious Affections*, published in 1746, Edwards offered his answer to that question in what emerged as the most subtle and sophisticated defense of the Awakening and the role of emotion in the religious life. Deep emotion was not only legitimate in religion, he argued, it was essential to genuine religion. For without the emotions or "affections," one is not moved, one's life is not altered. Religion was not a matter of intellectual apprehension alone, Edwards declared, not a matter of doctrinal knowledge alone, not a matter of mere propositions. Faith rested upon knowledge, but moved beyond the faculty of understanding to the faculty of the will or what we often speak of as the heart. Edwards explained that to have a change of mind was not the same thing as to have a change of heart. The latter involved deep feeling, new direction, transformed life. Edwards asserted that there was a great difference between being told that honey is sweet and having the experience of tasting honey. The latter knowledge is direct, intuitive, certain and rests upon experience that can be neither doubted nor denied. This knowledge comes to us by what may be called a "sense of the heart." "Spiritual wisdom and grace is the highest and most excellent gift that ever God bestows on any creature," Edwards declared. Furthermore, "it is not a thing that belongs to reason . . . it is not a speculative thing, but depends on the sense of the heart."

WORSHIP

Puritanism began in England most visibly as an effort to reform the nature of worship. What went on in the churches of the nation seemed to the Puritan still too Catholic, too "papist." Worshippers should not kneel when receiving the sacrament at communion (or Eucharist or Lord's Supper) for that suggested a kind of idolatry, an acceptance of the Catholic idea that the wine and the bread were in fact transformed into the very body and blood of Jesus Christ. Vestments should not be worn that implied a spiritual distance between clergy and laity as if those persons belonged to separate castes. Academic gowns might be worn, for that indicated a special training or preparation, but not a higher spiritual order. If one reads the New Testament carefully, the Puritan argued, one finds no ground for the high office of bishop with such special prerogatives as confirmation and ordination. Moreover, if one reads the New Testament carefully, one finds only two sacraments or ordinances specified there, not the seven that Catholicism embraces (baptism, confirmation, confession, communion, marriage, ordination, and extreme unction). Puritans would narrow that list to only two: baptism and communion.

Baptism represented an initiation into the Christian community; it may appropriately be bestowed upon infants, properly sponsored by their natural parents (church members, of course) as well as by their godparents. Infant baptism was a pledge for the future by all who witnessed it: to support and sustain this child, nurturing his or her faith and bringing that youth into a full and faithful participation in mature Christian life. The Lord's Supper sustained the Christian community, as ordinary food sustained the common life. Bread was the most basic food, the "staff of life"; similarly, the bread served in the Lord's Supper was basic to one's spiritual life. Wine, said Samuel Willard, symbolized the work of Christ: "Wine is a cordial, it comforts the heart, recruits the fainting spirits, and greatly refresheth them that drink it." It even drove away sorrow and could purge all wounds. These sacraments were observed because Christ commanded that they be; they served as key symbols, pregnant with meaning, but not (as in Roman Catholic worship) as saving channels of grace.

The minister was no intermediary standing between the worshippers and their God, nor did the saints of medieval Christendom have any special role to play. Sunday was a special day, of course, to be strictly observed: not a time for frivolity or sports or unnecessary travel and labor. But feast days, saint days, even Christmas and Easter had no special sanctity and called for no special observance: that would be popish, that would be worship uncleansed of the remaining taints of Catholicism. No priest or bishop should "intermeddle" in the personal piety of the Christian; no altar should suggest that the sacrifice of Christ must be repeated over and over; no statues or pictures or stained glass windows should tempt the faithful to honor anything other than God. Worship should be as simple as it was sincere, not fixed in accordance with the Book of Common Prayer or with any other book except the Bible. One came to church to praise God from the heart, to hear the Word expounded and interpreted, not ritually intoned or read without comment (the latter was called "dumb reading").

All of this took place in the meeting house which was the center of not only all ecclesiastical life but all other life as well in the New England town. It was the place of "meeting," whether the purpose was a call to worship or a call to the militia. On Mondays, citizens met to decide what roads or fences needed to be repaired, what bridges must be built, whose pigs required better control, and what new lands should be surveyed. The meeting house belonged to the town, for the whole population therein (whether churchmember or not) contributed to its support and paid for its repair. Congregationalism was the official religion of New England, not just one denomination among many; the alliance between the civil and ecclesiastical authorities was both intimate and strong. Ministers did not rule the colonies of Massachusetts and Connecticut; there was no "theocracy." But clergy and magistrate, governor and people, worked in mutual understanding of common obligations all carried out under the watchful eye of Providence.

The settlement patterns of New England, differing markedly from the "scattered plantings" of Virginia, centered around the creation in towns, just as those towns centered around the meeting house. Ironically, New England did better at re-creating the parish life of old England than did Virginia which set such a re-creation as its goal. And New England ended up as the most thoroughly "churched" region of colonial North America. By 1740, Congregationalists had well over four hundred churches, concentrated largely in Massachusetts, Connecticut, and southeastern New Hampshire. Anglicanism at that same time had little more than half that number, spread all throughout the South as well as widely scattered in colonies north of the Chesapeake. No other denomination began to approach these two in number of churches, and no group, not even Anglicanism, rivalled Congregationalism in its saturation and ecclesiastical control.

The revivalism of the 1740s on the one hand "awakened" the New England churches to a more earnest and committed spiritual life. On the other hand, that intense movement divided those churches into two "armies" (as Jonathan Edwards said), the New Lights who favored the revivals and the Old Lights who opposed them. Revivalists and itinerant ministers, Britain's George Whitefield being foremost among them, alarmed and alienated many. Whitefield challenged the Standing Order and questioned the sincerity or spirituality of some of its clergy. The neat and orderly pattern of one church in one town with one minister solemnly appointed thereto found itself threatened by noisy and critical itinerants who preached where they had not been invited, who left in their wake angry ministers and divided towns. One itinerant from New Jersey wrote of "The Danger of an Unconverted Ministry," an inflammatory and disturbing tract that suggested that regularly ordained pastors might not even be Christians! A New England minister responded with "The Danger of an Unqualified Ministry," suggesting that many of the itinerants were obnoxious and mindless troublemakers who simply did not know what they were talking about.

Such tracts hardly settled matters, but they did point to the sharp divisions that ultimately spelled doom for the Congregational monopoly in New England. Many of the New Light churches, separating from the town's control, argued that only a zealous ministry and a regenerate membership faithfully reproduced the pure Christian church of New Testament days. A large number of these Separate New Light churches turned to the Baptist denomination, making that non-Congregational group suddenly a powerful force in New England and well beyond. Even before the Awakening, other unwelcome religious forces such as Anglicanism and Quakerism, had invaded the Congregational domain. Quakers initially received the harshest treatment of all, four of them being hanged in Boston Common in the second half of the seventeenth century. Since Anglicans had the force of all England behind them, they could not be hanged, but they could be resisted. One Boston pastor, Jonathan Mayhew (1720–1766), ridiculed the absurd practice of having Anglican missionaries sent to New England. Missionaries to New England! The very thought was appalling. Why, missionaries have been sent, Mayhew exploded, into those very towns "where the public worship was regularly upheld, and his word and sacraments duly administered." This proved that Anglicans were not interested in converting the ignorant and heathen to Christianity, but only in subverting the orderly and established New England Way.

By the end of the colonial period, Congregational worship still dominated New England and still infused the entire culture of the region. But no longer did it exercise an unchallenged monopoly. In the final decades of the eighteenth century, seeds of ecclesiastical revolution no less than of political revolution began everywhere to grow.

EDUCATION

In New England, where no bishops ruled but Bibles did, education had a high priority. The first ministers in the Great Migration of the 1630s were themselves university educated men, chiefly from Cambridge University in England. So far as primitive conditions and meagre resources would allow, the Puritans resolved that education would not be inferior in New England to that available to them in Old England. In Massachusetts, each town of fifty households or more would maintain its own teacher of reading and writing; each town of one hundred or more families would, by legal requirement, build and support its own grammar school. Connecticut soon followed suit with similar demands, so that by 1671 all Puritan New England—alone among the American colonies—had its own public system of compulsory education. As the missionary to the Indians, John Eliot (1604–1690), exclaimed in 1679: "Lord, for schools everywhere among us! That our schools may flourish!"

Grammar schools constituted a good and necessary beginning, but grammar schools were not enough, certainly not for a Bay Colony that dreaded "to leave an illiterate ministry to the churches, when our present ministers shall lie in the dust." Very soon after the Puritans' arrival, therefore, leaders began to plan for some higher form of education. As Thomas Shepard (1605?–1649), pastor in a new community on the Charles River, reported: "The Lord was pleased to direct the hearts of the magistrates . . . to think of erecting a School or College, and that speedily to be a nursery of knowledge in these deserts." The Puritans' "nursery of knowledge" was placed in Shepard's town, promptly renamed Cambridge in honor of the English alma mater so many of the immigrants called their own. The college itself took the name of Harvard when a young citizen died, unexpectedly leaving a legacy of nearly £800 and an entire library. Founded in 1636, only a mere half-dozen years after the beginnings of Massachusetts Bay, Harvard testified to the keen commitment that the Puritans made to education.

No mere bible school or parochial seminary, Harvard from the beginning was dedicated to the "advancement of all good literature, arts and sciences." Students were obliged to know Latin and Greek, not in order to graduate from Harvard, but in order to be admitted. Of course, the school was permeated with the religious commitment that characterized the colony as a whole, a 1646 rule stipulating that every student "shall consider the main end of his life and studies to know God and Jesus Christ which is eternal life." Students had to read their bibles twice every day, studying the scriptures carefully and being prepared "to give an account of their proficiency therein, both in theoretical observation of language and logic, and in practical and spiritual truths."

Two generations later, in 1701, Connecticut followed with Yale College. Longing for "a nearer and less expensive seat of learning" than that at Harvard, Congregationalists in the "land of steady habits"

8. The early donor, John Harvard, watches over "his" college, the first founded in North America. *Harvard University News Office*

launched their school first at Saybrook, then in 1716 moved the infant institution to New Haven. In 1718 the "Collegiate School" took the name of Yale after a wealthy trader, Elihu Yale (1649–1721) who, responding to a plea from Cotton Mather (1663–1728) and others, made a significant contribution to the institution that then agreed to bear his name. Mather's argument was that bestowing his name upon the school would, years hence, prove to be a better monument than even an Egyptian pyramid. The argument of the colony's colonial agent in London (where Elihu Yale then lived) was that even if the school were not Anglican, as its benefactor was, what better way to convince young men of the truth of the Anglican cause than to make them "sensible of it by giving them good learning." Yale, like Harvard, dedicated itself from the beginning to "the liberal and religious education of suitable youth . . . under the blessing of God." The founding trustees declared in 1701 that they had too long neglected their "grand errand" to "propagate in this wilderness the blessed reformed Protestant religion in the purity of its order and worship." Yale, like Harvard, would be a vital instrument directed toward the achievement of that great end.

After the Great Awakening (in which Yale joined more heartily than Harvard), one of Yale's alumni, Eleazar Wheelock (1711–1779) of the class of 1733, took a special interest in the education and the redemption of the Indian. Founding a small school in Connecticut, Wheelock attained only a modest success in his enterprise, though one pupil, a Mohegan Indian named Samson Occom, became a successful minister to many tribes throughout New England. Wheelock's greater success lay in New Hampshire where he founded a school chiefly for Indians—he declared and hoped. Finding its patron in the Earl of Dartmouth, this New Hampshire college opened its doors in 1770 to both Indian and non-Indian, the latter quickly becoming the principal constituency of the school. Dartmouth, chartered in 1769, emerged from the revived piety of the Awakening, a movement in which Wheelock himself was heavily involved. But it also sprang from that motive as old as Richard Hakluyt in the sixteenth century: namely, the earnest desire (in Wheelock's words) "to save the swarms of Indian Natives in this land from final and eternal ruin, which must unavoidably be the issue of those poor miserable creatures, unless God shall mercifully interpose with his blessing upon endeavors to prevent it."

New England Congregationalists, by means of these and other educational efforts, gave a distinctive coloration to their own culture and a lasting imprint throughout much of the later nation. We can speak of a "New England mind" in the colonial period in a way that is not possible for any other colony or region. It is a mind that powerfully influenced literature, history, politics, and religion—all across the Midwest and even to the Pacific Coast.

It was a "mind" of such force that we may forget it was also a mind filled with many pre-modern suppositions. This mind, for example, enveloped Salem, Massachusetts, in the 1690s during the famous witchcraft episode. A seventeenth-century mentality, European or American, accepted the reality of witches and wizards, of demonic possession and supernatural evil. Persons suspected of doing the devil's work were as feared as, in a more modern age, persons suspected of carrying a dread communicable disease would be. In either case, one must isolate in order to protect the community as a whole. And in the case of witches, the biblical commandment was clear: Thou shalt not suffer a witch to live. In Salem in 1692, twenty persons, so accused and then judicially found guilty, met their deaths. Soon the hysteria subsided and one of those judges, Samuel Sewall, stood before his church in 1697, acknowledging his blame and shame, and asking the pardon of both his fellows and his God that this sin "and all his other sins" would be forgiven.

In 1630 William Bradford, encouraged by the rush of immigrants into New England, saw in these beginnings far greater developments ahead. "As one small candle may light a thousand," he wrote, "so the light here kindled hath shone unto many, yea in some sort to our whole nation." By means of a carefully considered theology, a scrupulously corrected form of worship, and a zeal for minds as well as for souls, New England Puritans-become-Congregationalists illumined the dark forests of primitive America.

CHAPTER 7

"A Full Liberty in Religious Concernments": RHODE ISLAND

The phrase "Puritan New England" deliberately excluded Rhode Island, and all Puritans would have preferred it that way. The tiny colony of Rhode Island, founded in 1636, never became part of "the New England Way," never pursued a religious conformity, never created anything that might be called the Rhode Island mind. Nonetheless, this much-despised colony managed to leave its imprint upon a later nation, that mark relating to a new and daring liberty in religion.

The efforts of the Massachusetts Bay Colony to maintain a strict religious conformity exacted a high price: intolerance, persecution, and exile. One of those persons whom Massachusetts sought first to silence, then found necessary to expel, was Roger Williams (1603?–1682). Coming to Boston in 1631 as a Puritan minister himself, Williams soon found his views diverging from those of the other Puritans. In the first place, he did not believe that one could, in good conscience, claim to be still part of the Church of England while pursuing distinctly different paths of worship and of thought. One cannot have his cake and eat it too; or, in Williams' words, one cannot build a square house on top of a ship's keel. And if one be so foolish as to try, the result will never be "a soul-saving true ark or church of Christ Jesus."

Massachusetts Puritans were trying to walk some invisible narrow line, trying to find some imaginary middle path, wherein they could walk not totally inside the Church of England, but at the same time not totally outside of it either. No such path exists, Williams asserted. "This middle walking" was really nothing more than a dangerous if not fatal compromise: one must make a clean break, separating the "holy from the unholy, penitent from impenitent, godly from ungodly." Anything less was to betray the great dream, to fail on the grand errand.

In the second place, Williams was disturbed to discover that the first immigrants from England had simply taken over and occupied the land without any reference to or acknowledgment of the Indians. No one paid for the land or bartered for it. No one asked permission of the Indians to occupy it on terms that might be mutually agreeable. Puritans in general thought this notion utter nonsense: the Indians neither farmed nor fenced most of the land. They roamed here and there, hunted and fished; now and then they planted some corn. One could hardly believe that they actually held title to specific parcels of land, as Englishmen did. Besides, the land had been assigned to them quite legally: King Charles I, by terms of their charter, had given them the land on which they had built. Agreed, said Williams, but pray tell, who had given the land to King Charles?

A third and even more unsettling difficulty regarding "the New England Way" presented itself to the mind of Williams. Puritans had fled from England to escape the cruel penalties of law and the religious persecutions resulting therefrom. Yet, in Massachusetts they forged the same kind of fatal alliance between the civil and the ecclesiastical authorities, having so poorly learned their lessons. "It has been England's sinful shame," Williams wrote, "to fashion and change [her] garments and [her] religions with wondrous ease, as a higher power or a stronger sword has prevailed." Will Massachusetts repeat that folly? Nothing is more absurd, Roger Williams contended, than "the setting up of civil power and officers to judge the conviction of men's souls." If history teaches us any lessons at all, it teaches us that force applied to religion creates not a purity of faith but a river of blood.

The Massachusetts authorities listened, at first with patience, then with incredulity, at last with horror. Here was a man gone mad, a zealot who heeded neither the voice of reason nor of God. Williams had gone so far as to declare that their churches were impure, their title to the land unclear, their enforcement of true religion both cruel and absurd. As Cotton Mather later wrote, he was reminded of the story of a Dutch town where a violent wind caused the windmill to whirl around so fast that it overheated the millstone, first setting the mill on fire, then because of the winds the entire town. "But I can tell my readers," Mather noted, that "there was a whole country in America like to be set on fire by the rapid motion of a windmill in the head of one particular man." That man, Roger Williams, would not be allowed to set all of Massachusetts on fire.

The colony's General Court therefore ruled in 1635: "Whereas Mr. Roger Williams . . . hath broached and divulged diverse new opinions against the authority of the magistrates and churches here, . . . it is therefore ordered that the said Mr. Williams shall depart out of this jurisdiction." This opinion was rendered as the harsh winter season approached, so that the court agreed to allow Williams to stay until spring, if and only if he would keep silent with respect to these "diverse new opinions." But if the sun cannot stop shining nor the ocean cease its roaring, Williams could not stop speaking to those who visited him in his home. In January the authorities made plans to arrest him and set him aboard a vessel bound for England. When Williams heard of these plans, he left home "in the bitter winter season," making his way on foot out of the Bay Colony's jurisdiction to the headwaters of the Narragansett Bay. There he established a settlement which he called Providence "in a sense of God's merciful providence unto me in my distress." And so another colony was born, a colony whose official name remains Rhode Island and Providence Plantations.

Williams' complaints against Massachusetts were much on his mind as he founded his new colony. He therefore (1) bought the land from the Indians; (2) helped to organize a separated church; and (3) determined that the civil government would have nothing to do with religion except to maintain a peaceable social order. He and others spent many years seeking guarantees for the colony's territorial borders and assurances that their "livelie experiment" in religious liberty could be pursued. Finally in 1663, a generation after its founding, Rhode Island received from King Charles II a charter which, without equivocation, declared that the experiment could indeed continue. "No person within the said colony," the royal charter affirmed, "shall be any wise molested, punished, disquieted, or call[ed] in question for any differences of opinion in matters of religion." The colony would, on the contrary, be founded on the premise—no, on the conviction, "that a most flourishing civil state may stand and best be maintained . . . with a full liberty in religious concernments." No other colony, state, or nation had yet dared to make a claim of such frightening extravagance.

Williams, concerned about his own religious liberty, was equally dedicated to the religious liberty of all others. His colony would be a haven for all dissenters, for persons of all shades of religious opinion, or of no religious opinion at all. Whoever wished might come. And come they did, in considerable number and near-infinite variety.

One year after the colony's founding, Anne Hutchinson (1591–1643) fell afoul of those same authorities that had banned Roger Williams. Like Williams, Hutchinson saw herself as a very good Puritan, perhaps a somewhat better or more insightful Puritan than many of those around her. More purely theological than ecclesiastical in her concerns, Anne Hutchinson wished to magnify the role of God's grace, to clarify the distinction between religion and morals. Unlike Roger Williams, Anne Hutchinson thought she was only explicating the theology of her pastor, John Cotton, only drawing out implications already present in Puritan thought. But in drawing those implications, she went farther than the fathers were willing to go, and certainly farther than those fathers were willing for a woman to go. Mrs. Hutchinson talked too much, knew too much, and presumed too much; she did things not "fitting for your sex."

So she too was brought to trial before Boston's General Court, and she too found it necessary to flee to Rhode Island. Her enemies brought two charges against her, employing loaded scare words of the seventeenth century: she was both an antinomian and an enthusiast. Because she regarded "good works" as unrelated to the evidence of salvation, she undermined the social order of New England and destroyed all basis for moral law. In this sense she was "against the law," which is what the word *antinomian* literally means. To be an *enthusiast* in that early day meant much more than being excited or zealous: it meant that one presumed—the grossest presumption of all—to be inspired directly by God. Anne Hutchinson, during the course of her farcical trial, confessed that some of what she knew and taught came to her by "immediate revelation." That seemed to bypass the Bible, the clergy, the Church, thereby once again threatening the entire social fabric of New England. As the court deliberated, the outcome never really being in doubt, the defendant declared: "You have power over my body, but the Lord Jesus hath power over my body and my soul." Exercising what power it had, the court found her guilty, exiled her from the commonwealth, while her church cast her from its fellowship. Removing to Rhode Island in 1638, Anne Hutchinson and her family remained

9. Intimately connected to Brown University, the First Baptist Church in America honors Roger Williams as one of its founders; this structure was built in 1775. *First Baptist Church, Providence, Rhode Island*

in the colony until 1642; then she departed for Long Island where the following years she and some of her children were slain by Indians.

While the Hutchinson family lived in Rhode Island, Baptists took advantage of that colony's liberty to settle there in significant numbers, this a full century before Baptists reached Virginia. The Baptists, emerging out of English Puritanism early in the seventeenth century, settled in Newport in 1639 and in Providence shortly before that. Roger Williams participated in the founding of America's earliest Baptist church in Providence, though he remained within the denomination only a short time. He left the Baptists not for any other church, but on the conviction that a truly pure church must await the return of Christ and the initiation of a new apostolic age. In Newport, the physician and clergyman, John Clarke (1609–1676), gave steady and significant leadership to the infant denomination throughout the colony, and beyond. When in 1651 he and two companions journeyed to Massachusetts to help advance the Baptist cause, Bay Colony authorities quickly arrested all three. Four years earlier Massachusetts had passed a law against Baptists as having historically been "the incendiaries of commonwealths and the infectors of persons in main matters of religion." Such persons should be banished from the colony or, if they did not live in the colony, then some other form of punishment must be inflicted.

One of Clarke's companions, Obadiah Holmes (1607?–1682), learned just what that meant. Publicly whipped with thirty lashes in Boston's Market Street, Holmes responded by declaring that he was pleased to share in the kind of suffering that Jesus knew "that so I may have further fellowship with my Lord. [I] am not ashamed of His sufferings, for by His stripes am I healed." Roger Williams was not ashamed of what happened to Holmes, but he was enraged. Protesting to Massachusetts Governor John Endicott, Williams again made the point that the civil magistrate has no business meddling "in matters of conscience and religion." Further, if you persecute everyone who disagrees with you on any point, sooner or later, Williams wrote, you will end up persecuting Christ himself. Ask yourself this question, John Endicott: "I have fought against several sorts of consciences; is it beyond all possibility and hazard that I have not fought against God?" Not until 1682 did Boston concede the right of Baptists to hold their own services of worship there.

Long before then Baptists had established themselves firmly in Rhode Island, not so firmly, however, as to enjoy or maintain a religious monopoly. Roger Williams' colony was open to Baptists, but open to all others as well. The Society of Friends, or Quakers, shortly after their founding by George Fox in England in 1651, moved in strength into Rhode Island, especially around Newport. Soon they were strong enough to dominate the colonial government and to become by 1676, in the words of an Anglican missionary, "the Grandees of the place." Authorities of Puritan New England, horrified that a sanctuary for Quakers existed so close to their own borders, urged authorities in Rhode Island to shut its doors against them. But that colony's General Assembly serenely declined, asserting that "freedom of conscience we still prize as the greatest happiness that man can possess in this world."

Cotton Mather was not amused. Rhode Island had become a sink, a cesspool, a latrine into which all the refuse of the world could be dumped. Never in history had there been "such a variety of religions together on so small a spot of ground," wrote Mather. One could find there anything that fancy might conjure up: "Antinomians, Anabaptists, Antisabbatarians, Arminians, Socinians, Quakers, Ranters— everything in the world but Roman Catholics and real Christians." What for Mather was a shattering indictment was for Williams and others a cherished freedom: "a full liberty in religious concernments."

Rhode Island never grew to the strength of its neighbors in population or wealth. By 1700 when Massachusetts was over fifty thousand strong and Connecticut over twenty-five thousand, Rhode Island had fewer than six thousand. Seventy years later, the latter had only one-fourth the population of Massachusetts, only about one-third that of Connecticut. By then, Baptists and Quakers had been joined by Anglicans, Congregationalists, and Jews—among others. Under the auspices of the Society for the Propagation of the Gospel, Anglicanism established its first outpost in Newport in 1704. By 1726 Anglicans there had sufficient strength to erect a magnificent wooden church near the water's edge and, one year later, the missionary in Newport joined with other nearby Anglican clergy to write London that England's National Church did much to produce "a great reformation in life & manners, & vice and immorality." Rhode Island, they admitted, was quite a challenge. "That fertile soil of heresy & schism" somehow finds new strength to resist the Anglicans, this sad fact due in no small part to having Baptists and Quakers in the highest civil offices of the colony. But if London could only send us a bishop, all would be well.

London did not send them a bishop in 1727, or at any later date. From Ireland, however, came an ecclesiastical dignitary that gave them some hope and encouragement. George Berkeley (1685–1753), who as a younger man had written philosophical works of lasting brilliance, determined to build in the New World a college that would be a fountain of learning and religion for all the colonies. While waiting for Parliament to fulfill its pledge of a major grant, Berkeley lived near Newport from 1730 to 1732. As an Anglo-Irish clergyman and Dean of Londonderry, Berkeley often preached in that handsome wooden church, Trinity, and offered comfort to the Anglican clergy seeking a friendly following in a hostile land. Berkeley's sojourn in America gave special encouragement to a philosophical soulmate in Connecticut, Samuel Johnson (1696–1772), the latter becoming the first president of King's College (forerunner of Columbia) in New York City. Berkeley's own college, however, was never built, as Parliament reneged on the grant and Berkeley returned in disappointment to his native Ireland. His interest in New England remained, however, testified to notably by handsome gifts of books to Harvard and Yale, as well as of an organ to Trinity Church.

Congregationalists, while disdainful of Rhode Island's wild and willful varieties of religious experience, by the 1720s felt some obligation to see that "real Christians" be introduced there too. From Boston's Old South Church, Josiah Cotton (1703–1780) came as a "missionary" to Providence where he organized a church in 1728. In Newport, Ezra Stiles (later president of Yale) exercised an effective ministry from 1755 to 1776. A man of broad sympathies and even broader intellectual capacities, Stiles (1727–1795) helped move Congregationalism out of its parochial shell toward a vigorous participation in civil and religious life throughout America. This was especially true during the American Revolution, a movement which Stiles (unlike New England's Anglicans) supported with vigor and effect.

Jews also took advantage of the colony's offer of religious freedom. Arriving in the seventeenth century, Sephardic Jews, that is Jews whose liturgical practices stemmed from Portugal and Spain, had to wait many decades before their numbers and resources permitted the building of a synagogue. They finally broke ground in 1759, completing in 1763 the finest of colonial synagogues and one that is still in use. Home of the Congregation of Jeshuat Israel, Touro Synagogue, named after its rabbi at the time of construction, had its plans drawn by Peter Harrison (1716–1775), distinguished master builder and designer who also gave to Newport other notable buildings. A tiny minority of America's colonial population, Jews also had synagogues in New York City, Philadelphia, Richmond, and Charleston. The first federal census of 1790 showed how modest Jewish population was prior to the major immigrations of the nineteenth century: only twelve hundred could be tabulated in the expanse from Maine to Georgia.

In 1764 the colony of Rhode Island acquired a college which ultimately came to reside in Providence under the name of Brown University. With the support of Baptists from Pennsylvania as well as all of New England, Brown purposed to educate young men "for discharging the offices of life with usefulness and reputation." Furthermore, the original charter, in an effort to remain true to the spirit of Roger Williams, stated: "Into this liberal and catholic institution shall never be admitted any religious tests; but on the contrary, all the members hereof shall forever enjoy full, free, absolute and uninterrupted liberty of conscience." Williams would have been pleased. Over a century earlier, he had written: "Having bought truth dear, we must not sell it cheap—not the least grain of it for the whole world."

10. The interior of Touro Synagogue in Newport, Rhode Island: designed by Peter Harrison and erected in 1763. This is the oldest synagogue building in North America. *Library of Congress*

CHAPTER 8

"The Gospel into a Fruitful Bosom": MARYLAND

Alone among the British colonies in North America, Maryland came into existence under Roman Catholic auspices and served as a haven for English Catholics. Just as relations between Catholics and Protestants were stormy in England, so that turbulence characterized most of Maryland's colonial years. The "haven" was rarely either safe or secure.

In 1632 King Charles I granted a charter to Cecil Calvert (1605–1675) for lands on both sides of the Chesapeake Bay. Calvert who inherited from his father the title of Lord Baltimore thus became the founder of the first proprietary colony in America, a colony in which all the land legally belonged to Calvert himself. As landlord in a quite literal sense, Calvert wished his colony to attract numerous settlers and to become quickly an economic success. To that end he encouraged both Protestants and Catholics to emigrate, even on the first ships, the *Ark* and the *Dove*, that set sail in 1634. He instructed his fellow Catholics aboard those ships to "preserve unity and peace among all the passengers," giving neither scandal nor offense to any of the Protestants. All occasions of Roman Catholic worship aboard ship were to be conducted as privately as possible, with all Catholics instructed "to be silent upon all occasions of discourse concerning matters of religion." If diplomacy and tact were the keys to religious harmony, Maryland's future would seem assured.

Jealousies and suspicions and political cabals, however, prevented serenity, both in Maryland and back home. In England, many protested against the very notion of giving land to a Catholic family, such a grant inevitably offering encouragement to a religion against which the kingdom had set its face. In 1633 the proprietor and his friends attempted to soften the protests by explaining that sending Catholics off to Maryland was not necessarily doing them any great favor. "Banishment from a pleasant, plentiful, and one's own native country into a wilderness among savages and wild beasts" might not be such a fair exchange. True, Catholics were persecuted in England, but an exile in the New World might be departing "from one persecution to a worse. For diverse malefactors in this Kingdom have chosen rather to be hanged than to go to Virginia." Besides, some political service can be rendered to England by the fact that Englishmen, even if Catholic, rather than foreigners would possess the land. No one should worry about some sort of Catholic coup in British territory, Lord Baltimore pointed out, for already three times as many Protestant lived in Virginia and New England than all the Roman Catholics together in England. In that respect, Calvert spoke more truly than he knew: Protestant coups, not Catholic ones, would threaten his royal grant.

In March of 1634 the two ships with their nonquarreling passengers aboard arrived at the mouth of the Potomac River, then made their way northward up the Chesapeake Bay to St. Clement's Island. One member of the group, Jesuit Father Andrew White (1579–1656), offered the first mass on the twenty-fifth of that month, then he and his fellows bearing "a huge cross, moved in procession to a spot selected" where "we recited with deep emotion the Litany of the Holy Cross." Soon after this solemn event, the Jesuits directed the building of the first Catholic chapel in St. Mary's City, the original capital of Maryland.

Father White attempted missionary work among the Indians, but their unyielding hostility made his recall to St. Mary's mandatory. Yet Jesuit missions among the Indians remained a major objective in and around the settled areas, White noting that "It is more prudence and charity to civilize and make them Christians than to kill, rob, and hunt them from place to place, as you would do a wolf." Again, the alternative to Christianization was extermination, not tribal purity and cultural integrity. Like other priests and ministers, White saw the whole colonial venture as an exciting opportunity to expand the cause of Christ, both among Europeans and native Americans. "The English nation," he stated, "never undertook anything more noble or glorious than this. Behold, the lands are white for the harvest, prepared for receiving the seed of the Gospel into a fruitful bosom."

That harvest fell into "enemy" hands quite soon, as Protestants in the early 1640s wrested control from Lord Baltimore and expelled the Jesuits from their own land. In 1646, when lawful authority was restored, the Jesuits returned to resume their labors. In an effort to prevent future religious conflict, the Maryland Assembly in 1649 passed a Toleration Act (well before England's Act of 1689) that guaranteed to all Christians the right of free worship and immunity from all coercion in religion. This would seem to have been enough to keep the neighbors at bay, but it was not. England's Civil War, the execution of the king, the ascendancy of Oliver Cromwell—all these events afflicted Maryland. A Protestant rebel named William Claiborne (1587?–1677?) managed to win full control of the colony by 1655, moving quickly to bar Roman Catholics from any civil office and to restrain any person from practicing "the popish (commonly called Roman Catholic) religion."

When in 1660 the monarchy was restored to England, Calvert regained his authority and a comparative peace settled once more upon

Maryland. But England was not finished with her turbulence nor Maryland with her distractions. The Glorious Revolution of 1688 which brought William and Mary to the throne brought a resurgence of anti-Catholic feeling both at home and abroad. In 1692 Maryland lost its proprietary status forever, becoming at that time a royal colony under the control of very Protestant sovereigns and a very Protestant Parliament. Maryland's own assembly, in that same year, hurried to pass an act that provided "for the service of Almighty God and the establishment of the Protestant religion." For much of the seventeenth century, the Calverts had tried to delicately balance the competing interests of Catholic and Protestant, of nation and church; they had tried a policy of open immigration and religious toleration. To no avail. For by the final decade of that century, Maryland had, like her neighbors to the south, become just another Anglican colony, with officialdom moving quickly to make England's church as strong and unchallenged as it could possibly be.

In 1696 the three Anglican clergy in Maryland wrote to the Bishop of

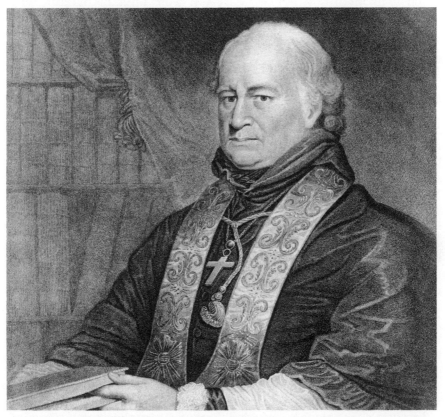

11. The first bishop of the Roman Catholic church in the United States, John Carroll, built upon the earlier labors of Father Andrew White and the large hopes of Cecil Calvert. *National Portrait Gallery*

London, complaining that Anglicanism suffered from the presence of not only Roman Catholics but also from that of Quakers and "wandering preachers" who "deluded not only the Protestant Dissenters from our Church but many of the Churchmen [Anglicans] themselves by their extemporary prayers and preachments." Furthermore, new immigration augmented the Catholic presence, with "great numbers of Irish Papists brought continually into this province" and even, in disguise, a few Irish priests. Some Catholics are so misguided as to think that Lord Baltimore's authority will be restored, the Anglicans reported; thus, they refuse to be quiet and subdued. So, even though the Church of England now enjoyed official status, it did not enjoy a great deal of respect. The solution? For the Maryland churchmen as for those in Rhode Island, the solution was for England to dispatch a bishop without further delay. What Maryland required above all else was "an Ecclesiastical rule here, invested with such ample power and authority . . . as may capacitate him to redress what is amiss, and to supply what is wanting in the Church." If no such rule was established, the clergy noted with mournful despair, Maryland shall soon be overrun with "enthusiasm" (that is, Quakerism), with "idolatry" (that is, Catholicism), and with "atheism" (that is, all else outside of and opposed to Anglicanism).

Again like Rhode Island, Maryland received no bishop. The colony did receive, however, Thomas Bray (1656–1730) who came as a commissary at the very end of the century and who came as one already identified in the public mind of England as thoughtfully concerned about ways in which to advance the Anglican cause. Anglicanism needed more than mere legislative fiats that created parishes on paper but failed to give those parishes any real life or force. In 1695 Bray had set down his "Proposals for Encouraging Learning and Religion in the Foreign Plantations." These proposals pointed to the real weakness of Anglicanism throughout so much of North America: insufficient attention to any means for education, inadequate supply and inappropriate quality of clergy. A graduate of Oxford, Bray was a gifted student, pastor, and teacher who, when appointed a commissary by the Bishop of London, took his responsibility with singular seriousness. It would not be enough to travel to Maryland, observe the deficiencies, deplore the weakened condition of the Church, and come home to detail same in a report that no one would ever read. Bray conceived of a corporation, perhaps two, that would be empowered to receive gifts, collect monies, dispatch goods and services: in short he proposed to create agencies that would for the first time really take charge of a situation for which no one in England felt any keen obligation. And it was time, Bray concluded, that someone did.

In 1699, therefore, Bray founded the Society for Promoting Christian Knowledge which would go into the book business, not for England's sake, but for the sake of her colonies, her "foreign plantations." This society would print and distribute literature, would encourage the creation of parish libraries, and would resolve to make each Anglican church a center of education and religious training. While noble in its intent, this society did not make the impact in colonial America that Bray's second agency did: The Society for the Propagation of the Gospel in Foreign Parts, founded in 1701, after his return from Maryland. This body would attack the clerical problem and try mightily to solve it. On its own, it would hire ministers, send them as missionaries where they were most needed, continue to support them financially as long as necessary, and continue to give them all the encouragement possible from home. To sell England on the idea, Bray painted a picture of religion in the colonies darker than it really was, but dark enough certainly with respect to the fortunes of Anglicanism. We are credibly informed, King William III declared in the Charter of 1701, that many of the foreign plantations "are wholly destitute and unprovided of a maintenance for ministers and the public worship of God." Indeed, "many of our loving subjects" appear to have been abandoned "to atheism and infidelity"; to correct that deplorable circumstance, this society is hereby constituted and ordained.

In some respects, Bray did not exaggerate. The effectiveness of the ministry to Indians and blacks was virtually nil. His society should certainly assist those that "shall most hazard their persons in attempting the conversion of the Negroes or native Indians." A generation later, however, the secretary of the Society for the Propagation of the Gospel had to report most regretfully that little progress had been made. David Humphreys, writing in 1730, noted that while some converts had come into the church, "what hath been done is as nothing with regard to what a true Christian would hope to see effected." Humphreys added that blacks rarely had enough time off to receive religious instruction, Sunday being their only time to clear ground and plant crops "to subsist themselves and families." Masters, moreover, did not take seriously any obligation with respect to the conversion of their slaves. "Some have been so weak as to argue [that] the Negroes have no souls; others, that they grew worse by being taught and made Christians." Distressing reports these were, so much so that Humphreys felt obliged to add that he would not even mention them "if they were not popular arguments now," arguments that had "no foundation in reason or truth."

By 1750 Anglicanism was far ahead of all other religious groups in Maryland, but Catholicism had not been extinguished. One Catholic family in particular, the Carrolls, gave Catholicism a political and social visibility that enhanced its status, especially during the revolutionary years and beyond. Charles Carroll (1737–1832), a wealthy and eloquent spokesman for the Catholic cause, served as an adviser to the First

Continental Congress and a delegate to the Second, in which capacity he became the only Catholic to sign the Declaration of Independence. Like Cecil Calvert a century and one-half earlier, Charles Carroll manifested more tolerance and forbearance than he received. Attacked by fellow Marylander Daniel Dulany (1727–1797) for his Catholicism, for his presumed sympathies with the Stuart kings, for his being a threat— as Dulany saw it—to religious and civil liberty, Carroll responded that he despised "knaves and bigots" of whatever sect or denomination. And he added that Dulany "would make a most excellent inquisitor."

John Carroll (1735–1815), cousin to Charles, played an even more powerful part in rescuing Catholicism from the widespread suspicion with which it was regarded. Educated abroad, Carroll returned to his homeland in 1774, just as tension between England and her colonies reached the point of war. His sympathies wholly with the American cause, he joined in efforts to win France's aid and to keep Canada (which had been bounced back and forth between France and England) at least neutral in the event of war. In 1784 Carroll was named Vicar Apostolic for the new nation, this title a prelude to his being elevated to the dignity of America's first Roman Catholic bishop. Carroll chose Baltimore as the site for his cathedral and there Benjamin Latrobe designed a classical structure in the style of the Pantheon in Rome. In 1785, Carroll reported to Rome on the state of Catholicism in America: a grand total of only about twenty-five thousand members in the entire country, the vast majority of these being in Maryland and Pennsylvania. Clergymen were few, but Carroll wisely warned that it was better to have no priests at all than "incautious and imprudent" ones, especially in a country ever ready to find fault with a religion still widely feared and widely distrusted. Catholicism enjoyed no great health in America when Carroll became bishop in 1789; upon his death in 1815, he left behind a far more vigorous ecclesiastical body than he had found.

That Maryland should serve as the colonial center for Catholicism occasions no surprise. That it also served as the colonial center for Methodism was less predictable. As previously noted, Methodism emerged out of the Church of England as a more evangelical, more personal religious movement, carried in its earliest years often by the voices and efforts of dedicated laymen and laywomen. So it was in Maryland when in 1766 Robert Strawbridge (d. 1781) first introduced the Methodist message. The "cradle of Methodism" in America, Barrett's Chapel near Frederick, soon resulted from Strawbridge's lay preaching. A Methodist conference meeting in 1773 reported more Methodists in Maryland than in any of the other colonies, though Methodism quite swiftly spread south into Virginia and north into Pennsylvania, New Jersey, and New York. In 1774, however, over half of the country's Methodists were still to be found in Maryland.

One decade later Methodists gathered in Baltimore to declare themselves separate from the Church of England and to begin a march of conquest that would reach far beyond the borders of Maryland. Francis Asbury (1745–1816) emerged as the leading voice from that famous 1784 Christmas Conference, also as the leading itinerant in advancing the Methodist word. Setting the example as a "circuit rider," Asbury traveled incessantly as so many others would do after him. Methodist clergy did not settle into a single parish, but moved across great expanses, visiting hamlets and isolated families who otherwise would be devoid of any Christian ministry at all. Methodists seemed always to be in a hurry, always on the move, growing so rapidly in so many places that observers trying to keep up were flabbergasted. The Methodists, Jedidiah Morse (1761–1826) reported in 1792, number somewhere around forty thousand, but then again, who knows? Everytime one turns around, they seem to be in some other place where they had not been before, and every new account places them well above the numbers of only a year or two before. "It would be a matter of no small difficulty," Morse concluded, "to find out their exact amount."

While this was true up and down the Atlantic Coast, it was conspicuously true in Maryland where Methodists soared in number, reaching both blacks and white, utilizing both laity and clergy, employing devout women no less than zealous men. In 1787 the General Conference exhorted its ministers to make a special effort to reach the slaves. That effort paid off as blacks, both slave and free, responded

12. Designed by the influential Benjamin Latrobe, the Baltimore Cathedral drew its inspiration in part from the Pantheon in Rome. *Archdiocese of Baltimore*

warmly to a gospel made accessible to them. As ex-slave Richard Allen (1760–1831), bishop of the African Methodist Episcopal Church, explained: "The Methodists were the first people that brought glad tidings to the colored people. I feel thankful that ever I heard a Methodist preach." He added that blacks were "beholden to the Methodists, under God, for the light of the Gospel we enjoy; for all other denominations preached so highflown that we were not able to comprehend their doctrines." Unmistakably, Methodism moved in power, across racial lines, across mountains, across the categories of class and gender. And Maryland provided a powerful base, proving once more to be (as Father White had foreseen) a "fruitful bosom" in which tiny seeds could be nurtured to a swift and full-flowered maturity.

CHAPTER 9

"Religions of All Sorts": NEW YORK, NEW JERSEY, DELAWARE

Pluralism is not a product of the twentieth century alone. New York and New Jersey in the seventeenth century displayed a remarkable variety in religion, without anyone having really planned it that way and without laws that officially recognized the bubbling diversity. Freedom in religion there, never complete, arrived in spite of efforts to prevent it, in spite of theories that condemned it. As in so much of American history, diversity itself set the agenda. In the earlier periods of that history, the presence of numerous religious options, a novelty beyond the experience of most seventeenth-century Europeans, demanded notice. It astounded, it amused, it offended; chiefly, however, it prevailed.

Under the auspices of their West India Company, the Dutch in 1626 sailed into the mouth of the Hudson River, then later up the river to establish trading posts that would bring to Holland some share of New World riches. A major seafaring power at this time, Holland ignored the overlapping English claims of the Virginia and Plymouth Companies to purchase Manhattan Island from the Indians and to establish Fort Orange near the present-day site of Albany, far to the north of Manhattan. Here furs could be received from Indians to the west, in or near the Mohawk River valley, and from here oceangoing vessels could sail down to Hudson to that larger port called New Amsterdam. Trade with Europe and throughout the Caribbean would make Holland a major player, along with France, Spain, and England, for the markets of the world and in the search for that elusive shortcut to India.

While the company's interest was clearly commercial, merchant promoters urged that ministers be sent to instruct both the few settlers and the many Indians "in religion and learning." Those ministers would naturally represent the Dutch Reformed Church, Holland's legal religious institution. Amsterdam's Company would direct the economic life, while Amsterdam's church (more specifically its synod or classis) would direct the spiritual life. The first ordained clergyman, Jonas Michaelius (1603–1670), arrived in April of 1628 to find "a rather rough and unrestrained people" and Indians whom he characterized as "entirely savage and wild" as well as "proficient in all wickedness and godlessness." If these comments suggest that Michaelius was not wholly charmed by the delights of New Amsterdam, the hints are correct. Nor was the West India Company wholly charmed with him. Within four years, he sailed for home, with little regret being expressed from either side.

In 1629 the Dutch Reformed Church received official recognition as the established church of New Netherland, an establishment technically excluding the presence of other religions. Just as in Holland, however, the company preferred to follow a relaxed policy that would not make religion an issue of such difficulty or magnitude as to interfere with commerce and economic growth. Peter Stuyvesant (1592–1672) who in 1647 took over as the director general of the colony had trouble understanding or applying that liberal company policy. In his view, the populace of New Amsterdam had by 1647 become an undisciplined mess. The town had too many nationalities, too many languages, too many religions, and not nearly enough strict Dutch obedience. Stuyvesant would clean it all up, making New Amsterdam look like the neat Dutch village that it ought to be.

Already dismayed by the presence of Lutherans, Quakers, Presbyterians, and Catholics, Stuyvesant was in no mood to put up with a couple of dozen impoverished Jews who arrived in his city in 1654. Thinking only of the good of "this weak and newly developing place and the land in general," Stuyvesant reported to the company, he "deemed it useful to require [the Jews] in a friendly way to depart." Accustomed to a broader toleration in old Amsterdam than they found in New Amsterdam, the Jews protested to the West India Company. From these merchants, they received the assurance that they could "travel and trade to and in New Netherland and live and remain there, provided that the poor among them shall not become a burden to the company or to the community." Jews did live and remain there, first holding religious services in their homes, then purchasing land for a cemetery, and finally (in 1729) organizing America's first synagogue, the Congregation Shearith Israel in what had by that time become New York City.

Stuyvesant had even greater difficulty with the Quakers and they with him. For years Stuyvesant attempted to stamp out this "abominable heresy," though the more he stamped the more the young sect grew. Outside of the law as the Pilgrims had been in England, Quakers, like the Pilgrims, met in private homes and kept their newfound faith alive and flourishing. In Jamaica on Long Island, Stuyvesant was informed in 1662, a majority of the citizens gathered on Sundays in secret Quaker meetings. An outraged director-general arrested the man in whose home such meetings had been held, hauled him to New

Amsterdam for trial, and quickly found him guilty of harboring and encouraging a religion that "vilifies the magistrates and preachers of God's Holy Word, that endeavors to undermine both the State and Religion," and that seduces "others from the right path with the dangerous consequences of heresy and schism." The Quaker, John Bowne (1628–1695), was fined, a penalty he refused to pay; he quickly found himself, therefore, thrown in prison. But Bowne, like the Jews, argued his case (in person) before the West India Company which, once more, took Stuyvesant to task. Old Amsterdam, the company noted, "has always practiced [a] policy of moderation and consequently has often had a considerable influx of people." New Amsterdam should do no less.

Stuyvesant fought against not only his own company but the temper of his own people. In 1657 the inhabitants of Flushing protested against his edict that any ship which dared to bring a Quaker into his colony would be confiscated and anyone who allowed a Quaker to spend the night in his home would be fined fifty Flemish pounds, with half of that amount going to the informer. The residents of Flushing, deciding that they had had enough, issued a Remonstrance that took a different stance, advocating that "love, peace, and libertie" be extended "to all in Christ Jesus." Whether we talk of Quakers or Baptists, Independents or Presbyterians, "we cannot in conscience lay violent hands upon them."

13. This Dutch Reformed Church, erected in Albany, New York, in 1715, no longer survives. *Library of Congress*

Any and all shall have the right of free entrance into our towns and our homes "as God shall persuade our Consciences." And you, Mr. Director-General, will simply have to make your peace with that.

Meanwhile, Swedish Lutherans had settled along the Delaware River near the modern city of Wilmington. Like the Dutch, the Swedes saw the New World as a potential source of wealth and trade but, also like the Dutch, the National Church would go wherever merchants and governors went. The governor who arrived in the small colony in 1643, John Printz (1592–1663), was instructed to "exert himself to obtain a good breed of cattle," to obtain all kinds of sheep, to plant grapes and make wine, to search for metals and minerals, and to consider "what kind of advantages may be expected from oak-trees and walnut-trees." But in the midst of all this economic preoccupation, the governor should "above all things . . . consider and see to it that a true and due worship, becoming honor, laud, and praise be paid to the Most High God in all things." Worship would be conducted according to the "unaltered Augsburg Confession" and the "ceremonies of the Swedish Church."

While the colony of New Sweden represents the first formal introduction of Lutheranism to North America, the real strength of that continental denomination had to await the arrival of much larger numbers from Germany in the eighteenth century and from Scandinavia in the nineteenth century. The few hundred Swedes who lived at Fort Christina (named in honor of their nation's seventeen-year-old queen) could not greatly advance the Lutheran cause, though one minister, John Campanius (1601–1683), tried to gather in the Delaware Indians by learning their language and by translating the catechism of Martin Luther into the "American-Virginian" tongue. When in 1654 a few hundred more Swedes arrived in such strength as to enable the colony to take over a nearby small Dutch fort, Stuyvesant to the north reacted with predictable outrage. He led seven armed vessels from New Amsterdam down to the mouth of the Delaware, then up the Delaware where he forced the surrender of Fort Christina.

While the Swedish flag came down, the Swedish mission itself remained until the American Revolution. In New York, Peter Stuyvesant's effort to guarantee a Dutch Reformed monopoly soon became academic, as the Dutch outposts fell to the English in 1664. In September of that year, England landed its soldiers at Gravesend "and marched them over Long Island to the Ferry" opposite Manhattan. British ships "came up under full sail . . . with guns trained to one side." "They had orders," reported the Dutch Reformed Minister Samuel Drisius (1600–1673), "if any resistance was shown to them, to give a full broadside on this open place, then take it by assault, and make it a scene of pillage and bloodshed." Wisely, the Dutch surrendered as

New Netherland became New York. Drisius gratefully reported, however, that the Articles of Surrender provided "that our religious services and doctrines, together with the preachers, shall remain and continue unchanged."

English authorities were prepared to acknowledge another national church, that of Holland, as being more or less on a par with their own Church of England. They were not prepared, any more than Stuyvesant had been, to look with favor on the religious hodge-podge all around them. Governor Edmund Andros (1637–1714) in 1678 painted the shocking picture: we have here, he wrote, "religions of all sorts, one Church of England, several Presbyterians and Independents [Congregationalists], Quakers and Anabaptists of several sects, some Jews . . . " Eight years later, nothing had improved, according to Governor Thomas Dongan (1634–1715) who found also Catholics, preachers male and female, lots of Quakers (both "singing Quakers" and "ranting Quakers") and much besides: "In short, of all sorts of opinion there are some, and the most of none at all."

Early in the eighteenth century an arrogant governor, Lord Cornbury (1661–1723), resolved to harass or persecute, penalize or imprison, in order to make the establishment of Anglicanism more the true reality and not simply the nice ideal. He turned against even the Dutch Reformed who up to this time had been left rather much alone (as indeed the Articles of Surrender required). When Dutch churches lost their ministers, Cornbury arbitrarily appointed Anglican ones in their place. When Dutch ministers arrived directly from Holland, Cornbury refused to grant them licenses to preach or to recognize the congregations' right to install them. The Dutch naturally protested that Cornbury had changed the rules which had been in effect since 1664, but the Governor replied that what had been done before was by mere courtesy, not by right. He, on the other hand, had the right and would exercise it to the hilt to establish the Church of England fully and firmly.

If Lord Cornbury treated the Dutch Reformed Church with contempt, one can readily imagine the scorn that would fall upon other dissenters. In 1707 he took on the Presbyterians, arresting Francis Makemie (1658–1708) and John Hampton (?–?) for preaching without a license. When these traveling preachers claimed the protection of England's 1689 Declaration of Religious Toleration, Cornbury calmly replied that the benefits of this act did not extend to New York. Makemie held out for a trial by jury where he argued that he was "morally persuaded there is no limitation or restriction [of] the Law to England." English law, he added, had been extended to the Barbadoes, to Virginia and Maryland: why not to New York? Unimpressed by precedent, Cornbury did admit that in general English law took effect in the colony of New York, "but the Act of Toleration does not extend to the Plantations by its own intrinsic virtue . . . but only by Her Majesty's Royal Instructions signified unto me."

Cornbury who felt no obligation even to read the act declared that it had been passed precisely to prevent "strolling Preachers" such as Makemie. The latter, who had read the law, observed that it contained "not one word against traveling or strolling Preachers." At Cornbury's request, the judge directed the jury to render a verdict of guilty. With minds of their own, twelve good and true men found Makemie innocent. Cornbury was soon recalled to England, having done the cause of Anglicanism far more harm that good.

Anglicanism in New York prospered more in spite of Cornbury than because of him. The city's first Anglican church, Trinity, was chartered in 1697; a mere half century later, New York had twenty such churches,

14. The Swedish venture up the Delaware River in 1638 has a continuing witness in this "Old Swede's Church" located in Wilmington, Delaware. *Keystone-Mast Collection, UC–Riverside*

with an additional eighteen in New Jersey, and fourteen in Delaware. Once again, Bray's Society for the Propagation of the Gospel deserves major credit for this rapid expansion. By midcentury New York Anglicans felt strong enough to consider the possibility of a college that would represent their cause in the North as the College of William and Mary did in the South. New York's General Assembly in 1746 authorized a public lottery "for the advancement of learning and toward the founding of a college," while the city's Trinity Church donated farm land for this purpose. In 1754 King George II granted a charter to "the College of the Province of New-York in the City of New-York in America." Calling their school King's College, Anglicans launched an institution which would in 1784 take the name of Columbia.

Presbyterians and other protested against New York's one college being so distinctly Anglican in liturgy and in rule. Since the colony was mixed religiously, so should the rules and regulations of the college reflect that heterogeneity. William Livingston (1723–1790), Yale graduate and Presbyterian lawyer, led the forces opposed to a strictly Anglican school. He pointed out that Congregationalists, Presbyterians, and Dutch Reformed were all more numerous than Anglicans in the 1750s; moreover, we also have here in New York "Anabaptists, Lutherans, Quakers, and a growing Church of Moravians, all equally zealous for their discriminating tenets." To give any one group exclusive control of "King's College" would, Livingston argued, "kindle the jealousy of the rest, not only against the persuasion so preferred, but the College itself." Livingston lost the battle, but won the war. While the schools' trustees, the majority of whom were Anglican, specified that morning and evening services would be conducted every day according to the liturgy of the Church of England and that the college president would be an Anglican "forever hereafter," diversity would not be denied. All academically qualified New Yorkers were eligible to attend, and by the time of the Revolution the very idea of an Anglican school lost any chance of continued public support. "Columbia" was clearly a more patriotic name than "King's," as the Church of England suffered from its intimate identification with those authorities against whom Americans were now at war.

Far more than in Virginia or the South generally, Anglicans in New York and New Jersey opposed the Revolution and clung to England's side. The clergy, almost all missionaries sent out by the Society for Propagation of the Gospel, put down only the shallowest of roots in America, seeing England as their home and their "exile" in America as merely temporary. As they regarded it, their main mission was not to identify with American interests or condemn the Stamp Act or argue for a larger degree of local liberty. Rather, it was their task to advance the cause of Anglicanism everywhere; that meant loyalty to the king no less than to his church. It also meant, from their point of view, that sending a bishop to America had the highest urgency. A New Jersey Anglican, Thomas Bradbury Chandler (1726–1790), wrote in 1767 *An Appeal to the Public* where he declared that "arguments for sending Bishops of the Church of England to America" were so strong, so rational, so readily apparent that none could resist. Bishops were necessary for Anglicanism to conduct its affairs, and to deny this church its bishops was to deny its religious freedom. Bishops would not persecute in America, Chandler promised, as they may have done in England, nor would they necessarily require support by taxes and other public monies. And then in an argument that could hardly have appealed to the American public in the late 1760s, Chandler gave his case away by asserting that "Episcopacy and Monarchy are, in their Frame and Constitution, best suited to each other. Episcopacy can never thrive in a Republican Government."

Thomas Bradbury Chandler was right. As republicanism spread throughout the colonies, the Church of England did not thrive, and would not thrive until it reconstituted itself with American-elected bishops who had no more taste for monarchy than did their fellow citizens. Bradbury found it expedient to return to England in 1775, while his fellow clergyman in New York City, Charles Inglis (1734–1816), hung on to continue, even in 1776, the plea for a bishop and to condemn the American Revolution in no uncertain terms as "one of the most causeless, unprovoked, and unnatural" rebellions "that ever disgraced any Country." Inglis proudly reported to London that the clergy of his colony as well as those in New England and New Jersey retained their loyalty to the king; in the South, however, it was another story, but "I never expected much Good of those Clergy."

While Anglicanism suffered, other denominations took up any slack that might appear: Baptists, Methodists, Quakers, Lutherans, and especially the aggressive Scotch-Irish Presbyterians and the long-suffering Dutch Reformed. Colleges founded in New Jersey reflected the prestige and strength of the two latter groups. Following the Great Awakening, Presbyterian forces sympathetic to the revival established in 1746 the College of New Jersey, later to take the name of Princeton. Aided by the support of Presbyterians in all the colonies as well as of many in the British Isles, Princeton suffered no reversal during the Revolution. On the contrary, it identified itself wholly with the patriotic cause, its clergyman president, John Witherspoon (1723–1794), being the only minister to sign the Declaration of Independence. And Presbyterians, unlike Anglicans, made the revolutionary cause their own, so much so as to provoke an English statesman to call the Revolution "a Presbyterian rebellion." The Synod of New York and Philadelphia, organized in 1758, directed the growth of Presbyterianism in all the Middle Colonies, a large proportion of that growth resulting directly from the hundreds of thousands of Scottish immigrants from both Scotland proper and the Ulster Province of Northern Ireland.

The Dutch Reformed, like the Presbyterians, participated in the Great Awakening and benefitted from it. Under the leadership of Theodore Frelinghuysen (1723–1760?), churches found new strength and membership during the course of the evangelical revival. A later Frelinghuysen in 1755 directed the plan for a Dutch Reformed college, the church's synod affirming their resolve "to strive with all our energy, and in the fear of God, to plant a university or seminary for young men." Like the Puritans who founded Harvard, the Dutch desired to raise up and educate their own young men so that they might "enter upon the sacred ministerial office in the church of God." Queen's College, later Rutgers, resulted a decade later from this resolve, training ministers but also offering a European liberal education to all its students. While the Dutch Reformed Church never swept across the country in the manner of the Presbyterians or Methodists, it continued to be a major cultural force in New York and New Jersey where, a century and a half earlier, Dutch adventurers had so tentatively explored the reaches of the Hudson River.

Quakers also survived in New York and New Jersey, despite the determined effort of both Stuyvesant and Cornbury. But Quakers flourished most dramatically in a colony of their very own, founded across the Delaware River from New Jersey. And when it came to encouraging "religions of all sorts," Pennsylvania far outdistanced what even New York and New Jersey had managed to do.

CHAPTER 10

"In No Ways Molested or Prejudiced": PENNSYLVANIA

Unlike all the colonies considered to this point, Pennsylvania came into existence not in the early decades of the seventeenth century but many decades later. This deserves emphasis, for much more than simple chronology is involved. Penn's colony, founded in 1682, had the advantage of learning from all the others: learning above all else what mistakes to avoid in bringing a new colony into being. Thus, the "Quaker colony" avoided the "starving time" of Jamestown, the struggle for survival in Plymouth. It avoided encouraging any and all to emigrate to the New World, expecting bounty without labor, harvest without planting. "I would," Penn wrote in 1681, have all prospective settlers to understand "that they must look for a winter before a summer comes; and they must be willing to be two or three years without some of the conveniences they enjoy at home." Penn encouraged none to venture across the ocean without due reflection nor from a "fickle" mind, but to consider carefully "the providence of God in the disposal of themselves." But for those willing and ready to work, a rich land promised rich reward.

William Penn (1644–1718), born in London and student at Oxford in the early 1660s, turned in 1667 to the Society of Friends (the Quakers). Engaging upon an active ministry in their behalf in England and elsewhere, Penn first tried to reform his own nation and its church, then (like the Pilgrims) tried to save the small sect itself from harsh persecution and possible extermination. In 1670 Penn wrote a lengthy treatise, *The Great Case of Liberty of Conscience*, where he argued against the senseless intrusion of civil power into the tender area of religious conscience. A great and good God has given us reason, understanding, and judgment to use in matters religious. These instruments, not sheriffs or armies, courts or jails, properly decide matters of the heart and of the soul. Man is not king over conscience: that is alone "the just claim and privilege of his Creator."

So Penn argued vigorously but largely in vain for a far more liberal policy of toleration in England, making his argument long before England took such a step in 1689. Before that date, Penn found in the

New World an even happier solution. King Charles II owed a large debt to Penn's father who had served him in a military capacity. Charles discharged that debt by giving to the son a vast tract of land on the west side of the Delaware River. Pennsylvania (or "Penn's woods") would offer English and Irish Quakers a refuge from persecution and a path to prosperity. It would offer such not only to them, however, but (in the words of the 1682 Frame of Government) the same to "all persons living in this province who confess and acknowledge the one almighty and eternal God to be the creator." All such citizens, agreeing "to live peaceably and justly in civil society," would in "no ways be molested or prejudiced for their religious persuasion or practice in matters of faith and worship, nor shall they be compelled at any time to frequent or maintain any religious worship, place, or ministry whatever." Thus, the Holy Experiment was set upon a path that would avoid another earlier and common mistake: namely, that of religious harassment and persecution. Penn's colony would grant not merely "moderation" in the Dutch manner, or "toleration" in the English fashion, but a much bolder invitation to freedom in religion. And, to the amazement of all, the colony did not suffer thereby; on the contrary, it quickly prospered.

Another mistake that William Penn wished to avoid pertained to the Indians. Both Virginia and Massachusetts had offended and alienated the Indians; both suffered from costly Indian wars. Even before coming to America, Penn sent agents ahead to let the Delaware Indians know of his intention to occupy the land only "with your love and consent." I am well aware, Penn added, "of the unkindness and injustice" that Indians have suffered from previous English settlers and traders. "But I am not such a man, as is well known in my own country." Penn sent presents as well as promises that, when he arrived himself, he would seek a fair treaty and "a firm league of peace." And in laying out the city of Philadelphia ("brotherly love"), Penn charged his commissioners to "be tender of offending the Indians . . . but soften them to me and the people; let them know that you are come to sit down lovingly among them." The treaty itself, finally concluded in 1701, set Pennsylvania on a course of better relations between Indian and English than any other colony had known. Not all problems were solved nor all tragedies avoided, but Penn had at least made a far better start.

Quakers settled in large numbers in Philadelphia, William Penn's carefully laid out "green country town," and in nearby lands along the river. German emigrants soon added to the ethnic and religious mixture, founding Germantown (a section of some six thousand acres) in 1683. Later, Mennonites and Amish moved into Lancaster County, west of the early Quaker settlements. Still later, in the 1730s and beyond, many German Lutherans and German Reformed (Calvinist) developed magnificent farms as well as an enduring folk culture. Then Scotch-Irish Presbyterians, Welsh Baptists, free African Methodists,

Irish Catholics, and missionary Anglicans added to a diversity that either attracted or repelled. Earliest settlers and administrators soon learned that the "blessings of liberty" also seemed to carry a few curses.

For Penn himself, disappointment followed disappointment. Quakers even quarreled among themselves, while trusted deputies mismanaged their funds and abused their positions. Many mistook liberty for license and freedom for the equivalent of moral anarchy. In a sobered mood, Penn later noted that "Liberty without obedience is confusion, and obedience without liberty is slavery." While he continued to work earnestly for "a blessed government and a virtuous, ingenious, and industrious society," Penn felt the reins of the Holy Experiment slipping from his grasp. Even his own family embarrassed him and, at last, disease disabled him; in 1718 Penn died a broken and saddened man.

Nonetheless, the colony flourished economically and proved by 1750 to be the major center for Lutheranism, German Reformed, and Presbyterianism. Lutheranism, itself largely German at this time, found strong leadership in Henry Muhlenberg (1711–1787) who arrived in Philadelphia in 1742. An accomplished linguist, Muhlenberg could preach in English and Dutch as well as German, doing so far beyond the confines of Pennsylvania itself. He journeyed to New York, New Jersey, Delaware, Maryland, the Carolinas, and Georgia. Everywhere he went, he not only preached in whatever language seemed most appropriate, but he conducted catechism classes, settled congregational disputes, introduced some measure of Lutheran liturgy and discipline, and carried on an extensive correspondence with those whom he could

15. Benjamin West's famous painting portrays William Penn making a treaty with the Indians in 1701. *Pennsylvania Academy of the Fine Arts*

not reach in person. Clearly a man of inexhaustible energies, Muhlenberg served Lutheranism well, serving it the better because he ministered not to Lutherans alone.

As he noted in his valuable journal, Muhlenberg left some persons unsure whether he was even a Lutheran! The German Reformed thought he was one of them because "I had not reviled and run down" all other denominations, "but simply preached the order of salvation." An Anglican clergyman (Alexander Murray) came to him, convinced that some sort of coalition could be worked out between them. Murray "expressed the opinion," Muhlenberg recorded, "that this was just the most suitable period in which to establish a bishop in America. And if this were to come to pass, native German sons of good intelligence and piety could be educated in the English academies, ordained, and usefully employed for the best welfare of the Church of Christ in both the German and the English languages." Muhlenberg listened to what must have been a surprising proposal, commenting only that one "could travel from one pole to the other in a few minutes on a map, but in practice things went much more slowly and laboriously." Such a diplomatic reply revealed Muhlenberg to be a pastor of broad and catholic spirit.

One aspect of Quakerism, however, got under his skin as it did that of many other Pennsylvanians: namely, their pacifism. Quakers believed that the command of Christ to "love your enemies and bless them that persecute you" meant at the very least that any follower of Christ could not in good conscience take up arms for the purpose of killing those enemies and persecutors. In addition to the Quakers, Pennsylvania was filled with other pacifists: Mennonites, Amish, Schwenkfelders, Dunkers or German Baptists, Moravians and more. This disproportionate number of persons unwilling to bear arms threw the burden of defense upon those who were left, a burden sometimes resented and protested against. When during the course of the French and Indian War (1756–1763), some frontiersmen murdered twenty Conestoga Indians, then marched defiantly upon pacifist Philadelphia, at that point—according to Muhlenberg—the Quakers at last were willing to bear arms, not against the French or the Indians, but against their fellow colonists! It was amazing, Muhlenberg stated, to see these "pious sheep" who had comfortably sat out the long war and who "would rather have died than lift a hand for defense" now arm themselves to "shoot and smite . . . suffering fellow inhabitants and citizens from the frontier." A great many of those frontier fighters were Scotch-Irish Presbyterians who fully shared Muhlenberg's impatience and would have welcomed his biting sarcasm, if they had known of it.

Pacifism proved even more difficult, of course, during the equally long American Revolution which lasted from 1776 to 1783. Benjamin Franklin (1706–1790) in that troubled period advised all pacifists to render some kind of service on behalf of the united colonies: to help care for the wounded, to provide food, to form emergency fire brigades, or whatever. If they only sat on their hands like "pious sheep," their neighbors would understandably feel great hostility against them and perhaps even give vent to it. In a petition to the Pennsylvania Assembly in 1775, Mennonites indicated that they were quite ready to accept such advice "with Cheerfulness towards all Men of what Station they may be—it being our principle to feed the Hungry and give the Thirsty Drink." A few Quakers overcame their scruples long enough to enlist in the Revolutionary Army, but most did not, holding themselves aloof not only because of pacifism but because of doubts about the colonial cause. Earlier English kings had befriended the Quakers and made Penn's colony possible; now they would stand by the present king, the Philadelphia Yearly Meeting in 1774 reminding its members that they were indebted to King George III "and his royal ancestors for the continued favour of enjoying our religious liberties."

German Reformed immigrants, like the Lutherans with whom they shared an ethnic bond, displayed no fondness for pacifism. Moving first into the upper Hudson River valley in 1708, German Calvinists made Pennsylvania the place of their largest settlement. By mid-eighteenth century, over sixty German Reformed churches had been planted in Pennsylvania, far more than in all other colonies combined. And like others who arrived a half century or more after the colony had

16. Pacifism received artistic expression here in Edward Hick's painting where the lion rests besides the lamb, as the Bible predicted. *Randolph-Macon Woman's College*

been founded, these Germans settled farther to the west, in such coun-
ties as Montgomery, Lehigh, Northampton, Berks, and York. In their
earliest years, feeling especially estranged in a land of many religions
and tongues, these Calvinists often joined with those Lutherans who
spoke a common tongue and shared a common national heritage. In
the 1730s, for example, Lutheran and Reformed together rented "an old
and dilapidated butcher's house," sharing the space and sometimes
even the minister until each group gathered sufficient strength to establish its own church and hire its own clergy.

Presbyterians moved in force toward the colony's western frontier,
many of them migrating from that point down the valleys into the
backcountry of Virginia and the Carolinas. Suffering no persecution in
Pennsylvania, of course, they continued to press beyond the Susque-
hanna River into the Cumberland Valley and along the banks of the
Juniata River. England at the conclusion of the French and Indian War
tried to halt all overland migration across the Allegheny Mountains, but
Presbyterians would not be halted. In 1773, Presbyterian minister
David McClure (1748–1820) made his way into the "western country,"
observing that the many families he overtook displayed "a patience and
perseverance in poverty and fatigue" that he could only admire. They
looked forward, he said, to abundant land, full freedom, and "happy
days." Well before that time, Presbyterians at midcentury had over two
hundred churches throughout America, the largest number being in
Pennsylvania and New Jersey.

The earliest Baptists in Pennsylvania came from Wales, settling in or
near Philadelphia before the end of the seventeenth century. In 1707
Baptist churches banded together to form the Philadelphia Association,
the first such interchurch fellowship among Baptists in America, and
one of enduring strength both before and after the Revolution. By 1750
Pennsylvania was second only to Rhode Island in its number of Baptist
churches, and by the time of the Revolution Pennsylvania (along with
much of the South) had moved well ahead of Rhode Island. Baptists
who spoke much of liberty found the rhetoric of resistance to all tyranny, civil or ecclesiastical, congenial to their interests and readily
adaptable to their theology.

Spilling over from nearby Maryland, as well disembarking directly
upon the docks at Philadelphia, Roman Catholics also freely conducted
their services of worship in Penn's colony. Much of colonial America
continued throughout the eighteenth century to keep doors against
Catholics tightly shut, but not Pennsylvania. In 1750 Catholics had
thirty churches in the colonies, all but four of these to be found in
Maryland and Pennsylvania. Even these colonies, however, could not
escape rumors of "popish plots" and "Jesuit intrigues." In 1757, during
the early years of the French and Indian War, many feared that Catholics would make common cause with France against the interests of

England and her colonies. Prompted by this concern, British authorities ordered that a census of Pennsylvania Catholics be taken, the results indicating a grand total of only about fourteen hundred in the entire colony, and the majority of these were German. In the Revolution, of course, France shifted from the status of enemy to that of ally, thereby helping to soften the near-automatic suspicion of all things Catholic.

Philadelphia also became a major center for Jews in America. Though synagogue services did not begin until the middle of the eighteenth century, the Philadelphia Jewish community grew by the end of the colonial period to be the largest in the new nation. The social and economic status of this community enabled it to erect the Cherry Street Synagogue in 1782, and to remodel that structure early in the nineteenth century in the Egyptian style, giving Philadelphia its first example of this architectural mode. Much later in the nineteenth century, Rabbi Isaac Leeser (1806–1868) would make Philadelphia an important center for Jewish educational and theological life in America.

After the Revolution, Methodism made its presence felt in Pennsylvania as it did everywhere else. But Philadelphia was uniquely important in the organization of and ministry to black Methodists. In 1787 Richard Allen along with other blacks led an exodus out of the predominantly white St. George's Methodist Church in Philadelphia. A few years later, he founded Bethel Church as a fellowship for others of his own race, this "mother church" being dedicated by Francis Asbury in 1794. Here the seeds were planted for what was to become the first denomination in America working specifically with blacks: the African Methodist Episcopal Church. For a time, Allen hesitated between remaining with the Methodists or turning to the Episcopalians, but opted for the former, explaining that "I was indebted to the Methodists, under God, for what little religion I had" and was "convinced that they were the people of God." A companion of Allen's, Absalom Jones (1747–1818), did accept ordination in the Episcopal Church, taking over in 1796 the ministerial duties of the African Episcopal Church of St. Thomas in Philadelphia.

The Anglicans had only a single church in Pennsylvania prior to 1700, but after Thomas Bray created his Society for the Propagation of the Gospel, prospects sharply improved. By 1750, nineteen Anglican churches had been erected in the colony, these being concentrated in its southeastern corner. Anglicanism seemed headed for even larger successes in the prosperous colony when it foundered on the hard rock of anti-English sentiment in general, anti-bishop sentiment in particular. Like Anglicans elsewhere in the Middle Colonies and New England, Pennsylvania's clergy felt unable to cope with all the religious diversity and indifference unless strengthened and supported by a resident bishop. And when revolutionary passions rose, these clergy who had taken oaths of loyalty to the king found themselves placed upon a cruel rack. On the one hand, they could not in good conscience omit offering the prescribed prayers for the king and the Royal Family; on the other hand, if they did offer such prayers, they placed themselves and their churches in danger from angry mobs. What to do? Most solved their dilemma by simply closing their churches, continuing to minister in a private fashion as best they could.

Even that strategy failed to save them from all public outrage. As Thomas Barton (1730?–1780), society missionary in Lancaster, reported to London in 1776, "I have been obliged to shut my Churches to avoid the fury of the populace." By the end of 1776 when Barton's letter was written, passions ran high. Even though he had acted with all prudence and tact, Barton noted, "yet my life and property have been threatened upon mere *suspicion* of being unfriendly to what is called the American cause." And with respect to my fellow clergy, what manner of indignities have been heaped upon them! "Some of them have been dragged from their horses, assaulted with stones & dirt, ducked in water; obliged to flee for their lives, driven from their habitations & families, laid under arrests & imprisoned!" Certainly, the year 1776 was no time to indicate any hesitation with respect to "the American cause" or to reveal any sympathy with either England's Parliament or king. Nor was it a time, in the words of Philadelphia's Thomas Paine (1737–1809), to put up with the summer soldier or sunshine patriot who would, when the going got rough, surrender his rifle and shed his patriotism.

Anglicanism suffered not only from its identification with England but also from its strong distaste for the wide diversity in religion so flagrantly manifest in Pennsylvania. Anglicanism adjusted far more readily to those situations in which it alone bore the title of "Church," while all other groups, if present at all, would be identified as dissenters or nonconformists or worse. Thomas Barton in his capacity as missionary to all of Lancaster County could find no more than five hundred Anglicans there. The rest, he glumly reported, "are German Lutherans, Calvinists, Mennonites, New Born, Dunkers, Presbyterians, Seceders, New Lights, Covenanters, Mountain Men, Brownists, Independents, Papists, Quakers, Jews." Then, obviously out of breath as well as patience, Barton added a final "et cetera." Clearly, the Church of England had little chance to make its way "amidst such a swarm of sectaries." Barton would hang on, he would pray, and he would try to hope, but "headquarters" back in London simply had to understand that Pennsylvania posed a challenge unlike that which his church had ever before been accustomed to face.

For the direction that America would later take, Pennsylvania made two critical contributions. First, it offered religious liberty on a wider scale than had been available anywhere before, that offer being accepted by a greater number than had been the case anywhere before.

Second, and probably even more important, Pennsylvania demonstrated that religious liberty and economic progress could go hand in hand. Despite all that diversity, Pennsylvania prospered in a most remarkable fashion. Though it began half a century after Massachusetts and even longer than that after Virginia, Penn's colony by the time of Revolution had caught up with both. And Philadelphia by then had become the cultural capital of America, a center of light and learning as well as of prosperity. All this despite a rampant religious variety. Could such success possibly be *because* of that liberty?

CHAPTER 11

"An Excellent School to Learn Christ In": CAROLINAS AND GEORGIA

Like Pennsylvania, the founding of Carolina came in the second half of the seventeenth century rather than in the first. Unlike all the other colonies, Georgia alone was founded in the eighteenth century, the last effort of the British Empire to thwart the ambitions of Spain abroad and to solve some of its own social problems at home.

THE CAROLINAS

When the monarchy was restored to England in 1660 and Charles II elevated to the throne, the mood of that nation called for a repudiation of the chaos and religious boiling over that characterized the turbulent Cromwellian period. All stability and order, it was now assumed, lay in unquestioning loyalty to the king. Republican experiments and religious innovations should be left to the past. All land was the king's and he could, if he so chose, grant large portions of it to merchants and planters and loyal supporters. In 1663, Charles did give land between the latitudes of thirty-one and thirty-six degrees, extending from the Atlantic Ocean in the East to those mythical "South Seas" of the West. Honoring the king, that whole territory would take the name of Carolina, and if the Latin form were not enough, the major settlement and port would be called Charlestown, the only real city in the colonial South.

Settlement did not come swiftly, with fewer than two hundred persons living in the colony by 1670. By the end of the century, the numbers had risen to around eight thousand, with half of that population being black. The slave population, much of it imported from the Barbados, continued to grow even more rapidly than the white, with the result that South Carolina became the only colony in which the white settlers were a minority. (In 1750 the colony had a population of around sixty-four thousand, of whom nearly forty thousand were slaves.) The numerical dominance of blacks, together with the heavy dependence on slave labor, especially in the cultivation of rice, helps to account for a sharp severity in the slave code. Blacks knew both harsh treatment and cruel punishments; life expectancy in Carolina, as in the Caribbean, was low. For their part, white settlers, knowing what deprivation of freedom could ultimately mean, jealously guarded their own liberties and asserted their own freedoms.

Population centered in and around Charlestown ("Charleston" after 1787) which served as center for the trade in furs and slaves. Immigrants from France, Germany, Ireland, as well as from the Caribbean and England, poured into the town. Even from New England, settlers came. And, as has often been noted before, diversity simply defied all careful plans to reproduce an English society and village in an American environment.

One element of that diversity resulted from a happy coincidence of timing. The Edict of Nantes which had granted a measure of toleration to Protestants in France was revoked in 1685. Finding it prudent to flee their homeland, these Protestants or Huguenots sought safer shores. Carolina, at that time still in its earliest years of settlement, presented itself as a welcome possibility with the result that about five hundred Huguenots had settled there by 1700. Many of these were artisans, following trades in the New World that they had learned in the Old: blacksmiths, coopers, gunsmiths, and clockmakers. And many were young and newly married, a younger population being more willing to undertake the long and dangerous ocean voyage. These French-speaking settlers quickly moved into the political life of the young colony, also quickly organized their own church in Charlestown.

Both political and religious instability kept the French community disquieted and unsure of the best path to follow. Some Huguenot ministers thought it best to develop close relationships with official Anglicanism, even seeking ordination in that church. Others who recognized the need for an accommodation of sorts nonetheless determined to maintain their own liturgy, their own language, their own Calvinist theology. One clergyman, John La Pierre (d. 1755), found Anglican pressures for conformity so irksome that in 1726 he took the unusual step of complaining by letter to the Bishop of London concerning his mistreatment by the leading Anglican clergymen in the colony, Commissary Alexander Garden. This man, La Pierre affirmed, has charged me with "open contempt and defiance of the ecclesiastical laws and constitutions" of Carolina. La Pierre's crime, if such it was, consisted of his having baptized an infant within Garden's parish and without Garden's consent. Garden reported the offense to both the Governor and the Bishop of London, leaving La Pierre dismayed that he was not given an opportunity "to have made him all reasonable satisfaction in a meeting of the clergy, as our former custom was." The case has sig-

nificance only as a symbol of the uneasy relations between the Huguenots and the Anglicans in a colony that could certainly have used some
bridges of understanding between its many religious groups. Huguenots nonetheless maintained a visible presence in and near Charlestown, as they did much farther to the north, in New Rochelle, New
York.

The Church of England itself struggled through many political shifts
from the initial charter which offered a large measure of religious toleration, to a proprietary establishment of the Church of England that
made few concessions to dissenters, to a royal colony (after 1719) that
again granted to non-Anglicans some latitude for their own worship
and some relief from harassment. Missionaries sent out by the Society
for the Propagation of the Gospel filled their reports with complaints
about the difficulties of their assignments, the disinterest of English
settlers, the resistance of Indians and blacks to their preaching, and the
irrepressible growth of "libertines, sectaries, and enthusiasts," particularly in the Carolina backcountry. One such missionary, Gideon
Johnston (d. 1716), noted in 1710 that he lived in the midst of hardship,
poverty, and disease, with the prospects for the Church of England
dependent on empty promises of better pay, better crops, and a better
life. Johnston thought little of such promises, seeing around him in
Charlestown mainly "the Vilest race of men upon the earth" who have
"neither honour, nor honesty nor Religion enough to entitle them to
any tolerable Character."

Years later Alexander Garden (1685–1756) found the population
somewhat improved, but the prospects of the Anglican church still
greatly dimmed by all of the unchecked competition that, like weeds,
choked out its normal development. The Huguenots along with other
dissenters troubled him, but when one of his very own fellow Anglicans, George Whitefield, came bounding into the colony in 1740,
preaching to and even encouraging all the dissenters, Garden exploded. That explosion is made the more understandable by Whitefield's explicit attack upon Garden himself and upon the general spiritual state of Anglicanism in Carolina. Whitefield attended one service
in Garden's church, then advised the people to worship in the dissenting meeting houses "since the Gospel was not preached in the
Church." The revivalist added that perhaps the society should send no
more missionaries to the Carolinas since those that had been sent were
such poor representatives: "the Established Church is in excellent order
as to externals," Whitefield wrote in 1740, but its chief ministers were
in fact "bigots."

Commissary Garden succeeded in summoning an ecclesiastical court
in Charlestown and tried to suspend Whitefield from exercising the
ministerial office of an Anglican minister. Garden informed the Bishop
of London that, if it were in his power, he would excommunicate

Whitefield altogether. For this evangelizer only weakened the church further, holding it up to ridicule, encouraging illiterate and untrained men to imitate him in a traveling ministry, and creating the illusion that salvation was "a sudden, instantaneous Work" rather than "a gradual and cooperative work of the Holy Spirit, joining in our understandings and leading us on by Reason and Persuasion." But it was not in Garden's power either to excommunicate Whitefield or to prevent his continuing ministry. He did succeed in driving Whitefield even more fully into the arms of the dissenters, Charlestown's Baptists, Presbyterians, and Congregationalists welcoming him warmly.

The Great Awakening proved therefore another trial to Carolina's Church of England, even as dissent and disinterest had been trials from the beginning. Nonetheless, Anglicanism could boast of at least sixteen churches in 1750, some of them impressive structures. An Anglican observer in 1766 thought that the church was healthy enough to turn down more mission money, carrying on its work in such grand churches as St. Phillips and St. Michaels, the former being, according to Charles Woodmason (b. 1720?), the "most elegant Religious Edifice in British America." Even the rural churches deserved praise for their buildings as well as their orderly services. But Anglicanism in this area still had a Revolution to endure (Charlestown, like New York City, was long occupied by the British), a disestablishment to survive, and by 1790 a "free exercise and enjoyment of religious profession and worship" to absorb.

Much later to be settled were the regions well to the north of Charlestown, regions that would eventually be designated as North Carolina. To the extent that it was ruled at all in the seventeenth century, that rule came from Charlestown. In 1711, North Carolina had its own governor and in 1729 its full status as a distinct royal colony. If South Carolina seemed inhospitable to the careful cultivation of orderly religion and moral community, North Carolina by comparison made its southern neighbor look like a model society. Both Virginia and South Carolina regarded the wilderness that lay between them with hostility and derision. Virginia's acerbic William Byrd (1674–1744) in the 1730s spoke of North Carolinians as not knowing Sunday from any other day. This would be a great advantage, he added, if only they were industrious. "But they keep so many Sabbaths every week that their disregard of the Seventh Day has no manner of cruelty in it, either to Servants or Cattle." Missionaries have on occasion ventured into that wild land, but (wrote Byrd) "unfortunately the Priest has been too Lewd for the people, or . . . they too Lewd for the Priest." Under these circumstances, no reformation in either doctrine or morals would ever take place.

Anglicans were not reassured when in 1707 a Quaker was named as deputy governor of the province. Quakers had migrated down from inhospitable Virginia, finding in this region of Carolina no government strong enough or near enough to persecute them or drive them away. By the early years of the eighteenth century, they had become a significant body in North Carolina, the only southern colony in which a Quaker presence endured. John Archdale (1642?–1717), the Quaker deputy governor, tried to play down the whole issue of religious distinctiveness, arguing that what really mattered was whether colonists could clear and develop the land. "For cannot Dissenters kill Wolves and Bears, etc. as well as Churchmen; as also fell Trees and clear Ground for Plantations, and be as capable of defending the same generally as well as the other?" To Archdale, the answer was obvious. And the reality of the dissenters' abilities could be demonstrated if only the Anglicans did not try to take too seriously their legally privileged status. For those who might argue that North Carolina could never prosper if dissent were not checked, Archdale had his response ready: Look at Pennsylvania. Surely it "can bear witness to what I write." Let the Scotch Presbyterians flourish here as they do there, for these were people "generally Ingenious and Industrious . . . a People generally zealous for Liberty and Property, and will by no Persuasion be attracted to any [place] where their Native Rights are invaded." Let the dissenters come, and let us all leave their religious scruples alone.

Dissenters did come to North Carolina, arriving in such force and variety as to scandalize Virginia and South Carolina even more. By 1750 Baptists had more churches than Anglicans, joining with Quakers and Presbyterians, with Moravians and German Reformed, to make that colony a rich repository of religious dissent. And if Charles Woodmason was encouraged by the progress of Anglicanism in South Carolina, has reaction to what passed for religion in the northern province was precisely the contrary. Everything about the evangelical Baptists in North Carolina offended Woodmason: what he observed was bad enough, what he imagined was even worse.

Among other things these "new-born" Christians placed too much emphasis upon religious experiences. "It seems that before a Person can be dipped he must give an Account of his Secret Calls, Conviction, Conversion, &c. &c." These accounts were either hilarious or blasphemous; many were "too horrid" to be repeated. Young men and young women gathered in the evenings at "what they call their Love Feasts and Kiss of Charity," these inevitably becoming occasions for much more than just religious instruction. "Lasciviousness, Wantoness, Adultery,"—these were more common now than they had been before these new "Holy Persons" arrived, Woodmason reported in disgust. Indeed, he concluded, religion was "brought into Contempt," and if steps be not taken to make the Church of England strong in North

Carolina, then we shall see "the End of Religion: Confusion, Anarchy, and every Evil Work."

This was a harsh judgment, and certainly harsh far beyond that which even a modicum of objectivity would have allowed. But Woodmason was interested in making a case: namely, that without an official Church, the colony was doomed and much of American religion along with it. Despite so negative a "press," Baptists spurred by the Great Awakening raced all across North Carolina and through all of the South. When westward migration got underway into Alabama and Mississippi and beyond, the Baptists' horses were saddled and ready to go.

17. A restored "Old Salem" in North Carolina reminds the visitor of the Moravian eighteenth-century settlement; the Salem Community Store illustrated here was owned and operated by the church. *Old Salem, Inc.*

In Salem, North Carolina, a close-knit communitarian body, the Moravians, made their mark. This pacifist European body had for a time escaped persecution by taking refuge in Saxony on the large estate of a leading pietist, Count Nicholas von Zinzendorf (1770–1760). America promised to be both a larger and more lasting refuge for these settlers who found permanent homes in Pennsylvania as well as North Carolina. The latter settlement resulted from their purchase of a large tract of wilderness in the northwestern portion of the colony, a land they named Wachovia. Salem became the "capital" of Wachovia as in

1766 the Moravians began to build their community store and tavern, their homes and "congregation house." We "were rejoiced and strengthened," a Moravian writer reported in that year, "by the safe arrival of the first company of Brethren and Sisters coming to us direct from Europe by way of Charleston." Resources were scarce and numbers few, "but for this small beginning we thank our Heavenly Father, and He will help us further next year." The promise of better times "next year" kept many a knot of believers clinging to their small plot of ground and subsisting on their meagre harvests.

"Next year" offered little hope to the black slave who found this life on earth an unrelieved burden. It was the next life more than the next year that gave what comfort and promise one might find. "All God's chillun' " would someday be gathered into that home where all tears would be wiped away and all burdens laid "down by the riverside." Slaves who converted to Christianity did so only by overcoming stupendous obstacles, most notoriously that of adopting the religion of their oppressors. In the Carolinas, as in Virginia, missionaries reported the reluctance of many masters to see their slaves become Christian; and, in the Carolinas more than in Virginia, they also reported barbaric cruelties practiced upon the slaves.

Francis Le Jau (1665–1717), Anglican missionary in the Goose Creek parish near Charleston, wrote early in the eighteenth century that he had great difficulty watching one of the white overseers kneel in his church in an attitude of prayer when he knew of that overseer's merciless treatment of his slaves. Some maimed or crippled, others whipped and chained, still others placed in a coffin where they "could not stir" for several days and nights—these and other horrors Le Jau recounted. Mistreatment was of such severity as to cause slaves to commit suicide when the opportunity presented itself, but I and much of my congregation, Le Jau noted, look upon those deaths as nothing less than murder.

Nonetheless, and it is an incredible "nonetheless," many slaves turned to the Christian religion and its promises of a loving God and a heavenly home. After careful examination and instruction ("I do nothing too hastily in that respect"), Le Jau baptized some slaves and carefully supervised their behavior thereafter. He would have baptized more, he wrote the society's headquarters back in London, but for the masters who "seem very much Averse to my Design." They continue to argue that "Baptism makes the Slaves proud and undutiful," while Le Jau continued trying to "convince them of the Contrary from the Example of those I have baptized." In a plaintive tone, Le Jau urged the society to publish something "to induce the Masters to show more Charity towards their Slaves." He also tried to reach the nearby Indians with his Christian message, but confessed that the Carolina practice of "fomenting of War among them for our people to get Slaves" doomed his efforts from the start. Indeed, the behavior of the English with respect to both Indian and black "afflicts and discourages me beyond Expression."

GEORGIA

Thomas Bray, whose societies had so significant an impact in all of North America, was even more intimately involved in the founding of Britain's last colony on American soil. Bray's idealism by itself could never have brought Georgia into being, but that idealism joined with certain social and political necessities in England could make it happen. Britain needed another military outpost against Spain that threatened to creep up from Florida all the way to the very borders of Carolina. Britain also needed some place to send the "worthy poor" with whom her debtors' prisons were filled to overflowing. Bray in the 1720s received a bequest specifying that monies derived therefrom be "employed in the erecting a School or Schools for the thorough instructing in the Christian Religion the young Children of Negro Slaves & such of their Parents as show themselves inclinable & desirous to be so instructed." Bray, now aged and ill, formed yet another organization, this one known as "Dr. Bray's Associates" which would oversee the expenditure of this money and, as it turned out, also oversee the founding of the colony of Georgia, named after King George II who reigned from 1727 to 1760.

Launched with great idealism, Georgia was initially under the control of trustees from 1732 to 1752. This body of men decreed that Georgia should be free of slavery, free of liquor, and profitable to England. None of these ideals endured. By the time that Georgia became a royal colony in 1752, it began to resemble it neighbors farther north, with an established church, with the adoption of slavery, and with the usual quarrels about land as well as the usual absence of any profits to be sent back home. Population, moreover, remained sparse, with scarcely more than two thousand souls by then in that vast expanse, most of these huddled around Savannah.

In its brief experimental period, Georgia did prove a haven not only for the "worthy poor," but also for the persecuted from Europe. Lutherans from Salzburg, Austria, escaped their tormentors and, under the sponsorship of Bray's Society for Promoting Christian Knowledge, made their way in 1734 to the just-launched colony. These "Salzburgers" emigrated as a religious community, led by their pastor who conducted services aboard ship, sustained the faltering, and led the entire group in a service of praise when land was sighted on the fifth of March. (They had sailed out of Dover two months before.) "The Sixty-sixth Psalm, which came next in order of our readings, brought us great pleasure because it fitted our circumstances exceedingly well. At last we read from the fifth chapter of Joshua, with the admonition that those who needed it should use the last few days at sea to open their hearts."

Though it had not been planned for Jews to be part of the early colony, they nonetheless came in 1733. James Ogelthorpe (1696–1785), resident governor, not only welcomed them but gave them land, and soon synagogue services were heard in Savannah. Scottish Presbyterians were encouraged to settle farther to the west where they could be defenders against Spanish encroachment. Moravians also arrived early but, being less interested in serving as part of a military defense against anybody, soon moved northward to Pennsylvania. And the poor came, lured by the promise of land abroad and driven by the harshness of life at home. In the words of an early chronicler of Georgia's first years: "No wonder then, that great numbers of poor subjects, who lay under a cloud of misfortunes, embraced the opportunity of once more tasting liberty and happiness." The account continued, speaking of others who soon arrived: "Jews, attracted by the temptation of inheritances, flocked over"; also "Germans, oppressed and dissatisfied at home, willingly joined in the adventure." And then even "gentlemen of some stock and fortune willingly expended part of the same in purchasing servants [indentured whites, nor slaves], tools, commodities, and other necessaries."

With these gentlemen came, of course, the Church of England which later found official protection in laws passed by the Georgia Assembly. This church's progress, like that of the colony as a whole, was painfully slow. Even John (1703–1791) and Charles (1707–1788) Wesley, before their separation from the church, came to Georgia in 1736, John laboring in Savannah and Charles on St. Simon's Island. Neither finding much satisfaction in his labor, the two soon returned to England having done little for the Anglican cause, but having had their piety strengthened and hearts warmed through contact with the Moravians. As the Wesleys left Georgia, George Whitefield arrived, making a much greater impact there than his predecessors. In 1740 he started an orphanage near Savannah, raising money (and suspicions) for that project up and down the Atlantic Coast. After his first visit to Georgia in 1738, he noted in his journal that he left it with great regret. For in my opinion, he wrote, it was "an excellent school to learn Christ in." He had particularly high hopes for Savannah, "because the longer I continued there, the larger the congregations grew. And I scarce knew a night . . . when the church house has not been full."

While Georgia may have been "an excellent school to learn Christ in," the learning came much too slowly for most. The solitary Anglican clergyman in Augusta complained in 1768 of "a famine, not a famine of bread, nor a thirst for water, but of hearing the word of the Lord." Savannah offered no more promise, for the colonists there "seem in general to have but very little more knowledge of a Savior than the aboriginal natives." At midcentury, Georgia harbored only a pitiful scattering of churches and, by the time of the Revolution, a population of less than fifty thousand. The youngest of the colonies was in 1776 still too young to have its religious patterns fixed. After the Revolution, the learning came more quickly, especially as taught by Baptists, Methodists, and Presbyterians.

18. Throughout the South and all up and down the East Coast, the "awakener" George Whitefield attracted enormous crowds; his statue stands on the campus of the University of Pennsylvania. *University of Pennsylvania*

Suggested Reading for Part Two

Primary sources pertinent to Part Two may be found in the Gaustad *Documentary* previously cited, Vol. 1, 93–258. On the much debated question of church membership and church attendance in colonial America, see the excellent analysis in Patricia Bonomi, *Under the Cope of Heaven* (New York, 1986).

The standard treatment of Anglicanism in Virginia is the two-volume work by George M. Bryden, *Virginia's Mother Church* (Richmond, Va., 1947; Philadelphia, 1952). More recently John F. Woolverton has provided a much broader survey: *Colonial Anglicanism in North America* (Detroit, 1984). Carl Bridenbaugh's *Mitre and Sceptre* (New York, 1962), along with Frederick V. Mills' *Bishops by Ballot* (New York, 1978) concentrate on the special difficulties confronting Anglicanism before, during, and immediately after the American Revolution. The powerful sweep of evangelical religion all across the Old Dominion is the subject of Rhys Isaac's masterful book, *The Transformation of Virginia, 1740–1790* (Chapel Hill, N.C., 1982). An architectural historian, Dell Upton, has given life to the bricks and mortar of colonial Virginia's Anglican churches in *Holy Things and Profane* (New York, 1986).

The literature on New England's early religious history is vast, a few of the authoritative guides thereto being the following: G. D. Langdon, Jr., *Pilgrim Colony* (New Haven, Conn., 1966); E. Brooks Holifield, *The Covenant Sealed* (New Haven, Conn., 1974); Joseph Ellis, *The New England Mind in Transition* (New Haven, Conn., 1973); Charles E. Hambrick-Stowe, *The Practice of Piety* (Chapel Hill, N.C., 1982); and, Harry S. Stout, *The New England Soul* (New York, 1986). Biographical entry into both the New England mind and the New England soul may be gained via these studies: Edmund S. Morgan on John Winthrop, *The Puritan Dilemma* (Boston, 1958); Charles Akers on Jonathan Mayhew, *Called Unto Liberty* (Cambridge, Mass., 1964); Morgan again on Ezra Stiles, *The Gentle Puritan* (New Haven, Conn., 1962); Kenneth Silverman, *The Life and Times of Cotton Mather* (New York, 1984); and, Patricia Tracy, *Jonathan Edwards, Pastor* (New York, 1980). Even in Puritan New England, religion was not all of a single piece, as Philip F. Gura skillfully explains in *A Glimpse of Sion's Glory* (Middletown, Conn., 1984). On the interplay between magic and religion, between clergy and ordinary folk, see David D. Hall's fine study, *Worlds of Wonder, Days of Judgment* (New York, 1989).

Always the exception to generalizations about religion in New England, Rhode Island should first be approached on its own terms; this can best be done by reading Sydney V. James, *Colonial Rhode Island: A History* (New York, 1975). William G. McLoughlin's monumental study of *New England Dissent, 1630–1833*, 2 vols. (Cambridge, Mass., 1971) traces in remarkable detail the Baptist interaction with society throughout all New England. The best analysis of Roger Williams' much misunderstood ideas can be found in Edmund S. Morgan, *Roger Williams: The Church and the State* (New York, 1967). A minor figure who has suffered major neglect, Obadiah Holmes, is resurrected in E. S. Gaustad, *Baptist Piety* (Grand Rapids, Mich., 1978).

A good place to begin the examination of Maryland's earliest years is Thomas Brien O'Hanley, *Their Rights and Liberties* (Westminster, Md., 1959); later Catholic history there centers around the career of John Carroll, and Hanley has edited *The John Carroll Papers* in three large volumes (Notre Dame, Ind., 1976). The most recent one-volume survey of *American Catholics* (New York, 1981), by James Hennesey, S. J., offers a wide-angle view of colonial Catholicism along with a chapter specifically on the Maryland scene. Since the Chesapeake region proved so important to the young Methodist movement, one should follow that story in Wade C. Barclay, *History of Methodist Missions* (New York, 1949), as well as in the three-volume work edited by Emory Bucke, *History of American Methodism* (New York, 1964); building on a narrower geographical base, William H. Williams describes *The Garden of American Methodism: The Delmarva Peninsula* (Wilmington, Del., 1984). For the important work of Commissary Bray, see H. P. Thompson, *Thomas Bray* (London, 1954), as well as John Calam, *Parsons and Pedagogues: The SPG Adventure in American Education* (New York, 1971).

Both the commercial and ecclesiastical ventures of the Dutch are carefully treated in George L. Smith, *Religion and Trade in New Netherland* (Ithaca, N.Y., 1973), while the fortunes of Holland's church itself are more closely followed in G. F. DeJong, *The Dutch Reformed Church in the American Colonies* (Grand Rapids, Mich., 1978). The latest treatment of the cultural interaction between the Dutch and the English in New York and New Jersey with excellent attention to religion is that of Randall Balmer, *A Perfect Babel of Confusion* (New York, 1989). Also see James Tanis, *Dutch Calvinist Pietism in the Middle Colonies* (The Hague, the Netherlands, 1967). John W. Pratt paints a broader picture of religion in the Empire State in his book, *Religion, Politics, and Diversity* (Ithaca, N.Y., 1967). For the early years of Presbyterianism in the Middle Colonies generally, see Leonard J. Trinterud, *The Forming of an*

American Tradition (Philadelphia, 1949); the fortunes of Anglicanism in New York, especially during the Revolutionary period, may be followed through John W. Lydekker's biography, *The Life and Letters of Charles Inglis* (London, 1936); and, the story of America's oldest Jewish congregation is unfolded in appreciative detail in David and Tamar de Sola Pool, *An Old Faith in the New World* (New York, 1955).

One may most profitably begin the examination of both Quakerism and Penn in the documentary history edited by Jean R. Soderlund, *William Penn and the Founding of Pennsylvania, 1680–1684* (Philadelphia, 1983). Sydney V. James offers a valuable account of Quaker social concern in the eighteenth century in his *People Among Peoples* (Cambridge, Mass., 1963), while J. William Frost emphasizes the role of *The Quaker Family in Colonial America* (New York, 1973). Both Melvin Endy and Mary Maples Dunn give major attention to the colony's founder, the former in *William Penn and Early Quakerism* (Princeton, N.J., 1973), and the latter in *William Penn: Politics and Conscience* (Princeton, N.J., 1967). James T. Lemmon helpfully maps the settlement patterns of Pennsylvania's many religious groups in *The Best Poor Man's Country* (Baltimore, Md., 1972). For the Great Awakening's impact in Pennsylvania, see Dieter Rothermund, *The Layman's Progress; Religious and Political Experience in Colonial Pennsylvania, 1740–1770* (Philadelphia, 1961). And for excellent insight into Philadelphia's important black community, consult Gary Nash, *Forging Freedom* (Cambridge, Mass., 1988).

The religious history of Carolina may be followed in John W. Brinsfield, *Religion and Politics in Colonial South Carolina* (Easley, S.C., 1983). To the older treatment of French Protestants by Arthur H. Hirsch, *The Huguenots of Colonial South Carolina* (Durham, N.C., 1928), one may now add the sophisticated monograph for all the colonies by Jon Butler, *The Huguenots in America: A Refugee People in New World Society* (Cambridge, Mass., 1983). For lively observations of the Church of England and its competitors in the 1760s, see Richard J. Hooker, ed., *The Carolina Backcountry on the Eve of the Revolution: The Journal of Charles Woodmason* (Chapel Hill, N.C., 1953). And the depressing conditions of slavery are clearly seen in Frank W. Klingberg, ed., *The Carolina Chronicle of Dr. Francis Le Jau, 1706–1717* (Berkeley, Ca., 1956). For Georgia's brief life as a colony, see Harold E. Davis, *The Fledgling Province: Social and Cultural Life in Colonial Georgia* (Chapel Hill, N.C., 1976). The heavy involvement of Thomas Bray and of his "Associates" receives its fullest coverage in John C. Van Horne, ed., *Religious Philanthropy and Colonial Slavery: The American Correspondence of the Associates of Dr. Bray, 1717–1777* (Urbana, Ill., 1985).

Part 3

AGE OF EXPANSION

CHAPTER 12

Liberty and Law

A long War of Independence, successfully concluded with a surprisingly generous peace treaty in 1783, set the thirteen colonies—now sovereign states—upon an uncharted course. Much uncertainty lay before them, as they grappled with the question of central or national authority, and as they struggled for some security or at least recognition as a nation among nations. One common thread bound the states together in peace even as it held them together in war: the fear of tyranny, of ALL tyranny, civil or ecclesiastic, foreign or domestic.

Americans in the eighteenth century, far more than their descendants in the twentieth, understood tyrannical authority to be all of one piece. Lordly bishops like lordly princes paid little attention to ordinary folk, made few if any concessions to "majority will," and spoke seldom if at all of natural or inalienable rights bestowed upon humankind. For fourteen hundred years, church and state had joined in a powerful alliance designed to cramp or suppress those rights. For fourteen hundred years, tyranny presented a united front, thereby forcing those who would declare their independence to fight a revolution to resist all tyranny, whether of church or of state, for in the final analysis all tyranny was one. Such at least was the pervasive assumption of those Americans who had won a revolution and signed a treaty of peace. And because of that common conviction, the American Revolution must be seen as a struggle for ecclesiastical no less than civil liberty.

"NO LORDS SPIRITUAL OR TEMPORAL"

Resistance to "spiritual lords," more specifically, to sending bishops from England to America, grew especially strong in the 1760s just when the mother country tightened her control over the colonies and attempted to gain a firmer grip. On their part, many Anglican clergy in the Middle Colonies and New England raised their voices even higher in pleas that bishops be sent before it was too late, before the colonists turned away from not only the Anglican church but against England itself. Even as late as the fall of 1776, the rector of Trinity Church in New York City, Charles Inglis, argued that England's cause could be rescued if only a bishop were quickly dispatched to America. "Upon the whole, the Church of England has lost none of its members by the Rebellion as yet," Inglis wrote, "none, I mean, whose departure from it can be deemed a loss." Like many other observers, Inglis saw the colonists' chances for a military victory as quite slim: "I have not a doubt but, with the Blessing of Providence, His Majesty's Arms will be successful, and finally crush this unnatural Rebellion." When that happens, then England's "Church will indubitably increase, & these confusions will terminate in a large accession to its members."

If the hopes of Charles Inglis were real, so were the fears of those who saw religious liberty as well as civil liberty hanging upon the outcome of the "rebellion." As Presbyterian William Livingston argued in 1768, the concerted effort to impose an Anglican bishop upon Americans posed a threat to liberty, property, and conscience even greater than the "deservedly obnoxious Stamp Act itself." That Act had been repealed, but the pressure for bishops continued, even increased. So Americans who loved their liberty must be ever watchful, for (as Boston's Jonathan Mayhew pointed out) "People are not usually deprived of their liberties all at once, but gradually, by one encroachment after another, as it is found they are disposed to bear them." Those who remembered the persecutions carried forward by England's bishops (and who had not read Foxe's *Book of Martyrs*?) could never consent to "lords spiritual" of that stripe and heritage ever coming to America. Such imperious bishops the colonists had fled England to escape; such bishops they would never allow to land upon their own shores.

No bishops arrived, so that the Revolution did not require a forced exile or imprisonment of such men. What the Revolution did require was a swift abandonment of those privileges that the Church of England enjoyed wherever it had been legally established. In Virginia, the legislature moved quickly to relieve all non-Anglicans from any further taxation for the support of Anglicanism. Laws that attempted to enforce orthodoxy of belief were dropped, as toleration became the norm. But did not the Revolution require more than toleration? Did not its spirit call for a full liberty in religion, for those of all religious persuasions and even for those of none?

Here the events in Virginia must be followed closely, for they determine the course that the nation itself chose to follow. Here dissenters and deists, pietists and rationalists, worked together to abolish all vestiges of an established church, substituting in its place a full and free liberty. Thomas Jefferson (1743–1826) in 1777 wrote a Bill for Establishing Religious Freedom that, as governor, he sent forward to the legislature. The latter body, dominated by members from the older Tidewater region of Virginia, was not yet ready to move away from all governmental alliance with or encouragement of religion. After all, Virginia had known more than a century and one-half of close connection between the church and the state. Should this tie be totally severed? Should the Anglican church be reduced to a struggling sect, competing with all the other newer religious groups? Or could some compromise be found that would honor the Revolution without at the same time turning all history and society upside down?

One compromise proved particularly tempting to the legislature in Virginia: namely, to establish not any single church or sect, but to establish Christianity itself as the official religion. Patrick Henry (1736–1799) made several efforts to have his Bill Establishing a Provision for Teachers of the Christian Religion approved by his fellow legislators. His proposal, supported by several leading Anglicans, seemed a happy

19. The Liberty Bell in Philadelphia's Independence Mall carries this inscription from the Book of Leviticus: "Proclaim liberty through all the land." *Library of Congress*

solution, for it would not discriminate against dissenters, yet it would help safeguard the social and moral order that a new state needed even more than before. It would be more broadly tolerant than previous laws had been, but at the same time it would not act as though the church and the state should have nothing whatsoever to do with each other. Christianity, if Henry's Bill should pass, would be officially declared "the established Religion of this Commonwealth; and all Denominations of Christians demeaning themselves peaceably and faithfully shall enjoy equal privileges."

Dissenters in the backcountry of Virginia suspected that this bill might be just a trick to restore the Church of England to its old favored position. Or they firmly believed that the confounding of civil and ecclesiastical authority, no matter how well intended, was both a bad and a dangerous idea. Baptists urged the legislature to continue in its push for a full religious liberty until "every grievous yoke be broken." Presbyterians questioned whether legislators had the authority to make laws in the field of religion, urging such mere mortals not to presume their "Supremacy in Spirituals." Dissenters had been too long discriminated against, too long persecuted and jailed, to trust a legislature that had for so many decades been the instrument of that persecution and maltreatment. But dissenters alone could not have successfully countered Patrick Henry's moving oratory and considerable prestige.

James Madison (1751–1836), also a member of that Virginia legislature, assumed the task of insuring Henry's defeat. He did so by gathering many signatures to a "Memorial and Remonstrance" against the bill and, even more, by gathering many arguments from history and from logic that could prevail against mere oratory and popular passion. Religion, Madison had argued since he was twenty-two years of age, is a matter for reason to decide, not for legislature to promote or armies to enforce. Now in 1785, a thirty-four-year-old Madison felt even more strongly about keeping civil power far removed from matters of worship and belief. Legislators simply do not have the right, much less the wisdom, to set themselves up as judges of religious truth, Madison argued. Beyond that, however, if today Virginia can lawfully establish Christianity to the exclusion of all other religions, what then will prevent Virginia tomorrow from lawfully establishing a particular denomination of Christians to the exclusion of all others? And if we do that, Madison pointed out, then we are right back where we started from before we fought a revolution to rid us of ALL tyranny, civil or ecclesiastic. Let us, Madison urged, leave all laws pertaining to religion to the only truly qualified authority in this area: namely, "the Supreme Lawgiver of the Universe."

James Madison prevailed; Patrick Henry lost. Thomas Jefferson (far away in Paris at the time) also prevailed as now the Virginia legislature at last prepared itself to pass that bill that Jefferson had written long ago. In January of 1786, Jefferson's language, somewhat modified, became the Statute for Religious Freedom, making Virginia's disestablishment complete and Virginia's contribution to the nation's religious liberty crucial. Jefferson began with the fundamental premise that "Almighty God hath made the mind free." It follows therefrom that mankind should do all that it can to keep minds unshackled and uncoerced. Let us consider, Jefferson noted, that if an all wise and all powerful God restrained himself from coercing either the bodies or the minds of men and women, how utterly absurd it must be for "fallible and uninspired men" to arrogate to themselves the right to exercise "dominion over the faith of others." But, someone will say, without the authority of the state all sorts of errors and heresies will spread. Jefferson responded that error can be conquered only by truth, and that "truth is great and will prevail if left to herself."

With these presuppositions and affirmations, Jefferson's statute elevated rhetoric into law. "Be it enacted," therefore, "that no man shall be compelled to frequent or support any religious worship, place, or ministry whatsoever." One will suffer in no way for his or her religious opinions; on the contrary, all persons "shall be free to profess, and by argument to maintain, their opinions in matters of religion." And whatever their opinions, this will in no way affect their citizenship or their rights. The statute provided for the freedom of religion, but also the freedom from religion. What Jefferson had sought for so long in his "country" of Virginia was now assured; quite soon he and Madison would concern themselves with the even larger country and its liberties.

When delegates gathered in Philadelphia the very next year, 1787, to draft an entirely new frame of government, religion was not their most pressing concern. An effective union of the several states took highest priority. Nonetheless, the Constitution did not entirely ignore religion, paying attention to it only long enough to reduce potential sources of friction or division. Article Six provided that no religious test would ever be required of those holding federal office. The Constitution also allowed those taking the oath of office to "affirm" rather than "swear" their allegiance, this concession being a kindly gesture to Quakers (and others) who believed that biblical injunctions forbade such swearing. Other than that, the Constitution proper made no reference to religion, failing to offer even a token recognition of God's sovereignty over the people.

In a mere three months the delegates, led to a considerable degree by the astute and skillful Madison, managed to write a document that has proved remarkably resilient and enduring. When their work was done in the early fall, Madison quickly dispatched a copy to Jefferson, still in Paris. Jefferson complimented his younger colleague on a job well done, but then wrote: "I will now add what I do not like." And the very first item on that list was the Constitution's failure to provide explicit guarantees for human liberties, the one Jefferson noted at the beginning being freedom of religion. The United States, no less than Virginia, must build liberty into its foundation, must not leave to chance or caprice or politics the security of those natural rights for which so many had died.

In the process of winning approval, state by state, of that Constitution written in Philadelphia, Madison discovered that many others shared Jefferson's passionate concern. He therefore promised that if the Constitution were ratified, he would make the framing of a Bill of Rights the very first order of business in the newly elected Congress. As good as his word, Madison helped guide such a "bill" through Congress in 1789. Ratified by a sufficient number of states by 1791, these first Ten Amendments to the Constitution gave liberty its solid base. The first phrase of the First Amendment spoke to the freedom uppermost in Jefferson's mind when it provided that "Congress shall make no law respecting an establishment of religion, or prohibiting the free exercise thereof." Here a double guarantee could be found: first, that government would do nothing to favor religion; second, that government would do nothing to inhibit religion. In this sensitive area of the soul, government would simply keep its hands off. And for the first time in Western civilization, citizens of a nation could claim as their fundamental right their religious beliefs to be nobody's business but their very own.

So novel was this daring experiment in religious freedom, so unprecedented in European history, that none could be entirely sure just what it meant. Did the promise of "free exercise" extend to all Protestants? Even to Roman Catholics? To Jews, Moslems, and beyond? Did the prohibition against "establishment" rule out federally promoted days of fasting or feasting? Did it require a rigid neutrality that might at times appear to be even a hostility? And did it determine what the states might or might not do in the religious arena? These questions were not readily answered in the 1790s, nor two hundred years later. For Jefferson himself, the language of the First Amendment seemed explicit enough. Those words, he wrote early in 1802, erected "a wall of separation between Church and State." This phrase, written during his first term as president, guided his own actions in that high office, even as to some degree it guided the nation after his death. Jefferson understood the American Revolution to have been a struggle equally against all "Lords Temporal or Spiritual."

"TO BIGOTRY NO SANCTION, TO PERSECUTION NO ASSISTANCE"

When George Washington (1732–1799) assumed the office of president in 1789, all eyes fastened upon him in order to learn whether the untried nation had merely exchanged a foreign tyranny for a domestic one. Since the history of religious persecution had been such a long and cruel one, many persons could hardly believe that the promises of freedom could survive the realities of politics. Those Americans who had been viewed with particular suspicion or unease had the most to fear. Roman Catholics, for example, knew firsthand the force of laws against "popery," against receiving immigrants from Catholic countries, against "divers Jesuit priests and popish missionaries." With understandable concern, they wrote to President Washington, first, to congratulate him upon his election and, second, to inquire concerning their status under a new form of government. With sensitivity and assurances, Washington replied (March 12, 1790) that he hoped to see "America among the foremost nations in examples of justice and liberality." With reference to the Catholics in particular, Washington added: "I presume that your fellow-citizens will not forget the patriotic part which you took in the accomplishment of their Revolution, and the establishment of their government." He also noted the critical assistance that France, "a nation in which the Roman Catholic religion is professed," had rendered to the nation in its struggle with Britain. Catholics, still a beleaguered minority confined mainly to Maryland and Pennsylvania, found hope in such promises of justice and liberality.

An even tinier minority, America's Jews, wondered if this still-vulnerable nation would continue on its Madisonian course of "offering an asylum to the persecuted and oppressed of every Nation and Religion." Newport's Hebrew congregation expressed their concern to the country's first president and received from him equally comforting words. Liberty of conscience, Washington noted (August 17, 1790), applied to all Americans alike, without distinction or discrimination. We no longer speak of "toleration," he wrote, but rather of "inherent natural rights." Then picking up an apt phrasing that the Newport congregation had used in its letter, Washington replied that "happily the Government of the United States . . . gives to bigotry no sanction, to persecution no assistance." He concluded with the wish that "the Children of the Stock of Abraham who dwell in this land [will] continue to merit and enjoy the good will of the other Inhabitants." The President envisioned a future in which "every one shall sit in safety under his own vine and fig tree, and there shall be none to make him afraid."

So to many other religious groups, Washington affirmed that liberty was what this country was all about, that none should fear, none should waver. To the Quakers, he declared that liberty in religion was not only among the nation's choicest "blessings," it was among its citizens most certain "rights." To the Baptists, he avowed that none would be more vigorous than he himself "against the horrors of spiritual tyranny, and every species of religious persecution." An old age had passed away; a *Novus Ordo Seclorum* was at hand.

It took that New Order of the Ages some time to extend its liberty to all. America's blacks continued to labor under the harsh burden of slavery and indifference. Even though the air rang with cries of liberty in the latter decades of the eighteenth century, few concluded that this liberty extended absolutely and unequivocally to all. In 1772, in Philadelphia, the Quaker Anthony Benezet (1713–1784) called for an end to the slave trade, "this unnatural and barbarous Traffic" and "the destruction & intolerable suffering it entails" both in the slave's country of origin as well as in the country of adoption. That same year in Boston, Baptist John Allen (?–?) argued that just as white Americans had scorned to be slaves to Britain, so black Americans should be emancipated from their bondage. "Every sensation of humanity, every bowel of pity, every compassion as a Christian" demanded that liberty be granted to "the most distressed of all human beings, the natives of Africa." Slavery in any land or nation is unforgiveable, but for "those who love the Gospel of Christ" to engage in and even encourage "this bloody and inhuman Trade of Man-stealing and Slave-making," this staggers the imagination and shocks all sensibility. But the Declaration of Independence suffered major deletions, the Constitution made major compromises, and the nation later confronted major consequences that inflicted incalculable costs.

If the federal government moved timidly with respect to the slave trade and to slavery itself, the states moved timidly with respect to a full religious freedom, or failed to perceive the implications of a liberty that they generally embraced. Few states took steps as unambiguous as those taken by Virginia in 1786. Delaware's 1776 constitution required all public officials to swear their belief "in God the Father, in Jesus Christ His only Son, and in the Holy Ghost." Maryland, which stipulated that its office holders be of the Christian religion, extended its benefits of religious liberty to Christians alone. Pennsylvania in 1790 vowed to deny state offices to any atheist as well as to any person who did not believe in "a future state of rewards and punishments." Only Protestants could be elected in New Hampshire, Massachusetts, New Jersey, South Carolina, and Georgia—according to their constitutions of the 1770s and 1780s. Though all states supported the idea of religious liberty, their application of the concept was both uneven and gradual.

This was conspicuously so in the case of Connecticut and Massachusetts where a measure of establishment continued well into the nineteenth century. Unlike the Church of England which suffered great unpopularity during the Revolution and therefore experienced swift disestablishment, Congregationalism in New England was "locally owned and operated" and wholly committed to the revolutionary cause. No popular wave of resentment or suspicion washed over the Congregationalists who continued to encourage local governments "to make suitable provision . . . for the institution of the public worship of God, and for the support and maintenance of public Protestant teachers of piety, religion, and morality" (to quote from the 1780 Massachusetts Constitution). In Connecticut, Baptists, Quakers, and Episcopalians joined with Jeffersonian Republicans in a long struggle to sever the last remaining ties between Congregationalism and the state. In 1818 the knot was finally cut, with Jefferson writing happily to John Adams (1735–1826) that he rejoiced to see that "this den of priesthood is at length broken up, and that a protestant popedom is no longer to disgrace American history and character." Several more years passed before Massachusetts managed, after considerable involved litigation, to remove from its constitution all vestiges of an alliance between church and state that had endured for two hundred years. Step by faltering step, the sentiment responsible for the First Amendment filtered down to state and county, parish and town.

"A GOVERNMENT OF THE UNIVERSE"

If the Founding Fathers had much to say about liberty in religion, they also regularly acknowledged the overseeing Providence that directed all affairs of persons and of nations. In 1789 George Washington called for the country to express its gratitude to "that great and glorious Being who is the beneficent Author of all the good that was, that is, or that will be." In his First Inaugural Address, the Anglican-reared president sounded the same theme: "No people can be bound to acknowledge and adore the invisible hand which conducts the affairs of men more than the people of the United States. Every step by which they have been advanced to the character of an independent nation seems to have been distinguished by some token of providential agency." "The Grand Architect," the "superintending Power," the "Governor of the Universe," the "Great Ruler of Events"—these were the terms, vaguely impersonal and broadly rational, in which Washington spoke of God. He rarely cited the bible and never spoke of Jesus Christ, but he hardly needed to. For Washington had himself become a kind of Moses, leading his people from submission and captivity to a rich and bountiful Promised Land.

Washington's successor, John Adams, grew up in the Congregational milieu of colonial New England. He shared in the liberalism that eventually resulted in the separation of Unitarianism from its more orthodox ancestry; he also shared fully in the European Enlightenment that sought its religious ideas more from "Nature" and "Reason" (both words being regularly capitalized by these thinkers) than from biblical revelation or Christian tradition. From Adam's youth to his old age, the subject of religion fascinated him: he could never quite let it go.

Adams had little patience with creeds, and less patience with those who tried to impose them upon others. "Let the mind loose," he urged in a letter to his son in 1816; "it must be loose," uncramped by dogmatism, unfettered by superstition. The Christian religion is good—indeed "as I understand it"—the very best. But Adams understood Christianity to be primarily the sturdy ally of morality. Conduct rather than creed was the true measure of one's faith. At its best, Christianity introduced millions to "the great Principle of the Law of Nature and Nations: Love your Neighbour as yourself, and do to others as you would that others should do to you." Where Christianity has gone astray was in its endless and barren disputing about theological issues that did not alter the way in which women and men lived. Every church acted as though it had a complete monopoly on truth, Adams wrote, as though it had "the Holy Ghost in a Phial." Every church thinks only its members have guaranteed tickets of admission into heaven. I simply refuse to believe, Adams noted in 1821, that "millions and millions of men are to be miserable and only a little handful of Elect Calvinists happy forever." Like Washington, Adams preferred to honor "the Power that moves, the Wisdom that directs, and the Benevolence that sanctifies" this grand and mysterious universe.

If Adams spent much time indicating what he rejected from the old orthodoxies, he also spent much time and effort emphasizing why religion was essential to the welfare of humanity in general and of the United States in particular. To a cousin, John Adams wrote in the early years of the American Revolution that all must remember, amid the excited cries for liberty, that "it is religion and morality alone which can establish the principles upon which freedom can securely stand." People will be free, he added, only so long as they are virtuous. "Without virtue, people may change governments, but in so doing they only trade one tyranny for another." If nations cannot survive without religion, neither can individuals. It is religion that teaches duty, that makes us responsible and honorable. Without religion, the Adamses themselves would have been "rakes, fops, sots, gamblers, starved with hunger, frozen with cold, scalped by Indians." Let us not talk about Original Sin, Adams cautioned, or about the absence of free will; rather, let us talk about our own responsibility and our own free choice to be "good husbands and good wives, good parents and good children, good masters and good servants." This is what religion calls us, and helps us, to be.

Thomas Jefferson who succeeded Adams in the presidency shared the view that religion often got off its proper track by getting lost in a wasteland of doctrinal absurdity and dogmatic perversity. Even more strongly than Adams, Jefferson condemned those who buried the "genuine precepts" of Jesus under a pile of priestly jargon and philosophical subtleties. In his retirement at Monticello, Jefferson spent many hours compiling the *Life and Morals of Jesus* from a careful examination of the New Testament in Greek, Latin, French, and English. Extracting that which emphasized the ethical content of Jesus' teaching, Jefferson hoped to make Christianity appear less the abstruse metaphysical system and more the clear moral code by which all people could live. "The sum of all religion," Jefferson noted, was proclaimed by "its best preacher: fear God and love thy neighbor." That's all there was to it: no mystery to be unravelled, no elaborate catechism to be memorized, no initiatory rite to be administered.

Why has that which was all so simple been changed into something all too complex? Jefferson's answer to that question was to blame the Platonists who turned the pure morality of the Sermon on the Mount into "unintelligible jargon" and nonsensical whimsy. And the clergy from the fourth century down to the eighteenth have preserved their

20. The Jefferson Memorial in Washington, D.C., recognizes the contribution of the third president to *all* liberty, civil and ecclesiastical. *Baptist Joint Committee on Public Affairs*

power only by preferring mystery over clarity, Jefferson argued. Jefferson who had little sympathy for religious institutions and their "priests" declared that the paid ministry had been far more interested in profit and power than in the moral nature of man or of the universe. Endlessly spinning out their theological formulas and defending their entrenched positions, the priests have kept their followers in ignorance and servility. But I wish it to be known to all, Jefferson wrote, that "our Saviour did not come into the world to save metaphysicians only." We have, lamented Jefferson, given up "morals for mysteries, Jesus for Plato."

The Jeffersonian theme was just this: keep Christianity simple, but also keep it moral. Like Adams, Jefferson thought morality essential to the well being of the country, and that Christianity—a purified, reasonable Christianity—was the best instrument for instructing and enforcing the moral duties. No system of morality would work, Jefferson believed, "without the sanction of divine authority stampt upon it." But this was where the emphasis of religion must lie: upon our deeds more than our words, upon our good works more than our declarations of belief. If I were to found a new sect, Jefferson observed in 1819, my fundamental principle "would be the reverse of Calvin's: that we are saved by our good works which are within our power, and not by our faith which is not within our power." Often called the infidel or atheist or archdemon, Jefferson sincerely believed that he had not rejected Christianity, only purified it. He was more attached to the "pure wheat" of Jesus' teaching than were many others who accepted the wheat all mixed up with the chaff. "I am a real Christian," Jefferson explained in 1803, in that I am "sincerely attached" to the instructions of Jesus, preferring Jesus' teaching to that of all others. Jesus taught a morality broader than that of the Greeks who concentrated largely on the self, and more compassionate than that of the ancient Hebrews whose ethics were "often irreconcilable with the sound dictates of reason." Jesus returned us to the Jewish idea of one God (away from all the polytheism of Greece and Rome), but gave us "juster notions of his attributes and government." Jesus, moreover, corrected the defects of ancient moral systems by "gathering all into one family, under the bonds of love, charity, peace, common wants, and common aids."

Like both of his presidential predecessors, Jefferson had no difficulty affirming a "government of the Universe." And like other deists of his time, Jefferson found the argument from design compelling. To explain a world of pattern and order and causation, one must assume a Creator and "Grand Architect." Trusting to our senses and our reason (not to biblical revelation), we know that God exists. He creates, regulates, preserves. Our reason tells us that God is One, not many, Jefferson rejecting what he called "the incomprehensible jargon of Trinitarian arithmetic." And eventually, in a newly enlightened age, all will come to recognize the unity of God. "The religion of Jesus," Jefferson declared, "is founded on the Unity of God, and this principle, chiefly, gave it triumph over the rabble of heathen gods" so widely believed to exist in the Graeco-Roman world. "I have little doubt," Jefferson wrote in 1822, that "the whole of our country will soon be rallied to the Unity of the Creator." This was the religion of the earliest Christians, Jefferson argued, and would have been the religion of all later Christians had not the philosophers and priests so muffled the doctrines of Jesus in "mysticisms, fancies, and falsehoods." There would never have been an infidel, Jefferson concluded, if there had never been a priest.

In the minds of the nations's founders, liberty in religion was of critical importance to all humankind. Also critical, however, was a commitment to religion on the part of the citizens of the young nation. Washington, Adams, and Jefferson all agreed and in various public addresses asserted that ours was a universe of morality and reason, and a universe in which right would ultimately prevail—if not in this life, then in the life beyond. "A future state," John Adams affirmed in 1823, "will set all aright; without the supposition of a future state I can make nothing of this Universe but a Chaos." The whole world, without divine justice, would be only "a boyish Fire Work." Providence sustained, Providence guided, and the future both within history and beyond history rested firmly in the control of a providential and "All Wise Creator." Liberty was a matter of human law, but destiny was shaped by divine law.

CHAPTER 13

Freedom and the Frontier

In the early decades of the nineteenth century, freedom proved to be not so much a proposition to defend as an experience to enjoy. Freedom in religion was no tired cliché, but a prize of war, now to be energized into daily life and national expansion. Lyman Beecher (1775–1863) who had so passionately resisted the disestablishment of the Congregational Church in Connecticut confessed, after the event, that severing the ties between church and state was "the best thing that ever happened to the State of Connecticut." He discovered that churches, cut "loose from dependence on state support," found a renewed vigor and forcefulness. Relying "wholly on their own resources and on God," they moved forward with swift and astonishing speed to meet the challenges of a rapidly moving frontier and a rapidly expanding population.

Relying on their own resources, the churches and synagogues of America engaged in a voluntary effort of unprecedented magnitude. "Voluntarism," that is, action unaided by the state and undirected by any supreme ecclesiastical authority, came to be the distinguishing feature of religion in America, and at no time more conspicuously so than in the early decades of the nineteenth century. Robert Baird (1798–1863), an early religious historian, explained to Europeans that what was happening in America was different from anything that they had known. And the difference lay chiefly in "the voluntary principle." For this principle, Baird noted, represented an energy and self-reliance that extended itself "in every direction with an all-powerful influence." By means of free and spontaneous effort, men and women became instruments of this new force "wherever the Gospel is to be preached, wherever vice is to be attacked, wherever suffering humanity is to be relieved." In a young nation, so much needed to be done, and done quickly.

A SECOND GREAT AWAKENING

The challenge seemed enormous, perhaps well beyond the resources and will of the religious institutions themselves. First, an American

Revolution had removed government from any significant role in religion. Second, a French Revolution had attacked the churches and their clergy with a force and virulence that threatened the very fabric of society. Third, a hostile rationalism, personified in such men as Thomas Paine, Ethan Allen (1738–1789), and Elihu Palmer (1764–1806), sought to undermine the very foundations of the Christian religion, attacking biblical revelation and characterizing traditional religion as "an empire of superstition" (to quote Palmer). Fourth, the nation daily received new waves of immigrants that might forever alter the familiar patterns of belief and behavior. Could any merely voluntary force be strong enough and swift enough to meet these challenges, to turn the tide, to preserve and perpetuate the religious heritage of America?

What has come to be called the Second Great Awakening was the bravest effort to answer that question in the affirmative. Through the creation of many new agencies and organizations, through the founding of academies and schools, through the development of new techniques for recruitment and commitment, the religious forces mounted a powerful counteroffensive against indifference and hostility.

First, new agencies sprang into existence with a profusion like that of spring flowers. In 1816 the American Bible Society arose out of individual and voluntary concern that the Scriptures be widely and inexpensively distributed all across the country and even beyond. Such printing and circulation would help counter that false philosophy, masquerading "under the imposing names of liberality and reason," that would "seduce mankind" away from the truths of the Christian religion and away "from all which can bless the life that is, or shed a cheering radiance on the life that is to come." Like most of the voluntary agencies springing up in the early nineteenth century, the Bible Society saw itself as rising above denominational differences and sectarian jealousies to present a "united evangelical front" in the conquest of "the prodigious territory of the United States" and its rapidly increasing population.

Similarly, the American Sunday School Union, formed in 1824, would help to organize this new movement so that it might defeat or diminish all ignorance or faithlessness. The Sunday school at this time was really a school, often the only school on the frontier, where reading and writing could be taught. Not dependent upon an ordained clergy for its operation, the Sunday school frequently preceded the organization of a church and could exist for years independently of any church. The laity, male and female, took charge of such schools, with women playing an especially active and determinative role in their development. Sunday schools did exist, of course, prior to and apart from a "union" that attempted to coordinate and strengthen their efforts. But the union, in the words of its founders, represented "a combination of talent, of energy, and of means, and of the most approved plans of instruction." With this supervision, the schools would "become more successful, and their influence more extensive."

The very next year, the American Tract Society dedicated itself to the printing and distributing of "short, plain, striking, entertaining, and instructive Tracts" that would assist in the spread of good morals and sound religion. Noting that a ten-page tract could be produced for a single penny, the society saw such inexpensive printing as a boon particularly to the poor, most surely the "poor of an extended population." If necessary, such tracts could be given away, with the probable result that they would be used over and over, read and re-read. "The traveler may scatter them along the roads and throughout the inns and cottages. . . . Merchants may distribute them to ship-masters, and ship-masters to seamen; men of business may transmit them, with every

21. Native American Samson Occom, ordained into the Congregational ministry in 1759, had great success in England raising money for the missionary efforts among the Indians back in America. *National Portrait Gallery*

bale of goods, to the remote corners of the land and globe." In this fashion, so much good could be achieved at so little expense. "Next to the Bible and the living Ministry," nothing else could be so useful as the pervasive sprinkling of the land with booklets expressing "some of great and glorious truths of the Gospel."

Agencies such as the American Bible Society, the American Sunday School Union, and the American Tract Society reveal a strong commitment to and confidence in education. That commitment is seen even more clearly in the establishment in the East and all along the frontier of academies and colleges that would operate under denominational influence if not control. In the early years of the young nation, states moved to support and supervise their own colleges and universities, the creation of the University of Virginia in 1816 being a conspicuous symbol of this effort. Under the sway of the Second Great Awakening, however, religious forces continued to dominate even most state institutions until well after the Civil War When the state of New Hampshire sought in 1816 to take over Dartmouth College, then still under Congregational control, the stage was set for a major contest between religious and secular interests in higher education. When this famous case finally reached the U. S. Supreme Court in 1819, Chief Justice John Marshall's decision—to the dismay of Thomas Jefferson—upheld the right of the religious and private trustees to continue their control of the school without interference from the state.

Such a decision gave great encouragement to denominations to launch their own colleges and maintain their long-standing dominance of higher education in America. So Congregationalists and Presbyterians together founded such schools as Western Reserve (1826) in Ohio, Knox (1837) in Illinois, Grinnell (1847) in Iowa, and Ripon (1851) in Wisconsin. Methodists were responsible for such early frontier schools as McKendree (1835) and De Pauw (1837) in Illinois, and Ohio Wesleyan (1842). Before the Civil War, Baptists brought these schools into existence: Denison (1832) in Ohio, Shurtleff (1835) in Illinois, and Baylor (1845) in Texas. These four denominations accounted for about half of all institutions of higher learning begun before 1860. By that latter date, Roman Catholics had started St. Louis University in 1832, St. Xavier in Illinois a decade later, and Indiana's Notre Dame in 1844. Episcopal schools included Ohio's Kenyon (1826) as well as Tennessee's University of the South (1858). Even such smaller groups as German Reformed, Quakers, and German Lutherans moved onto the frontier in sufficient force to create colleges in Ohio and Indiana. Religion, declared the Society for the Promotion of Collegiate and Theological Education in 1847, must be prepared to do for the frontier "what Yale, and Dartmouth, and Williams, and Amherst have done for New England: to call forth . . . a learned and pious ministry; to send life, and health, and vigor through the whole system of popular education; and, to . . .

found society on the lasting basis of religious freedom and evangelical truth." Nowhere else, the society concluded, were the opportunities greater at that time than in "the valley of the Mississippi."

Finally, the Second Great Awakening rode on the waves of revivalism, a revivalism planned and promoted most effectively by Charles G. Finney (1792–1875). Professor of theology and sometime president of Oberlin College (founded in 1833), Finney led revivals not only on the frontier but with equal if not greater effectiveness in the major cities of the East. Revivals stressed the importance of individual response to Christian proclamations just as they gave the churches a renewed and enlarged membership. Under the pressures of voluntarism, churches could not live by the law of inertia alone, nor could they count on long-standing traditions to maintain their community status. To exist, churches had to persuade and recruit, win and enlist vast multitudes to their own fellowships and budgets. Revivalism proved a most valued technique for accomplishing these life-sustaining tasks, and Finney proved the most expert practitioner in the first half of the nineteenth century.

More than just a practitioner, however, Finney also defended conscious effort in promoting revivals. Some said that since revivals were given of God, one should sit back and wait until God sent a revival down to earth. Well, Finney responded, it's true that revivals like all blessings, like harvests of corn, are ultimately the gift of God. But that did not mean that we as human beings have nothing to do but wait! Suppose one simply waited for a harvest without ever tilling the earth and planting the seed and clearing the weeds. That would make no sense at all. Nor does it make sense to suppose that we can make no preparation for the harvest of souls. "In the Bible, the word of God is compared to grain, and preaching is compared to sowing seed, and the results to the springing up and growth of the crop," Finney wrote in 1835. And just as we will reap a natural crop if we have done all our work properly, so we will reap a supernatural crop of converts if only we will do our work properly. One is as scientifically and philosophically certain as the other: proper means lead to worthy ends. Because the churches have lost sight of that simple connection between cause and effect, "more than five thousand million have gone down to hell, while the church has been dreaming, and waiting for God to save them without the use of means." Now was the time, America was the place to demonstrate the willingness of Christians, the eagerness of Christians, to gather as many lost sheep as possible into the churchly fold.

Roman Catholics also found the revival or "retreat" an effective means for recruitment and renewal on the frontier. The bishop of the first frontier diocese, centered in Bardstown, Kentucky, Joseph Flaget (1763–1850), made his See an instrument of vigorous evangelical activity. Prompted by the declaration of Pope Leo XII that 1825 would mark the opening of a Jubilee Year for Roman Catholicism everywhere, Bishop Flaget encouraged his own followers to celebrate not for one but for two years in order to cover his vast territory with preaching and calls to greater repentance and dedication. Flaget "put himself at the head of his missionaries," an account written a few years later reported, "and despite the fatigue inseparable from long journeys, he wished to share with them in all the labours as well as in all the consolations." Even in the middle of winter, people crowded to the churches, coming from miles around to attend the Mass, to offer their confessions and "share in the graces flowing from the Sacrament of Penace." Evidences of repentance abounded, as even "sinners of the most inveterate habits were seen weeping over their past wanderings." Laborers and farmers, "who constituted the majority of the Catholics," displayed their fervor and zeal, but so also did merchants, physicians, magistrates, and legislators show "themselves equally eager to profit by the graces of heaven."

Such descriptions of Catholic retreats matched the more familiar accounts of the frontier camp meeting where members of many denominations or of none gathered for days or for weeks to hear sermons delivered with unusual power, to offer prayers and sing hymns, to find new strength in the fellowship of so many earnest Christians. The drama and passion of such meetings greatly impressed the frontier reformer, Timothy Flint (1780–1840), who found it nearly impossible to portray the eager anticipation and the unrestrained excitement that characterized these great gatherings. Speaking of the Cumberland Valley of Tennessee in the late 1820s, Flint explained how publicity had been circulated for two or three months in advance of the actual time appointed for the meeting to begin. Then, as the day approached, "coaches, chaises, wagons, carts, people on horseback, and multitudes traveling from a distance on foot" hurried from every direction to the grove of trees selected for the encampment. There tents were pitched "and the religious city grows up in a few hours under the trees, beside the stream" which offered the necessary supply of water.

Persons of all ages and classes and backgrounds congregated: those running for office, those who wished merely to enjoy the spectacle, the young and beautiful "with mixed motives which it were best not severely to scrutinize," the middle-aged parents with their families, and the "men and women of hoary hairs . . . with such thoughts, it may be hoped, as their years invite." Such was the congregation "consisting of thousands," Flint reported. When lamps were hung on all the trees, when preachers of simple and native eloquence began to speak upon the "awful themes" of eternity, when all assembled in solemn excitement, then one beheld "the most brilliant theatre in the world," "a temple worthy of the grandeur of God."

Testimony from these camp meetings demonstrate their potency and their capacity to change the direction of lives and the intensity of loyalties. One black convert to Methodism, Zilpha Elaw (1790?–1846?) tells of her first attending such a meeting in 1817 where she observed that "the hardest hearts are melted into tenderness; the driest eyes overflow with tears, and the loftiest spirits bow down." All sensed the presence of God, she added, in the midst of the "magnificently solemn scene." Worship began before sunrise, with a blowing of trumpets "to awaken every inhabitant of the City of the Lord." After devotions and breakfast in the family tents, trumpets announced the beginning of public prayer, this followed at ten o'clock by the first round of public preaching which lasted until nearly noon. Then after lunch in the tents, another period of prayer and preaching in the afternoon. "At six o'clock in the evening, the public services commence again, as before," this continuing until around ten when all retire. Religious services of this intensity might go on for a week or more, concluding with a "solemn love feast" after which all tents were struck as the thousands prepared to depart. The ministers, Zilpha Elaw wrote, "form themselves in procession and march round the camp, the people falling into rank and following them." After this formal processing, everyone stood still while a farewell hymn was sung. Then the people broke rank to shake hands with all the clergy, bidding them a tender adieu. "This farewell scene is a most moving and affecting occasion. Hundreds of Christians, dear to each other and beloved in the Spirit, embrace each other for the last time, and part to meet no more, until the morning of the resurrection." The camp meeting was in its essence neither carnival nor county fair but a time of spiritual regeneration and sustaining hope. And that, by one means or another, was the task to which the Second Great Awakening dedicated itself.

UTOPIAN EXPERIMENTATION

While the Second Great Awakening sought to save the whole country, some smaller groups of believers sought to save themselves from the country. Or at least they, like the seventeenth-century Puritans, wished first to save themselves and then, perhaps by example, to save others. In the first half of the nineteenth century, hopes were high, land was cheap, and experimental visions abounded. As Ralph Waldo Emerson commented to Thomas Carlyle in 1840, "Not a reading man but has a draft of a new community in his waistcoat pocket."

An early utopian community, the Shakers, arrived in America from England in 1774 under the direction of "Mother" Ann Lee (1736–1784). Ann Lee taught that procreation was unnecessary since the Kingdom of God was near at hand; this being so, Shaker men and women should live apart, leading celibate lives. If a married couple joined the Shaker community, the marital relationship ended as the common life began. The founder also held that God had first appeared incarnate in a male,

Jesus of Nazareth; now, the divine essence has its second incarnation in a female, Ann Lee of England. The movement initially took hold in New England and New York, there scandalizing the Congregational geographer, Jedidiah Morse, by its mode of worship. Shaker worship, "if such extravagant conduct may be so called," included (Morse reported) "dancing, singing, leaping, clapping their hands, falling on their knees, and uttering themselves in groans and sighs." Behavior of this sort, far removed from the sober decorum of the New England meeting house, led Morse to hope that Shakerism would swiftly disappear.

Rather than disappear, Shaker communities multiplied in the first half of the nineteenth century as these visionaries moved into Ohio, Indiana, and Kentucky. Reaping some of the harvest of frontier revivals, Shakers grew to about six thousand by midcentury. Typical of most

22. Richard Allen, distinguished leader of Black Methodists, served as bishop of the African Methodist Episcopal Church from 1816 to 1831. *National Portrait Gallery*

utopian groups of the day, Shakers held all property in common and believed that spiritual power along with proper diet could conquer physical disease. Like the early Christians at Pentecost, Shakers did "not called the least thing their own." Also, first-century Christians "took no part in the heathen government, either in being officers or electing officers. They would not swear, or take oaths. They would not fight, or engage in war." Shakers saw themselves as reviving "The Pentecost Church" in their own time, one feature of that church being the commitment "to live a virgin life." Celibacy, the most distinctive doctrine of the Shakers, doomed this society to decline and ultimate extinction since no natural progeny kept membership stable. When frontier revivalism waned, so did the growth of the Shakers. A single century after their peak membership of six thousand, only a handful of Shakers remained. Toward the end of the twentieth century, the sinful world remembered Shakers chiefly for their furniture, their herbs, and their songs.

John Humphrey Noyes (1811–1886) of Putney, Vermont, led his small band of followers in 1847 from that New England locale to the town of Oneida in western New York. True, this was an age of hope, Noyes observed; so much of mankind's hope, however, was misplaced, being centered in an idealization of the past or in expectations of some divine fulfillment in the future. We on the other hand, said Noyes, believe in a spiritual revolution now at hand: "an outburst of spiritual knowledge and power—a conversion of the world from sensuality, from carnal morality, and from brain-philosophy, to spiritual wisdom and life." To bring about a spiritual revolution, a sexual revolution was first required.

Rejecting the celibacy of the Shakers ("they virtually castrate themselves"), Noyes advocated what he called "complex marriage." Under his utopian system, the community itself would determine who should mate with whom, that decision being guided by the best principles of eugenics or "scientific propagation." Monogamy "is an absolute bar to scientific propagation." Consider, Noyes wrote, "how much progress would the horse-breeders expect to make if they were only at liberty to bring their animals together in exclusive pairs." No, monogamy made no more sense than celibacy did. What did make sense was bringing together the best specimens of the human race to procreate and thereby to lift all humankind up to the level where a truly spiritual revolution could occur. Surely, Noyes argued, this was better than the present system which "restricts each man, whatever may be his potency and his value, to the amount of production of which one woman, chosen blindly, may be capable." What we have in effect done, he added, was choose the worst over the best, for "the good man will be limited by his conscience . . . while the bad man, free from moral check, will distribute his seed beyond the legal limits as widely as he dares."

It all made sense—except to the neighbors. Suffering from every harassment and ridicule, the Oneida Community limped along without recruiting many new members, gaining rather only in the number and intensity of its enemies. By 1880 this utopian experiment turned to economics for its salvation, so that the descendents of this vision are remembered more for their silverware than for their social engineering. (For information on the most successful of these nineteenth century utopian visions, the Mormons, see Chapter Fourteen.)

GREAT EXPECTATIONS

Other visions depended not so much on questions of private property and marital proprieties but on God's plan for the future or his revelation in the past. Millennialism wrestled with the Book of Revelation (and other prophecies) in order to determine just when Christ would come again to usher in the thousand years of peace and virtue, when the Devil would be chained and the earth cleansed of all unrighteousness. So much that was promising and good seemed to be happening in and to America in the early decades of the nineteenth century: could it be that the Kingdom of God was just around the corner? Many thought so, including Charles G. Finney who in 1835 announced that "the millennium may come in this country in three years."

An even more fervent and convinced announcer, William Miller (1782–1849) of upstate New York, predicted that Christ would come again sometime between March 21, 1843 and the following twenty-first of March. Basing his prophecy on the Daniel 8:13, Miller argued that the "two thousand and three hundred evenings and mornings" spoken of there really meant a time period of twenty-three hundred years. That period began, Miller calculated, with the command of the Persian King Artaxerxes in 457 B.C. to rebuild Jerusalem. If one subtracted 457 from 2,300, the mathematical remainder pointed unmistakably to 1843—the year when the New Jerusalem would be established as Christ descended from the heavens. Attracting wide audiences from among the Baptists, Methodists, Presbyterians, Congregationalists, and Shakers (whose proper title is the United Society of Believers in Christ's Second Coming), Miller drew many into his net of great expectations. "If I have erred" in my calculations, he wrote, we shall all soon know. But if on the other hand I have announced the truth, then "how important the era in which we live! What vast and important changes must soon be realized! And how necessary that every individual be prepared, that [this] day may not come upon them unawares."

Miller did err, with the consequence that all those great hopes led to the Great Disappointment, as this period is known in the history of later millennialists. Baffled by the prophecy that failed, many returned to their former denominational homes while others, disenchanted, turned away from biblical religion altogether. Still others, convinced that the expectation was right and only the dating wrong, regrouped to await a later (and not so clearly specified) Second Coming of Christ. Among the most significant survivors of the Millerite disappointment, the Seventh-Day Adventists followed the visions of their new leader, Ellen G. White (1827–1915), who drew her disciples from dismay and disintegration to renewed confidence in God's sovereignty over human history and eventual intrusion into that history.

These Adventists (the word *advent* means coming or arrival) moved from their early New England base to Michigan in 1855. By 1863 they could claim over one hundred churches and more than three thousand members, numbers that would grow dramatically during the next century. In addition to their emphasis upon the "advent," Mrs. White's followers believed that the ancient commandment to "keep the Sabbath day holy" had not been cancelled or revoked; therefore, one must keep the Sabbath, the seventh day of the week, and not Sunday as the day set aside by divine law. Moreover, one must keep one's body free of the defilement that comes from eating meat; drinking alcohol, coffee, or tea; smoking tobacco; or indulging in anything that works against a pure mind in a sound body. Since one of the main difficulties in maintaining a vegetarian diet was its sheer monotony, Adventists set about to offer variety. Their most conspicuous success came from Battle Creek, Michigan, where Adventist W. K. Kellogg (1860–1951) created a whole new cereal empire. But health reform moved beyond breakfast foods to include sanitaria and hospitals along with doctors, dentists, and nurses trained in Adventists schools and dispatched as missionaries all around the world. Out of great disappointments great new energies were born.

Another kind of expectancy looked not so much to a Millennial Age yet to come but to an Apostolic Age now to be revived. "Restorationism" is the term applied to those earnest Christians who wished to bring back, to restore, the New Testament church in its purity and power. In western Pennsylvania, Alexander Campbell (1788–1866) bemoaned the many divisions within Christendom, most of these (in his view) having no essential reason for being in the nineteenth century. Denominations arose because of special historical conditions or through the influence of powerful personalities. Now, was it not time to rise above these largely meaningless or accidental separations and return to the fount from which all have come and to which all owe their ultimate loyalty? In the 1820s Campbell, traveling throughout Ohio, Indiana, Kentucky, and Tennessee, observed that the "different regimentals" and the "different standards" did not mean all that much: "one is heroic and daring, another dastardly and timid under any insignia." "The flag"—that is, the denominational label—simply did not make that much difference. It was time, Campbell concluded, for all churches to become just "Christians," just followers or disciples of Christ.

The Christian world has seen too much of bickering and warfare,

Campbell argued, too much of a family "torn by factions." Consider, Campbell wrote, that Protestants around the world are about forty million strong, except that being so divided they were not strong at all. "How do they muster?" Campbell asked, and then answered: "Under forty ensigns? Under forty antagonist leaders? Would to God there were but forty!" Geneva alone, Campbell added, can provide that many. Protestant divisions were beyond calculating: "I will not attempt to name the antagonizing creeds, feuds, and parties that are in eternal war, under the banners of the Prince of Peace. And yet they talk of love and charity, and of the conversion of the Jews, the Turks, and pagans!!!" One could weep over the seamless robe of Christ, ripped to shreds and scattered across the globe.

What could be done? Alexander Campbell, along with a leader in Kentucky's famous Cane Ridge revival, Barton Stone (1772–1844), preached the gospel of restorationism with energy and expectation. "There is but one Body, and one Spirit, even as we are called in one hope of our calling," Stone wrote. We will "pray more and dispute less," looking not to men's words but only to the Bible. We will trust not in churches or denominations, presbyteries or synods, but build only on "the Rock of Ages, and follow Jesus for the future." By 1833 most of the followers of Stone and Campbell merged into a single movement known variously as the Christian Church or Disciples of Christ or the "Campbellites." A frontier church, this new institution had its earliest successes in Ohio, Indiana, Illinois, Kentucky, Tennessee, and Missouri. By the end of the century, these Disciples had passed the half-million mark. In growth, they flourished; in unity, they failed. For not only did the Disciples fail to heal the divisions within Christendom, they added to them by bringing new denominations (three in the twentieth century) and new "insignia" into the still-quarreling camp.

THE POST-REVOLUTIONARY SOUTH

In the early decades of the nineteenth century, Southern religion presented a dramatically new face. Wholly changed from the Anglican-dominated region which it had for so long been, the South had been transformed by 1800 into a bastion of evangelical religion. Presbyterians, Baptists, and Methodists created a kind of cultural and religious unity that eluded Campbell and Stone. Not that denominational differences disappeared, but only that they mattered much less. Baptists with their farmer-preachers, Methodists with their circuits riders, Presbyterians with their local and sometimes independent presbyteries managed to move freely across boundaries of class and race, of gender and bases of political power. The aristocracy of an older Anglicanism fell before a democracy of emotional fervor and pietist conviction.

Women assumed roles of leadership in the churches, gradually achieving numerical dominance in membership. Where clergymen grew weary in their well-doing, evangelical women seemed ever ready to perform the tasks that needed to be done, giving moral instruction to their children and sensitive direction to their churches.

Generally without ordination and largely unhampered by their non-clerical status, women served as deaconesses, raised funds for the support of missionaries both at home and abroad, then undertook themselves the role of missionary teachers, missionary doctors, and missionary evangelists. Women helped promote revivals, even as many had experienced their own conversions within that context. Women became evangelists even in their own communities, and even among that southern community which suffered serious neglect: the slaves. In Virginia, Ann Page Randolph wrote in 1825 of her anxious concern for those "who inhabit the smoky huts and till our fields" but remained untouched by the Christian message. In her diary, Mrs. Randolph confessed her fears that some terrible divine wrath awaited those who "neglect to labor for souls committed to their charge," souls that were as dear to God as those of the masters. "Awake us—arouse us—strike an alarm from the vast ocean of eternity which rolls so near!" It was our solemn duty, she concluded, to care for both the bodies and souls of our slaves, "knowing that we must give an account of our stewardship."

Evangelical religion bridged the gap, as few forces could, between black and white. Slaves in surprising numbers turned to that religion which spoke of a freedom in Christ, of a fellowship that knew no barriers, of an eternal life that knew no sorrows. Taking his text from Romans 8:37, the black preacher John Jasper (1812–1901) explicated the meaning of the words, "Nay, in all these things we are more than conquerors through him that loved us." Biblical history was filled with examples of how God had taken the lowly and despised and turned them into conquerors: Moses, Joshua, David, and many more. God's power had even been made manifest in a lowly Jew, executed on a cross like a common criminal. The gospel made its promises not to the rich and mighty, but to the poor and lowly, the oppressed and imprisoned, Jasper explained. Christianity was neither the monopoly of the white master nor the reason for slavery. God would judge all men and women alike, bringing a harsher judgment to the powerful and a merciful one to the powerless. With faith and fervor Jasper proclaimed that one day the valley would be exalted and the mountains laid low; one day the mighty would fall and the weak be lifted up. One day, the evangelically committed slaves agreed, we shall be more than conquerors through him who loved us.

THEOLOGY IN NEW ENGLAND

Theological variety in New England matched the ecclesiastical variety of the frontier. The Calvinism revived most forcefully in the writings of Jonathan Edwards continued into the nineteenth century where it bore the label of *the* New England theology. But, as it turned out, it was only one theology among many. Reactions against the prevailing Calvinism first took the form of an entering Arminian wedge which emphasized man's free will and the significance of good works. Charles Chauncy (1705–1787), Edwards' opponent in the First Great Awakening, moved from Arminianism to Universalism which proclaimed the "Salvation of All Men" to be "the Grand Thing aimed at in the Scheme of God," to cite the title of Chauncy's 1784 work.

23. Absalom Jones, ordained into the ministry of the Protestant Episcopal Chruch in 1796, led a black congregation in Philadelphia. *National Portrait Gallery*

Elhanan Winchester (1751–1797), native of Massachusetts, moved from a Baptist ministry to a Universalist one by the end of the 1780s. A careful study of the Scriptures, Winchester declared, convinced him that a moral and loving God would not rest until all his creatures had been gathered to his bosom. We are told that, in the fullness of time, every knee shall bow and every tongue confess that Christ is Lord. Winchester took these words seriously, amazed and shaken to discover "that any danger could have arisen from my expressing a hope that the Scriptures were true." But dangers there were, as former friends forsook him and condemned him as a heretic for having embraced the doctrine of "Universal Restoration." The new convert, however, stood firm, for "the truth appeared to me more valuable than all things and . . . I was determined never to part with it." By 1850 Universalism had spread throughout New England and across New York, but displayed little strength elsewhere in America.

Unitarianism, far more than Universalism, shook Congregational orthodoxy to its very foundations. Rejecting the Calvinists' low view of unredeemed man, a wormlike creature without the capacity either to do good or think well, the Unitarians spoke of man's moral nature, his rational capacity, his freedom to choose or to reject the doctrines taught and the promises offered by the Christian religion. In an important sermon delivered in 1819, Boston Unitarian William Ellery Channing (1780–1842) laid down the basic presuppositions of New England's newfound faith. We accept that which is "clearly taught in the Scriptures," Channing said, though we do not "attach equal importance to all the books in this collection." In general, the New Testament supercedes and supplants the Old. When it comes to understanding what the New Testament says about God, Channing concluded that it taught the oneness, not the threeness of God, a Unity, not a Trinity. We do "with all earnestness, though without reproaching our brethren, protest against the irrational and unscriptural doctrine of the Trinity."

Christ's mediation and mission was of great historical moment since "we believe that he was sent by the Father to effect a moral or spiritual deliverance of mankind." This does not mean, however, that Unitarians accept the prevailing orthodox notion that man's sin has in some way been paid for by a sacrifice on the cross, "that man, having sinned against an infinite Being, has contracted infinite guilt, and is consequently exposed to an infinite penalty." This and all the other complexities of the Calvinist teachings regarding salvation are, said Channing, both "unscriptural and absurd." We ask our adversaries, he added, "to point to some plain passage [in the Bible] where it is taught." Since they cannot do so, it follows that such teachings are "the fictions of theologians," and Unitarians will dismiss them out of hand.

New England Unitarianism came not so much as a new denomination, with its charismatic founder or its supplementary revelation;

rather, it arose within Congregationalism itself, especially in eastern Massachusetts, as it rejected an ancestral orthodoxy in favor of "a larger intellectual and religious life, free of the restraints imposed by a doctrinal system." But for the first fifty years of its corporate life, Unitarianism scarcely moved beyond the bounds of the Congregational churches that gave it birth. Only in and around larger Boston did the church, as a church, exercise any real authority. But as a system of ideas and as a network of attitudes, its influence grew out of all proportion to its numbers.

Among the famous names associated with Unitarianism, none is better known than that of Ralph Waldo Emerson (1803–1882). Ordained a minister of Boston's Second Church in 1829, Emerson resigned that position three years later to continue a philosophical and religious search to which the name Transcendentalism was given. Reacting against the overemphasis on community, especially sectarian community, as well as against the overcommitment to material goods and worldly prosperity, Emerson called for a self-reliance that affirmed the wisdom found within one's own soul. Intuition was more reliable than a syllogism, even as an arid rationalism robbed humankind of its noblest passions and deepest truths. "The materialist," Emerson wrote in 1843, "insists on facts, on history, on the force of circumstances, and the animal wants of man; the idealist on the power of Thought and Will, on inspiration, on miracle, on individual culture." To embrace inspiration and miracle was to put great distance between himself and the Unitarians, but even greater distance separated Emerson from the Calvinists. Would New England continue to divide itself until, as Emerson predicted, every person became his or her own sect?

In Hartford, Connecticut, the Congregationalist pastor, Horace Bushnell (1802–1876), thought that New England had seen enough intellectual warfare to last several lifetimes. Enough of the quarrels between revivalists and antirevivalists, between Trinitarians and anti-Trinitarians, between moralists and rationalists, between literalists and symbolists. Bushnell would if he could gather together all the opposing forces, transcend their differences with a theology that rejected neither this nor that entrenched position but moved the argument to a higher ground. To accomplish all this, Bushnell advanced his theory of language in which he explained that a totally precise, totally accurate, totally "correct" theology was simply not possible. The reason that it was impossible lay in the severe limitations of theological language; such language, moving far beyond the data gathered by the five senses, employed metaphor and figure to suggest, to hint at, to provoke the imagination into a reflection on things of God. What? No science of theology? None whatsoever, Bushnell calmly replied. "Human language is a gift to the imagination so essentially metaphoric, warp and woof, that it has no exact blocks of meaning to build a science of." This was hardly reason for despair, however, since neither can we build a science out of Homer or Shakespeare or Milton. "And the Bible is not a whit less poetic, or a whit less metaphoric, or a particle less difficult to be propositionized in the terms of understanding."

Unitarians who rejected the literalism of Calvinism substituted a literalism of their own. And Transcendentalists swept old metaphors away only to introduce new metaphors of their own. How dreary and how sad, Bushnell noted, for "Nothing makes infidels more surely than the spinning, splitting, nerveless refinements of theology." Never content with suggestive allegory, we demand absolute propositions. We never get them, of course, but what we do get is "a history of divisions, recriminations, famishings, vanishings, and general uncharitableness." The gospel, like language itself, Bushnell wrote, is above all else a "gift to the imagination," and we can say nothing more exalted of Christ than to regard him as "the metaphor of God." Theology must be kept alive like a beautiful flower, fragrant and fresh, ever growing, ever appealing. In New England, Bushnell concluded, we take that flower, pull it apart petal by petal, squeeze all its juices out, rob it of all vitality and allure. Then we pack it all away in a dry herbarium. The result of our labors, that tasteless, odorless, lifeless thing, we are pleased to call "theology."

CHAPTER 14

Civilizing and Redeeming
the West

In the early nineteenth century, the American West both attracted and repelled. Yale President Timothy Dwight (1752–1817) who visited the West (not very far west, to be sure, but at least beyond the bounds of New England) was not favorably impressed. He found an independence bordering on anarchy, an egalitarianism bordering on comedy. The pioneers, Dwight noted, "cannot live in regular society. They are too idle, too talkative, too passionate, too prodigal, and too shiftless to acquire either property or character." In their own estimation, however, frontier dwellers think of themselves, wrote Dwight, as possessed of "uncommon wisdom," knowing more about law, medicine, politics, and religion "than those who have studied them through life." President Dwight did not expect much from the West.

In sharp contrast, fellow Congregationalist Lyman Beecher who brought his family to Cincinnati in 1832 thought the West would fulfill all the rich promise of America. People were moving all the way to the Mississippi River in tremendous numbers. From the Appalachian Mountains to the great river, new states sprang up almost overnight and population increased in a single generation from about one hundred fifty thousand to "little short of five millions." Stretching his imagination to the limit, Beecher prophesied that by the end of the century perhaps as many as one hundred million people would live in that region "half as large as all Europe, four times as large as the Atlantic states, and twenty times as large as New England." Without religion and morality, the West—it was true—would sink into barbarism, but with religion and morality, then the future of the West "will be glorious." In an optimism that would not be reined in, Beecher exulted that "the sun and rain of heaven are not more sure to call forth a bounteous vegetation" than will Bibles and Sunday schools, colleges and clergy, in this promised land. Listening to travelers return from New Orleans, St. Louis, and even the Pacific Ocean with their wondrous tales, only then (Beecher confessed) "did I perceive how God, who seeth the end from the beginning, had prepared the West to be mighty."

Not much common ground could be found between Timothy

145

Dwight and Lyman Beecher with respect to the West. And interested Europeans had similar difficulty in reconciling reports of their visitors to interior America, some praising the openness of the people and the land, others speaking only of its barbarism and bad manners. All could agree on one point, however: in the first half of the nineteenth century, the United States added to its domain an enormous amount of "west." The purchase of the Louisiana Territory in 1803 virtually doubled the territory of the nation, this great gulp of land to be augmented in 1846 by the spoils of the Mexican-American War that included all of the Pacific Southwest and by a treaty with Great Britain that ceded all of the Pacific Northwest. From ocean to ocean a single flag now flew, as the wonder and fury of it all left citizens breathless. It also left churches and synagogues stunned by the enormity of the tasks thereby spread before them.

PROTESTANTISM

Less than a decade after the Louisiana Purchase, the Missionary Societies of Massachusetts and Connecticut sent observers westward to report on the state of religion and morals in territory that, for most easterners, remained unknown. What these observers found in Louisiana offered little encouragement but much challenge. "The state of society in this country is very deplorable," they wrote, their Protestantism preventing them from finding much solace in the French Catholicism that had managed to survive, even long after the Jesuit withdrawal. "The people are entirely ignorant of divine things, and have been taught only to attend mass and count their beads." Intemperance prevailed, vice flourished, and Sunday was treated more as a "high holiday" than an occasion for sober reflection and worship. Probably, the travelers asserted, more actual sin was committed on Sunday "than during the whole week besides." Even the newly appointed Roman Catholic bishop, Louis William DuBourg (1766–1833), "mourns over the depravity and wickedness of [this] place," the itinerant missionaries noted. Surely, much must be done before the rest of the country has reason to regret that Thomas Jefferson ever signed that treaty and made that purchase.

Another missionary tour which followed a couple of years later (1814–15) saw little improvement, only more urgency. Not a single Bible in any language could be found anywhere in New Orleans, either to be bought or given away. Protestantism was virtually nonexistent, and what Protestant clergy could be located were seldom of the educated and responsible sort. "What shall be done? Shall we leave one of our fairest cities to be completely overwhelmed with vice and folly? The dreaded inundation of the Mississippi would not be half so ruinous." The solution proposed was to apply the proven instruments of the Second Great Awakening: send missionaries, distribute tracts, teach people to read and write, and instill some sense of duty and of right. "Send us someone to break to us the bread of life."

One of these missionary observers, John F. Schermerhorn (1786–1851), reported to the Society for Propagating the Gospel Among the Indians concerning the status of Native Americans in the newly added territories. The society, having originally ministered to Indians in New England, now determined to use its funds for "tribes in the remote parts of North America." Schermerhorn, like all missionaries before him, expressed amazement at the diversity of tribes, the insularity of their cultures and languages, their independence from or hostility toward one another. He also joined others in noting the negative effect that contact with Europeans wrought upon tribal life. In his 1814 report, he suggested to the society that a mission might be most successful among the Chickasaws and the Choctaws since they were relatively "uncontaminated by the vices of the whites." In Louisiana itself, it was most difficult to find any Indians not adversely affected by contact with Spanish or French, British or American traders. With respect to Indians west of the Mississippi River, Schermerhorn confessed that

24. Spokesman and apologist for the West, Lyman Beecher exercised his prodigious energies on behalf of Christianizing and taming the frontier. *National Portrait Gallery*

he could only repeat the words of the few explorers—such as Lewis and Clark—who had actually made first-hand observations.

These observers represented the reconnaissance troops for Presbyterians and Congregationalists who, by a Plan of Union drawn up in 1801, determined to pool their resources in order better to meet the challenge of so much "west." Congregational missionaries even reached beyond California's shores to the Hawaiian Islands with whom New England's whaling vessels had established contact. One native Hawaiian, Henry Obookiah (1792?–1818), made his way to Yale College, there to be brought into the Christian fold by Samuel J. Mills (1783–1818) another of those missionaries sent out to the trans-Appalachian West. In 1820 the first contingent of Connecticut missionaries and their wives arrived in the islands, establishing their mission on the largest island, Hawaii, in the village of Kailua. By 1837, over eighty missionaries had been dispatched to the Pacific outpost, with seventeen churches established there. Hawaii even had its own version of a Great Awakening in the late 1830s and 1840s, with a marked increase in the number of Polynesian Christians being the most conspicuous result. All this American activity helped smooth the way for annexation of the islands before the end of the nineteenth century.

Also before the end of that century, Protestantism penetrated another westernmost territory: namely, that of Alaska, purchased by the United States in 1867. A Presbyterian missionary, Sheldon Jackson (1834–1909), moved from his successful labors among the Indians in Oklahoma, Minnesota, Wyoming, Montana and elsewhere in the continental West, to the land which Russian Orthodoxy had claimed as their mission since 1792. Jackson, first visiting that northern tundra in 1877, discovered how much the native Alaskans needed in the way of medicine, education, "republican government" and "industrial pursuits." Appointed as a U. S. General Agent for Education in 1885, Jackson fought lawlessness, corruption, slavery, and starvation. With respect to the latter, he succeeded in introducing reindeer from Siberia to alleviate the Eskimo and Aleut dependence on seal herds, now depleted by the aggressive hunting techniques of others. In changing the natives from "hunters to herders," Sheldon Jackson rescued a population from near-certain decline and death. He, along with his successors, also firmly planted Protestantism in Alaska's frosty soil.

Presbyterians and Congregationalists reached into Oregon Territory, into California (added to the Union in 1850), and elsewhere in the West, working both with newly arriving settlers and with often retreating and resentful Indians. One northwestern mission, identified with the labors of Marcus (1802–1847) and Narcissa (1808–1847) Whitman, was established in 1835 near Walla Walla, Washington, part of a string of missions spread out along the Columbia River. Among the first white women to cross the Rockies, Narcissa Whitman wrote often of her work in giving bible instruction, in helping with the singing, in assisting in many ways as her somewhat frail health would allow. She also wrote of her loneliness and depression, far removed from family and friends back in Prattsburg, New York. All came to a tragic end for both of the Whitmans when in 1847 the Cayuse Indians, frustrated and angered by the growing pressure of white settlements, attacked the mission, killing Marcus and Narcissa Whitman along with a dozen other whites present at the time. Accounts of missionary efforts among the Indians do not always have happy endings, either for the missionaries themselves or for those among whom they labored.

Even more successful in helping to bring Protestantism to the West were the Baptists and Methodists. A rapidly expanding nation, crossing mountains and fording streams, seemed perfectly suited to the circuit-rider Methodist and the farmer-preacher Baptist. The former moved out on the postroads leading westward just as soon as such roads were laid out or, if too impatient to wait for the road builders, the Methodist parson simply mounted his horse and made his own trails to where any tiny knots of settlers or isolated families might be found. Whether a church could be built and sustained was not as important as bringing the ministrations of religion to Americans on the move. But churches were built, one measure of Methodist success being that this denomination by 1850 had more churches than any other group in such western lands as Mississippi, Louisiana, Texas, Arkansas, Tennessee, Ohio, Indiana, Illinois, Michigan, Wisconsin, and Iowa.

By midcentury, Methodists had also reached all the way to California and Oregon Territory. One of their number, Jason Lee (1803–1845), led the way into Oregon Territory even before it became American soil. Convinced that the Pacific Northwest was ripe for plucking by some nation or people, Lee argued that it should be part of the United States' domain. In an 1839 letter to a U. S. Congressman, Lee wrote: "The country will be settled, and that speedily, from some quarter. . . . It may be thought that Oregon is of but little importance; but, rely upon it, there is the germ of a great state." Less than a decade later, Oregon belonged to America with Lee's labors, especially in the Willammete Valley, providing solid foundation on which not only Methodists but many others could build.

Baptists also followed, or sometimes led, the western migrations, racing with the Methodists toward a membership mark of one million by 1850. Like the Methodists, the Baptists by that year had reached all the way to the Pacific Ocean, and like the Methodists they endeavored to serve both Indians and the advancing settlers. One missionary to the Indians, Isaac McCoy (1784–1846), argued for the creation of an Indian Territory in the West that would offer some insulation from greedy and corrupting white traders. Cherokees, Creeks, Choctaws, and Chickasaws all gathered well before midcentury in what became Oklahoma.

Like Sheldon Jackson, McCoy himself worked with and for the federal government, seeking ways to forestall the "ultimate solution" of extermination and to reduce the bloody conflicts between the tribes and the U. S. government. In 1849 the Bureau of Indian Affairs was transferred from the War Department to the newly created Department of Interior, a symbol but not yet a reality of significant alteration in Indian policy.

In working with settlers in the West, Baptists leaned heavily upon local preachers who were most likely also themselves new pioneers and hard-working farmers. Fully employed like their fellows in clearing land and raising food, some in addition responded to what they

25. Narcissa Whitman met her death in the Oregon Territory in 1847. *Presbyterian Historical Society*

believed to be a divine call to preach. No hierarchy needed to approve such a ministry, no college or advanced education was required to enter upon such a ministry. While farmer-preachers may have lacked many a qualification and many a degree, they possessed one attribute that outweighed most others: they were there, on the scene, ready to be used by the Spirit, ready to serve the people. But Baptists also had their missionaries sent from the East, John Mason Peck (1789–1858) arriving in St. Louis in 1817 and working both sides of the river thereafter. Founding schools, distributing tracts, organizing denominational life, preaching countless sermons, and traveling thousands of miles, Peck saw the American West as God's new Zion, his prodigious labors helping to give considerable substance to that fair dream.

ROMAN CATHOLICISM

Alone among the denominations moving from the East out to the West, Roman Catholicism entered lands that had already known the presence of the Catholic missionary. In the Louisiana Territory itself, French Cath-

26. Methodist successes on the frontier owed much to the tireless labors of the circuit rider who gained near-mythological status. *Library of Congress*

olics (notably the Jesuits, but also others) had labored since the seventeenth century. When that territory came under United States control in 1803, French Catholicism—even if not in the best of health—continued to flavor the land. When William DuBourg was appointed Bishop of "Louisiana and the Floridas" in 1815, the area had been without any effective episcopal supervision for many years, being (in John Carroll's gentle words) in a "relaxed state of civil and ecclesiastical authority." Since DuBourg had been appointed by the American Archbishop Carroll, the French in New Orleans would have little to do with him, while the Spanish in East and West Florida calmly continued to take their orders from the Bishop of Havana. Four years after Du-Bourg's elevation to the episcopate, the last portion of foreign soil east of the Mississippi, Florida, passed from Spain to the United States. DuBourg endured great difficulty with his remaining charges in Louisiana, being so unwelcome in New Orleans that he initially resided far to the north in St. Louis.

Though distracted by the internal quarrels and defiance of his authority, Bishop DuBourg nonetheless recognized those major religious needs, especially among the Indians, which required attention. He appealed to the Jesuits (their order having now been restored) of Belgium to come to his aid, one such man doing so with unusual effectiveness. Pierre Jean DeSmet, S. J. (1801–1873), left St. Louis in 1840 for the first of many trips to Indians in the West, notably among the Flatheads whose advocate he became. Unlike many who served as missionaries to the Indians, DeSmet was neither scandalized nor offended by their culture. The Flatheads, he wrote in 1841, "are scrupulously honest in their buying and selling; they have never been accused of committing a theft . . . lying is hateful to them beyond anything else. . . . They are polite, always of a jovial humor, very hospitable, and helpful to one another in their duties." Incredulously, DeSmet asked: How do we dare to call such people "savages"? And he explained the high culture that he found among the Flatheads by noting that they had not yet "learned the vices of the whites."

Like a few other missionaries in colonial times and beyond, Father DeSmet found his trust in the Indians matched by a corresponding Indian trust in him. At the request of the Secretary of the Interior, DeSmet in 1868 persuaded the Sioux to accept a treaty of peace, accomplishing the delicate negotiations with skill and maintaining the respect of both sides. Admiring the Osage and the Sioux, the black-robed Jesuit also admired and entertained high hopes for the nation in which he labored for over fifty years. America, he wrote his brother in 1849, has within it the possibility, "the germ and the sinew, to raise a greater people than many of the proud, now tottering, principalities of Europe." This confidence, shared by so many who loaded wagons and set out on the Oregon Trail, prevented the West from being a mere appendage to the nation: it was a fulfillment of the nation.

By 1850, the Roman Catholic church had become the largest denomination in the country, a status never thereafter surrendered to any other church. Its magnitude came chiefly as the result of massive emigration from Ireland, the potato famine encouraging hundreds of thousands to leave their poor and inhospitable land. Of the five million immigrants who settled in America from 1815 to 1860, two million came from Ireland. "Anti-popery" which in early America lay only slightly below the surface raised itself above ground once more as nativist fears and Know-Nothing parties challenged the right of Catholics to live freely in the United States. In Massachusetts in 1834 an angry mob

27. Missionary to the western Indians and member of the Society of Jesus, Pierre Jean DeSmet served as intermediary between retreating tribes and advancing settlers from the East. *Library of Congress*

burned an Ursuline convent to the ground, and in Philadelphia a decade later riots broke out, directing their wrath against Catholic churches in that city. A Thomas Nast cartoon warned against "Anti-Republic Romanism," while Samuel F. B. Morse (1791–1872) in 1835 published a tract entitled "Imminent Dangers to the Free Institutions of the United States Through Foreign Immigration." The imminent danger uppermost in his mind was that of a rapidly increasing Irish Catholic presence. "It is a fact," he patiently explained, "that Popery is opposed in its very nature to Democratic Republicanism; and it is, therefore, as a political system, as well as religious, opposed to civil and religious liberty, and consequently to our form of government."

On the contrary, argued Orestes Brownson, a New England convert to the Catholic church in 1844, Roman Catholicism "is necessary to sustain popular liberty because popular liberty can be sustained only by a religion free from popular control, above the people, speaking from above and able to command them." Even the Catholic bishops themselves could not ignore the many clamorous voices raised against their church. Lamenting the outbreaks of religious discrimination, the bishops in 1833 encouraged the faithful to stand firm against all the "vituperation and offense," against the misrepresentations of Catholic beliefs and the vilification of Catholic practices. We urge you, the bishops wrote, to ignore all of this and continue "to discharge honestly, faithfully, and with affectionate attachment your duties to the government under which you live." And in 1841 Bishop John England (1786–1842) of Charleston, South Carolina, called for an end to all attempts to divide the country along religious lines. "Men are beginning to perceive," he declared in a Boston address, "that the greatest curse which could befall our country would be the encouragement of any spirit of sectarian persecution."

While fending off both the quiet suspicions and active hostilities of other Americans, Roman Catholics were also busy attempting to cope with the enormous ethnic diversity that confronted their own church in America. German Catholics were not happy when placed under the supervision of Irish brothers, sisters, and priests. Irish Catholics were not happy to find themselves saddled with French fathers who understood little of Irish feasts or Irish saints and sometimes less of the English language. Making matters even worse, some Catholic laity, observing the practices of their Protestant neighbors, decided that they too should have the right to hire or fire their own pastors, to own their own church property and control the parish finances. All of these difficulties, manifesting themselves east of the Mississippi, were compounded as American Catholicism joined with the Hispanic Catholicism of the Far West.

Spain's labors in North America left, as previously noted, a lasting mark in the Southwest: notably in New Mexico, Arizona, California, and much of Texas. Spanish missions constituted the most obvious feature of the landscape, standing high above the sage brush and chapparal. From the famed Alamo (formerly the San Antonio de Valero Mission) of Texas history to the even more famed chain of missions in California, Hispanic Catholicism shaped an entire geographical region. The Jesuit Eusebio Kino (1645–1711) labored in southern Arizona in the final years of the seventeenth and the first years of the eighteenth centuries, drawing maps, learning Indian languages, building chapels, and teaching farming. The beautiful San Xavier del Bac Church near Tucson, though a product of the 1790s, was erected on the site of Kino's first mission in that region. In California the Franciscan Junipero Serra (1713–1784) established missions from San Diego (1769) to Ventura (1782), with his brown-robed successors continuing his work until a total of twenty-one missions extended from San Diego in the South to San Francisco de Solano (Sonoma, 1823) in the North.

Mexico, winning its independence from Spain in 1821, a dozen years later passed the long-feared act of secularization which turned over the abundant California mission lands to secular hands, reserving in each area only a single parish church to ecclesiastical authority. Monks and nuns were released from their vows, as an anticlerical Mexico encouraged many of the religious to leave for Spain, the government even agreeing to pay the traveling expenses for those who had not sworn to uphold Mexico's independence. Then, as a result of the Mexican-American War of 1846 to 1847, all of the vast Southwest passed into American hands. None could know just what that shift in sovereignty would mean in religious terms, though the military governor, General S. W. Kearney (1794–1848), assured Californians that their religious rights would be secured "in the most ample manner." What threatened Catholic rights was not so much the American flag as it was the American "invasion" of those easterners who came for gold or trade or Protestantizing.

Easterners left behind them a culture predominantly Anglo-Saxon to find the culture ahead of them predominantly Mexican or Spanish. Protestant missionaries in northern New Mexico, confronted by late medieval Spanish Catholic practices that included severe whipping and self-mortification (notably among the Penitentes), denounced the "barbarities" and ignorant superstitions of what seemed to them a particularly odious example of foreign fanaticism. French Catholic prelates in Santa Fe also objected to the Penitentes, trying as early as 1833 to bring them into greater conformity with Catholic practices as found in eastern America or non-Iberian Europe.

In California, easterners generally regarded themselves as superior in both education and religion to the Hispanics they encountered there. An English Catholic, Herbert Vaughan (1832–1903), visiting that state in 1864 thought otherwise. Consider, he wrote, the ways in which the two cultures treat the Indian, then decide which is superior. "The Spaniard went with the tenderest devotedness to serve and save the Indian," while the "Yankee came, straining every nerve and energy in the pursuit of wealth." For the latter, the Indian was only "fair game, just as bear or elk were, and men would shoot them by way of pastime. . . . Murder became thus a relaxation." If one required any further evidence of high culture or the utter absence thereof, then regard, said Vaughan, the names which Anglos and Hispanics give to their respective towns and villages. The latter bestow such dignified titles as Jesus Maria, Buena Vista, and Nuestra Señora de Soledad, while the former afflict their settlements with such labels as Bloody Run, Rat-Trap Slide, and Jackass Gulch. Let any fair-minded person decide which civilization considered all men and all races as people of God, and which endeavored to give a Christian flavor to all they discovered and explored and inhabited.

Hispanic Catholicism, however, did not enjoy many such defenders, not even within its own ecclesiastical institution. Catholicism would continue to be directed from the East not the West, which meant its hierarchy would continue to be heavily Irish or French, lightly (if at all) Hispanic. Despite the fact that something like one-fourth of America's Catholics were now Hispanic, Mexican-Americans had to wait until the second half of the twentieth century before making any inroads into the upper clerical ranks of the Roman Catholic church. The problem of ethnic diversity continued to prove difficult for the church to solve readily or with total ease. Nonetheless, Catholicism could and did claim the American West as uniquely its own, with Catholics dominating the Southwest from the seventeenth century through the twentieth.

28. San Xavier del Bac Mission, located near Tucson, Arizona, is associated with the labors of Jesuit Eusebio Kino. *Keystone-Mast Collection, UC Riverside*

JUDAISM

Though far smaller in membership than either Catholicism or Protestantism in the early nineteenth century, Judaism managed to move well beyond its early centers of worship along the Atlantic Coast. With a significant number of emigrants from Germany arriving in this period, Judaism found its fortunes rising from that of a tiny and scarcely visible colonial minority. German Jews, many having achieved a large degree of emancipation in their homeland, saw America in general, the West in particular, as a place where that freedom could find even fuller expression. Rabbi Isaac Mayer Wise (1819–1900), moving to the Ohio frontier at midcentury, urged his fellows to discard old European ways for new American ones. He also pushed for Judaism itself to reform its archaic rituals and presuppositions, recognizing that modern times have "revolutionized each other's thought, feelings, and conceptions." This age of the railroad and steamboat called for something more than the ideas and practices appropriate to the age of oxcart and of mule. "The Jew must be Americanized, I said to myself, . . . in order to gain the proud self-consciousness of the free-born man." Once fired by this vision, Wise began "to Americanize with all my might." Hebrew Union College, founded in Cincinnati in 1875, helped keep alive Wise's vision and give substance to his hopes for a "reformed Judaism."

Traveling even more widely throughout the West, Rabbi Isaac Leeser (1806–1868) tried to help isolated Jewish communities hold together in obedience to the Torah and to their ancestral traditions. The greatest danger for Jews, so few, was to become lost in an America so vast. That danger was accentuated in California where many went not to "settle" but to "acquire all the wealth possible in the least imaginable space of time." Under such circumstances, Jews were reluctant, Leeser reported, to contribute much money to erect a "suitable house of prayer" or to hire "ministers of the mental capacity and moral qualifications" demanded in a new and lawless country. Isaac Leeser nonetheless remained optimistic, looking forward to that day when he would hear of many synagogues being consecrated in the West and of many thousands faithfully keeping the Sabbath.

Judaism before the Civil War remained of modest size, with probably fewer than fifty synagogues to be found in the United States, East and West combined. Partly because of its restricted numbers, Judaism at this time also remained largely free of internal quarrel and dissension. When Jewish immigration sharply accelerated after the Civil War, bringing millions of East European Jews to the nation, then differences did arise regarding just what living in America required of or offered to the religiously observant Jew. Was a free nation an invitation to amend one's loyalty to the Torah, or was it on the other hand an opportunity to observe it more faithfully than was possible elsewhere? Like the Roman Catholics, Jews found it necessary to deal with ethnicity and culture, trying to determine what principles remained, what forms might be changed. Jews, Isaac Mayer Wise pointed out, no longer perform animal sacrifices in their temples, no longer believe in a hereditary priesthood. So while ceremonies do change, the essence of Judaism must remain.

THE WEST AS RELIGIOUS REGION

Nearly everyone recognizes that religion in the South demonstrates features peculiar to that area of the country. The uniqueness of the West is not so widely recognized; yet, it too has elements which set it apart from American religion at large. Three such elements will be noted here: (1) the "kingdom of the saints," that is, Mormonism; (2) the adaptation by or insulation of Hispanics and Indians; and, (3) the harbinger of social stress, that is, the growth of pluralism.

The Mormons managed to give utopianism a good name by refusing to wither away, by avoiding the sacrifice of a religious vision to an economic one. Though originating in the East (Fayette, New York) in 1830 and dwelling for a time in Ohio, Missouri, and Illinois, the Church of Jesus Christ of Latter-Day Saints made the Far West its very own. Forced by the hostility of neighbors to move again and again, Mormons in Nauvoo, Illinois thought that perhaps their last ejection notice had been served. Arriving there in 1839, they built a temple (one had already been abandoned in Ohio), established a government, and readied themselves against "Gentile" attack, if such should come. Gentiles in Mormon terminology included all those not of the inner community, all of those rejecting the revelations and the authority of the founder, Joseph Smith (1805–1844). The "outside world" objected to Mormons holding property in common, objected to their adding to the Bible scripture revelations of their own, objected to their zealous determination to be a "peculiar people," and certainly objected to the practice (rumored or real) of polygamy. When in 1844 Joseph Smith, arrested on a charge of destroying property, was placed in jail, a Gentile mob seized its opportunity: armed men stormed the jail, broke in, and assassinated both Joseph and his brother, Hyrum. At such a critical and difficult juncture, utopian colonies are supposed to fade quietly away. But Mormonism refused to die.

Under the strong leadership of Brigham Young (1801–1877), these Saints determined to take one more step, this one a giant step, away from states that would not welcome them and from neighbors who would not tolerate them. This time they would move where there were no states and where the only neighbors would be their own brothers and sisters. "The exodus of the nation of the only true Israel from these United States," said Brigham Young in 1845, "to a far distant region of the west, where bigotry, intolerance, and insatiable oppression lose their power over them, forms a new epoch, not only in the history of the church, but of this nation." In 1847 the long and painful march began, from Nauvoo, Illinois to Omaha ("Winter Quarters"), Nebraska until at last a great Salt Lake Basin received them. To that barren land but that land which by imitating the diligence of the honeybee (Deseret in the Book of Mormon) could blossom and flourish, converts flocked as to a New Jerusalem. They came not just from the East, but from England, Scotland, Wales, Germany, and Scandinavia—many arriving in ships sent out from Liverpool, their passage paid for by the church, their trek from New Orleans arranged by the church, their welcome in Utah Territory (by 1850) assured by the church. Why did the recruitment of new members succeed on such a scale?

Mormon historians Leonard Arrington and Davis Bitton explain the many-sided appeal of this new and remarkably successful church. First,

29. Martyred founder of the Church of Jesus Christ of Latter-day Saints, Joseph Smith fell before a "gentile" mob in 1844. *National Portrait Gallery*

like the Disciples movement, the Mormons emphasized a return to the pure and primitive church of the New Testament. Second, though Joseph Smith stressed the importance of the Bible, he provided his followers with their own additional scriptural base: the Book of Mormon, first published in 1830. This book brought the New World and its native peoples into the whole divine plan, acclaiming America to be a "land choice above all other lands." Third, successive revelations to the prophet and leader created more distinctiveness, making this church not just another frontier variant, but a new religion: for example, the practice of baptism for the dead (which created an entire genealogical industry) and the teaching of an eternal progression of humankind, even beyond death (which gave the nineteenth-century doctrine of progress its most ambitious expression). Fourth, like the Millerites of upstate New York, Mormons also looked forward to an imminent end of the world, a Second Coming of Christ that Mormons were called to prepare for and thereby help bring about. The New Jerusalem, moreover, would be in America (Utah), not Palestine. Finally, Mormonism with its certain answers and strong central authority created a sustaining, enveloping community: this community would defend and protect, feed and house, make clear the difference between the Saints and all the rest of a hostile or indifferent or godless world. Like the seventeenth-century Puritans, the Saints had founded a new kingdom, the new Israel, an empire that would not, could not fail.

If numbers can measure success, then this Mormon claim cannot be denied. As Brigham Young declared in 1849, "We have been kicked out of the frying pan into the fire, out of fire into the middle of the floor,

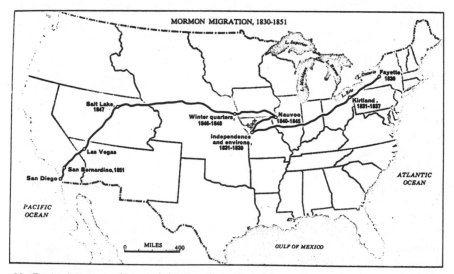

30. Beginning as a religion of the American East, Mormonism ended up as emphatically a religion of the American West. *Gaustad, Historical Atlas of Religion in America*

and here we are and here we will stay." In the Great Basin of the Salt Lake Valley, the Saints would irrigate and plant, harvest and prosper. And that they would do, knowing that God "will rebuke the frost and the sterility of the soil, and the land shall become fruitful." A century after Young's prophecy, all had been fulfilled as Mormons dominated not only all of Utah but much of the western regions on all sides of Deseret. At that point, Mormonism had become a fixed feature, often a determinative feature, of the Western landscape.

Hispanics and Indians also colored and shaped the culture of the southern deserts, the Great Plains, and the Pacific slopes. The former remained in those regions that had once been Spain's, then Mexico's, declining to surrender their culture when a United States, once confined to the lands east of the Mississippi, moved westward with dazzling speed. Nor did Hispanics surrender their religion to Anglo missionaries or, for that matter, to Irish and French Catholics. Catholic authorities in the East, burdened by the heavy nineteenth century immigrations arriving on the Atlantic shores, had few resources remaining to expend on the immense Southwest. A population, predominantly agricultural and rural and even anticlerical, would largely have to fend for itself, supervised lightly (if at all) by a hierarchy not yet prepared to elevate priests and bishops out of these silent and often invisible masses. That would all someday change, but the day was long in coming. Hispanics nonetheless remained, in fact enlarged, rising to ever-increasing visibility across the entire West.

Indians remained in the West because that was as far as they could be "removed" from the more settled areas of the East. Beginning with the removal of the Cherokees in the 1830s from northwest Georgia to "the West" (that is, Oklahoma "Indian Territory"), one solution to the Indian "problem" was simply to keep them as many steps as possible ahead of westward expansion. When that did not work, extermination and war (the two at times being virtually synonymous) were the major alternatives. As early as 1828 Congressman Edward Everett (1794–1865) found official policy with respect to the Indian empty of all integrity and good faith. We have violated treaty after treaty, he noted, until the Indian has no reason to trust us and no security living among us. "We shall sign and seal, but we shall not perform. Let them go to Texas; let them join the Comanches, for their sakes, and for ours." That way, we may be spared further shame, Everett concluded. But further shame descended, in the Battle of Wounded Knee in South Dakota at the end of 1890 as well as in many other forms. Understandably, Indian population declined steadily throughout the nineteenth century, but in its comeback in the twentieth, the Indian presence in the West could be neither gainsaid nor ignored.

Finally, the West entered early into a pluralistic age that much of the rest of the nation would not know until decades later. The West was

Protestant, Catholic, and Jewish; the West was experimental in ways that went far beyond historic Christianity or Judaism; the West was more secular than the East; and the West found Asia. While most of the country did not encounter Asian religion until the World's Parliament of Religions met in Chicago in 1893, California knew Chinese emigrants before the Civil War, coming not only to know them but to fear them as something foreign to America and foreign to its familiar religious patterns. When as many as three million Chinese reached western shores by the early 1880s, political leaders decided that the time had come to halt all further immigration. Similarly, the influx of Japanese along the West Coast, even more into Hawaii, led to sharp restrictions

31. Sequoyah developed an alphabet for his own tribe of Cherokees; neither their literacy nor their Christianity, however, helped to spare their homeland in Georgia. *National Portrait Gallery*

of those who would introduce Buddhism and Shinto, even as the Chinese had brought with them Confucianism and Taoism. Nonetheless, despite unmistakable anti-Oriental prejudices and actions, Asian religions established their beach heads all along the Pacific shores, never to be successfully dislodged therefrom. With Alaska as its base, Russian Orthodoxy also infiltrated the West all the way down to northern California, this in the early decades of the nineteenth century.

The American West, therefore, revealed a rich variety that gave to its religious life a character sharply different from that of any other region in the country. If in Boston or Philadelphia or Charleston or Atlanta, men and women might continue to think in terms of a "Protestant Empire," western diversity and western individuality subjected such a concept to uncertainty and serious question. In religious terms, deviation from the Protestant norm had in the West become the norm.

CHAPTER 15

A House of Faith Divided

In the first half of the nineteenth century, the voluntary energies of the Second Great Awakening along with the military and diplomatic successes of the nation created a sense of invincibility and assurance. Nothing could halt the progress, nothing could stem the tide of reform, nothing could diminish or cloud the religious vision. Except slavery. This was the fire bell that rang in the night, this the dark cloud that grew ever more ominous and menacing.

For a time, early in the nineteenth century, one could believe that all the nation agreed on the point that slavery was wrong, slavery was doomed; it was only a matter of time—and not too much time at that—before slavery would be eliminated from the land. Churchmen of both North and South condemned the institution: Presbyterians at their General Assembly in 1818 unanimously declared that "We consider the voluntary enslaving of one part of the human race by another as a gross violation of the most precious and sacred rights of human nature; as utterly inconsistent with the law of God . . . and as totally irreconcilable with the spirit and principles of the Gospel of Christ." By constitutional provision, the slave trade had come to an end and "if we have no right to enslave an African," Angelina Grimké (1805–1879) pointed out, "surely we can have none to enslave an American." It seemed so logical, so inevitable, that once the trading in slavery ended, so must slavery soon thereafter wither away. Above all else, Americans would agree—would they not?—that slavery must not be expanded into other territories, into Missouri for example, where it had not existed before.

The costly Missouri Compromise of 1820 preserved the Union, but postponed answering the question whether that union could continue half slave and half free. Within a decade following the admission of Missouri into the nation, one no longer felt much confidence that slavery would quietly wither away. As some pressed for an immediate emancipation, others expounded a ringing defense of the institution. As some concentrated on the moral issue, others spoke only of the political issue. As some cried out regarding human rights, others passionately defended their property rights. As abolitionists and apologists arrayed themselves in opposing stances, the rhetoric grew steadily harsher, the positions even firmer and unyielding.

THE ABOLITIONISTS

With the founding of William Lloyd Garrison's radical newspaper, *The Liberator*, in 1831, anti-slavery voices and forces grew visibly stronger. The New England Anti-Slavery Society was formed the very next year, that followed two years later by the creation in Philadelphia of the American Anti-Slavery Society. Calling for complete and immediate emancipation of slavery, the abolitionists offered no hint of compromise or concession. Slavery must go; it must go now. Unitarian clergyman, William Ellery Channing, in 1835 composed a powerful treatise against slavery, arguing from every philosophical, moral, and religious perspective that slavery was intrinsically, tragically wrong. "An institution so founded in wrong, so imbued with injustice, cannot be made a good." The essence of Christianity, Channing argued, is the spiritual kinship, the brotherhood of all humankind. "Human nature is not set before us in a few forms of beauty, magnificence, and outward glory"; rather, it appears in forms that may be unattractive, humble, even "repulsive" in outward circumstances. But that is the test set before us: to be able "to recognize our own spiritual nature and God's image in these humble forms, to recognize as brethren those who want all outward distinction." If we fail in this test, Channing concluded, then we fail "him who came to raise the fallen and to save the lost."

Two years after Channing published his addresses in Boston, the Reverend Elijah P. Lovejoy (1802–1837) affirmed his right to speak and to publish in Alton, Illinois. A Presbyterian clergyman and newspaper editor, Lovejoy defended the abolitionists for they rejected the view that black men and women were mere chattel or "an article of personal property" or "a piece of merchandise." Slaves were human beings, possessed therefore of natural and inalienable rights, created by and responsible to the same God and Father of us all. The only master of human beings was Almighty God, declared Lovejoy, and slavery usurped his prerogative "as the rightful owner of all human beings." And "whatever is morally wrong can never be politically right." Slavery, Lovejoy added, "is a political evil of unspeakable magnitude and one which, if not removed, will speedily work the downfall of our free institutions, both civil and religious."

Such sentiments were not popular in the South, nor in the North, nor on the frontier. In the process of printing and proclaiming his views, Lovejoy had one printing press after another destroyed and dumped into the Mississippi River. Determined to defend a fourth press from similar attack, Lovejoy appealed to his fellow citizens in Alton to assist him. Not asking that they agree with him, Lovejoy pleaded only that his own right to life, liberty, and property be respected, that he be allowed to go home safely at night to his family "without being assailed," that his wife not be driven night after night "from a sick bed into the garret to save her life from the brickbats and violence of the mobs." He could flee from Alton, as he had fled from other places, Lovejoy added, but sometime, somewhere one must take his stand. "I have concluded . . . to remain at Alton, and here to insist on protection in the exercise of my rights. If the civil authorities refuse to protect me, I must look to God; and if I die, I have determined to make my grave in Alton." On November 7, 1837, this Presbyterian abolitionist was shot and killed, the issue of slavery having ceased to be a matter for polite or rational debate.

Blacks likewise became active in arousing public opinion against slavery. The most famous black abolitionist of all, ex-slave Frederick Douglass (1817?–1895), spoke not only throughout much of America but abroad as well, contending that slavery was "a system of such gigantic evil, so strong, so overwhelming in its power, that no one nation is equal to its removal." Speaking before a packed house in London in 1846, Douglass attacked slavery, of course, but in addition he attacked

32. Presbyterian clergyman, Elijah P. Lovejoy, died for both the freedom of the press and the freedom of the slave. *Library of Congress*

a Christianity that seemed content to permit, even encourage, its continuance. "There has not been any war," he said, "between the religion and the slavery of the south." Indeed, the two seem as partners. "The church and the slave prison stand next to each other. . . . The church-going bell and the auctioneer's bell chime in with each other; the pulpit and the auctioneer's block stand in the same neighbourhood." Beyond all that, the profits from slave buying and selling go to build more churches that will defend more masters. "We have men sold to build churches, women sold to support missionaries, and babies sold to buy Bibles and communion services." "Between the Christianity of this land and the Christianity of Christ," Douglass wrote in his autobiography, "I recognize the widest possible difference."

Daniel Payne (1811–1893), ordained as a Lutheran clergyman in 1839, then for a time a Presbyterian minister, found his lasting niche as a leader (becoming a bishop by 1852) in the African Methodist Episcopal Church. Dedicated to the cause of black religion and a major figure in improving its fortunes, Payne joined Douglass and other blacks in the call for slavery's abolition. He condemned slavery, he said in 1839, "not because it enslaves the black man, but because it enslaves *man*." The unnatural and immoral relationship corrupts master as surely as it does slave, destroying the will of the latter and all moral restraint in the former. And of course it corrupted or destroyed the allegiance of men and women to the Bible which has been turned into a pro-slavery tract by some whose only text was this: "Servants, obey your masters."

So abolitionism, black and white, North and South, rushed across the land. Pulpits rang with calls for slavery's swift and sudden end; newspapers editorialized on the necessity of action now; books, such as Theodore Weld's *The Bible Against Slavery* (1837) and *Slavery As It Is* (1839), and even more Harriet Beecher Stowe's *Uncle Tom's Cabin* (1852), reached a wide and increasingly agitated audience. Addresses were delivered, public protest meetings held, revival meetings (such as those of Charles Finney) turned into anti-slavery crusades. Wendell Phillips (1811–1884), addressing the Massachusetts Anti-Slavery Society in 1853, declared that every means at the disposal of the abolitionist must be utilized in a cause that for the slave grew increasingly hopeless. "We dare not, in so desperate a case," Phillips said, "throw away any weapon which ever broke up the crust of an ignorant prejudice, roused a slumbering conscience, shamed a proud sinner, or changed in any way the conduct of a human being. Our aim is to alter public opinion." And on that battlefield, opposing forces drew themselves up in ever increasing numbers.

THE APOLOGISTS

As the rhetoric of abolitionism grew more strident and uncompromising, so did the language of those now prepared to defend slavery on political or moral or religious grounds. The frontier Methodist preacher, Peter Cartwright (1785–1872), described the insidious process by which many came to see slavery as something to praise rather than condemn. Methodist preachers, Cartwright said, started out poor, unable to afford any slaves and unready to be participants in the institution of slavery. In that circumstance, "they preached loudly against it." But then, said Cartwright, their economic circumstances improved, as many of them even married into slave-holding families. "Then, they began to apologize for the evil; then to justify it on legal principles; then on Bible principles—till lo and behold! it is not an evil but a good! it is not a curse but a blessing!" With rich sarcasm, Cartwright concluded that Methodist preachers in this last stage of their "education" about slavery even implied that "you would go to the Devil for not enjoying the labor, toil, sweat of this degraded race—and all this without rendering them any equivalent whatever!"

Just as abolitionism was not limited to the North, so apologies for slavery came not exclusively from the South. From New Jersey, a Dutch Reformed minister, Samuel B. How (1790–1868), argued in 1855 that the biblical record demonstrated that slavery was no sin. The New Testament no less than the Old, How stated, "entirely agree" on the legitimacy of slavery as a social institution. The Bible teaches us "that there are rights of property; that there are masters and that there are slaves, and bids us to respect the right of the master, and not to covet his man-servant or his maid-servant" (Exodus 20:17). Samuel How emphasized the significance of property rights in the intensifying dispute, affirming that "the desire and the attempt to deprive others of property which the law of God and the law of the land have made it lawful for them to hold, is to strike a blow at the very existence of civilization and Christianity."

In Charleston, South Carolina, the Roman Catholic bishop, John England (1786–1842), also defended slavery as an institution approved by both God and man. Natural law does not prohibit, England explained, "a state in which one man has the dominion over the labour and the ingenuity of another to the end of his life." Natural law may not establish slavery, since in "pure nature all men are equal," but natural law does not prohibit slavery. Slaves voluntarily surrendered their freedom in order to receive protection and care from their human masters. This situation "insures to him food, raiment, and dwelling, together with a variety of little comforts; it relieves him from the apprehensions of neglect in sickness, from all solicitude for the support of his family; and, in return, all that is required is fidelty and moderate labour." Many slaves, England concluded, are neither interested in nor would they accept their freedom. The arrangement is one of mutual benefit.

Similarly, the Baptist spokesman Richard Furman (1755–1825) explained that the "right of holding slaves is clearly established in the

Holy Scriptures, both by precept and example." Furthermore, the golden rule, so often cited by the abolitionists as the ultimate argument against slavery, cannot be applied as though in a social vacuum. One must always consider the context, Furman pointed out, having "a due regard to justice, propriety, and the general good." For example, he asked: "A father may very naturally desire that his son be obedient to his orders; is he, therefore, to obey the orders of the son?" Social relationships as well as family ones require ordinary reason to be applied when implementing the rule to "do unto others as you would have them do unto you."

The problem with abolitionists, some apologists argued, was that they had left their religion and their Bibles far behind as they embraced foreign philosophies and radical thinkers. Such persons can never be persuaded that they read back into Scripture what simply is not there. Abolitionists act as though "Moses and Paul were moved by the Holy Ghost to sanction the philosophy of Thomas Jefferson!" Or, said Presbyterian Frederick A. Ross (1796–1883) in 1857, they leave the Bible in disgust because they cannot "torture" it any further into support of their cause; they then go off in search somewhere else of "an abolition Bible, an abolition Constitution for the United States, and an abolition God." Meanwhile, those who see slavery as totally "in harmony with the Bible," will cling even more faithfully to their holy writings and to their holy religion. The slaveholder, Ross wrote, "with the Bible in his heart and hand . . . will do justice and love mercy in higher and higher rule. Every evil will be removed, and the negro will be elevated to the highest attainments he can make, and be prepared for whatever destiny God intends."

If slavery could not be defended as a good, it could perhaps be justified as a political and economic given with which the churches should not interfere. South Carolina Lutherans in 1836 protested the "impropriety and injustice of the interference or intermeddling of any religious or deliberative body with the subject of slavery or slaveholding, emancipation or abolitionism." For themselves, they would henceforth have nothing to do with the subject, nor "at any time enter into a discussion of slavery." Others were willing to discuss it, but in terms of their own choosing only: Christianity against atheism. On one side, said Presbyterian James H. Thornwell (1812–1862), we find "Atheists, Socialists, Communists, Red Republicans, [and] Jacobins." On the other, the "friends of order and regulated freedom" who see the workings of society not as the creation of man but the ordinance of God. Our task, said Thornwell, is to maintain "the principles upon which the security of social order and the development of humanity depend." Abolitionists think that "the duties of all men are specifically the same," while their opponents understand that men's duties "are as various as the circumstances in which men are placed." "Some are tried in one way, some in another," Thornwell explained, "but the spirit of true obedience is universally the same."

Like a rag doll, the Bible was tossed back and forth, now quoted to support slavery, not to attack it. The Christian religion was now the slave's dearest friend, now his betrayer and deceiver. The church could be a station in the underground railroad, helping to spirit the runaway slave on his way to freedom. Or the church could be the gathering place from which to send out patrols to recapture slaves or to break up their religious meetings. Both sides, as Abraham Lincoln later and sorrowfully observed, "read the same Bible, and pray to the same God." The prayers of both, he added, could not be answered.

THE CHURCHES

While some churches managed to avoid bitter recrimination and lasting schism, churches with the largest following in the South could not escape being torn apart. Refusing to talk about the issue did not resolve it; praying about the matter did not alleviate it; creedal loyalty did not help nor did a common denominational bond prove strong enough to hold. In the two decades immediately prior to the Civil War, the Methodist, Baptist, and Presbyterian fellowships all fell apart. If Christian love proved not to be the tie that binds, what of civil law and national loyalty? Could either the nation or its churches long endure, half slave and half free?

In 1844 the youngest of the three denominations, the Methodist, was the first to suffer schism. Such painful parting of the ways could be readily anticipated in the sharply contrasting statements regarding slavery that came from the North and the South. In 1836 Bishop William Capers (1790–1855) of South Carolina took aim at the abolitionists, charging them with loyalty to "a false philosophy, overreaching and setting aside the Scriptures." Whatever may be the motives of these northern radicals, the conclusions reached "are utterly erroneous and altogether harmful." Bishop Capers held out no olive branch, allowed for no "good faith" on the part of those determined to eradicate slavery and to do it now.

A Methodist Anti-Slavery Convention, meeting in Boston in 1843, proclaimed views wholly unacceptable to their brothers and sisters in the South. Holding slaves, treating human beings as property rather than persons, was (said the convention members) "a flagrant violation of the law of God: it is sin itself; a sin in the abstract and in the concrete; a sin under all circumstances." Not much room for negotiation there either. Then, addressing specifically the denominational issue, the Boston Methodists declared that neither unanimity nor harmony could exist within their church as long as slavery continued to flourish there. "We feel it our imperative duty," they concluded, "to use all such means as become Christians in seeking an immediate and entire abolition from the church of which we are members."

The very next year, therefore, the Methodist church in America, founded only sixty years before and successful all across the nation beyond anyone's expectations, ceased to be a single church. Splitting into two branches which followed sectional north-south lines, these two churches were predominantly white in membership. Two predominantly black Methodist bodies, the African Methodist Episcopal (formed in 1816) and the African Methodist Episcopal Zion (formed in 1821), continued their independent existence, operating initially in the North but eventually throughout the country. Active Methodist abolitionists, impatient for their whole church to act with respect to slavery, had formed the Wesleyan Methodist Church in 1840, but that separation involved only about twenty-five thousand members as contrasted with the million members caught up in the schism of 1844.

The immediate cause of that separation was the question of whether a slave-holding clergyman could be appointed a bishop in the national Methodist Episcopal Church. As early as 1836 when the general conference of the church met in Cincinnati, that issue was raised, with Southern delegates arguing that it was wholly inappropriate to make not holding slaves a condition of elevation to the episcopate. Northern delegates, on the other hand, contended that the Methodist Book of Discipline had from the beginning taken a strong stand against slavery, condemning it as a "great evil." Gradually, the church relaxed its position to the extent that it did not expel members who held slaves, but never did the church (so the Northerners held) approve of slavery. "What, then, has been done to force the South to separation? What *new* grievance or injury has been inflicted by church action upon our brethren of the South? We are compelled to answer," a northern editor wrote in 1844, "None—absolutely none!" Southerners reasoned, on the other side, that if a Methodist member could hold slaves, then why not a Methodist bishop? Why make that the sticking point? Neither side would yield; the Methodist bond could not hold.

If, however, slavery should be outlawed by presidential proclamation (as it was in 1863), then nothing would prevent Northern and Southern Methodists from reuniting—or so it would seem. By that time, however, twenty years of bitter recrimination and mutual accusation had only widened the chasm between the two branches. Southern bishops in 1865 indicated that a majority of their northern brethren had "become incurably radical." They had substituted politics for theology, social dogmas for churchly creeds. "Their pulpits," the bishops continued, "are perverted to agitations and questions not healthful to personal piety, but promotive of political and ecclesiastical discord." "Preach Christ and Him crucified," the bishops advised; "Do not preach politics." Earlier the U.S. Supreme Court had even had to settle property disputes between the two great divisions of Methodism, this further aggravating the wounds and postponing reconciliation. Not until nearly one hundred years later, in 1939, did north and south come together again.

In 1845 the Baptists, operating as a national entity only since 1814, similarly separated into northern and southern bodies, though in this instance the Southern Baptist Convention far outdistanced its northern counterpart in membership and expansion. Slavery once again served as the fulcrum around which opposing sentiments revolved, with the appointment of a slave-holding missionary here bringing the issue to the fore as among the Methodists it had been the appointment of a slave-holding bishop. In 1844 Alabama Baptists had put to the Boston-based Board of Missions a question concerning its willingness to appoint a missionary who held slaves. The Board indicated that the question had never come up, but if it should the Board could not appoint any such person who insisted upon retaining his slaves. "We never can be a party to any arrangement which would imply approbation of slavery." Southerners felt excluded by such a pronouncement, since they contributed to missionary support but had no effective voice in missionary appointments. Shall the South "participate in all the burdens of the Convention," one writer inquired in 1845, "and be excluded from all its privileges?" Slavery is part of our land, our culture, our economy: "We do not choose the place of our birth." We only claim the right, this author asserted, to act "according to the dictates of our own consciences, without foreign control or interference."

Although denominational structures among black Baptists came after the Civil War rather than before, many blacks took active roles in resisting and condemning slavery long before the war. Baptist churches provided opportunities for such leadership and audiences for such sentiments, as Nathaniel Paul (1775?–1839) demonstrated in the Hamilton Baptist Church of Albany, New York. Celebrating that state's own Emancipation Day (July 4, 1827), Paul denounced slavery as blocking the path to salvation and to God's otherwise freely available mercies: "it stands as a barrier . . . to ward off the influence of divine grace; it shuts up the avenues of the soul, and prevents its receiving divine instruction; and scarce does it permit its miserable captives to know that there is a God, a Heaven or a Hell!"

In even more frightening rhetoric, another black Baptist, Boston's David Walker (1785–1830) issued an *Appeal* in 1829 that warned that the continued toleration of slavery would spell doom and ruin to the entire country "For Almighty God will tear up the very face of the earth!!!" Anxieties that Walker aroused seemed totally fulfilled when yet another black Baptist preacher, Nat Turner (1800–1831) of Southampton County, Virginia, two years later led a slave rebellion that resulted in hundreds of deaths, black and white. Seeing himself as an instrument of God's long-delayed justice at last made manifest on earth, Turner reported in his *Confessions* that "it was plain to me that the Savior was about to lay down the yoke he had borne for the sins of man, and the great day of judgment was at hand."

Apocalyptic judgments came in sermons, in rebellions, and at last in a long and costly war. Despite all that and despite all separations and schisms, Baptists both black and white continued to grow before, during, and after the Civil War. Within a generation black Baptists passed the million mark before 1890, one of their number rejoicing in an increase "without precedent in the history of mankind. Truly we were once weak; but out of weakness we are made strong." Blacks turned to the Baptist denomination in greater force than to any other church, attracted by a relaxed polity that allowed them full independence in their own institutions and by an informal worship that permitted their own free and full expression. Meanwhile, the white branches of the denomination, with over nine thousand churches in 1850, increased fourfold in the subsequent century. Yet, for those branches no reconciliation came, as the Baptist house of faith remained divided long after the issue of slavery had finally been laid to rest.

Presbyterians, the last of the three great churches to divide, took its fateful step in 1857. Decades before, however, churchmen of North and South found their disagreements over slavery firmly set. In 1835 South Carolina Presbyterians affirmed that slavery was "far from being a sin in the sight of God." On the contrary, it was nowhere condemned in Scripture. In fact, slavery accorded with the example set by "patriarchs, prophets, and apostles" and was wholly consistent with "the most fraternal regard to the best good of those servants whom God may have committed to our charge." But in that very same year, Michigan Presbyterians avowed that slavery was most certainly "A Sin Before God and Man." It was an evil from every conceivable point of view, the synod declared—"moral, political, physical, and social." We are obliged, these Presbyterians of the North stated, "to endeavor to hasten the happy day of universal emancipation." If Presbyterians felt that strongly and that differently in 1835, none of the fast-moving events of the next twenty years would soften their disagreements or reveal any common ground.

Presbyterian abolitionists believed that to use the Bible to defend slavery was the surest way to bring calamity down upon that repository of religion as well as to defame and possibly even destroy all effectiveness of the Christian religion in America. Apologists for slavery on the other hand argued that the Bible had little to do with the matter: abolitionists drew their ammunition from radical French philosophy or acted as though Jefferson had in all his assertions been divinely inspired. The argument, southern Presbyterians believed, was not between Christian and Christian but between orthodox believer and foreign radical. Northerners believed time and history to be on their side: the idea that slavery was wrong, everywhere and always wrong, "is becoming as fixed as the everlasting hills."

Not as strong in the South as Methodists and Baptists had been, Presbyterians after the separation grew more rapidly in the North and West, the southern Church limiting itself largely to the confines of the Confederacy. Approximately four times the size of the southern branch of Presbyterianism, the northern branch grew from about one-half million in 1870 to around three million a century later. By that time overtures for reunion between the two sections grew more serious, a merger finally being consummated in 1985.

The cost to American religion of these divisions can hardly be overestimated. All of the crusading spirit of reform and conquest suffered enormously, as clerical leadership now spoke for regions more than for a nation or a world, and now reflected local biases more obviously than ever before. Members, meanwhile, found themselves defending positions taken earlier or resenting attitudes and expressions revealed earlier. Religion retreated from culture more than it shaped it, a retreat

33. Author of *Uncle Tom's Cabin*, Harriet Beecher Stowe hoped for a great religious and moral revival that would forestall the Civil War; none came. *National Portrait Gallery*

compounded by continuing theological and ecclesiastical conflicts marring the remainder of the nineteenth century.

THE NATION

Harriet Beecher Stowe (1811–1896) concluded her famous novel, *Uncle Tom's Cabin* (1852), with a plea to both North and South to repent of their respective injustices and cruelties while there was yet time. "A day of grace is yet held out to us," she wrote, and "the Christian church has a heavy account to answer." She hoped even in the decade of the 1850s to turn aside "the wrath of Almighty God," a wrath visited upon all the unjust and a wrath not to be escaped except through "repentance, justice, and mercy."

Revivalism had proved before to be a powerful instrument for healing differences and solving critical social or moral problems. Could revivalism rise to the challenges posed in America in the 1850s? Some thought that it just might work as in 1858, a year of miracle and wonder, revivalism swiftly ignited city after city. Starting out in Boston and New York, the revival moved quickly beyond those centers to other towns and villages that anticipated another Great Awakening. "It swept over the land with such power," Charles G. Finney reported, that an estimated fifty thousand or more conversions occurred in a single week. Then one could hardly make reasonable estimates, since the number of meetings increased so rapidly and since "all classes of people were inquiring everywhere." But then Finney added ominously, "Slavery seemed to shut it out from the South. The people there were in such a state of irritation, of vexation, and of committal to their peculiar institution . . . that the Spirit of God seemed to be grieved away from them."

Harriet Stowe continued to hope that the "great revival" of 1858 would become the "great reformation" of 1858 wherein men and women would resolve to draw closer to God and to become more Christlike in all their ways. "The great turning of the public mind to religion" raises our hopes, the novelist noted, that the nation can avoid tragic bloodshed. Northerners need to repent of the "profitable wickedness" of the slave trade; Southerners need to repent of the continuing exploitation of the slave. What we so desperately need as a people is a genuine revival, Stowe concluded, that will "make men like Christ; or, if they do not make them like Him, at least set them on the road of trying to be like Him."

However powerful this revival and however numerous the weekly conversions, it failed to bring North and South together. Animosities turned into violence and violence became war, a war that tried the national soul more than any event in America's history. Early in the course of that struggle, President Lincoln meditating on the mind of

God declined to wrap the cause of either side in the mantle of righteousness and truth. "It is quite possible," he wrote, "that God's purpose is something different from the purpose of either party." Americans as a people have grown too accustomed to success, Lincoln observed in 1863, too self-sufficient, "too proud to pray to the God that made us." It is time, therefore, for humility and confession and earnest pleas for divine forgiveness.

The moral as opposed to the military climax of the Civil War came on the first of January, 1863, when Lincoln issued the Emancipation Proclamation freeing all slaves wherever federal authority could make that possible. This was a beginning, of course, rather than a concluding in the march toward racial justice, but it was a necessary and crucial beginning. In the District of Columbia where emancipation was immediate, black Methodist Daniel A. Payne preached a sermon entitled "Welcome to the Ransomed." There he urged that a responsible and disciplined freedom be pursued by those now set free: "As you are now free in body, so now seek to be free in soul and spirit, from sin and Satan." That person is freest of all, Payne declared, who is free in Christ.

34. Julia Ward Howe memorialized that bloody war in her "Battle Hymn of the Republic": "Mine eyes have seen the glory of the coming of the Lord." *Keystone-Mast Collection, UC–Riverside*

When the war itself ended in 1865, the losses in both body and spirit defied the imagination. Lincoln earlier that year in his Second Inaugural Address had called for all "to bind up the nation's wounds." Many wounds there were, and Lincoln, struck down by an assassin's bullet, could not assist in the binding up nor in the assuring of "malice toward none, with charity for all, with firmness in the right, as God gives us to see the right." In that same year Horace Bushnell, delivering the commencement address at Yale, placed the awesome costs of the war in a theological perspective. As Christians, Bushnell said, we have been taught that without the shedding of blood, there is no remission of sins. So it is, he added, that "without shedding of blood, there is almost nothing great in the world . . . for the life is in the blood, all life." Great has been the sacrifice, and great the suffering. But what has been given to us thereby is a nation reborn: "In this blood our unity is cemented and forever sanctified."

CHAPTER 16

Faithful Immigrants and the "Varieties of Religious Experience"

Although the history of the United States is indeed a history of immigration, the period after the Civil War symbolizes that fact in a uniquely powerful way. Between 1860 (when the population of the whole country was thirty-one million) and 1890, newly arrived immigrants numbered some ten million. In the briefer period from 1890 to 1914, the number soared to fifteen million. This mighty movement of peoples, largely from southern and eastern Europe, was augmented by migrations across the Mexican-American border and by an influx of Chinese and Japanese along the Pacific Coast. The multiplicity of cultural patterns gave religion new opportunities for colorful display, even as it raised anxieties regarding national unity and religious direction.

In the tumult of transplanting, religion often provided both personal security and ethnic cohesion. In a new land and generally faced with a new language, far removed from ancestral home and former national identities, uncertain immigrants turned hungrily toward synagogue and church for the comfort of the familiar. When so much had been so abruptly interrupted, religion stood steady, offering continuity and assurance. There, in the communities of faith, the uprooted still found roots—and they were sustained by them.

ETHNICITY AND RELIGION

While religion often reinforced ethnic cohesiveness, ethnicity sometimes challenged the unifying force of religion. Ethnic loyalty created social community at the same time that it threatened or shattered theological and ecclesiastical community. Nowhere were the challenges more dramatic than among America's rapidly expanding Roman Catholics. The Irish immigration before the Civil War was of such magnitude as to give the American Church a Hibernian stamp and flavor that would last for at least one hundred years. Among the bishops and archbishops of the Roman Catholic church in late nineteenth-century America, the Irish exercised a virtual monopoly. Like all monopolists, they jealously guarded their preserve, only reluctantly and tardily agreeing to share their power.

German Catholics who had in many cases arrived long before the Irish newcomers especially resented the domination exercised by the spiritual sons of Saint Patrick. In 1886 a Milwaukee priest, P. M. Abbelen (1843–1917), protested to the Vatican on behalf of his German brothers and sisters, asking that German parishes "be entirely independent of Irish parishes" and that "the rectors of Irish parishes . . . not be able to exercise any parochial jurisdiction over Germans enrolled in any German church." What was at stake, Father Abbelen pointed

35. The Jewish Market on the East Side of New York City found new immigrant buyers and sellers in 1900. *Library of Congress*

out, was more than merely a matter of the German language; the whole character of worship differed between Irish and German. The Irish "love simplicity" and "do not care much for pomp and splendor," while the Germans on the other hand "love the beauty of the church edifice and the pomp of ceremonies, belfries and bells, organs and sacred music, procession, feast days, sodalities, and the most solemn celebration of First Communion and weddings."

German laity, moreover, tend to exercise much more control of the administrative structure of the parish, while the Irish seem inclined to leave everything in the hands of the priests. "Finally, even manners and social customs of the two nationalities differ exceedingly," the most obvious example of this being that rarely do Irish boys marry German girls or German boys Irish girls. This is not said, the Milwaukee priest and vicar-general carefully noted, in order to argue that one group is superior to the other, only that they are different and that the Catholic church will be a healthier institution if it respects that difference, rather than attempting to suppress or obliterate it.

Similarly, the Italians and the Portuguese, and the Austrians and the Czechs, found themselves ruled over by Irish unfamiliar with their customs and their language, sometimes unsympathetic to their difficulties and concerns. An Italian Catholic, recalling his boyhood in New York early in the twentieth century, indicated that the Irish leadership was often responsible for driving Italians totally away from Catholicism and into the embrace of Protestantism. Italian males, he pointed out, had never been too fond of Italian clergy, but the American clergy they despised. Polish Catholics, more than others, found the adjustment away from homeland and language and long-standing custom extraordinarily difficult to make. And to some it appeared so difficult that schism from the church of their birth turned out to be the only possible path.

In Scranton, Pennsylvania, in the 1880s and 1890s Polish Catholics found themselves ruled not by a Polish bishop but an Irish one, governed not by a Polish mayor but an Irish one, outvoted even in their own parish by what they described as a "foreign priestly power." True catholicity was one thing, but too much Irishness quite another. When riots erupted, concerned laymen looked for assistance somewhere, anywhere. A Polish priest and former rector in Scranton came to the rescue, advising all those "who are dissatisfied and feel wronged" to set about organizing and building a new church of their own. In Buffalo, Chicago, and other cities where large Polish communities could be found, similar sentiments led to ecclesiastical independence. Mass was celebrated in Polish, religious journals were published in Polish, Polish saint days and festivals were celebrated; by 1904 the Polish National Catholic Church in America had become a reality. Although the vast majority of Poles remained in the Roman Catholic Church, the ethnic church continued to survive and prosper, as one symbol of ethnicity's awesome power.

On the whole, however, the Roman church successfully resisted the natural tendency of ethnic enclaves to run their own ecclesiastical affairs and to establish competing hierarchies. In this respect, Catholicism remained "catholic." On the other hand, the failure to assure some kind of proportional representation in the American hierarchy to the several ethnic groups led to continued tensions and struggles within a church striving, against great odds, to prove its universality and its inclusiveness. In the twentieth century, Hispanic Catholics made many of the same arguments that had been made by German and Italian parishoners before them.

In the post–Civil War period, the ethnic complexion of Judaism underwent radical transformation. Largely German dominated before that war, Judaism in the succeeding decades acquired a decidedly Eastern European cast. Especially from Russia and especially in response to the bloody massacres or pogroms of 1881, 1891, and 1905, Jews by the hundreds of thousands left a hostile Europe for a beckoning America. The most famous words of welcome to immigrants, written by the Jewish poet Emma Lazarus in 1883, found their way onto the Statue of Liberty:

> Give me your tired, your poor,
> Your huddled masses yearning to be free,
> The wretched refuse of your teeming shore,
> Send these, the homeless, tempest-tost to me,
> I lift my lamp beside the golden door.

That golden door did not stay open indefinitely, but it did stand wide long enough for the United States to become the major center of Jewish population.

More was changed than mere ethnicity, however, for the ethnic shift (from Jews of the German Enlightenment to Jews of the Russian persecutions) also led to a religious shift. German Jews, typified by Rabbi Isaac Mayer Wise, saw the reforming and the Americanizing of Judaism as a coordinated task. Here in America, Judaism need not hunker down behind ghettoed walls, need not live in isolation from nor in terror of the prevailing culture. Jews were free to worship as they chose, but more than that Jews were free to modernize their religion, if they chose. Wise believed that Judaism should free itself of ancient legislation and ethnic limitation to become a noble and highly ethical religion with appeal to all mankind. To do this, the Jew must become totally and proudly American, shorn of all foreignness. If the Jew continues "under German influences," Wise wrote, "he must become either a bigot or an atheist, a satellite or a tyrant. He will never be aroused to self-consciousness and independent thought." In short, Wise concluded, the Jew must become unambiguously an American rather than merely an ethnic or religious refugee.

Eastern European Jews, however, sought nothing so much as the opportunity to practice their ancient religion without hindrance or limitation. Arriving in New York City or other eastern ports, they hurried from the ship to create a synagogue: intimate, free, and above all orthodox. These Jews did not wish to reform the ancient law (or Torah); they wished only to obey it. Being or becoming Americans was not

36. Solomon Schechter arrived in America early in the twentieth century to lead the forces of Conservative Judaism. *Jewish Theological Seminary*

nearly so pressing or important as being or becoming faithful Jews. For decades they had been harassed or hindered, beaten or robbed, jailed or slain. Every obstacle that could be thrown in the path of ritual purity and communal worship had been thrown; every burden that could be thrust upon the observant Jew had been pressed upon him, his wife, his children. Now that he had come to a land where he could worship without fear, let him do just that. To such a one, do not speak of reform, speak of obedience.

Ethnicity represented, therefore, among America's newly arriving Jews more than just the competing allegiances found among America's newly arriving Catholics. Here one found a sharply contrasting psychology, a pointedly different stance with regard to culture. Reform Judaism argued for great change in Judaism; Orthodox Judaism argued for no change. In between these two groups, Conservative Judaism arose as yet another alternative, arguing for limited change, or perhaps better, for change only in the nonessentials with steadfast loyalty to the abiding, eternal truths. Solomon Schechter who arrived in America in 1902 to become president of the Jewish Theological Seminary in New York City defended the Conservative approach. "There is nothing in American citizenship," he wrote, "which is incompatible with our observing the dietary laws, our sanctifying the Sabbath, our fixing a Mezuzah [small portion of Hebrew scripture] on our doorposts, our refraining from unleavened bread on Passover, or our perpetuating any other law essential to the preservation of Judaism." In Europe, compromises were forced upon us, said Schechter. In America, they are not. "In this great, glorious and free country we Jews need not sacrifice a single iota of our Torah; and, in the enjoyment of absolute equality with our fellow citizens, we can live to carry out those ideals for which our ancestors so often had to die."

Ethnicity together with the vagaries of historical conditioning introduced sectarian or denominational differences among America's religious Jews. Many of the new immigrants, however, found their interests to be more political or economic than religious with the result that perhaps only about one-half of the nation's Jews belong to the synagogues or temples of the Reform, Orthodox, and Conservative branches. No hierarchy from abroad had directed the development of Judaism in America; thus no schism from or rebellion against external authority has ever been necessary. Synagogue government is local and democratic, a fact which enables ethnicity in the large urban centers to survive with its own leadership and traditions, its own intimacy and enduring, sustaining sense of community.

Protestantism also enjoyed ethnic enriching in the period following the Civil War. Lutheranism in particular revealed a pattern of development in which ethnic loyalty prevented the creation of any single Lutheran church. The large Scandinavian immigrations (Swedish,

Danish, Norwegian, Finnish, Icelandic) of the second half of the nineteenth century led to separate ecclesiastical entities whose reason for being was neither doctrinal nor geographical but ethnic. Affiliation with German Lutherans who had arrived in the eighteenth century was out of the question, but so also was affiliation with fellow Scandinavians. Each group wanted its own language, its own festivals, its own familiar patterns of life. In Minnesota, for example, as one Lutheran later recalled, "the Swedes and Danes and Finns kept to themselves in communities that had names like Swedish Grove and Dane Prairie and Finlandia. The groups could have made themselves understood to one another," he added, "and might have found they had much in common. But these exchanges did not occur." The twentieth century opened with twenty-four separate Lutheran groups in America, but the peak had been reached. Gradually, the process began to reverse itself, as ethnic distinctions gave way to identification more generally and more vaguely American.

Ethnicity did not always conquer theology and ecclesiology. In the case of the Dutch Reformed, for example, "Dutchness" was of itself insufficient to maintain unity between those Dutch who arrived in the nineteenth century and those who had arrived two centuries earlier. The newer immigrants found their countrymen who had been in America for half a dozen generations or so already too Americanized; their

37. Kosher wine produced and inspected in New York City in 1942. *Library of Congress*

theology, moreover, had lost some of its Calvinist precision, some of its careful fidelity to the Heidelberg Confession. Thus, the Christian Reformed Church in North America, organized in 1857, declined to be identified with the older Reformed church. Less than a hundred years later, the Christian Reformed itself suffered a separation, the charge again being one of doctrinal or theological inexactitude. In each instance, while ethnicity mattered, theology mattered more.

In the twentieth century, the close tie between ethnicity and religion was nowhere better illustrated than in the several branches of Eastern Orthodoxy. Russian, Greek, Albanian, Armenian, Bulgarian, Romanian, Syrian, Serbian, Ukrainian and more ethnic labels defined not just parish boundaries but all social relationships and family alliances as well. Part of Eastern Orthodoxy's relatively low profile in American public life is directly due to the persisting power of ethnicity, that power proving sufficient to hold assimilation at bay and ecclesiastical union at risk.

RELIGION AND RACE

The deeply scarred memories of a Civil War made it wholly unnecessary to demonstrate the power of race. None dared question its might. And what could divide a nation could certainly divide the churches, not only before the war but long thereafter. Black Methodists in the North had already created their separate institutions (African Methodist Episcopal in 1816; African Methodist Episcopal Zion in 1821), but black Methodists in the South did not create a denomination of their own until 1870. At that time, about one hundred thousand blacks withdrew from the Methodist Episcopal Church, South, to form what was then called the Colored Methodist Episcopal Church. After nearly a century of growth, the name "Christian" was substituted for that of "Colored." Growth of black Baptists following the war was, however, even more impressive than that among Methodists.

As early as 1880, black Baptists had formed their own missionary organization, a decade and a half later a fully developed denomination, the National Baptist Convention, came into being, its creation in part the result of blacks feeling less than totally welcome in the white-dominated parent bodies. As one black pastor, E. K. Love of Savannah, Georgia, noted in 1896: "It never was true anywhere, and perhaps never will be, that a Negro can enjoy every right in an institution controlled by white men that a white man can enjoy." Like many others, Love also believed that a "bright and glorious future" awaited America's blacks in religious institutions of their own creation and their own direction. In this way, noted another pastor from Helena, Arkansas, blacks could identify and develop "a host of intelligent, self-reliant practical leaders among us."

This is precisely how it turned out, as black Baptists created their own publishing house in 1898, their own mechanisms for educating missionaries to Africa, and their own lobbying machinery designed to improve the condition and future of the nation's black population. With about two million members by 1900, these Baptists felt strong enough to take the gospel message back to Africa, to "be a power as a missionary force for the evangelization of the world," as one of their number proclaimed in 1903. While all the world should receive missionaries, Africa in particular, "the original home of the race," called out for evangelists to come among them. "A great work remains to be done for the race in this and other lands," the spokesman concluded, "and every Baptist should therefore be intensely a missionary Baptist." Though the National Baptist Convention itself suffered a schism in 1915, now two major denominations pressed forward in growth and influence across the continent.

Blacks also actively participated in the lively Pentecostal movement which, like that first Pentecost recorded in the Book of Acts, emphasized the direct, visible impact of the Holy Spirit in the services of

38. Russian Orthodoxy found its way first into Alaska, then moved slowly down the Pacific Coast; this church in Sitka was photographed around 1900. *Keystone-Mast Collection, UC–Riverside*

worship. The powerful sway of the Spirit was evident chiefly in the practice of speaking in tongues and in the ceremonies of religious healing. In the 1880s the many manifestations of this Pentecostal surge were casually interracial, without self-consciousness. Gradually, however, the power of race again made itself felt, sometimes whites taking the initiative for separation and sometimes blacks. In 1897 in Lexington, Mississippi, two black Baptists created the Church of God in Christ, a body destined to become the largest black Pentecostal church in the world. Though its early centers of strength were in Alabama, Mississippi, Louisiana, Arkansas, and east Texas, this black church moved beyond the borders of the nation to the Caribbean, to Central and South America, and to Africa as well.

Though black Christians could frequently be found in such prevailing white institutions as the Episcopal and the Roman Catholic churches, by far the larger number of them served in denominations where the leadership was wholly theirs, where the worship more faithfully reflected their spiritual joy, and where their contribution to the total Christian community could be more freely rendered. The tragedy of involuntary segregation remained, but as E. K. Love noted at the close of the last century, black denominations may have this mitigating effect: "We can more thoroughly fill our people with race pride, denominational enthusiasm and activity, by presenting to them for support enterprises that are wholly ours." The religious life of blacks in the second half of the nineteenth century turned out to be another way of echoing Bishop Daniel Payne's "Welcome to the Ransomed."

In the generation or two that followed the Civil War, prejudice in the United States found many targets conveniently at hand. As immigration increased, one could find dark threats in the growing number of Catholics and Jews, in the growing "foreignness" in general. Blacks, of course, though not part of the immigration surge, encountered prejudice on many other grounds. Then into the West came Orientals, creating even more unease as they found the path to total assimilation either exceedingly difficult or totally blocked. Bringing with them such exotic religions as Confucianism and Buddhism, Chinese and Japanese emigrants also posed an economic threat as they bartered their labor at the cheapest rates. With over three million emigrants from China by 1882, public pressure led to the adoption of the Chinese Exclusion Act which suspended all immigration from China for ten years. The Act was renewed ten years later, and a decade after that, Chinese immigration was suspended indefinitely. By that time, public feeling against the increased Japanese influx led to similar anxieties about the "Yellow Peril" and the racial dilution or "mongrelization" (to use a Ku Klux Klan term) of the nation. A so-called Gentlemen's Agreement of 1907 and 1908 between Japan and the United States effectively halted the flow of the Japanese into the West Coast states.

The nation's religious forces were no more effective in promoting a blindness to race with respect to the Oriental than they had been with respect to the black. Missionaries and schools were charged with the responsibility of Christianizing and Americanizing these distinctive immigrants, but initial successes were limited. Converts, moreover, tended to be placed in ethnically restricted churches: the Korean Baptist Church, the Chinese Methodist Church, the Japanese Presbyterian Church. Ethnicity, sometimes seen as enriching and brightening the whole fabric of American society, could also be regarded as detrimental to social cohesion and religious destiny. The large Oriental presence was a major factor in making the nation's immigration policy far more restrictive in the early decades of the twentieth century, in closing that "golden door" of which Emma Lazarus had written.

RELIGION AND GENDER

In the wake of the Emancipation Proclamation and in the gradual extension of voting rights to a wider segment of the population, women began to participate more broadly in public affairs. In religion, female leadership (as in the case of the Shakers and in Christian Science) drew comment and attention, as it did in the rapidly multiplying Holiness and Pentecostal bodies where a female ministry was commonplace. In more traditional religious settings, however, the drive for true equality, especially in ministerial roles, was both difficult and uneven. The long shadow of tradition, along with the selective support of biblical injunction, combined to keep women from sharing in leadership and authority. Emancipation came with much reluctance and, in many cases, it did not come at all.

Antoinette Brown Blackwell (1825–1921) had no trouble being admitted to Oberlin College, a school founded under the joint auspices of the Congregationalists and the Presbyterians and a school that had early taken a firm stand in favor of coeducation. But then, after her undergraduate studies, Blackwell did what no female student had done before: she applied for admission to the theological department where, at the conclusion of one's advanced study, ordination to the ministry was the normal result. After much discussion, the faculty decided that Blackwell would be admitted to advanced study, but would not be granted a degree and would presumably therefore not be ordained. Somehow, it seemed the perfect academic compromise. Nonetheless, the determined lady finally won her ordination in 1853, being the first of her sex to be set apart for the ministry by one of the major denominations (Congregational). She spent the remainder of her long life in raising a large family and in raising the consciousness of her fellow citizens to the questions of equity and fair play with respect to female rights in general, a female ministry in particular.

Among those not persuaded by Blackwell's argument or example was Professor Robert L. Dabney (1820–1898), a Presbyterian minister and theologian in Virginia. Writing in 1879, he explained that not all social novelties were healthy, not all "progressive" developments were biblical. Ordaining women to the ministry was, according to Dabney, an example of innovation without scriptural foundation and without any socially redeeming quality. The Old Testament, he argued, "allowed no regular church office to any woman." "No woman ever ministered at the altar as either priest or Levite." And the Old Testament pattern was very much followed in the New. Moreover, Dabney added, woman really was the "weaker vessel," not designed by God for all the responsibilities nor to all "the franchises in society to which the male is entitled." We hear much of "women's rights" these days, Dabney observed; this is a "common movement," not supported by scripture. It is a movement which threatens biblical authority at large and undermines the foundation of Christian marriage in particular; it is, in short, "simply infidel," and good Presbyterians will have nothing to do with that general trend and certainly not with the specific effort to create women preachers.

Dabney based his argument heavily on the Bible, and just there, said Elizabeth Cady Stanton (1815–1902), lies much of the difficulty that besets American women. "The Bible teaches that woman brought sin and death into the world," Stanton wrote in 1895, "that she precipitated the fall of the race, that she was arraigned before the judgment

39. Lucretia Mott served as a Quaker minister from 1821 to 1880 in which capacity she fought for the rights of both slaves and women. *National Portrait Gallery*

seat of Heaven, tried, condemned and sentenced." Marriage was to be her bondage, childbearing her curse, and intellectual dependence her earthly fate. "Here is the Bible position of woman briefly summed up." On that foundation, Feminist Stanton believed, little emancipation for women can be based. What is required is a new understanding, a new translation if you will, of those Scriptures which have been used to justify centuries of bondage. This new foundation Stanton sought to provide in what came to be known as *The Woman's Bible*, issued in two volumes in 1895 and 1898. To those shocked by the thought that liturgies and scriptures might be thus revised, Stanton offered this counsel: "Come, come, my conservative friend, wipe the dew off your spectacles, and see that the world is moving." So it did move as equality in education, in political participation, in career opportunity, and in positions of religious authority all advanced. But that world, especially in religion, moved slowly.

NATIONAL UNITY AMID DIVERSITY

With millions of new immigrants, with dozens of new ethnic strains, with concerns about both race and gender, many worried in the late nineteenth century about the oneness of the nation. Whether the language of "melting pot" was used or not, the image for which it stood had strong appeal: taking all that "foreignness" in language, custom, dress, and religion and somehow melting it all down into a familiar, domesticated, English-speaking "American." The religion of such an American would preferably be Protestant—at least Bible-believing and informed by a moral code essentially biblical. Temperance (if not abstinence) would be required so far as alcoholic beverages were concerned. Sunday as a day of rest and worship (not of recreation and carnival) would be encouraged, sometimes with the force of law. Public schools would serve as a major instrument of the Americanization process, with private or parochial schools being regarded with considerable suspicion as divisive and almost "un-American."

These uneasy anxieties informed and gave momentum to the broad-gauged revivalism identified with Dwight L. Moody (1837–1899). A Boston shoe clerk, Moody, impressed by the earnestness of his Sunday school teacher, joined the Congregational Church when he was eighteen years of age. Later that same year, 1856, he left for Chicago to make his own way in the world of business, but soon he decided that money-making should take second place to gospel preaching. Moody spent his after-business hours organizing Sunday schools, distributing tracts, raising money for the building of churches, and ministering in a dozen ways to Chicago's poor and distressed. By 1860 he emerged from "the hardest struggle I ever had in my life" with the decision to give himself totally to the cause of religion.

During the Civil War he worked in army camps, offering aid to the wounded and counsel to those uprooted from family and home. After that conflict, he returned to the slums of Chicago to direct relief, establish missions, and acquire a reputation as a Christian leader who repeatedly managed to get things done. He won his greatest fame, however, as a revivalist, and he won that fame far from Chicago. His earliest evangelistic successes came in Great Britain, and from his victories there he returned to America in 1875 to become as much the popular hero at home as he had been abroad. When he joined forces with the song leader and hymn writer, Ira D. Sankey (1840–1908), his revivals gained even greater acceptance.

Unordained and uneducated (he never finished the seventh grade),

40. Dwight L. Moody dominated revivalism in the second half of the nineteenth century, as Charles G. Finney had in the first half. *Library of Congress*

Moody preached sermons of simple style. Stressing the need for personal redemption, he called upon his hearers to respond to clear and compelling divine initiatives. "Now, let me say, my friends," he declared from the pulpits, "if you want the love of God in your hearts, all you have to do is to open the door and let it shine in. It will shine in as the sun shines in a dark room. Let him have full possession of your hearts." Such straightforward sentences were spoken earnestly, quietly, without theatrics or bombast. No great emotional display on the part of the congregation was encouraged, no hysterics countenanced, as ushers were instructed to remove persons who became overly demonstrative. A simple gospel, simply presented: that was the heart of Dwight L. Moody.

And it so obviously worked in the final quarter of the nineteenth century. In New York City's Madison Avenue Hall in 1875 crowds gathered in such abundance that hundreds had to stand outside, straining to hear what went on within. A reporter covering the meeting could not help but note the great air of expectancy, the eagerness with which the five thousand persons crowded inside joined in the singing of hymns taken from the *Moody and Sankey Hymnbook*, the rapt attention during the sober sermon. "The quiet of the audience during Moody's preaching and Sankey's singing," the reporter noted, was remarkable. Even the rough fellows who crowd the gallery passages make no sound." And in city after city, the scene was repeated in hippodromes and auditoriums, in churches if they were large enough and in public parks if they were not. Once again, as in the First Great Awakening and the Second, revivalism swept over much of the land.

But revivalism is notoriously fleeting, a surge of heightened excitement inevitably followed by a decline and a lull. Moody himself, recognizing the ephemeral nature of such excitement, gave much attention to the creation of longer lasting institutions, especially in the area of education. Aware that the common heritage of most Americans was rapidly disappearing, Moody pleaded for "teachers who shall teach and show what the gospel is." In 1879 he founded a school for girls near his old home in Northfield, Massachusetts; the Mount Hermon school for boys opened two years later. In 1889 he transformed Chicago's Evangelization Society into a coeducational religious school, later to be known as the Moody Bible Institute. From these centers as from the impact of wealthy and powerful supporters (Cyrus McCormick, John Wanamaker, Anson G. Phelps, T. DeWitt Talmadge, Phillips Brooks, James McCosh, and Henry Ward Beecher, among others), Moody's name and fame covered not only North America but far beyond.

With respect to the larger social and political issues of his day, Moody was no radical, no zealous reformer prepared to turn tables upside down or drive moneychangers from the temple and from the marketplace. Reform was possible, said Moody, only when "the reformer gets into [people's] hearts." The principal business of religion, he argued, was to change those hearts, to see that Christianity met the personal, private needs of the individual. His clerical supporters generally pursued a similar path, the persuasive Phillips Brooks (1835–93), rector of Boston's Trinity (Episcopal) Church, maintaining that the only way to a better world was through patience, prayer, Bible reading, and churchgoing. In an address to the working men of Boston in 1882, Brooks spoke not of capital and labor, not of municipal corruption or the widening inequalities of wealth. The great enemies of the working man, Brooks pointed out, were "intemperance, slothfulness, unskillfulness, and the rest." The salvation of the working man, on the other hand, lay "in sobriety, in intelligence, in industry, in skill, in thrift." "Until the heart is made right," said Dwight L. Moody, "all else will be wrong."

A fellow Congregationalist, Josiah Strong (1847–1916), saw more reason for social reform but, like Moody, worried about the increasing diversity in America, the growing variety in religion and the growing secularity in culture. In a widely read book published in 1885 (*Our Country: Its Possible Future and Its Present Crisis*), Josiah Strong was not content with a simple call to repentance or a generalized homily about changing one's heart. He presented hard data about the economic woes of capitalism, the exploitation of labor, the growing self-indulgence in money-making and pleasure-seeking, the delusions of a socialism that acted as though a brotherhood of man could be achieved without a fatherhood of God being recognized. But along with all his social statistics and his sense of promise for America, Strong did find a "present crisis." That crisis, in short, was the threat to Anglo-Saxon civilization and pure Christian religion. The Greeks brought beauty to the world, the Romans, law; the Egyptians brought the "seminal idea of life," while the Hebrews stressed purity. Now in the modern age, the torch has been passed to the Anglo-Saxons who have made two great contributions: the love of liberty, and a "pure spiritual Christianity."

Emigration to America, however, threatens to divide "our country" into "little Germanies here, little Scandinavias there, and little Irelands yonder." Foreigners profane the Sabbath, Strong asserted, and foreigners promote intemperance. Politically, we now have an Irish vote, a German vote, a Roman Catholic vote, a Mormon vote, a liquor vote, and who knows where all this will end, Strong asked. Religiously, the Protestant consensus is challenged, especially by the great flood of Catholic immigrants and by the rapid rise of the Mormons. Catholicism threatens America's free speech, free press, and free public education, Strong declared. Wherever the Catholic church has full sway, as in Italy or in Spain, the church totally dominates the educational system and generally limits educational opportunity to an elite minority of the population. Revealing his Protestant biases fully, Strong raised the question of the dual loyalty of Catholics in America: loyalty to the United States, but above that loyalty to an infallible pope and foreign prince. "Manifestly," Strong concluded, "there is an irreconcilable difference between papal principles and the fundamental principles of our free institutions." Strong particularly worried about the American West where Jesuits have "empires in their brains."

He also worried about the American West because Mormonism was strongest there. Many Americans think of the Mormon empire as more a disgrace than a danger; it is both, Strong argued. Polygamy was not the problem, for in 1885 that was already on its way out. No, said Strong, despotism was the problem. The real strength and the real threat of this new church lay not in its sexual ethics but in its political power. According to Strong, Mormonism was not a church but a state, exercising total control over the moral, industrial, social, political, and religious life of its people. Much of Mormon growth, like Catholic growth, resulted directly from immigration. Sending out between two hundred and four hundred missionaries a year, Strong calculated, this church imported a steadily increasing number of converts from abroad. This threatened the destiny not only of pure Christianity but of America as well, and in Strong's view of Western history, the destiny of America would to a large degree shape the destiny of the world. We speak of the immigrant being "Americanized," Strong observed; instead, the country is being "foreignized" and that, in a nutshell, was the "present crisis."

Within a few decades the foes of unlimited immigration won their point, but the proponents of a religious uniformity lost theirs. Diversity in religion increased, not only because of large scale immigration, but also because of repeated innovation. In 1872 a small Bible study group, led by Charles Taze Russell (1852–1916), planted the seeds of what became the Jehovah's Witnesses. Russell guided his group in a close study of those passages of Scripture relating to the Second Coming of Christ. Convinced that a great cosmic contest between Satan and Jehovah would end with a physical, visible return of Christ to earth and further convinced that this event was near at hand, Witnesses proclaimed that "millions now living shall never die." By 1879 Witnesses had their own publication (the *Watch Tower*), by 1893 their first national assembly (Chicago), and by 1909 their world headquarters (in Brooklyn, initially taking over the former parsonage of Henry Ward Beecher, Congregational pastor there from 1847 to 1887). Beecher's bowing out in favor of Witnesses typified for Josiah Strong and many others the "perils" confronting American religion. With only a few hundred in the 1870s, Witnesses in America and beyond numbered their ranks in the millions a mere century later.

Also in the 1870s Christian Science arose in Massachusetts under the leadership of Mary Baker Eddy (1821–1910). A native of New Hampshire, young Mary suffered much ill health from which traditional remedies offered little relief. Led to the discovery of a "science of health" through association with Phineas P. Quimby in the 1860s, Eddy was ready a decade later to strike out on her own. Her important book, *Science and Health,* first appeared in 1875 with the first Church of Christ, Scientist being chartered four years later. The founder explained that healing could not be accomplished by science alone; it required a specific religious understanding as well. The correlation between false belief and ill health was direct and inescapable. Disease had no independent reality of its own: it was mental error, error that could be corrected through appropriate metaphysical comprehension. Mind controls matter, and much more besides, she wrote. It controls and conquers "sin, sickness, and death." Jesus was the first Scientist, for he recognized that only God was real, all else was illusion and error. And the Bible, properly understood, gives "all our recipes for healing"—but it must be properly understood. In 1883, therefore, Mary Baker Eddy provided a "Key to the Scriptures" that would thereafter be a fixed part of *Science and Health*. By the time of the founder's death in 1910, Christian Science was firmly established with more than a thousand churches spread from the Atlantic to the Pacific. Christian Science reading rooms, public lectures, and carefully centralized organization kept its message before the American public.

In 1875 Madame H. P. Blavatsky (1831–1891) organized the Theosophical Society, dedicated to blending the ancient wisdom of India with the religions of the West for the cause of a common humanity. In the 1880s mind-cure institutes, metaphysical clubs, and New Thought exponents multiplied the religious options in ways that both Moody and Strong would find dismaying. The purchase of Alaska in 1867 and the annexation of Hawaii in 1898 only widened the religious alternatives more and more.

The most dramatic manifestation of religion's variety in the final quarter of the nineteenth century, however, came in Chicago in 1893 with the opening of the World's Parliament of Religions. Now for the first time Americans saw and heard about the religions of the East from the actual devotees of those religions. Islam, Buddhism, Hinduism and others of the world's faiths came not in distorting stereotypes or dismissive tones, but in colorful costume, earnest testimony, and often persuasive power. Brainchild of Congregationalist John Henry Barrows, the parliament provided a platform not only for Oriental religions, but for Judaism, for Catholicism (both Eastern and Western), even—as something of an afterthought—for American blacks. It also provided incontrovertible evidence of what philosopher and psychologist William James was to call the *Varieties of Religious Experience* (1902), variety far wider than anything Americans of a hundred years before could have begun to imagine.

The variety on the world stage would sooner or later be reflected in the American drama, many observers in 1893 agreed. But could not Christianity at least get its own brawling, bewildering house in order? Could not denominations that had divided come together as a family once more? In the last year of his life, the noted church historian, Philip Schaff, spoke to the Parliament of Religions of his hope for greater harmony among the churches, greater unity in spirit if not in organization. Briefly reviewing the nineteen centuries of Christian history (and Christian schism), he accentuated the positive. "Let us forget and forgive their [the denominations'] many sins and errors," he said, and "remember only their virtues and merits." Greek Orthodox, Roman Catholic, Lutheran, Presbyterian, Baptist, Methodist, Moravian, Unitarian, Universalist, even the Salvation Army with "its strange and abnormal methods"—all have merit, all have made major contributions. "There is room for all these and many other churches and societies in

41. Mary Baker Eddy, founder of Christian Science, is shown here in a photograph taken in 1910. *Library of Congress*

the Kingdom of God," Schaff concluded, a kingdom "whose height and depth and length and breadth, variety and beauty, surpass human comprehension." His optimism and his charity were more often praised than vigorously pursued.

CHAPTER 17

New Challenges and the Responses of Faith

The face of America altered radically between 1850 and 1900. Two forces drove that alteration: the move from the villages and ships to the cities; the move from the farms to the factories. Such moves, never easy under any circumstances, were aggravated by deep distrust between capital and labor, by deep suspicion of or hostility toward the rapid urbanization. Symptoms of the social stress came in the form of strikes, financial panics, riots, slums, sweatshops, immorality, poverty, bribery, and graft. Rural America, Jefferson's land of the yeoman farmer, was rapidly disappearing; many were uneasy about its passing, unsure about its successor.

Immigration of course doubled or tripled the population of the coastal cities, but urbanization was by no means a coastal phenomenon alone. Americans in the Midwest and elsewhere left hamlet and homestead for the city—any city. By 1900 Chicago had become the nation's second largest city, with sharp growth also evident in Detroit, Milwaukee, Minneapolis, St. Paul, Indianapolis, Cleveland, Columbus, Toledo, Kansas City, and Omaha. The city lured its newcomers with promise of economic opportunity and uninhibited freedom. Behind those promises, dark dangers lurked.

In this same half century, from 1850 to 1900, the Industrial Revolution reshaped the nation, especially in the North. "Revolution" does not exaggerate the nature of those changes that transformed so many areas of life: transportation (steam engine, combustion engine, and electric engine); communication (telegraph, telephone, transatlantic cable, wireless, typewriter, and linotype press); agriculture (binders, threshers, cutters, and improved harvesters); and domestic life (electric lights, sewing machines, phonographs, and gas stoves). The greatest revolution, however, occurred in the labor market itself where thousands of propertyless men and women had nothing to barter but their toil and their sweat.

To all of the ills and pains of social dislocation and change, institutional religion could not long remain indifferent. Though many continued to believe that changing the individual heart was sufficient cure for all troubles, others found disease in the very character of the city itself, in the grinding impersonal nature of the factory itself, or perhaps even in the greed and indifference of the economic system itself. Could religion offer any cure for diseases of this deep-seated sort? Or for some the question went like this: should religion allow itself to become involved in political, economic, and social questions far beyond its own area of expertise and competence? Salvation of souls had been the traditional business of much American religion. Did it now have any business going beyond that private domain, venturing into dangerous waters and unexplored territories?

THE CITY

In health, housing, education, and moral standards, the metropolis presented both church and synagogue with a wide array of pressing problems. The immigrant journalist, Jacob Riis (1849–1914), looking at the poorer neighborhoods in New York City, was shocked at what he found. He soon shocked the nation by reporting in 1890 on *How the Other Half Lives*. The tenements in which the poor live, Riis wrote, were "dark and deadly dens" where the home loses all sanctity, where character was smothered, where children were "damned rather than born" into the world. And where is the church in this neighborhood? The church is outnumbered by the saloon, ten to one or more. "Either the devil was on the ground first, or he has been doing a good deal more in the way of building." The congregation was also larger in the saloons than in the churches, Riis reported, "and the contributions more liberal the week round."

Roman Catholic Bishop of Peoria, Illinois, John Lancaster Spalding (1840–1916), worried most about the city's effect upon the family, the social unit which most Americans then (and now) regarded as fundamental to all human relationships and moral development. What Bishop Spalding found in the city, however, was not moral development but moral degradation. "The conditions of life are not favorable to purity," he wrote, "and the grossest sensuality prevails." In the city "where people have no settled home and no local traditions, the loss of good name is often looked upon as a mere trifle." Even the simplest sort of moral education, such as the teaching of courtesy and good manners, "cease to be handed down as sacred heirlooms." We all carry around with us, Spalding observed, a kind of romanticized ideal of the American home: the vine covered cottage, the fireside gatherings, the mother and father bringing up healthy, happy children in "love and religion . . . nurtured by traditions of honor and virtue." So far as the city is concerned, that image is hopelessly shattered, said the Peoria bishop. "Lodging-houses were people sleep and eat are not homes.

Hired rooms which are changed from year to year, and often from month to month, are not homes." What one finds in these urban dwellings "is the grave of the family, not its home."

Such pessimistic assessments would certainly seize the attention of the city fathers (would it not?) so that they could correct the terrible housing, the intolerable levels of sanitation, the high rate of infant mortality, the explosion of prostitution, drunkenness, and major crime. Unfortunately, the city fathers were often part of, even agents of, the problem. Municipal corruption was widespread and seemingly built into the very structure of the city itself. Graft, greed, and partnership with crime afflicted the local governments and their agencies, this fact requiring religion to exercise whatever moral power it might.

42. Congregationalist Washington Gladden fought urban corruption and moral indifference close to home in Columbus, Ohio. *Library of Congress*

A Columbus, Ohio, Congregational pastor, Washington Gladden (1836–1918), realized that a voice crying in the wilderness (or even from the pulpit) might not be nearly so effective as a voice on the city council itself. He therefore, with "no special fitness" for the office, announced that he would run in 1900; he was elected and served for two years, educating himself to be sure but also bringing some measure of his own moral commitment to bear on the many problems that Columbus, like so many other American cities, confronted. He argued for public ownership of such utilities as water, lights, and gas, pointing out that these monopolies "furnish us with the necessaries of life; and monopolies of that nature must belong to the people." If we grant such power to a private corporation, Gladden noted, then we might as well give a private corporation the right to tax us as well.

Gladden identified two fundamental problems at the base of municipal evil. First, responsible citizens "think it bad form" to get involved in local politics, and "so long as anything resembling this is true, we shall, of course, have bad government in our cities." Second, city authorities were not so much corrupt as they were simply incompetent, and this to some degree prevailed at the level of state government as well. Major policy decisions "are generally in the hands of men who have no fitness to deal with them; and this is mainly because the men who have the necessary equipment for such work almost uniformly refuse to undertake it." Gladden not only set an example by serving on the city council; he wrote widely and well of the necessity of what he called *Applied Christianity: Moral Aspects of Social Questions* (1886); in this and some thirty-eight other books Gladden raised consciousness and conscience in a time when the nation so urgently needed men and women of good will and moral courage.

In Kansas City, Missouri, machine politics, under the direction of Thomas J. Pendergast, generally helped to give city government a bad name. Rabbi Samuel S. Mayerberg (1892–1964), on the other hand, tried to give the forces of religion a good name as he urged his own members as well as other religiously motivated people into organized battle against the Pendergast machine and all its flagrant violation of every principle of dignity, equity, and honesty. "The tyrants," Mayerberg reported, dominated not only all municipal life but had invaded private life as well. "People were actually told what physicians they might use, what lawyers might practice, what merchants might do business." All of this was carried on in close alliance between the affairs of the city and the bosses of the underworld. Every attempt was made to turn the rabbi aside in his reforming crusade. As he noted in his autobiography, "The racketeers began to fight back in their vicious ways": they tapped his telephone "in my Temple study"; they ransacked his files, stole the records of the resistant organization that Mayerberg had helped form, and tried to get members of his congregation to bring pressure upon him to quit the crusade; the racketeers "threatened me and attempted to bribe me." Like Gladden, Mayerberg found the entire experience difficult but educational, concluding that the only solution to such problems across the country was for honorable people, driven by "conscience and the power of religious conviction," to enlist in the battle against all forms of municipal corruption and cancerous greed.

In the neighboring state of Kansas, a Congregational pastor in Topeka tackled the problem of the city's sins in yet another way. In the place of sermons or civic service or crusading leagues, Charles M. Sheldon (1857–1946) wrote a novel: *In His Steps*, first published in 1897 and reprinted or serialized innumerable times thereafter. An all-time best-seller, this fairly simple story encouraged the modern city dweller to ask repeatedly, "What would Jesus do?" While this approach could have led to a mere repetition of the calls to private piety, Sheldon demonstrated a full awareness of the growing gap between rich and poor, the growing irrelevance of religion for those whose basic needs for food, clothing, and housing remained unmet, and the growing unwillingness of good churchpeople, "honorable people" in Mayerberg's phrase, to confront forthrightly the problems in their own neighborhoods, their own towns. "Every day I have more and more confidence," Sheldon told his congregation in 1895, "in the wonderful results which I believe God is going to bring about in the social and political life of the world." Such results will come, he added, as God "uses us who are Christians as instruments to do his great will."

In Chicago Jane Addams (1860–1935) founded her famous Hull House in 1889, this institution becoming the centerpiece of the Settlement House movement. Being a missionary to the city slum was not nearly so helpful as being a steady presence in that slum. As one reformer put it: "Suppose that the Lord, when he came on the earth, had come one day at a time and brought his lunch with him, and then gone home to heaven nights." To put the issue that way was to invite the answer: neighbor love can come only from a neighbor. So the settlement house arose in the midst of the tenements, among the neediest; there it became a school, a church, a library, a bathhouse, a theatre, an art gallery, a bank, a hospital, a refuge, a hope. Whatever it needed to be, that it became.

In Hull House, Jane Addams, in harmony with the Quaker principles of her father, determined to recognize the good in all persons, "even the meanest." One must be filled with "the overmastering belief that all that is noblest in life is common to men as men." Addams threw herself into the battle for social justice on a wide front, for women's rights and civil liberties, for child labor laws and for international peace. But the settlement movement in general and Hull House in particular remained her most influential commitment, a commitment which (as she wrote in *Philanthropy and Social Progress* in 1893) "will not waver when [the human] race happens to be represented by a drunken woman or an idiot boy." Those who reside in a settlement house "must be emptied of all conceit of opinion and all self-assertion. . . . They must be content to live quietly side by side with their neighbors until they grow into a sense of relationship and mutual interest." With a firm belief in the oneness of all humankind, Jane Addams argued that moral improvement must come to all, or it would surely come to none. Salvation is as certainly social as it is individual; the two cannot be divorced, and neither can be ignored. "Save our cities" was never her slogan; it was only her life.

THE FACTORY

In the turmoil of the Industrial Revolution, class struggles and class consciousness were born. Karl Marx's *Das Kapital*, written over the long period from 1867 to 1895, was one kind of response to the Revolution. The Social Gospel or Social Action of American religious institutions was another kind of response. Theologians and religiously motivated reformers—Protestants, Catholics, and Jews—joined in the effort to bring justice into the marketplace and the mill, to soften the antagonisms between capital and labor, to mitigate the cruelties of unemployment and grinding poverty. In the year of the Haymarket Riots (1886), Episcopal Bishop Frederic D. Huntington (1819–1904) noted that "Man has killed or maimed his fellow-man" only because he did not recognize the common humanity that bound them all. Brotherhood was more than a nice idea: it had become a necessary condition for survival in an industrialized world. In the contest between the rich and poor, the New York bishop observed, the duty of the church toward the latter is compellingly clear. In the New Testament itself, one must concede that "it is the rich and prosperous, not the less successful and disfavored, who are most severely denounced, most in danger of ruin, and most in need of a changed and watchful mind, and of a quickened conscience."

With so many of the nation's Roman Catholics recently arrived at the Atlantic shores, it is not surprising that Catholics constituted a large proportion of the laboring class. James Cardinal Gibbons (1834–1921) came to labor's defence, not only against the managerial and capitalist classes in America, but against European Catholic and Vatican attitudes as well. For laborers, especially when organized and potentially powerful, struck the conservative Catholic community abroad as a seedbed of radicalism and revolution, of socialism or communism. When the Knights of Labor (predominantly Catholic in membership) organized in 1869, Gibbons was forced to come to the defense of the very notion of a labor union of any sort. The exploitation of not only the laboring man but the laboring woman and child as well is evident to all, the Cardinal noted. In some airless, sunless tenement an entire family might have to work fourteen to sixteen hours a day, seven days a week, rolling cigars or sewing clothes, or whatever, just to earn, as a group, one barely living wage. Unsafe working conditions went uninspected, unrestrained. No insurance covered the worker injured on the job, no compensation came to him or her when unemployed, no independent arbitrator helped to determine a just or living wage.

Under such deplorable conditions, did not the laborer, particularly the Catholic laborer, have a right to organize, to unite? After all, Gibbons pointed out, association and organization are recognized as the most natural, the most just, the "most efficacious means" by which to attain any worthy public end. In the Knights of Labor, Catholics may be associated with Protestants, perhaps even with atheists or communists (as its enemies had charged). But, said Gibbons, this fact cannot be allowed to discredit the Knights of Labor, for Catholics in this country must at almost all times associate with those not of their own faith. "In a mixed people like ours, the separation of religious creeds in civil affairs is an impossibility." Even were it possible, it might not be desirable, for citizens need to work with and understand each other, not insulate themselves from all others. But most of all, Cardinal Gibbons pointed out to the Vatican in 1887, to condemn the Knights of Labor would be to risk "losing the love of the children of the Church, and of pushing them into an attitude of resistance against their Mother." The Catholic worker is obedient to the Church, but not blindly so.

43. Roman Catholic James Cardinal Gibbons defended labor's right to organize and to receive fair compensation for fair productivity. *Library of Congress*

Condemnation of the union would "be considered both false and unjust." Catholic laborers "love the Church, and they wish to save their souls, but they must also earn their living." For this just end, affiliation with a labor union is the appropriate means.

In Rochester, New York, a Baptist seminary professor, Walter Rauschenbusch (1861–1918), agreed that such unions were legitimate and necessary for the worker to achieve any measure of economic justice. True, labor unions exist to serve the interests of their members, but few people manage to pursue interests that transcend all limits of race or class, country or creed. "Why should we demand of one of the lowest classes, fighting on the borderland of poverty," Rauschenbusch inquired, "an unselfish devotion to all society which the upper classes have never shown?" The unions, he argued, stand "for human life against profits," while capitalism "makes the margin of life narrow in order to make the margin of profit wide." It is time, the Baptist reformer wrote in 1907, to turn the spiritual force of Christianity "against the materialism and mammonism of our industrial and social order." It is time to stop treating human beings as "things," things put to the dreary task of only producing more things. Jesus asked, Rauschenbusch noted, "Is not a man more than a sheep?" "Our industry says 'No.' It is careful of its live stock and machinery, and careless of its human working force."

Rauschenbusch was not encouraged by what appeared to him to be the indifference of many in the religious community to the fundamental problem. Modern day revivalists, he scornfully observed, produce only "skin deep changes. Things have simmered down to signing a card, shaking hands, or being introduced to the evangelist." A torn and bleeding society needed more than that; a hungry and exploited working class needed more than that. "It is the function of religion," Rauschenbusch wrote, "to teach the individual to value his soul more than his body, and his moral integrity more than his income." At the same time, however, it is equally the function of religion "to teach society to value human life more than property, and to value property only insofar as it forms the material basis for the higher development of human life." The Industrial Revolution is in danger of killing the goose that laid the golden egg, and "humanity is that goose." We have been taught that "man does not live by bread alone." Let us then have the courage of our religious faith, Rauschenbusch urged, to stand by that claim and to boldly assert it, to help our nation to understand that its true life consists not in the abundance of the things that it produces, "but in the way men live justly with one another and humbly with their God."

From Baltimore's Catholic Gibbons to Rochester's Baptist Rauschenbusch and across an entire spectrum of denominational life in between, advocates of social and economic justice dedicated themselves to shaming a whole nation—if that's what it took—into a greater faithfulness to both its religious heritage and its democratic promises. These advocates also dedicated themselves to speaking, insofar as possible, with a united voice, not allowing themselves to be lost or drowned out in the noise of an industrial boom. American religion was not yet in the position of having only a single voice, nor would it be a hundred years later, but early in the twentieth century it had begun to move away from every-increasing schism and separation. In 1908, some twelve million Protestants came together to form the Federal Council of Churches, this group taking as one of its first orders of business the adoption of a "Social Creed" that would emphasize "the mighty task of putting conscience and justice and love into a "Christian' civilization." The creed took stands that might have been radical in the first decade of the twentieth century, but would be thought of as tame and commonplace in the last decade of that century. With Methodists having often taken the lead in many of these areas of concern, the Federal Council followed them in calling for the abolition of child labor, the careful regulation of "toil for women" in order to "safeguard the physical and moral health of the community," the "release from employment one day in seven," and for "the principle of conciliation and arbitration in industrial dissensions." Radical then, commonplace now.

In 1918 the Central Conference of American Rabbis (Reform Judaism) also confronted that same "mighty task" of implementing conscience, justice, and love. Declaring that "the dignity of the individual soul before God cannot be lost sight of before men," the conference argued for a "fundamental reconstruction of our economic organization." But the rabbis, not content with generalities, proceeded to be specific in their call for reform, also advocating the abolition of child labor "and raising the standard of age wherever the legal age limit is lower than is consistent with moral and physical health." Workmen's compensation—a new phrase as well as a new idea—should be granted in the case of all "industrial accidents and occupational diseases." Labor's right "to organize and to bargain collectively" must be recognized, and a "minimum wage" must be established that would "insure for all workers a fair standard of living." The government should concern itself with proper housing, with "constructive care" of dependents, with some method of "social insurance" for "meeting the contingencies of unemployment and old age." Radical then, commonplace now.

World War I had helped to encourage united and responsible social responses on the part of Roman Catholics, just as it had among all of the nation's religious communities. A National Catholic War Council, formed in 1917, was created in specific response to the urgencies of war, of course, but it proved too useful an entity to be allowed to fade away once that war was over. Renamed the National Catholic Welfare Conference a few years later, this organization gave Catholicism a unity and a public voice which it had hitherto lacked in America. In 1919 the conference adopted the Bishop's Program of Social Reconstruction that called for "a reform in the spirit of both labor and capital." Under the guiding hand of Monsignor John A. Ryan (1869–1945), the bishops opposed child labor, advocated a minimum wage and vocational training, urged controls upon the rapidly rising cost of living, and declared that a "Christian view of work and wealth" would do much to ameliorate the industrial ills. There is such a thing, the bishops concluded, as a "human and Christian" ethics of industry; this rather than commercialism run wild must regulate as well as enrich our common life.

Because these socially sensitive, forward-looking statements were perceived as radical, they aroused strong opposition among persons of all religious persuasions, or of none. Preach the gospel, stick to the Bible, obey the popes, follow the Torah—many brakes were applied in the effort to keep religion from being applied where it hurt the pocketbooks of some, the politics of others, and the theology or ecclesiology of still others. But Protestants, Jews, and Catholics dedicated to reform were not readily turned aside or easily silenced. Their collective and courageous voices continued to be heard, heard long enough for the radical then to become the commonplace now.

WOMEN AND REFORM

After the Civil War women played an increasingly public role in social reform. Much of their effort was understandably aimed at increasing the voting privileges for women, but often joined to that suffrage movement (the Nineteenth Amendment finally passed in 1919) were such reformist matters as temperance, world peace, and civil liberties in general. The Woman's Christian Temperance Union (WCTU), organized in Ohio in 1874, endures as one of the best known manifestations of public reform directed by women. Frances E. Willard (1839–98) gave the Union its impetus and for nearly twenty years served as its president. Not only was the religious motivation made evident in the very name, but the official purposes emphasized the necessity of following scriptural injunctions to make one's body the "temple of the Holy Ghost." The WCTU, moreover, would "help forward the coming of Christ into all departments of life," correlating "New Testament religion with philanthropy" and the "church with civilization." Both nicotine and alcohol were identified as enemies to a purer and nobler spirituality.

By the second half of the nineteenth century, more and more Americans had concluded that the key to any successful social reform lay in organization. The WCTU, therefore, represented much more than a sentiment in favor of prohibition: it offered a "Plan of Work" that could "focus scattered influence and effort." Public sentiment would be reshaped by such techniques as these: mass meetings, wide circulation of temperance literature, school prizes for essays on the evil effects of alcoholic indulgence, "organizing temperance glee clubs of young people to sing temperance doctrines into the people's hearts as well as heads," and the like. Much attention has been given to the attack on saloons with axe in hand, Carry Nation style, but members of the WCTU wisely recognized that the real problem lay with the consumer, not the distributor. "If nobody would drink, then nobody would sell." "Dear sisters," warned the WCTU officers in 1874, "we have laid before you the plan of the long campaign." Hard realism, not soft sentiment, guided the effort; careful organization, not insular protests, made the effort count.

The Salvation Army was not the creation solely of women, though women assumed major leadership roles in the early years and again in the 1980s. Women also were as much in evidence as men, often more so, as the "hallelujah lasses" and "Sally Anns" played tambourine and trumpet, collected coins in their kettles, and "exhorted" as freely and frequently as the males. Organized in England in 1865 by William and Catherine Booth, the Army marched quickly across that island and soon set sail for North America. Evangeline Booth (1865–1950), daughter of the founders, served as field commissioner in the United States

44. In the period of World War I, the Salvation Army in the United States was directed by Evangeline Booth. *Library of Congress*

from 1904 to 1934 and as general of the whole international movement for some years thereafter. During her thirty-year leadership role in America, Booth helped the Army to win a reputation for social service that knew no limits, especially in serving "the lowest fallen, the most depraved, and the most neglected." The sick were visited, the hungry fed, the naked clothed, as charity—now organized and vigilant— alleviated the hardships that industrialization and urbanization brought.

Slum brigades fought filth and disease, while rescue homes for pros- titutes sprang up all across the nation. Services then provided by no other agency—legal advice, first aid, life insurance, even a missing per- sons department—were extended to all but seized with desperate ea- gerness by the "lowest fallen." Men roused at night from freight cars and empty wagons found their way to an Army shelter where "for ten cents a night, or its equivalent in work," the destitute could find sleep. Revivals were fine, one Army leader pointed out, but they appealed to the middle class churchgoer, while "the godless multitudes drifted past their doors." For those godless multitudes, other methods were re- quired and the Salvation Army demonstrated its capacity to develop those methods. The effective ministry of women, as Frederick Booth- Tucker readily acknowledged in 1899, was a vital ingredient in those new methods. Of their courage and skill, he wrote: "Problems that statesmanship and philanthropy have failed to solve have yielded to the gentle magic of these heroines of slumdom." Both their deeds and their words, "powerful in their simplicity, go straight to the hearts of their hearers and result in wonderful reformations."

In the Roman Catholic community, the emphasis upon woman's domestic role and her submission to male authority made participation in public social reform more difficult. Within the many orders of sisters, to be sure, one found great social sensitivity and service: to the ill, the poor, the illiterate, the orphaned, the fallen. Even there, however, the demands of teaching in the parish schools absorbed an increasing amount of the sisters' energies and commitment. Nuns labored in the nearly four thousand parochial schools that had been established by 1900, and to a lesser extent in private academies attended by both Cath- olic and non-Catholic children. They also served in over two hundred hospitals, frequently bearing the full administrative responsibility. In times of epidemic, as of cholera or yellow fever, as well as in times of war, the work of the women religious helped enormously not only the immediate objects of their solicitude but the reputation of the Catholic church at large for its charity and social commitment.

The path to public service for the Catholic laywomen was harder to establish. Writing in the *Catholic World* in 1893, Alice T. Toomy declared that there was a legitimate public sphere for Catholic women. A Cath- olic Women's Congress held that year in Chicago would permit a genuinely organized effort on behalf of "day nurseries and free kindergartens, protective and employment agencies for women, and clubs and homes for working girls." We are behind in these respects, Toomy noted, as "tens of thousands of our ablest Catholic women are working with the WCTU and other non-Catholic philanthropies, because they find no organization in their own church as a field for their activities." But in the very same issue of the *Catholic World* Toomy was answered

45. An 1874 Currier & Ives engraving emphasized the prominent role that women played in moral reform, especially with respect to alcohol.

by another Catholic female who asserted that it was settled "beyond question that women, as women, can have no vocation in public life."

Also in 1893 as part of the World's Parliament of Religions, a Congress of Jewish Women was formed, this group permitting a more collaborative participation of Jewish women in social and public reforms. Though largely attended by German Jews and though largely identified with Reform Judaism, the Congress (and its successor, the National Council of Jewish Women) found need for much social service to be rendered to Russian and largely Orthodox Jewry. As one speaker noted at the Congress, the history of Judaism is filled with women who rendered great service, both in the home and beyond. America's Jewish women, therefore should have no hesitation in playing significant public roles now. As Hannah Solomon (1858–1942) noted in 1897, the persecution that any woman may receive who places herself before the public is only a "sting" and lasts but a moment. Woman, she added with a touch of humor, must bear major burdens because instead of being created in the beginning out of dust, "the Lord waited until he could build her out of a strong, healthy, germproof bone." And so the germfree women in the National Council established schools, provided for manual and vocational training, established summer camps, encouraged philanthropy and in a host of other ways left their mark in the public sphere. Solving the problems of city and factory was everyone's task: male and female, religious and secular, new arrival and "old stock." But the magnitude of the problems became apparent at the same time that women were finding their voice and were about to find their vote. Thus, a happy partnership between women and reform accelerated a process that, even so, often seemed to move with frustrating deliberation.

EXTENDING RELIGION'S REACH

Religion in America had, since the earliest years of the nineteenth century, made a virtue out of voluntarism: that is, out of the necessity for the churches and synagogues themselves, not the government, to see that the related causes of religion and morality and human help were advanced. Ecclesiastical institutions did much more than just look after their own survival, pay their own bills, and care for their own members. Churches saw themselves as supply depots for—rather than as cozy retreats from—the needs of all those passing hurriedly by their doors. To serve those needs, perhaps ever more organization and initiative were required.

A distinctly American enterprise, the Knights of Columbus, beginning in 1882 as a kind of group insurance venture, soon included education, charity, and social service among its concerns. Under the leadership of Patrick H. Callahan (1865–1940), the Knights during World

War I operated over three hundred recreational centers for servicemen in the States and a like number abroad. But this was only a single dimension of the far-flung enterprises in which the Roman Catholic Knights were engaged. Himself a layman, Callahan encouraged other laymen to experiment with profit-sharing between management and labor. He served on the National Child Labor Commission and worked for greater racial understanding and for better relationships between Catholics and the nation's other religious groups. Meanwhile, the Knights of Columbus grew to over 300,000 members by the time of World War I, even spinning off a parallel women's society, the Daughters of Isabella.

The Catholic Young Men's National Union, formed in 1875, offered wholesome recreation, night school education, and vocational training, arguing that it made much more sense to assist the young before problems developed, not afterward. Similar ministries to young women were provided by the Sisters of Charity, the Sisters of Mercy, the Sisters of St. Joseph, among others. Finally, a National Conference of Catholic Charities, founded in 1910, coordinated much of the scattered efforts on behalf of improving society and the lot of those trapped by some of its impersonal cruelties. That conference, whose formation had been encouraged by a Catholic University sociologist, also represented a growing professionalism, as opposed to casual happenstance, in the area of religious good will.

That professionalism had been encouraged when, soon after the Civil War, the Catholic hierarchy issued a Pastoral Letter that commended "the great increase among us of Societies and Associations"; from these newly formed groups the bishops anticipated "the most beneficial results to the cause of morality and religion." They commended in particular the Society of St. Vincent de Paul, a lay organization that began in France but moved to the United States in 1845. By 1865, the Society had seventy-five chapters or conferences in this country, indicating the strength of motivation as well as the size of society's needs. Industrial schools and boarding homes gave youth the security, the training, and the religious discipline that would enable them to live productive and fulfilling lives. But the Society also, like the Salvation Army, gathered donations wherever it could in order to offer help wherever it must.

Protestant agencies also sometimes originated abroad, frequently to find in America the most inviting fields for labor. The Young Men's and Young Women's Christian Associations (popularly, simply the "Y") had their beginnings in England before the Civil War, but their most dramatic development in the United States after that conflict. Working first among the very poor, the Ys offered housing and job training, helped find employment, provided recreation and reading material for the lonely and bored. Evangelism was very much a part of the early Y activity, as efforts to win converts were made in jails, hospitals, poor-houses, rescue missions, and even among the sailors temporarily in port. Religious tracts, printed inexpensively, were scattered like seed in the hope of reaping a harvest of newly enlisted young people. But evangelism was never interpreted in narrow terms. Young people simply had to be helped, whatever the problem, whatever the means for its solution. One enterprising YMCA director, James Naismith, in desperation even invented the game of basketball in order to provide some indoor activity for his youth during the long winter months.

Similarly, Young Men's and Young Women's Hebrew Associations arose in the nineteenth century, working at first with German Jewish youth but soon finding themselves called upon to meet mushrooming needs as immigrant numbers swelled. Then the YMHA and the YWHA assisted in the difficulties of adjustment and assimilation, but always with special attention to and concern for the young. Just as World War I prompted the Roman Catholic community to "get organized" in order to respond more systematically to the nation's needs, so the Jewish Welfare Board was created to help advise the government on the choice of Jewish chaplains for the army. The very word "welfare," however, suggested the utility of a group that might be able to speak for all of American Jewry in certain matters of public interest.

The temperance issue, highlighted by the WCTU but shared by many others beyond its ranks, reached a political climax with the passage of the Eighteenth Amendment in 1917. That reality was made possible, once again, only by organization, in this instance the Anti-Saloon League formed in 1895. For over twenty years, the League supported politicians who would vote "dry," vigorously opposed all "wets" running for office. Individual churches had for decades been engaged in gathering pledges from those who would forswear the drinking of all alcohol. Then, the attempt was made to shut down the saloons, but none of this had really worked, a League Superintendent explained. Moral suasion has had its turn; now it was time for political compulsion. The League was formed in the conviction that "in most communities there were more anti-saloon than there were pro-saloon votes, and if the great mass of anti-saloon votes could be organized, the power of the saloon in politics would be broken." The League began its recruitment with the churches, especially the Methodists, arguing that the church must conquer the saloon or else be conquered by it. Passed at the end of 1917, the Eighteenth Amendment won ratification by early 1919. Fourteen years later, the Twenty-First Amendment brought the "noble experiment" to an end.

But by that time, religion was heavily involved in many other experiments of more enduring effect. Municipal corruptions had been cleaned up in city after city, many a reformer recognizing the critical assistance rendered by priests, ministers, and rabbis; by laymen and laywomen from many communities of faith. Also by that time, many of the grossest excesses of the Industrial Revolution had been curbed and a legitimate role for government recognized. Ecclesiastical bodies, moreover, now routinely had their Departments of Social Justice or their Social Action Committees or their Welfare Councils and Conferences. Many problems defied solution, of course, or arose in a somewhat altered form in later years. War did not vanish, racism did not disappear, equitable distribution of wealth proved elusive, and moral progress became harder and harder to demonstrate. Churches and synagogues climbed each hill only to find a still higher one in the road ahead.

Suggested Reading for Part Three

For primary material relating to the discussions in Part Three, see the Gaustad *Documentary*, Vol. 1, 259–524; Vol. 2, 1–199. Other source material for the nineteenth century may be found in Rosemary R. Ruether and Rosemary S. Keller, eds., *Women and Religion in America*, Vol. 1; in John Tracy Ellis, *Documents of American Catholic History* (Milwaukee, 1962; rev. ed., Chicago, 1967); and, Morris U. Schappes, *Documentary History of the Jews in the United States, 1654–1875* (New York, 1971).

For the early years of the republic, see Edwin S. Gaustad, *Faith of Our Fathers: Religion and the New Nation* (San Francisco, 1987). For particular attention to the origins and implications for religion of the First Amendment, one may turn to Thomas J. Curry, *The First Freedoms: Church and State in America to the Passage of the First Amendment* (New York, 1986); and, Leonard W. Levy, *The Establishment Clause: Religion and the First Amendment* (New York, 1986). See also the engagingly written work by William Lee Miller, *The First Liberty: Religion and the Republic* (New York, 1986). Madison's critical contributions in this area are explored in the anthology edited by Robert S. Alley, *James Madison on Religious Liberty* (Buffalo, N.Y., 1985). The role of Unitarianism is carefully documented in Sydney E. Ahlstrom and Jonathan S. Carey, eds., *An American Reformation* (Middletown, Conn., 1985).

The many religious experiments along the frontier and behind that westward advance have received much attention. A recent volume by R. Laurence Moore, *Religious Outsiders and the Making of Americans* (New York, 1986) helps to correct the imbalance resulting from too great a concentration on the "mainline" religious groups. Lawrence Foster explores the Shakers, the Mormons, and the Oneida Community in *Religion and Sexuality* (New York, 1981); related to his perspective is the earlier volume by Raymond Lee Muncy, *Sex and Marriage in Utopian Communities* (Baltimore, Md., 1974). John Humphrey Noyes is the subject of Robert D. Thomas's study, *The Man Who Would Be Perfect* (Philadelphia, 1977), while William Miller is the focal point of the important work edited by Ronald L. Numbers and Jonathan M. Butler, *The Dis-*

appointed: Miller and Millernarianism in the Nineteenth Century (Blooming-ton, Ind., 1987). On that most successful of the utopian colonies, one may rely on Leonard J. Arrington and Davis Bitton, *The Mormon Experience: A History of the Latter-day Saints* (New York, 1979), and the reader will be stimulated by Jan Shipps' interpretive work, *Mormonism: The Story of a New Religious Tradition* (Urbana, Ill., 1985). Two recent biographical studies by able historians should be noted: Richard L. Bushman, *Joseph Smith and the Beginnings of Mormonism* (Urbana, Ill., 1984); and, Leonard J. Arrington, *Brigham Young: American Moses* (New York, 1986). The Restorationist movement is revealed as a major theme of America's history in Richard T. Hughes and C. Leonard Allen, *Illusions of Innocence* (Chicago, 1988).

Revivalism, very much a part of the western frontier, was not limited to the West. The career of Lyman Beecher, instructive in this regard, can be followed in Stuart C. Henry's *Unvanquished Puritan* (Grand Rapids, Mich., 1973), and more broadly in Marie Caskey's *Chariot of Fire: Religion and the Beecher Family* (New Haven, Conn., 1978). Peter Cartwright's *Autobiography*, first published in Nashville in 1856, was reissued by Abingdon Press a century later. Finney's important impact on American culture may be best seen in the survey of *Modern Revivalism* by William G. McLoughlin (New York, 1959). For a good general discussion of religion on the frontier, see Charles A. Johnson, *Frontier Camp Meeting* (Dallas, 1955). That revivalism was not a Protestant monopoly is made evident by Jay P. Dolan in his *Catholic Revivalism: The American Experience, 1830–1900* (Notre Dame, Ind., 1978). I. H. Scharfman's *Jews on the Frontier* (Chicago, 1977) should be read along with Ira Rosenwaike's rich demographic study, *On the Edge of Greatness: A Portrait of American Jewry in the Early National Period* (Cincinnati, 1985). For a particularly insightful study of evangelical religion in the South, among both black and white segments of the population, see Donald G. Mathews, *Religion in the Old South* (Chicago, 1977); and for the much-vexed confrontation between Indian and missionary, consult Henry W. Bowden, *American Indians and Christian Missions: Studies in Cultural Conflict* (Chicago, 1981).

C. C. Goen's *Broken Churches, Broken Nation* (Macon, Ga., 1985) spells out how the denominational separations ominously foretold the political events to follow. Donald G. Mathews, *Slavery and Methodism: A Chapter in American Morality, 1780–1845* (Princeton, 1965) follows a single ecclesiastical tradition through its dark passage, while H. Shelton Smith's book, *In His Image . . . But: Racism in Southern Religion, 1780–1910* (Durham, N.C., 1972) offers a broader sweep, both chronologically and denominationally. Thanks to Albert J. Raboteau, we now have a much better understanding of *Slave Religion: The Invisible Institution in the Antebellum South* (New York, 1978) than ever before. And thanks to editor William L. Andrews, we have valuable primary material in his

Three Black Women's Autobiographies of the Nineteenth Century (Blooming-ton, Ind., 1986). Gerda Lerner's *The Grimké Sisters from South Carolina* (New York, 1971) nicely demonstrates the interrelationships between women's rights in particular and human rights in general. The religious consequences of the Civil War for the South are illuminated in Charles R. Wilson, *Baptized in Blood* (Athens, Ga., 1980). The most recent ac-count of black Baptist development, both before and after the war, is James M. Washington, *Frustrated Fellowship* (Macon, Ga., 1986).

Jay P. Dolan has given us the best account of immigration and its impact on American Catholicism in his *The Immigrant Church* (Baltimore, Md., 1975); but also see his general survey, *The American Catholic Ex-perience* (Garden City, N.Y., 1985). The story of the Knights of Colum-bus is fully told in Christopher J. Kauffman, *Faith & Fraternalism* (New York, 1982). On Chinese immigration, S. C. Miller, *Unwelcome Immi-grants* (Berkeley, Calif., 1969) is useful, while the article by Carlos E. Cortes on "Mexicans" will be helpful on south-of-the border move-ment: *Harvard Encyclopedia of American Ethnic Groups* (Cambridge, Mass., 1980). The best historical understanding of Judaism's denomi-national divisions can be found in Marc Lee Raphael, *Profiles in Amer-ican Judaism* (San Francisco, 1984). James F. Findlay's biography, *Dwight L. Moody: American Evangelist, 1837–1899* (Chicago, 1969) will supple-ment the McLoughlin survey cited above. Josiah Strong can be readily approached through the modern edition of his classic, *Our Country*, edited by Jergen Herbst (Cambridge, Mass., 1963). For the World's Par-liament of Religion and concomitant developments, the best contextual study is that of Martin E. Marty, *Modern American Religion*, Vol. 1 (Chi-cago, 1986).

Henry F. May *Protestant Churches and Industrial America* (New York, 1949) may be read along with the anthology edited by Robert T. Handy, *The Social Gospel in America, 1870–1920* (New York, 1966). With respect to Catholicism, Aaron I. Abell and David J. O'Brien serve as useful guides, the former in *American Catholicism and Social Action* (New York, 1960), and the latter in *American Catholicism and Social Reform* (New York, 1968). Similar developments in Judaism can be followed in Albert Vorspan and E. J. Lipman, *Justice and Judaism: The Work of Social Action* (New York, 1959). Recent biographies of social activists include Ruth Bordin, *Francis Willard* (Chapel Hill, N.C., 1986) and Timothy Miller, *Following in His Steps: A Biography of Charles M. Sheldon* (Knoxville, Tenn., 1987). A history of the Salvation Army in the United States is provided by Herbert A. Wisbey, Jr., *Soldiers Without Swords* (New York, 1955). *Women in American Religion*, edited by Janet Wilson James, con-tains helpful chapters on "Catholic Women Religious," "Protestant Women's Missionary Careers," and "Transitions in Judaism: The Jew-ish American Woman" (Philadelphia, 1980).

Part 4

RELIGION IN AN AGE OF EMPIRE

CHAPTER 18

The Church and the World

In the last two decades of the nineteenth century and the first four of the twentieth, the United States of America entered upon the world stage in a way that had not been true in the first century of its history as a nation. The country engaged in war well beyond its own borders, participated in international congresses and conferences, acquired territories and new responsibilities in the Pacific Ocean, and rediscovered and reaffirmed the Monroe Doctrine which in effect declared the entire Western Hemisphere to be uniquely an American concern. The United States had come of age.

So had its churches and synagogues. The boundaries of the parish now extended to the whole world as missionary movements stretched around the globe, as religious destiny often merged with Manifest Destiny. Municipal reform and factory safety continued as legitimate concerns, but religious institutions raised their sights beyond the local and near-at-hand to take in the whole continent, still being explored and settled, as well as the whole world, now being embraced and served. The command to "Go ye therefore unto all the world" had enjoyed a special standing in Christian history for eighteen centuries or more. In the closing years of the nineteenth century, those words acquired a special force and a timely relevance.

EMPIRE OR REPUBLIC?

In 1898 the United States annexed the Hawaiian Islands, for the first time adding to its domain territory far removed from the North American continent. That annexation resulted from a combination of national and commercial interests, but it also represented a culmination of religious and cultural ties dating back to the 1820s when New England dispatched Congregational missionaries to this Pacific outpost. Once drawn into the American orbit, Hawaii contributed dramatically to a religious pluralism that moved well beyond the more familiar contours of Judaism and Christianity. As the country established a foothold in the Pacific, so Buddhism, Confucianism, and Shinto established a significant port of embarkation for the mainland of America.

221

Even more dramatic was the Spanish-American War of that same year, a war entered into at least in part to rescue Cuba from the inhumanitarian treatment at the hands of a harsh Spanish regime. Of course, imperialism joined with loftier motivations to create a public mood that seemed ready for war. If Social Gospel advocates could resist cruelty and exploitation at home, many of them saw no reason to ignore cruelty and exploitation abroad, especially when that "abroad" lay only ninety miles off the coast of Florida. America had both a duty and a destiny, it was argued, to grant Cubans the same right of self-governance that Americans had themselves won more than a hundred years earlier. Understandably, Spain felt otherwise, the certain consequence being a declaration of war in April of 1898. Responding swiftly with its own declaration of war, the United States moved its navy with surprising effectiveness against Spain not only in Cuba but as well in the far distant Philippine Islands. In a few months, the "splendid little war" (as Secretary of State John Hay called it) was over; in those few months the United States entered into a new phase of its existence.

What was that phase to be called? More importantly, was this young nation about to follow the unhappy model of ancient Rome, leaving behind the virtues and restraints of its years as a republic to become now a greedy, grasping, and ultimately unvirtuous empire? This haunting question inspired heated public debate in which religious leaders were vocal and visible participants. To the general question of whether America should now become a conquering power imposing its will on other peoples, a more narrow question was raised with respect to the Philippines: namely, should this territory, essentially Roman Catholic, be subject to Protestant as well as American conquest? Should Protestant missionaries be allowed or even encouraged by the government to turn the Filipino people away from their old religious loyalty at the same time they were being encouraged to abandon their old political loyalty to Spain?

President William McKinley (1843–1901), an earnest Methodist, gave a religious spin to the public debate when he declared that through prayer he came to see that it was the nation's duty "to uplift and civilize and Christianize [the Filipinos], and by God's grace, do the very best we could by them, as our fellow men for whom Christ also died." But many church leaders needed little encouragement to see the American victory as an opportunity to spread American Protestantism to an ignorant and deluded people, whether in the Pacific or in the Atlantic. Congregational editor and clergyman, Lyman Abbott (1835–1922), viewed the Spanish-American War as altogether noble, a war that required neither apology nor defense. "We fought the American Revolution to free ourselves," Abbott explained, "the Civil War to free a people whom we had helped to enslave." This latest war, he concluded, was waged "to free a people to whom we owed no other duty than that of a big nation to an oppressed neighbor."

Well, perhaps, there was one other duty: namely, to rescue these poor people from the oppressions of Catholicism at the same time that they were rescued from the cruelties of Spain. Presbyterian missionary executive, Arthur J. Brown (1856–1963), argued that the old regime of the Philippines was of a single piece: the government, the educational system, the imposed national religion of Spain. To overthrow one was to overthrow all. Besides, Brown noted, Protestant missionaries did not thrust Protestantism upon the native population, nor did they depend on taxation or on the civil arm of government to enforce their doctrines. All was voluntary. "The Protestant Churches of the United States rely wholly upon moral suasion and the intrinsic power of the truths which they inculcate." Surely, no one could object to that.

Roman Catholics, however, could and did object, both on the grounds of the nation's moral posture in the war itself and on the grounds of a genuine religious liberty for the Filipinos. Arguing the first point, Bishop John Lancaster Spalding (1840–1916) of Peoria, Illinois cautioned against allowing an unquenchable thirst for expansion and empire to alter the fundamental character of the nation. We have stood for liberty, he explained, and, by the power of our example, may

46. Key figures in the Spanish-American War of 1898 gathered in Washington, D. C. soon after the war ended: President William McKinley, James Cardinal Gibbons, Admiral George Dewey. *Keystone-Mast Collection, UC—Riverside*

encourage others to seek liberty for themselves. Yet "we have never looked upon ourselves as predestined to subdue the earth," the bishop declared, nor are we obliged "to compel other nations, with sword and shell, to accept our rule." Our own articles of faith, derived from the Declaration of Independence and the Constitution, have bestowed great blessings upon the American people, "but we have never dreamed that they were articles to be exported and thrust down unwilling throats at the point of the bayonet."

Beyond the question of empire or republic, other Catholics rejected the notion that the Philippine Islands were now proper missionary fields for American Protestants. In Minneapolis, Archbishop John Ireland (1838–1918) took issue with action that seemed to him contrary to the spirit of the nation's commitment to freedom in religion. "As a Catholic," Ireland pointed out in 1899, "I cannot approve of any efforts

47. Archbishop John Ireland of Minneapolis defended the right of Philippine Catholics to continue undisturbed in the practice of their religion. *Library of Congress*

of Protestants to affect the religious duties of the inhabitants of the islands." Imagine the Protestant reaction were the situation reversed, Ireland suggested. Would Protestants rejoice to see Catholic missionaries sent *en masse* to a solidly Protestant land? "Now, as an American I will no less object to efforts to implant Protestantism in those islands." Besides, Ireland added, it is not prudent policy from the nation's point of view. Spain will say to her former subjects that they have lost more than their civil government: "they are also taking away your religion." In fact, "if I were America's enemy today, I would say to American Protestants," Archbishop Ireland observed, "Hurry your missionaries to Cuba, to Puerto Rico, and the Philippines, and have them tell the inhabitants of those islands that their historic faith is wrong." No swifter or surer way could be found, he concluded, to turn these populations against the United States and make its very flag a symbol of cruel oppression and religious tyranny.

Like the mythical Paul Bunyan, the United States had taken giant steps across the earth. But how steady and sure were those steps, religious and political leaders asked. And did they represent points of no return in the transformation of an agrarian republic into a military-industrial imperial power? In less than a generation the nation was plunged into another war, neither so splendid nor so limited. And if it was a case of Western civilization's ethnocentricity to call it a "world war," it was for the United States another bold step onto a far wider stage. In that brutal struggle, what role would religion in America be called upon to play?

A WORLD AT WAR

In August of 1914 England and France along with their allies declared war against Germany and the Austro-Hungarian Empire and their allies. Americans, forgetting that they had stepped half-way across the globe, initially took comfort in the fact, or the feeling, that this war was so very far away. They also, under the leadership of President Woodrow Wilson (1856–1924), a steadfast Presbyterian, took comfort in the promise of a neutrality that would give the United States a special role in helping to negotiate a lasting peace, once the cannons stopped their deafening roar and the submarines ceased their menacing prowl. The United States was enough of an ethnic medley that partisans on both sides of the conflict had their American supporters. Gradually, however, public sentiment—with Wilson again in the lead—shifted to the side of Great Britain. By 1917 World War I was neither far away nor of purely theoretical interest to Americans.

As in the instance of the Spanish-American War, religious leaders in 1917 were divided in the manner and degree of their support for the war effort. Lines this time, however, were not drawn along Protestant-

Catholic divisions, but along divisions with regard to the moral worth of war and of its long-term consequences. Does war make "the world safe for democracy" or does war, by its very nature, make men and women more barbaric, more inhumane, more prone to tyranny or revenge? Some religious leaders, especially those involved in the moral crusades of the Progressive movement, could be persuaded that war was an even greater, more glorious crusade. Wilson helped build this sentiment by declaring that the United States had no selfish interest in going to war: it sought no territory, it sought no compensation for losses already suffered or to be suffered. We go to war, Wilson said, to fight for the rights of mankind. "We shall be satisfied when those rights have been made as secure as the faith and freedom of nations can make them." A high purpose of this sort made it necessary to abandon neutrality, to surrender for the moment one's dedication to pacifist principles.

The abandonment of a religious pacifism did not come easily. Unitarian minister, John Haynes Holmes (1879–1964), in 1915 denounced all war as a "foul business." "From the standpoint of things spiritual as well as of things material," Holmes declared, "war is the antithesis of life. Its one end is to destroy." We talk of noble purposes and high ideals, but (said Holmes) "No man is wise enough, no nation is important enough, no human interest is precious enough, to justify the wholesale destruction and murder which constitutes the essence of war." A good friend of Holmes' and fellow-clergyman in New York City, Rabbi Stephen Wise (1874–1949), shared these strong views. In 1915 Wise wrote to President Wilson to condemn what seemed a steady build-up of a war mentality. We need to prepare for peace, not for war, Wise advised, adding: "I should not, my dear President, have written in this way nor would I burden you with my thought on this question if I did not feel conscience bound to dissent in pulpit and on platform from your position."

John Haynes Holmes had spoken of "the wholesale destruction" that modern warfare entailed. So indeed it did, as those closest to the conflict quickly discovered. Submarine warfare had indiscriminately murdered men, women, and children—combatant and noncombatant alike. Poison gas introduced new levels of horror; where it did not destroy, it maimed for life. Trench warfare, incredibly costly in the number of lives lost, reduced war from a theatre of romantic glamour to a ditch of filth, stench, disease, terror, and death. Yet another New York clergyman, Harry Emerson Fosdick (1878–1969), had by 1917 heard all about the "glory of war" that he was prepared to endure. Anyone who speaks of war that way, Fosdick asserted, "is morally unsound." We paint war in bright colors, Fosdick said, along with "rhythmic movement" and the "thrilling music of the military parade." But that is not war. "War now is dropping bombs from aeroplanes and killing women and children in their beds; it is shooting, by telephonic orders, at an unseen place miles away and slaughtering invisible men; it is murdering innocent travelers on merchant ships with torpedoes from unknown submarines." Who can dare call this kind of war a "crusade"—literally a bearing of the cross?

But even greater numbers of clergymen, like the public at large, did lend voice and energy to America's participation in the nation's first "world" war. Some even went far beyond a dedication to Wilsonian idealism to a vilification of the enemy, especially of Germany. Lyman Abbott despaired of any reform on the part of the German people, despaired of any solution except extermination. The German is my enemy, said another Protestant clergyman, because he "is a robber, a murderer, a destroyer of homes, a pillager of churches, a violator of women. I do well," this minister added, to hate an enemy like that. With a mixture of motives and with varying degrees of restraint, the majority of church members, like the majority of their leaders, fell into the ranks of those marching on to war.

Historic peace churches, that is those churches who throughout their history had made pacifism an article of faith, continued to stand strong, though their numbers were small. Church of the Brethren, the Moravian Church in America, Adventists, Quakers, and others were chiefly responsible for the over sixty thousand young men who, on the grounds of conscience, claimed exemption from the Selective Service Act of 1917. Not all of these were granted conscientious objector status, of course, and many of those who did receive such status were encouraged nonetheless to accept some position in the armed services that did not require their taking or threatening human life. Many served in such auxiliary efforts as the medical or engineering or quartermaster agencies. In 1917 the leading Quaker philosopher and historian, Rufus Jones (1863–1948), helped to form the American Friends

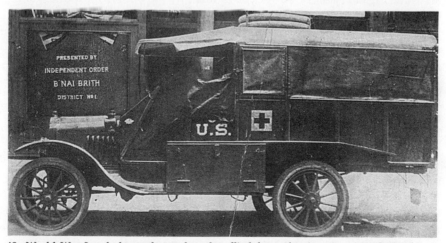

48. World War I ambulance donated to the allied forces by American members of B'nai B'rith. *B'nai B'rith, Washington, D. C.*

Service Committee, a group that aided Quakers (and many others) to stand firm in their testimonies for peace but that also encouraged active humanitarian activity both in the United States and abroad.

War, particularly large-scale war, requires activity to be organized and centralized. Religion in America, more than at any previous time, found it necessary during the First World War to speak and act with some degree of unity. Roman Catholics, for example, gathered in Washington, D. C., in 1917 in a general convention, the immediate consequence of which was the creation of a National Catholic War Council (as noted in Chapter Seventeen). Such a council could supervise the recruitment and training of Catholic chaplains as well as oversee the less formal ministries to young Catholics in military uniform. After the war was over, the newly named National Catholic Welfare Council (later Conference) took on far broader tasks: supervising Catholic education, "improving social conditions in accordance with the spirit of the Church," developing additional agencies among the laity, and promoting a more vigorous missionary program. As the Catholic bishops made clear in their Pastoral Letter of 1919, the overall purpose now far exceeded the narrow ones of the war; the new council would "promote more effectually the glory of God, the interests of His Church, and the welfare of the country."

Similarly, American Judaism, divided into varying theological orientations and among hundreds of largely self-ruled congregations, made some moves toward closer cooperation during World War I. Formal organization, however, did not come until 1926 when the Synagogue Council of America was born. Its purposes were explicitly announced in the preamble to the council's constitution: namely,

That a Council composed of representatives of national congregational and rabbinical organizations of America be formed, for the purpose of speaking and acting unitedly in furthering such religious interests as the constituent organizations in the council have in common . . .

Within a few years, the Synagogue Council estimated that its membership contained about sixty-five percent of all Jewish ministers in America, and that (as the council declared in 1931) "religious Israel had found a voice." Just as Catholics could speak with some degree of unity on matters of public policy and social welfare, so now could religious Jewry. Protestants, at least a large number of them, had found their public voice a decade or two earlier.

In 1908 thirty Protestant denominations created the Federal Council of Churches in order to "bring the Christian bodies in America into united service for Christ and the world." Protestants, of course, had the largest task of all, for schism and separation had by the beginning of the twentieth century seemed to be the most obvious feature of American Protantism. With pressures for unity increasing on the political level, it was time, or well passed the time, for larger unity at the ecclesiastical level. Over twelve million Protestants coming together for common tasks in 1908 represented an important first step toward unity; at the very least, it represented a reversal of a trend toward proliferation that apparently knew no limit. This Protestant organization, moreover, like its Catholic and Jewish counterparts, saw its role not so much to influence the affairs of the local congregation as to confront the challenges before the nation as a whole: war and peace, labor and capital, rich and poor, "equal rights and complete justice for all men in all stations of life," to quote from the council's 1908 "Social Creed of the Churches."

National life, especially during war time, dramatized the need for greater unity among the many scattered synagogues and churches. Once that unity was achieved in ecclesiastical terms, it managed to endure well beyond the war that gave it impetus. What did not endure was the idealism that Woodrow Wilson and others bestowed upon World War I itself. The decade of the 1920s constituted, in so many respects, a time of discouragement and disillusionment so far as heady optimism and grand dreams were concerned. A major element in the Wilsonian dream as early as 1916, the League of Nations came into being in 1919 as part of the treaty which brought the war to a formal end. The League was designed, above all else, to preserve peace. This it ultimately failed to do, but where it (and Wilson) failed immediately was in winning the support of the U. S. Congress and of many elements of the American public. This was the case even though the influential Church Peace Union (founded in 1914) favored the League by a proportion of twenty to one, even though the Federal Council of Churches cabled Wilson when he was in Paris that the League was the "political expression of the Kingdom of God on earth." Many others, however, saw the League as a way of perpetuating American involvement in those entangling alliances against which George Washington had warned. And so Wilson suffered the bitter disappointment of seeing even his own country turn its back on his last, best hope. The League, he had told the Senate on July 10, 1919, inspires the United States "to yet higher levels of service and achievement." Destiny calls us, he added, "by no plan of our conceiving, but by the hand of God who has led us into this way." But it was not to be. If a crusade at all, this world war, like those great crusades centuries earlier to retake Jerusalem and other holy places, would be remembered mainly for what it failed to accomplish.

Among other things, it failed to polish the moral reputation of war. In the years that followed the Treaty of Versailles, pacifism won a new respectability and popularity—and not just among those smaller "peace churches." Now large numbers of mainline Protestants along with many Catholics and Jews saw war as an unacceptable means for settling the conflicts and competition among nations. A Disciples of Christ minister, Kirby Page (1890–1957), in 1921 helped create the Fellowship for a Christian Social Order, the cardinal principle of such an order being that men and women (in the words of the old spiritual) "ain't gonna study war no more." More than twenty thousand clergymen in America petitioned President Warren Harding (1865–1923) to call a conference on international disarmament, with the result that such a conference was gathered in Washington on November 12, 1921. Promptly, churches and synagogues named November 6 as a day of prayer for peace and for all the delegates chosen for the Disarmament Conference.

Under the leadership of Secretary of State Charles Evans Hughes (1862–1948), a Baptist layman of note, the conference did not content itself with passing idle resolutions or appointing commissions for further study. It proposed actual disarmament according to a specific schedule, with the destruction of specific weapons and the sinking of a stated number of naval ships. Having learned their lesson from the rejection of the League of Nations, the nation's religious membership prayed, preached, lobbied, and maintained a keen public interest until the U. S. Senate ratified the resolutions of the conference. Hopes rose even higher in 1928 when the Briand-Kellogg peace treaty (Pact of Paris) resulted in fifteen nations renouncing war as an instrument of national policy. The agreement, Southern Methodists asserted, was illumined by "the light that shone in Bethlehem." Everywhere it seemed that peace was about to break out, and everywhere religious forces gave hand and heart to the pacifist effort.

In 1936 the General Conference of the Methodist Church officially pronounced war as "the greatest social sin of modern times." Even more strongly, the conference declared that "the Methodist Episcopal Church as an institution does not endorse, support, or purpose to participate in war." The Northern Baptist Convention agreed that war was "the supreme social sin," adding that as long as nations resort to war "there can be no safety for our homes or for our civilization and no realization of the kingdom of heaven on earth." A conference in London, representing worldwide Anglicanism, including this nation's Episcopalians, pointed out that just as "Christian conscience has condemned infanticide and slavery and torture, it is now called to condemn war as an outrage on the fatherhood of God and the brotherhood of all mankind." Congregationalists proclaimed: "The church is through with war!" Universalists declared that the Quakers had been right all along, and it was now time for all other churches to join them in "conscientious objection to all war." Disciples of Christ members, in convention assembled, pronounced war to be "destructive of the spiritual values for which the churches of Christ stand," and—like the Methodists—they would "serve notice to whom it may concern that we never again expect to bless or sanction war."

Without question, the First World War had done little or nothing to redeem the notion of war. Quite the contrary. But pacifism, explained

Quaker Rufus Jones, is not mere passivity. Pacifism, he wrote, "is not a theory; it is a way of life. It is something you *are and do*." So, what would the churches do? What would they become? The answer to those questions rested, to a great degree, upon the energies and undertakings of the missionary movement.

MISSIONS ABROAD

Even with a continent to conquer and with millions of immigrants to convert, Protestants in the nineteenth century found energy and resources to send missionaries abroad. The Student Volunteer Movement (SVM), for example, originating in 1886 as a device for recruiting missionary volunteers on college campuses, grew to prominence and surprising strength by the early decades of the twentieth century. Assuming leadership of the SVM soon after its founding, John R. Mott (1865–1955), a tireless Methodist layman, in 1895 created the World's Student Christian Federation and helped prepare for a World Missionary Conference held in Edinburgh in 1910. The organizational bustle was more than mere bureaucratic busy work: it pointed to a vision that was indeed worldwide, to an intention to scale all walls—linguistic, cultural, political—in the name of the Christian cause.

Mott had the pleasure of seeing some of his organizational structure duplicated in Britain, Holland, Germany, Norway, Sweden, Denmark, Finland, Switzerland, and South Africa. By the time of World War I, the SVM had sent out more than five thousand volunteers; in 1920 alone, the number reached twenty-seven hundred. Mott also had the pleasure of seeing his optimism, neatly capsuled in the title of his book *The Evangelization of the World in This Generation* (1900), widely shared in the Western world. Noting the growing hostility between nations and races in 1914, Mott declared that "The only program which can meet all the alarming facts of the situation is the worldwide spread of Christianity in its purest form." It was more important to change inner motivations, Mott argued, than external structures. "The springs of conduct must be touched. A new spirit must be imparted." Mott harnessed an enormous reservoir of youthful energy and good will toward all humankind in a way that President John F. Kennedy was to do with his establishment of the Peace Corps a generation later.

Protestant missions were, of course, broader than the inspired labors of a single man like John Mott. Protestant women, in fact, had been active in this realm for at least as long as the SVM itself. Congregationalist, Presbyterian, Baptist, and Methodist women had in the second half of the nineteenth century organized their own foreign missionary societies, with the steady increase of female involvement being such as to bring more than three million American women into active support of the worldwide enterprise by 1914. As Patricia Hill has noted, the woman's foreign missionary activity was, in fact, "the largest of the great nineteenth-century women's movements." Female commitment took the form of not only raising money and raising consciousness here at home regarding the world need; it many times included the dispatching of women "to foreign fields" in the capacity of doctors, nurses, teachers, and spouses of ordained clergy who labored side by side with their husbands, rendering selfless service of virtually every sort.

Organizational unity both before and after World War I gave even greater efficiency to a logistical effort of mammoth proportion. Writing of *The New Opportunity of the Church* in 1919, Presbyterian Robert E. Speer (1867–1947) found one of the few justifications for the war to be that moral ideals prevailed over material struggles. That war, he wrote, "has clarified and confirmed our fundamental religious ideas and revealed the power of their appeal to the present day mind." Given that confident assurance, Speer contended that missionaries should now go forward in greater numbers and with greater boldness to help heal the wounds of war and to counteract the political imperialism of the time. Speer acknowledged that Christians had done great damage to non-Christians, specifically in such matters as "commercial exploitation, the liquor traffic, the slave trade, . . . the opium traffic." But, he argued, the one element in the West that has protested against these and many other abuses has been the missionary enterprise. Year after year, he wrote, "it has joined with that wholesome moral sentiment existing among the people in a death struggle against the great iniquities that Western civilization [has] spread over the world."

In the 1920s the heavily populated nation of China received a major share of Protestant attention and monies. In 1922, for example, about three-quarters of a million dollars in totally voluntary offerings left the United States for China. At that time Protestants operated 219 kindergartens, 700 elementary schools, over 300 high schools, and more than 40 teaching training institutes in this one country alone. But that was only a beginning: colleges, seminaries, medical schools, orphanages, leper colonies, and a dozen institutions for the deaf and blind all resulted directly from Protestant endeavors. The American Bible Society by 1923 had sent nearly twenty thousand Bibles to China along with more than two million publications containing some portion of the Bible. This tremendous outlay could, though in numbers not quite so impressive, find its counterpart in Korea, Japan, Burma, Thailand, much of Africa, and throughout the South Pacific.

Roman Catholics in America, meanwhile, had not been idle, though special circumstances prevented their taking up an active missionary effort before the twentieth century. The Catholic Church in America was itself regarded by the Vatican as a missionary field until 1908; to be sure, the nineteenth-century American church, growing so rapidly and in such variety, needed all the help that it could get. But in the very

year that the Vatican declared the church in the United States no longer
a missionary dependent, some fifteen million Roman Catholics were
called upon to assume their proper responsibilities around the world.
Opening a Missionary Conference in Chicago in November, 1908,
Archbishop James Edward Quigley (1854–1915) of Chicago summarized
the purposes of the conference this way: "to crystallize the missionary
sentiment now being awakened in the Catholic clergy and people, to
the end that all may realize their common duty of preserving and extending the Church of Christ." And in closing the meeting, Boston's
Archbishop William H. O'Connell (1859–1944) sounded a similar note.
"It is time," he said, "for the Church in America to be vigilant in preserving the unselfishness and generosity of spirit which animated the
pioneer Catholic missionaries who planted on this continent the seed of
faith." Once France and the French language had been the major power
behind or vehicle of Catholic missions. Now, declared the Archbishop,
it was the turn of the United States and of the English language. "The
providential hour of opportunity has struck," he noted, sounding so

49. This medical mission, on the Amazon River, was a Seventh-day Adventist enterprise that well represents Protestant missions. *General Conference of the Seventh-day Adventists*

very much like John R. Mott. "We must be up and doing. All indications point to our vocation as a great missionary nation."

O'Connell's words found their most visible response in the creation of the Catholic Foreign Missionary Society of America in 1911 with headquarters in Maryknoll, New York. Maryknoll fathers and Maryknoll nuns carried on especially effective work in the Roman Catholic countries of Central and South America. After World War I, the National Catholic Welfare Conference coordinated the sporadic missionary efforts of the nation's dioceses, giving them greater effectiveness and wider visibility. As with Protestant missions, the tasks of Catholic missions were interpreted broadly to meet whatever human need was encountered. Schools, hospitals, orphanages, and the like regularly accompanied the more narrowly defined roles of offering spiritual counsel and conducting Mass. And like Protestants, Catholics gave much attention to the recruiting and development of a native clergy, so that the necessity to import ecclesiastical leadership from abroad would gradually fade away.

Other and newer groups in America, notably Mormons, Seventh-Day Adventists, and Jehovah's Witnesses carried on so vigorous a missionary effort as to attract almost as much attention as the far larger religious bodies. Mormons made missionary activity an obligation resting upon every young male Mormon, this duty leading to a large commitment in language training and to a broad cosmopolitanism in this church's membership. Adventists, putting great emphasis upon health both at home and abroad, created a missionary program in which doctors, dentists, and nurses played an even larger role than the clergy. And Jehovah's Witnesses, who expected all their membership to be vigorously engaged in missions around the world, soon found their membership abroad equaling, then surpassing, the membership at home. All groups encountered some hostility abroad, the Witnesses, however, excelling in this regard.

Hostility of "host" nations to the entire missionary enterprise led to a downturn of activity in specific areas. In China, for example, the very foreignness of foreign missions became an argument against encouraging or tolerating these emissaries from abroad. In the 1930s, waves of anti-Christian, anti-foreign, anti-Western sentiment spread across China. With the invasion by Japan in 1937, the position of Western missionaries worsened, a deterioration that continued for the next decade or more until hardly a foreign missionary was permitted to stay in China. Meanwhile, in the United States a severe depression of the 1930s undermined the financial base that had supported so much of the worldwide effort. Even more damaging to some aspects of Protestant missions, however, was the growing tension in America between conservative and liberal forces within Protestantism.

Those tensions had many ramifications and many manifestations, to be sure. Most of these will be explored in the following chapter. But on the mission field in particular, the tensions appeared in the form of a contest between how much the missionary movement should be allowed to drift off in the direction of general social service and how much it should remain focussed on evangelism and conversion. Early in the twentieth century, mission boards and commissions defended both approaches: to the body as well as to the soul, to concern about life here on earth as well as life hereafter. By the early 1930s, however, following the bruising battles of the 1920s between fundamentalists on the one hand and modernists on the other, much mainstream Protestantism came under attack from the more evangelically minded. Around the same time, many of those Protestants under seige themselves began questioning some of the perhaps culturally imperialist assumptions that lay behind the entire missionary movement. E. Stanley Jones (1884–1973), Methodist missionary to India, startled many in 1925 when he suggested that American Christians had as much to learn from Indian Hindus as was the case the other way around. "The religious genius of India," Jones affirmed, "is the richest in the world." Should the citizens of India adopt Christianity, it will be ultimately a very different sort of Christianity, Jones noted, than that familiar to most Americans: it "will be essentially Eastern and not Western."

Others questioned the effect of asking people to forsake cultural and tribal patterns, the effect of isolating them from centuries of tradition or

50. Maryknoll Fathers constituted the front line of Roman Catholic missionary effort in South America, in this case in the Andes Mountains. *Maryknoll Fathers*

bonds of communal affection. Still others wondered if the primary purpose of missions had not now become something quite different. "Starting with the purpose of saving souls, [missionaries] have been drawn on by necessity into efforts to build up the minds, and the bodies, and to improve the social life in which these souls are engaged. The educational and other associated interests have grown until in volume and variety they now outrank the parent activity." Those two sentences come from a 1932 report entitled *Re-thinking Missions: A Layman's Inquiry after One Hundred Years*. Leading the "inquiry" was Congregational churchman and professor of philosophy at Harvard, William Ernest Hocking (1873–1966). As a result of widespread second thoughts about missions in general, Hocking had been asked to undertake a major assessment of Protestant missions around the world, the point being to determine if the missionary enterprise should continue and, if so, in what revised or altered form.

The very fact of such an inquiry pointed to the pervasive doubts about Christianity's proper relationship to other religions of the world, about America's role in imposing its culture and often its will upon peoples possessed of less power. If missions had become largely social service, then was it not time to let other agencies, probably governmental, carry on that service? On the other hand, if Christian missions had ceased their primary business of saving souls, then was it not time for other Christian bodies to assume that which mainstream Protestantism seemed less willing to assume?

In the 1930s, therefore, conservative evangelical forces, including many Pentecostal and Holiness bodies, began to take up the slack so evident in the missionary resolve and purposiveness of liberal Protestants. The Federal Council of Churches represented much of Protestantism, but certainly not all. This was made clear in 1942 with the creation of the National Association of Evangelicals, with the introduction in America a few years earlier of the Intervarsity Christian Fellowship—conservative religion's answer to or revival of the Student Volunteer Movement. Protestant missions did not so much decline in the 1930s and 1940s as take on a different coloration and develop a different cadre of denominational supporters. In this later period, foreign missions became less a feature of establishment concern or public policy, more a subculture of zealous evangelization that would ride on the waves of new technological instruments and on the waves of strong religious passion. Meanwhile, many Americans, liberal and conservative, Protestant, Catholic, and Jew, found themselves challenged to solve pressing problems closer at hand.

MISSIONS AT HOME

In the two decades between the great wars, social ills and dislocations commanded the attention of organized religion. Immigration had effectively halted in 1924, but the task of Americanizing and Christianizing recent arrivals continued to press itself upon many religiousleaders. Before immigration ceased, a Lutheran church paper in 1920 addressed the momentous task of reaching the "seventeen million foreign-born in our midst, and the aliens arriving in our ports, now at the rate of five thousand daily." This concern found its echo in many other church groups as missions to the immigrant (preferably in his or her own language, preferably with a Bible that could be presented already printed in the appropriate language) constituted a preoccupation of many who saw the tasks at home as every bit as pressing as those abroad. With "melting-pot" imagery still enjoying high favor in the 1920s, churches tended to see themselves as major partners in the process of assimilation.

If some saw aggressive evangelical efforts among the immigrants in an unfavorable light, others adopted attitudes toward the new arrivals that won even less approval. Catholics and Jews found many Americans already turned against them, as a revived Ku Klux Klan tried repeatedly—and with some success—to make its case for an America that would be ruled by white Protestants only. America "must remain Protestant," declared the Klan's Imperial Wizard in 1926; the nation's destiny would be fatally damaged, he added, "if we became priest-ridden, if we had to submit our consciences and limit our activities and suppress our thoughts at the command of any man, much less of a man sitting upon Seven Hills thousands of miles away." Other religious voices protested this myopic view of what America or what being an American was all about. The rabbi of Temple Emanu-El in New York City asked, also in 1926, "What justification is there for this twentieth-century religious persecution on American soil?" The rabbi found none; indeed, what he found was that the "Americanism" of the Klan was the most un-American feature to be seen in all the land.

The presidential election of 1928 gave a sudden surge to anti-Catholicism in the country. For the first time, one of the major political parties had nominated a Roman Catholic to be president of the United States. Alfred E. Smith (1873–1944) had been a member of the New York legislature for many years and had been the state's governor for four terms, but to a large number of Americans the only biographical bit worth mentioning was that he was a Roman Catholic. All of the older nativism of the nineteenth century was reborn in an instant as broadsides and sermons, newspaper articles and editorials, explained the great danger to American liberty were a Catholic to be elected president. Smith himself found this attitude tragically un-American, noting how closely it reflected the mentality and bigotry of the Klan. "Nothing could be so out of line with the spirit of America," he pointed out during the campaign. Nor could anything be so out of line with the spirit of Christianity, Smith added. "The world knows no greater mockery than the use of the blazing cross, the cross upon which Christ died, as a symbol to install into the hearts of men hatred of their brethren, while Christ preached and died for the love and brotherhood of man." Smith was defeated and though, to be sure, other issues were at stake besides his Catholicism, the campaign dramatized in an unforgettable way that the "mission at home" had much work to do with respect to prejudice in the name of religion.

Similar prejudices took aim at the Jewish population, a population that grew very rapidly in the closing years of the nineteenth century and the early years of the twentieth. By 1913 the Jewish community found it expedient to create the Anti-Defamation League whose overriding purpose was to identify the sources of religious and racial prejudice, then through a program of education and persuasion try to alter attitudes so deeply ingrained. In the 1920s, the situation worsened as quota systems were applied to limit enrollment of Jews in major universities, and as housing covenants excluded Jews from many neighborhoods, and as "gentlemen's agreements" of several kinds regularized harassment of and discrimination against the Jews. No less a

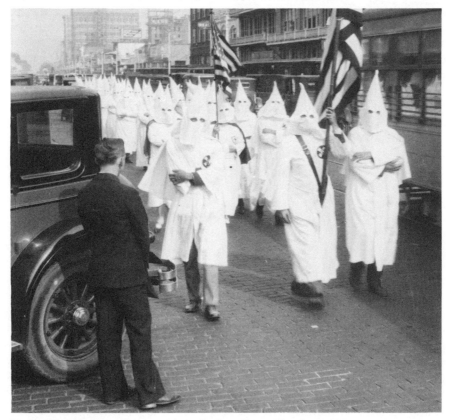

51. Ku Klux Klan members march in St. Petersburg, Florida, in 1926. *Keystone-Mast Collection, UC Riverside*

public figure than Henry Ford added his prestige to the rumors of conspiracy by international Jewry. The Jew was thought to resist assimilation or, if assimilated, to subvert both the economic and the political systems of the United States. Catholic voices such as that of Charles E. Coughlin (1891–1979) and Protestant voices such as that of Gerald B. Winrod (1899?–1957) sullied the 1930s with strident expressions of anti-Semitism, this at the very time when in Germany much more powerful voices were being raised against the Jew.

The black likewise suffered in this same period, not merely from petty persecution and humiliating segregation but from repeated instances of public murder. It was called lynching, and these ritualized hangings disgraced America over and over again. From 1882 to 1927, nearly five thousand lynchings took place, not all of the victims being blacks, though blacks constituted the vast majority. Nor were lynchings limited to the South; indeed, only four New England states wholly escaped this tragic blight. Racial discrimination was so blatant, so widespread, so much the "norm" that church bodies could neither ignore it nor dispute its omnipresence. For the most part, however, church leaders spent more time discussing the problem than taking concrete steps to solve it. Public revulsion against lynchings, nonetheless, did result in a steady decline in the 1920s and 1930s so that by the 1940s lynchings had virtually ceased. Other forms of racial injustice, however, continued apace, with the total immersion of the churches into the questions of racial injustice and human rights awaiting a later day.

The Great Depression of the 1930s concentrated the attention of all religion's forces in a way that nothing else had done since the First World War. As one instance of ecclesiastical concentration upon the economic woes and disorders, in 1931 the Federal Council of Churches along with the National Catholic Welfare Conference and the Central Conference of American Rabbis gathered together in an effort to find "Permanent Preventives of Unemployment." In that same year Pope Pius XI issued an important encyclical *Quadragesimo Anno* ("Fortieth Year," commemorating the socially progressive encyclical issued by Pope Leo XIII in 1891) that addressed itself specifically to depression-related problems that had by that time become worldwide. Urging men and women to avoid the extremes of individualism on the one hand and of collectivism on the other, the pope called upon the cooperation of governments "to make all human society conform to the needs of the common good; that is, to the norm of social justice."

Pronouncements, however, often failed to satisfy urgent human needs. As Roman Catholic activist, Dorothy Day (1898–1980), said with respect to the blacks, "We just went out and *did* things. We didn't form a Committee to Promote Interracial Relations. We took Negroes in our homes and lived with them." So also her Catholic Worker movement, founded in 1933, did not issue manifestos on poverty or hunger; the movement, with its Hospitality Houses, simply fed the hungry and clothed and sheltered the poor. The Society of St. Vincent de Paul, mentioned earlier, along with other groups discussed previously such as the Salvation Army, the YMCA and YWCA, the Jewish Welfare Board, and many more found in the 1930s more demands than they could readily meet for supplying thousands with the barest necessities of life.

The election of Franklin D. Roosevelt (1882–1945), an Episcopalian, in 1932 seemed to offer hope, though his New Deal took many years to rescue large numbers from their grinding poverty. For some church-people, Roosevelt began on the wrong foot by repealing the noble experiment known as Prohibition. The brevity of the experiment as well as the widespread flaunting of the law suggested that constitutional amendments were less than satisfactory solutions for religiously specific moral reforms. Roosevelt won back some of his detractors, however, by using the power of government more actively, more aggressively to deal with fundamental dislocations and prolonged human suffering. He, too, had a "mission at home," with it becoming increasingly clear as the 1940s approached that America and the wider world

52. Roman Catholic Dorothy Day was an activist and humanitarian. This photo was taken in 1974. *Religious News Service*

were mutually interdependent. And like politics, America's religious enterprises, in all of their many expressions, no longer stopped at the water's edge.

For a half-century or more, from the end of the 1880s to the beginning of the 1940s, the churches and synagogues recognized that they had mighty tasks to perform: in war and peace, in domestic matters as well as in international ones. Busy years for American religion. But the institutions of religion could not ignore even more immediate and anxiety-raising concerns. While aggressively pursuing crowded agenda both at home and abroad, the churches suffered great inner turmoil and dissension. Some of the vitality of the period found expression not in service, but in schism. How healthy, how whole were the nation's households of faith?

CHAPTER 19

Mainstream and Other Streams

In the final decade of the nineteenth century, the religious profile for the United States indicated that "mainstream religion" still dominated the ecclesiastical scene. "Mainstream" refers to the older, culturally established, comfortably familiar denominations—those with a history that could be studied, with a liturgy that could recognized, with a ministry that could be welcomed by civic organizations and trusted to pray on public occasions without giving offense. The mainstream in general could be relied upon to keep proselyting zeal under control and sectarian pride in check, at least most of the time.

In the 1890s the eight leading denominational families, in order of membership, were these: Roman Catholic, Methodist, Baptist, Presbyterian, Lutheran, Disciples of Christ, Episcopalian, and Congregational. The status of each of these groups on the eve of the twentieth century requires some comment. Roman Catholics, with about eight million members, had survived the resentments of Protestant neighbors, the tensions of the Civil War, the strains of ethnic jealousy, the suspicions of European Catholics—all with its organizational unity somehow still intact. A remarkable, an almost miraculous achievement this was, when one reflects upon the stupendous stresses that the church was subjected to in nineteenth-century America: wave after wave of immigration, wave after wave of nativist negativism, wave after wave of territorial assimilation. No other church confronted so great a challenge; no other church emerged so conspicuously victorious.

Methodism, unlike Catholicism, did not emerge from the nineteenth century with any conspicuous unity in organization. The Methodist family of about five and one-half million members was often a quarrelsome family: divided by race, by sectional sentiment, by argument over the authority of their bishops or superintendents, and by disagreement over the pursuit of John Wesley's "Christian perfection." Yet, the family as a whole continued to flourish with such zest that one hardly noticed the internal divisions and extravagant spinnings off of new religious bodies.

Like the Methodists, the Baptists enjoyed no structural oneness. They too had been divided by the Civil War; they too had watched the creation of separate entities for their black members; they too had found still other grounds for repeated separation. Baptists could not even agree on their own history, nor on the uniqueness of their mode of baptism, nor on the terms by which one might be invited to share in the Lord's Supper, nor on the authority of the congregation, nor, for that matter, on the precise wording of the Lord's Prayer. Yet, in some sense, the Baptist family did constitute a "family" of about four million strong in the closing years of the nineteenth century.

53. The National Shrine of the Immaculate Conception in Washington, D. C., is honored by all the nation's Roman Catholics, America's largest denomination. *The National Shrine of the Immaculate Conception*

Presbyterians, nearly as successful on the frontier as Baptists and Methodists had proved to be, elevated quarrelsomeness to a higher juridical level. With a more closely knit system of church governance, based on a pyramid structure of sessions, presbyteries, synods, and ultimately a General Assembly, Presbyterians tried heroically to maintain unity in doctrine, in practice, and certainly in organization itself. But in the free-wheeling environment of an open-ended American experiment, this effort often failed. Divided first over the "new measures" of revivalism, Presbyterians, like the Baptists and Methodists, divided just prior to the Civil War. And like their fellow evangelists on the frontier, they also saw black members create their own organization, even as they struggled with the question of proper ordination and educational requirements for all Presbyterian clergy. With about a million and one-half members in 1895, this family moved with some ease into all sections of the country, north and south, east and west.

Immigration in the second half of the nineteenth century gave Lutheranism significant numerical standing by 1895: nearly as numerous as the Presbyterians and fifth in ranking according to membership. But Lutherans did not have to wait until they arrived in America to find reasons for division and separation: they brought their reasons with them. Ethnic and national distinctions were inevitable, especially since no equivalent to the Catholics' Vatican could discourage or limit the natural tendency to gather in groups that spoke the same language, that shared the same memories. Thus, Lutherans who were just simply "Lutheran" in Sweden, for example, found it necessary in America to be identified as "Swedish Lutherans." Similarly, one could point to separate organizations for Norwegian Lutherans, Finnish Lutherans, Danish Lutherans, German Lutherans, and so on. This only began to account for the divisions, however, as one could (in truly American fashion) quarrel about theology, creedal loyalty, personal piety and many other matters judged sufficient to disagree and divide. At the beginning of the twentieth century, Lutheranism in America was separated into some two dozen distinct ecclesiastical bodies.

Alone among the top eight mainstream churches, the Disciples of Christ bore no European stamp. Its origin, described in an earlier chapter, belonged to the American frontier of the pre-Civil War period. The youngest of these eight nevertheless grew with vigor sufficient to claim nearly a million members by 1895, thus overtaking groups such as Dutch Reformed and Quakers who had enjoyed a far earlier planting on American soil. The movement's youth, however, as we shall see later in this chapter, did not prevent it too from suffering internal tension and ultimate division.

Ranking seventh and eighth in this census of the 1890s were the two churches that in the colonial period had been at the very top: the Episcopalians and the Congregationalists. Once it had seemed that they virtually divided the country between them, but by 1900, if not long before, this was obviously no longer the case. Still forces to bereckoned with, still unmistakably mainstream, Episcopalians and Congregationalists had fallen far behind their competitors, neither group proving to be all that effective on the frontier, neither group adjusting all that readily to the new realities of a totally open market in religion. With around six hundred thousand members apiece, these two churches entered the twentieth century with the assurance that earlier privilege and prestige bestowed. Their numbers, however, suggested already some narrowing of both these historic streams.

In 1900 the population of the country stood at seventy-six million, and church membership at around twenty-six million. Of that latter figure, more than four-fifths of the nation's church membership could be found in the eight "families" noted above. No other church body had as many as one-half million members, at least so far as the official census takers were able to determine. Much American religion then and now, however, eludes the census taker and escapes wide public notice. Religious, linguistic, and ethnic enclaves lead a kind of shrouded existence that conceals their numbers and sometimes stifles their voices. In the first half of the twentieth century, mainstream religion would find its channels neither so clear nor so deep as they had earlier been perceived to be. As with the Mississippi River, it sometimes became difficult to distinguish the proper course for heavy river traffic among the many new twists and turns that each bend in the river of religions exposed.

ERA OF CHURCH GROWTH

At the beginning of the twentieth century, about one-third of the nation's population could be found on the membership rolls of the

54. Mainstream Protestantism enjoyed much popularity in the 1940s and 1950s, as here at the New York Avenue Presbyterian Church in Washington, D. C. *Library of Congress*

churches and synagogues. By the middle of that century, membership had increased to well over fifty percent. In that same fifty-year period, the population as a whole doubled from around 76 million to over 150 million. As a consequence, church membership grew in absolute numbers as well as in percentage of the total population. The eight denominations noted above all participated dramatically in that growth: Catholics from 8 million to over 25 million; Methodists from 5.5 million to double that; Baptists from 4 million to more than 15 million (passing the Methodists); Presbyterians from 1.5 million to over 3 million; Lutherans from less than 1.5 million to more than 5 million; Disciples from less than 1 million to about 4 million (in the whole "family" derived from Alexander Campbell); Episcopalians and Congregationalists from well under a million each to around 3 million and 2 million, respectively. But church growth was by no means a monopoly of the mainstream alone. Others were growing—and gaining fast.

Mormon growth was as sharp as it was surprising. Surprising because utopian communities in nineteenth-century American had a way of quietly shrinking from public consciousness if not altogether from existence. Surprising because groups once deprived of their original charismatic leadership regularly splintered into countless insignificant fragments. Surprising because Mormons had been exiled to a barren and (it was widely assumed) soon-to-be-forgotten wasteland. The Church of Jesus Christ of Latter-Day Saints was not finished with still more surprises. The abandonment of polygamy in 1890 led to neither doctrinal nor communal decline; on the contrary, family values and family loyalties intensified. The admission of Utah as a state in 1896 led not to greater conflict with the church's old enemy, namely the United States, but to stronger embrace of the nation's pervading cultural values, indeed to patriotism distinguished by its unswerving passion. Perhaps most surprising of all, the acceptance of Mormonism into the mainstream led not to lassitude and complacency but to an increasingly fervent missionary enterprise abroad as well as at home.

One direct consequence of that last surprising feature of twentieth century Mormonism has been a growth curve that older religious bodies in America could regard with only envy and wonder. With a membership of a mere one-quarter million in the 1890s, Mormons by 1950 had more than twice that number in the state of Utah alone. In the United States, Mormonism stands as the best example of a large ecclesiastical institution whose power base in neither urban nor eastern but rural and western. The Utah branch (far larger than the more traditional Reorganized Church whose strength is mainly in and around Independence, Missouri) has spread across state boundaries into southern Idaho and Montana, northern Arizona and New Mexico, western Wyoming, and eastern Washington, Oregon, and California. Mormonism, once so commonly ridiculed and routinely dismissed by establishment religion, came of age in the twentieth century in ways hardly anticipated. With maturity came not a hardening of the arteries, but a continued adolescent energy and buoyant optimism.

Methodism helped to spawn a host of new denominations that, in their newness, quickly overtook the parent that spawned them so far as growth rates were concerned. John Wesley (1703–1791), founder of Methodism, had stressed the necessity for all Christians to press beyond the stage of mere justification to a higher plateau, a loftier goal of complete sanctification: that is, of being made holy. Taking his cue from the New Testament command to "be perfect, as your heavenly Father is perfect" (Matthew 5:48), Wesley and many of his followers pursued the ideal of a kind of Christian perfection in one's own life here on earth. Such striving could be quite individual or personal, but it could also characterize a whole church and eventually entire denominations.

After the Civil War a National Camp Meeting Association for the Promotion of Christian Holiness was formed to inspire greater commitment on the part of "brothers and sisters of the various denominations" to the steady pursuit of holiness. Though Methodists led in this early organization, the movement itself had too much vitality and lively spirit to be contained within a single ecclesiastical institution. In the 1880s and beyond, literally dozens of new denominations were born—all vying with each other to prove their restless passion as they pursued

55. Mormonism went west to the Salt Lake Basin—and forgot to stop. Here is the prominent temple in Hawaii, on Oahu. *Hawaii Visitors Bureau*

the high goal of Christian perfection. D. S. Warner's Church of God sprang into being in 1880, this quickly followed by A. B. Simpson's Christian and Missionary Alliance in 1887, then by J. H. King's Fire Baptized Holiness Church in 1895, then by the Pilgrim Holiness Church in 1897 and in the same year by the predominantly black Church of God in Christ—destined to become one of the largest of all. In 1914 a half-dozen smaller groups rested just long enough to agree on a new denominational name, the Church of the Nazarene, another body that exploded from a base of a few thousand to one-quarter million by 1950. If mainstream religions looked over their institutional shoulders, they saw someone gaining on them.

Also gaining were Pentecostal bodies, so-named from the description in the Book of Acts (2:1–4) of the Day of Pentecost when the Holy Spirit descended in power upon the apostolic worshippers, one manifestation of that power being that those present "began to speak in other tongues, as the Spirit gave them utterance." Speaking in tongues as well as practicing spiritual healing of physical infirmities became the chief distinguishing features of another whole array of rapidly growing denominations in America. An emotion-packed revival in Los Angeles in 1906 is often taken as the launching pad for these new churches that rocketed into the nation's religious space. Though in early years the Holiness and the Pentecostal movements were closely associated, the two gradually drew apart, the former concerned much more with a steady development of the Christian life, the latter more with the sudden manifestations of the Spirit's presence and power. In 1914 in Hot Springs, Arkansas, the Assemblies of God denomination gathered many scattered and ever-splintering Pentecostal churches into a single fold. This group, destined to become the largest representative of the whole charismatic (or spirit-filled) movement, resembled the Holiness bodies in that they saw the manifestation of the Holy Spirit's power as more progressive than instantaneous: that is, one did not in a moment achieve a new plateau of spiritual well being, but had to work at it, day by day, week by week, year after year.

In general Pentecostal churches grew more rapidly in the South than Holiness churches did, this in part because of the latter's emphasis on social reform to which the South, since slavery days, tended to be resistant. Pentecostal churches attracted membership that could be either black or white and, more surprisingly, sometimes both black and white. In the early days of the movement, many churches were interracial with no self-consciousness—this being simply another example of the Spirit moving how and where it would. Many of the major leaders, moreover, were black, making it inaccurate to think of Pentecostalism as a movement that whites spread among blacks. On the contrary, the Pentecostal phenomenon was every bit as much a black movement as it was a white one. Gradually, however, the patterns of the surrounding culture led to mainly segregated churches for these groups as they had for American religion at large. But in both segments of the nation's population, white and black, Pentecostalism proved to be enormously popular, quickly reaching a membership numbered in the millions as early as 1950.

Jewish population in America increased sharply from about one million in 1900 to five times that number a mere half-century later. Most of that increase resulted, of course, from immigration, especially prior to World War I, though some augmentation came from European refugees in the 1930s and 1940s. Not all Jews emigrating to America were conspicuously religious in behavior or institutional affiliation, though it would be difficult to draw neat lines between the sacred and secular aspects of what it meant to be Jewish in America. Certainly the

56. The rapid growth of Holiness and Pentecostal groups was due in part to a willingness to gather in rude and unpretentious structures such as this one near the New York-Pennsylvania border. *Library of Congress*

synagogue, especially among Eastern European Jews, provided the greatest sense of community as well as the strongest thread of continuity for the vast majority of newly arrived Jews. Particularly in New York City, many synagogues held together people from the same Old World towns, if not from the same ships that brought them to America. These religious centers often remained small, the sense of community and the degree of comfort being thereby heightened.

Jews proved their Americanness by duplicating the tendency to schism and separation that their non-Jewish neighbors had indulged in for years. Jews disagreed on the degree of accommodation to the wider culture that might be required or desired; they disagreed on the degree of loyalty demanded to ancient customs and ancient laws; they disagreed on the need for a single Jewish voice, in matters religious or otherwise, to speak for all; they disagreed on the relative merits of home, of faith, of culture, of history, or of tradition in arriving at the defining essence of Jewishness; and they disagreed on the question of a Jewish homeland under Jewish rule as the one feature essential to a secure Jewish future.

A Hungarian Jew, Theodor Herzl (1860–1906), gave Zionism (the program for a Jewish homeland) powerful leadership from the time that he published in 1896 a book entitled, *The Jewish State*. Here Herzl, dismayed by the continued outbursts in Europe of either quiet or violent

57. A modern synagogue in Jamaica, New York, has the Star of David built into the ceiling design. *Library of Congress*

anti-Semitism, argued that Jews would have no peace, no freedom from harassment and persecution, until they had a land of their own. Therefore, Herzl declared, "Let sovereignty be granted us over a portion of the globe adequate to meet our rightful national requirements; we will attend to the rest." Just where that homeland might be was not as urgent a question for Herzl as that there be one, so that the history of Jews in the twentieth century could differ sharply from their history in the preceding centuries, centuries that went all the way back to the Maccabees (a hundred or more years before the rise of Christianity) when Jews last enjoyed any political independence.

Soon after Herzl's book appeared, Jews in America began to organize on behalf of the Zionist idea—an idea that they were determined to turn into a reality. In 1912 Henrietta Szold (1860–1945) founded the Women's Zionist Organization of America, and six years later an even broader Zionist group was born. Conservative Judaism as represented by the Jewish Theological Seminary in New York City became a major recruiting center and training ground for American Zionists as the movement steadily gathered force in the 1920s and 1930s. Then, following World War II, the state of Israel at last came into being in 1948, this seen as a culmination of countless dreams and as a haven for thousands of homeless and often hopeless Jews from all around the world. From that point on, the existence of a Jewish homeland would play a determinative role in America's large Jewish community, arousing its moral passion and calling in new ways upon that community's spiritual as well as financial resources. For an increasing number of American Jews, the pressing question was no longer one of accommodation to a Gentile culture, but of dedication to a new Jewish political/religious reality.

Eastern Orthodoxy, despite its early presence in "Russian America" (that is, Alaska), is more a feature of twentieth-century America than of an earlier period. In the latter decades of the nineteenth century, one group of Byzantine-rite worshippers from the region around the Hungarian-Russian borders emigrated to the United States in significant numbers. Enjoying for a time a special relationship with the Roman Catholic church, the Uniates (who had a married clergy) ultimately found it more comfortable to renew and solidify their ancient ties with Orthodoxy—especially after a 1907 Roman bull that laid down conditions generally unacceptable to this group, sometimes also called Carpatho-Rusyns. Despite the fact that this body numbered perhaps as many as one-quarter million by 1900, they remained almost invisible to the larger populace. And that has been the story of Eastern Orthodoxy over and over, as separate immigrations of closely knit ethnic peoples took up residence in America in enclaves that resisted acculturation and escaped public attention.

The Russian revolution in 1917 did not, of course, escape public attention of the widest sort. Nonetheless, the significant emigrations resulting therefrom attracted little notice beyond the confines of the churches themselves. Even there, feuding and factionalism kept Russian Orthodoxy from becoming a recognizable force in American religion. In 1919 an "All-American Convention" meeting in Pittsburgh declared that Russian Orthodoxy in this country would be altogether independent of the Russian Orthodoxy in the Soviet Union. Such a proclamation was more easily announced than enforced, however, as the New York courts in 1925 and 1926 were called upon to settle the question of which group of Russian Orthodox in America held the legitimate title to Saint Nicholas Cathedral in New York City. Litigation and quarreling continued for another generation until in 1952 the United States Supreme Court (*Kedroff* v. *Saint Nicholas*) agreed that church law itself must determine the proper ownership. On that basis, the cathedral was deemed to be the property not of the largest group of Russian Orthodox living in America but of the group legally tied to the Patriarchate of Moscow. It was not a popular decision in Cold War days, its unpopularity captured in part by the remark of dissenting Justice Robert H. Jackson (1892–1954) who observed that he did not think "New York law must yield to the authority of a foreign and unfriendly state masquerading as a spiritual institution."

By 1952, and indeed long before, Orthodoxy in America had many more representatives than just those who had fled the Bolshevik Revolution. Syrians, Serbians, Rumanians, Albanians, and Bulgarians—among others—arrived in the intervals between World Wars I and II. It was the Greeks, however, who most conspicuously swelled the ranks of that ancient Orthodoxy whose allegiance was not to the Roman papacy but to one of any number of "superbishops" known as patriarchs. These patriarchs, usually residing in the capital city of the nation in question, were recognized, with varying degrees of consistency and fervency, as the true spiritual fathers. But Orthodoxy's progeny in America, like all other American progeny, found loyalties torn and tested as they tried to balance old world ties against new world realities. The Greeks, no less than others, faced this problem, especially as their number grew by World War I to around one hundred thousand.

In 1918 the Archbishop of Athens (historically under the Patriarch who ruled from Constantinople) came to the United States to form an all-Greek church where unity and love would prevail. Disorder and factionalism prevailed, however, frustrating his plans, just as those of the All-American Convention of the Russian Orthodox had been frustrated. But the archbishop (Meletios) persisted, his authority being dramatically increased when he was himself in 1921 named Patriarch of Constantinople. On a second visit to the United States that year, he created the Greek Orthodox Archdiocese of North and South America, this entity still serving as the ecclesiastical home for now some two million members. Factionalism did not disappear with one organizational stroke, however, as successive leaders struggled to make unity, at least among the Greeks if not among all the Orthodox in America, more nearly a reality. Archbishop Athenagoras who held the highest American office from 1930 to 1949 was especially successful in this regard, though he too often found it necessary to resort to the civil courts to untangle, if possible, many disputatious knots. When Athenagoras was in his turn named Patriarch of Constantinople in 1949, then President Harry Truman provided his own plane to assist the newly appointed Patriarch in his move from America to Turkey. Besides being a courteous gesture, this presidential action indicated that Orthodoxy had at last emerged from a near total invisibility in American public life.

By 1950 most Americans still did not regularly acknowledge the significant presence of Orthodoxy in the nation. One continued too casually to speak of "Protestant-Catholic-Jew" as encompassing virtually all of American religion. "Catholic" was understood almost without

58. Russian Orthodoxy had its impact in the East as well as the West, as seen here in Pittsburgh, Pennsylvania, in 1938. *Library of Congress*

exception to mean Roman Catholic, with that other church catholic and apostolic, the Eastern one, largely ignored. Given the antiquity of its history, the drama of its liturgy, the color of its iconography, and the richness of its cultural diversity, such unawareness became increasingly difficult, especially with respect to the two largest branches of Greeks and Russians. Both national and world events also conspired to bring greater attention to Orthodoxy: first, the public embrace in 1965 of Rome's Pope Paul VI and Constantinople's Patriarch Athenagoras I as a first step toward healing a bitter schism some nine hundred years old; and, second, the nomination for president in 1988 for the first time of a member of that ancient Orthodoxy.

So if "Protestant-Catholic-Jew" proved a label of insufficient breadth to cover all of American religion, stretching it to include Orthodoxy will help somewhat, but clearly not enough. For the United States by 1950 had become better acquainted with traditions well beyond the confines of Judaism and Christianity. The World's Parliament of Religions in 1893 in introducing the Orient to the Occident, the East to the West, had opened a gate to Hinduism, Buddhism, Confucianism, and Shinto. The annexation of Hawaii in 1898 opened that gate even more. Immigration to the mainland, especially to the West Coast, continued to widen those gates, both in the late nineteenth century and in the twentieth. Before 1900 Japanese Buddhism had become a major religion in Hawaii, and before that date the religious heritage of both China and Japan had long been represented in California. From that rich heritage, Buddhism emerged as the most vigorous, the most adaptable, the most "missionary-minded" of the Oriental religions, with the United States being seen in the twentieth century as an important mission field.

Formally established in San Francisco in 1899, the Buddhist Mission of North America grew out of the labors of two priests sent from Japan. By 1942 the "mission" was sufficiently well established to permit the name to be changed, more simply, to Buddhist Churches of America. Churches and temples had been established in the intervening years in sufficient number to suggest that Japanese (and to a lesser extent Chinese) Buddhism had found a permanent home in America. Not easily, however. First, in 1924 acts that restricted immigration in general included more specifically a Japanese Immigration Exclusion Act whose very name tells all. Then, with the outbreak of World War II, Japanese Americans by the thousands (about one hundred thousand in all) were relocated in internment camps, this unhappy action being taken on the grounds that national security required it. This injustice, for which the nation later officially apologized and provided financial reparation, was based less on national security considerations than on deep resentment over Japan's attack on Pearl Harbor (December 7, 1941) and on the long-standing racism of which the Exclusion Act was but one indisputable sign.

Like Eastern Orthodoxy, Buddhism represents not a single strand or "denomination" but several liturgical and national traditions. Zen Buddhism, of Japanese origin, with its focus on mediation and artistic simplicity (as well as intellectual conundrums) demonstrated appeal far beyond the Asian immigrants themselves. Many other forms of Japanese Buddhism (for example, Jodo Shin, Nichiren, and Shingon) flourished both in the Hawaiian Islands and along the West Coast of the United States. But Buddhist traditions from China, Korea, Vietnam, Tibet and other Asian countries also made their appearance in America, some more obviously in the decades after World War II. By 1950, in any case, one of the world's great religions, known for so long only as a strange and distant tradition, had taken up permanent residence nearby.

Hinduism, being closely identified with the culture of India, did not prove as exportable or missionary-minded as Buddhism. Nevertheless, a kind of reform or Westernized Hinduism did enter the United States following the World's Parliament of 1893. Swami Vivekanada established a local chapter of the Vedanta Society in New York City in 1894, and in 1920 Swami Yogananda moved to the United States, his ministry leading to the establishment of Self-Realization Fellowships around the country. This kind of Hinduism, shorn of much of its "India-ness," appealed not so much to the emigrant as to older Americans intrigued by the mystery and philosophy of such Hindu literature as the Upanishads. Other more popular expressions of Hinduism came to America in the decades following World War II. On a smaller scale, Confucianism and Taoism from China as well as Shinto from Japan found footholds in the United States, with the West Coast again predominating. As racism has somewhat diminished and as the claims to religious liberty have been more assertively pressed by the Oriental population, the many signs of an ever broadening religious pluralism became evident to all.

Churches of all kinds and from all countries generally enjoyed a period of steady growth, this increase being due to immigration, to a growing national population, and to a greater readiness to identify with some religious organization—at least up to around the middle of the twentieth century. But total growth could be deceptive. For in the very midst of statistics that seemed to move ever upward and onward, recrimination and strife weakened religion's voice, or perhaps better, raised the noise level of numerous competing voices.

STRUGGLES AND SCHISMS

A dramatic heresy trial held in the final decade of the nineteenth century pointed to troubled decades ahead in the twentieth. Charles A. Briggs (1841–1912), appointed in 1891 as Professor of Biblical Theology at Union Theological Seminary, New York City, was charged by the Presbyterian Church "with teaching that errors may have existed in the original text of the Holy Scripture." A Presbyterian himself, Briggs was brought to trial in 1893 where he was given an opportunity to defend himself. In his reply to the charges, Briggs explained that "The only errors I have found or ever recognized in Holy Scripture have been beyond the range of faith and practice, and therefore they do not impair the infallibility of Holy Scripture as a rule of faith and practice." This answer was judged to be unsatisfactory. It was enough that Briggs failed to declare Scripture to be without error of any kind, "inerrant." Found guilty of violating the essential standards of the Presbyterian Church, he was dismissed from the New York Presbytery of which he

59. A Zen Buddhist monitor here encourages proper posture and concentration. *Zen Center of Los Angeles*

was a member. He was not dismissed from the seminary, however, continuing to teach there until his death in 1912.

What happened in the 1890s in a single denomination was duplicated many times over in other denominations and, indeed, again with Presbyterianism itself. The struggle is most familiarly identified by the use of such labels as "fundamentalism" on one side of the battle and "modernism" on the other side. The intellectual and theological issues underlying these labels will be more fully discussed in the following chapter, but the ecclesiastical turmoil itself will be considered here. As in the Briggs trial, the issue often turned narrowly on attitudes toward the Bible, but the questions more broadly related to attitudes toward the modern world at large. And in this broader sense, the controversy was reflected in Catholicism and Judaism no less than in Protestantism.

In the sixteenth century Reformation, Martin Luther and other Protestant leaders regarded the role of Tradition (the teachings and authority of the medieval Church) as being less significant than the voice of Scripture. To reform the Church, they argued, one must take Scripture most seriously, using it to correct Tradition and to purify faith. "*Sola Scriptura*," that is, Scripture alone and above all else, became the watchword of Protestantism. It is not surprising, therefore, that when Scripture itself came under scrutiny (through new manuscript and archaeological discoveries, and through new historical and literary techniques), Protestantism would suffer most severely. And so it did as heresy trials multiplied, as churches quarreled, as seminaries struggled to survive, as denominations divided.

In the first third of the twentieth century, the three Protestant groups most severely torn by fundamentalist/modernist issues were the Presbyterians, the Northern Baptists, and the Disciples of Christ. Other bodies did not escape unscathed, but did escape without enduring schism. Episcopalians, for example, had their heresy trial early in the twentieth century as Algernon Crapsey (1847–1927) was charged with being unfaithful to that church's historic creeds; found guilty in 1906, he was deposed from the priesthood. Methodists, having lost many elements of their tradition to the Holiness bodies, weathered the storm somewhat better though not without charges and countercharges hurled by liberals and conservatives alike in the 1920s and 1930s. The Dutch Reformed suffered schism in the late nineteenth century, though this was related more to immigration patterns and disputes over the right of members to join secret organizations such as the Masons. In 1890 the Christian Reformed Church began its ecclesiastical life apart from the older parental body, the Reformed Church in America. Finally, Lutherans, still trapped in many ethnic enclaves, escaped the harshest aspect of the quarrels until much later in the twentieth century.

Presbyterians found that the Briggs trial settled very little. Other trials followed as did other attempts to define precisely the boundaries of Presbyterian orthodoxy. In 1910 the General Assembly emphasized five "fundamentals" that should not be compromised in any way: the inerrancy of Scripture, the virgin birth of Christ, his vicarious atonement (that is, substituting his death for the eternal punishment of others), his bodily resurrection, and the reality of his biblically recorded miracles. Though leading liberals such as Arthur C. McGiffert (1861–1933) and Harry Emerson Fosdick (1878–1969) came under heavy attack, the denomination as a whole rejected the fundamentalist stance. In 1929, for example, the leadership managed to pull Princeton Theological Seminary away from the control of the most conservative elements within the church. In the 1930s some conservatives, concluding that they no longer had a doctrinally comfortable home within the Presbyterian Church in the U. S. A. (a largely northern body), withdrew to create competing smaller denominations. Under the leadership of the scholarly John G. Machen (1881–1937), conservative forces drew lines that said in effect: Here we stand; we will concede not another inch; we will love the modern world less and the ancient truths more.

Northern Baptists were even more riddled by dissension and strife as the two opposing sides struggled for the soul of the denomination. (Baptists, like Presbyterians, were still divided at this time into northern and southern sections.) In the 1920s fundamentalists and conservatives sought to impose creedal uniformity upon all those identified with the Northern Baptist Convention, while modernists and liberals resisted such efforts as being contrary to the Baptist tradition of having no creed other than the Bible. In one sense, the liberals won since they maintained control of the denominational boards, seminaries, and agencies. Yet, in other senses they lost as schisms weakened the larger body and as evangelical energies were siphoned off into other causes. In 1933 fifty congregations withdrew from the parent group to form the General Association of Regular Baptists; fifteen years later more disaffected members separated to form the Conservative Baptist Association of America. Numbering about 1.5 million in 1925, Northern Baptists remained at roughly that level of membership for the next half-century. This was an era of growth—but also of schism and separation.

The Disciples of Christ, a frontier church that purposed to reduce denominationalism, ironically added even more labels to an already confusing situation. Early in the twentieth century, the conservatives who resisted many aspects of the creeping liberalism (as they perceived it) withdrew to create a new denomination: the Churches of Christ. These churches maintained a rigid congregational polity: that is, no denominational headquarters, no ecumenical participation with other religious bodies, no national programs or institutions or boards. They also held to the authority of the Bible in such a way as to resist any of the new interpretations or modifications becoming familiar in the fundamentalist/modernist contest. This conservative separation, however, was distinct from those among Presyberians and Baptists in one visible respect: it had a clear geographical component. The Churches of Christ found their centers of strength in Tennessee, Arkansas, and Texas, while the Disciples continued to be the major faction in Missouri, Illinois, Indiana, Ohio, and Kentucky. In 1927 yet another division afflicted Alexander Campbell's movement, this group taking the name of the North American Christian Connection. Neither southern nor border state in make-up, this third group challenged the parent group more directly in its own home territory. The older Disciples group, it was charged, had grown too fond of scholarship associated with the University of Chicago, too ready to surrender its denominational distinctives to a kind of undifferentiated Protestantism. Once again, the cry of the schismatic was heard across the land: "Come out from among them, and be ye separate, saith the Lord" (2 Corinthians 6:17).

Protestants, however, were not alone in their concern about where the modern world was leading traditional and historic religion. Roman Catholic authorities in the Vatican found much of what was happening in European scholarship to be worrisome in the extreme. In 1893 Pope Leo XIII condemned that biblical study "dignified by the name of 'higher criticism' " as an "inept method." It "pretends to judge the origin, integrity, and authority of each book from internal indications alone," without paying any attention to the views of the early church fathers or to the teaching authority of the Roman church itself. Then, in 1907 Pope Pius X in a long letter used the very word "modernism" in order to make clear that it was heretical, dangerous, and beyond enduring. Modernists talk of progress, the pope said, even progress in doctrine and dogma, but what they call progress is, in fact, "corruption." "To the laws of evolution everything" for the modernists "is subject under penalty of death—dogma, church, worship, the books we revere as sacred, even faith itself." Modernists question everyone's wisdom but their own, the pope added; they understand Scripture where all the Doctors of the Church have failed; they know "the needs of consciences better than anybody else"; they perceive the course of history where all others fail to do so. In fact, Pius X declared, though often rebuked and reprimanded, they continue undeterred, "masking an incredible audacity under a mock semblance of humility."

So sweeping was this 1907 condemnation that it left little room for maneuver or reinterpretation. Indeed, Pius X directed that all bishops and archbishops take care that in their own jurisdictions any hint or suggestion of modernism be rooted out, especially from the universities and seminaries. Some European scholars were disciplined, but in the American church no schismatic threat emerged. Yet, while the Roman Catholic Church escaped the kind of external break that many Protestant bodies suffered, the former did not emerge unscathed. Catholic scholarship in general, but biblical scholarship in particular, for more than a generation found itself confined and thwarted by the severe prescriptions of this papal letter.

A later pope, however, in 1943 sounded a very different note as he promoted biblical scholarship of the most responsible sort. Pius XII specifically encouraged a study of the original biblical languages of Hebrew and Greek, along with closely associated ancient tongues, as well as a full attention to "the historical, archeological, philological, and other auxiliary sciences." It was quite wrong, the pope pointed out, to assume that all truth was already known so that "nothing remains to be added by the Catholic" scholar of today. "On the contrary, these our times have brought to light so many things, which call for a fresh investigation and new examination." What was "fresh" and "new" had by the 1940s won a place in Catholic circles that had been denied to it in the 1890s and early 1900s.

Judaism did its dividing too along similar though not identical lines. As with the Dutch Reformed, immigration patterns (from what countries one came, in what time period one came) shaped some of the disagreements. But many of the familiar issues were present as well: attitudes toward the Bible (specifically toward the Torah or Books of Moses), attitudes toward history and tradition, attitudes toward modern civilization and the notion of progress. A platform adopted by Reform Judaism in 1885 highlighted issues that in other contexts would be called "modernist." The platform, for example, asserted that "modern discoveries of scientific researches . . . are not antagonistic to the doctrines of Judaism, the Bible reflecting the primitive ideas of its own age." The old Mosaic laws, moreover, were necessary as "a system of training" for Jews in ancient Palestine, but "today we accept as binding only the moral laws and maintain only such ceremonies as elevate and sanctify our lives." Judaism, like all religion that deserves to survive, must be "progressive," the platform declared, "ever striving to be in accord with the postulates of reason."

In the views of Orthodox Judaism and of much Conservative Judaism as well in the early twentieth century, this ready embrace of reason, this willingness to pick and choose among the demands of biblical law, was to love the modern world too much. Solomon Schechter (1850–1915), president of the Jewish Theological Seminary, argued in 1901 that Judaism was primarily not a progressive religion but "a revealed religion" that must continue to take the Bible very seriously. "Our great claim to the gratitude of mankind," Schechter asserted, "is that we gave to the world the word of God, the Bible. We have stormed heaven to snatch down this heavenly gift." And because that gift is so great, we have "allowed ourselves to be slain by the hundreds and thousands rather than become unfaithful to it." With passion and purpose, Schechter, speaking on behalf of many identified with

Conservative Judaism, dedicated himself to drawing lines too: Thus far and no farther will we go in accommodating and compromising, in sacrificing hoary tradition upon the altar of trendy progress.

Most religious bodies in America suffered severe strain if not actual break during those decades when the relative merits of the ancient versus the recent demanded daily evaluation or decision. Some groups escaped, such as the Eastern Orthodox and the Oriental, only because they had not yet absorbed enough of the West's modernity to be challenged or threatened by it. These groups had schisms of their own, to be sure, but these more often related to lands they left behind than to the new land in which they now dwelled. Others such as Quakers and Unitarians escaped because they had made the critical cultural choices long before. For the vast majority, however, not enough tranquility and calm repose prevailed to permit wild rejoicing over the statistical progress in religion. To a society still troubled by racism, still unsure of the status of women, still anxious about assimilation and Americanization, religion in the first half of the twentieth century was forced to concentrate more and more on its own internal, badly bruised affairs. Faith, one might well have argued at such a time, led not to social stability and order but to social unrest and disorder.

ECCLESIASTICAL AFTERMATH

In 1922 Harry Emerson Fosdick preached a sermon that captured wide attention across the country. Its subject, "Shall the Fundamentalists Win?," enabled Fosdick to sharpen the terms of debate as well as to endeavor to put the acrimonious decades of which he was a part into some kind of historical perspective. Terms were indeed sharpened when Fosdick explained that the modernists had collectively demonstrated the virgin birth to be "no longer accepted as historic fact, the literal inerrancy of the Scriptures [to be] incredible, the second coming of Christ from the skies [to be] an outmoded phrasing of hope." Such candid comment did little to lower the level of acrimony, Fosdick later noting that while he pleaded for good will, what he received was "an explosion of ill will, for over two years making headline news of a controversy that went the limit of truculence." But, did the fundamentalists win?

A token victory of sorts was theirs in 1925 when a young high school biology teacher, John Thomas Scopes (1900–1970), was brought to trial in Dayton, Tennessee. In what remains the most famous trial in the entire fundamentalist/modernist contest, the civil courts took up the question of whether Scopes had violated a Tennessee law that prohibited "the teaching of the evolution theory in all the universities, normals [teacher training institutions], and all the public schools of Tennessee which are supported in whole or in part by the public school funds of the state." The issue had drama, of course, but the courtroom had even more since the attorney for the prosecution was none other than three-time candidate for the presidency of the United States, William Jennings Bryan (1860–1925), with the defense attorney, Clarence Darrow (1857–1938), though not quite such a public figure, being nonetheless widely known as an outstanding trial lawyer from Chicago. In the battles of the giants, Bryan versus Darrow, young Scopes almost dropped from view.

The courtroom may seem an odd place to settle an issue of the science curriculum in the schools; and, indeed, it is. But, of course, the issue was far wider than that since for so many the question was not a narrow one of state law but the far larger one of the authority of the Bible and the authority, thereby, of many of the churches not just in Tennessee but across the nation. The national press was present in force, even as was the infant radio industry. The breadth of the issue

60. William Jennings Bryan, three-time candidate for the U. S. presidency, won another kind of fame as the leading force against the teaching of evolution. *Library of Congress*

was clearly identified in Bryan's closing remarks, remarks he was never able to deliver since he was stricken and died in the closing days of the trial. "This case," said Bryan correctly, "is no longer local; the defendant ceases to play an important part." Then Bryan said: "The case has assumed the proportion of a battle royal between unbelief that attempts to speak through so-called science and the defenders of the Christian faith, speaking through the legislators of Tennessee." If the jury votes to acquit Scopes, then, Bryan argued, Christ is crucified all over again. "If the law is nullified, there will be rejoicing where God is repudiated, the Saviour scoffed at, and the Bible ridiculed." But on the other hand, if the law is upheld, then "millions of Christians will call you blessed."

The law was upheld, Scopes was fined one hundred dollars, the country went on about its business: a nominal victory for fundamentalism. Nominal, because in so much of that national press the town of Dayton was portrayed as a rural backwater, fundamentalism as a know-nothing absurdity, and the trial itself as part carnival and part farce. In the cultural struggle for the hearts and minds of Americans, fundamentalism's victory in 1925 was far less clear cut. Indeed, liberalism retained control of most denominational seminaries and colleges, most publishing boards, most prestigious pulpits, and most endowed funds. One could argue that the Scopes trial was fundamentalism's last gasp. In so arguing, however, one would be utterly wrong. For not only did fundamentalism live to see the light of another day, stronger than ever before, but on the other side liberalism grew weaker, less self-assured, less a force capable of shaping those hearts and minds. How all of this happened we examine more closely in the following chapter.

CHAPTER 20

Faith and Reason

In the first half of the twentieth century, broad cultural shifts gradually moved religion away from its "king of the mountain" position of intellectual and ethical leadership in the nation. Increasingly, cultural rewards went to artists and novelists, to politicians and social engineers. Religion was, of course, not immune to the growing professionalization of the time, but the clergy as a profession steadily lost status in favor of physicians, lawyers, scientists, and others. One simple measure of that loss was financial: not only did the salaries of clergy fall far behind those of other professionals, they did not match those of most business and labor leaders nor of many civil servants and academicians. Such slippage in the professional standing of the clergy only symbolized far more significant losses in cultural authority at large: losses due in part to the growing importance of many other disciplines, but also due in part to the internal crises within the "religious mind" itself.

PHILOSOPHY AND RELIGION

Traditionally the closest of allies, philosophers and theologians found themselves drawing apart in the twentieth century as each group pursued its own agenda. Many philosophers turned away from the larger metaphysical questions in which religion had a keen interest to narrower ones of linguistic analysis or symbolic logic that, to the theologian, often seemed irrelevant. Many theologians, on the other hand, continued to be bound by creedal loyalties and biblical precedents in a way that made fruitful dialogue with philosophy unproductive if not impossible.

John Dewey (1859–1952), without question the most influential American philosopher in the first half of the twentieth century, deliberately took as his goal the reconstruction of American society. In art, logic, politics, science, and education, he influenced and reshaped in ways that defy precise measure. And he accomplished this "reconstruction" without much reference to religion, except to explain how irrelevant most ancient religious answers had become to the newer ways of investigation and discovery. "Anthropology, history, and literary criticism have furnished," Dewey wrote in 1934, "a radically different version of the historic events and personages upon which Christian religions have built." So also biology and psychology, geology and astronomy, challenged traditional religious points of view. But the principal issue, Dewey argued, is not a quarrel about the truth of this or that particular dogma or article of faith, but about the only valid method that humankind has come to accept for arriving at truth. Not by consulting sacred writings or ancient oracles, he explained, but by investigation and experiment and inquiry do we come to fresh and significant understanding.

As an exponent of pragmatism (which he also often called "instrumentalism"), Dewey saw the universe as open-ended, not closed; he saw truth as something not given but discovered, not fixed, but ever unfolding and enlarging. "For the educated man today," Dewey observed, "the final arbiter of all questions of fact, existence, and intellectual assent" are these new methods of investigation and verification. This was so dramatic a shift from older ways of looking at the world that it constituted, in Dewey's view, nothing less than a "revolution." Disputes about "this and that piecemeal item of belief" were irrelevant; the point is what methods does one accept as leading to new truths which will, in turn, lead to even more truths. "In this revolution, every defeat is a stimulus to renewed inquiry; every victory won is the open door to more discoveries, and every discovery is a new seed planted in the soil of intelligence, from which grow fresh plants with new fruits." The universe bubbles over with possibilities. To realize those possibilities, all that was necessary, Dewey believed, was for men and women to leave their outworn shells and with vigorous optimism fashion a finer future for all the world.

Outworn shells were represented, more often than not, by institutional religion which (for Dewey) seemed more interested in defending truths already known than in seeking truths yet to be found. In Dewey's world of the future, a place for religious language and for religious experience could still be found, but only as churches surrendered "the whole notion of special truths that are religious by nature, together with the idea of peculiar avenues to such truths." Somehow, one must be able to separate religion from the idea of intellectual assent to some special doctrine, "even that of the existence of the God of theism." To take the place of these old and outmoded ideas, religious persons can dedicate themselves, with faith and devotion, to that "one sure road of access to truth—the road of patient, cooperative inquiry operating by means of observation, experiment, record, and controlled reflection." Dewey did not think he was asking religion to give up much that mattered. For most theologians, however, what he called for was total capitulation and cowardly retreat.

Even more popular writers than Dewey carried similar messages in this same period of time. Walter Lippmann (1889–1974), for example, as a remarkably influential journalist and widely read author, convinced much of the literate American public that traditional religion was all washed up and finished. In *A Preface to Morals*, published in 1929, Lippmann explained that the old cultural cohesion had been dissolved by "the acids of modernity." Men and women have now become "brave and brilliant atheists who have defied the Methodist God," Lippmann wrote. Religious certainty, like the ocean floor, had given way to some momentous tidal shift, and nothing had yet replaced it. "Insofar as men have now lost their belief in a heavenly king," Lippmann observed, "they have to find some other ground for their moral choices than the revelation of his will." What that ground should be Lippmann was not sure, since for him even science failed to guarantee human dignity or offer sure promise of human destiny. One may turn, perhaps, to stoicism or humanism or objective detachment, but in any case one could no longer find strength in "leaning on the everlasting arms" of familiar faith. In subsequent books and regular newspaper columns, Lippmann continued his search for better certainties or at least "civilities" that would guide the society of which he was a part, but he would henceforth find neither certainty nor civility in American religion.

Not all philosophers, to be sure, dismissed traditional religion so swiftly and surely. Harvard professor William James, though also a pragmatist, found religious questions—and religious answers—to be significant and relevant. Such questions and such answers did have consequences for human behavior, and anything that had consequences the true pragmatist could not ignore. In many major areas of life, faith "is one of the indispensable preliminary conditions" for reaching some goal; "faith creates its own verification," James concluded. Alfred North Whitehead (1861–1947), also of Harvard, did not dismiss the idea of God though he altered it to emphasize "the tender elements in the world, which slowly and in quietness operate by love." For Whitehead God was not Aristotle's unmoved mover, nor was the deity some kind of "ruling Caesar, or ruthless moralist." God moved by persuasion rather than by coercion which was one reason, Whitehead pointed out, why the mills of the gods ground so slowly.

James and Whitehead and such other philosophers as Josiah Royce and George Santayana aside, however, professional philosophizing by midcentury had clearly distanced itself from any intimate or supportive alliance with theology. Faith had become a sign of intellectual weakness or closed-mindedness; reason, however defined, had become the only respectable path that those dedicated to a life of the mind could travel. Liberal religious thinkers tried to keep the bridges between faith and reason in good repair, but often in the process yielded more religious uniqueness than they should. Conservative religious thinkers kept pointing to the widening gap between reason and faith, between the sacred and the secular, often in the process yielding more cultural leadership than they should. In this philosophical distancing, theologians posed questions of tactics that also turned out to be matters of substance.

SCIENCE AND RELIGION

Far better known in this period were the contests and conflicts between scientists and theologians, the Scopes trial previously discussed being only a single if highly public example. From the point of view of the theologians, science kept invading their territory, answering questions about the origin and purpose of the world, about the nature and destiny of humanity—questions that were, fundamentally, religious rather than scientific. From the point of view of the scientists, theology blocked the pathways to knowledge, ruling the experiments of the laboratory as off limits, improper, and even dangerous. Each side saw the other as rude, ambitious, imperious, and uncompromising. Each side, to a degree, was right.

In the closing years of the nineteenth century, leading theologians searched for accommodations with the growing authority and prestige of science. But in this searching, they were often limited not only by their own religious convictions but by the authorities of the churches with which they were identified. Roman Catholics, for example, found their church's face set strongly against Darwin, as James Cardinal Gibbons (1834–1921) pointed out that crude theories not in accordance with revelation must be rejected. This was false science, he added, not true science, for between true science and religion no conflict is possible. "There is as much difference between true and false science, as there is between authority and despotism, liberty and license," the Cardinal noted, and it was the Church's duty to support one and resist the other. When the Church sees the scientist "raise his profane hands and attempt to touch the temple of faith, she cries out, 'Thus far shalt thou go and no farther!' "

A few years later, a Roman Catholic professor of Physics at Notre Dame tried to suggest that Darwinism was not irreconcilable with Catholic dogma. In a book published in 1896 (*Evolution and Dogma*), John Augustus Zahm (1851–1921) explained that there can be theistic evolutionists just as there can be atheistic or agnostic evolutionists. And to one who believed in God, everything within Darwinism "is a part of a grand unity betokening an omnipotent Creator." God's hand, Zahm argued, may be seen in all of creation, from the lowest to the highest, and God's handiwork can be found in all of nature. "His power and goodness are disclosed in the beauteous crystalline form of the snowflake, in the delicate texture, fragrance and color of the rose, in the marvellous pencilings of the butterfly's wing." All these and more, Zahm concluded, "are pregnant with truths of the highest order." But Catholicism was not yet ready for this synthesis of new biology with old theology, Zahm's book being denounced and withdrawn from further publication or circulation.

Protestantism likewise was unready for a full embrace of evolution, the popular Brooklyn preacher, T. DeWitt Talmage (1832–1902) denouncing the idea as both "atheistic and absurd." In arguing that man came from beast, man was made more bestial. In arguing against immortality, the evolutionist destroyed all foundation of morality and purpose. "We all die alike—the cow, the horse, the sheep, the man, the reptile. Annihilation is the heaven of the evolutionist," Talmage asserted. His advice followed immediately: "From such a stenchful and damnable doctrine, turn away." Talmage acknowledged that he believed in a kind of evolution, but one far different from that put

61. Lyman Abbott, Congregationalist minister and influential editor, argued in behalf of evolution; he is shown here in a 1905 photograph. *Keystone-Mast Collection, UC–Riverside*

forward by Charles Darwin. He believed, he wrote, in a "gracious and divine and heavenly evolution—evolution out of sin into holiness, out of grief into gladness, out of mortality into immortality, out of earth into heaven!" No stench in an evolution like that.

At the same time that Talmage was pronouncing against evolution, another Brooklyn Protestant, Henry Ward Beecher (1813–1887) contended that the whole history of Christianity was itself an instance of natural evolution. In a series of sermons preached in 1885, Beecher argued that evolution was but another example of "the diversified unfolding of God's plans on earth." Certainly, the idea of evolution had an effect upon religion in general, upon Christianity in particular, Beecher agreed. But the effect was for good rather than ill, for evolution weeded out the base and inferior, making room for the good and the strong. "Theology and the Church are undergoing a process of evolution, towards perfection," Beecher declared, "changing upwards and for the better."

Brooklyn could not contain the conflict which spread across the country and across the denominations. The popular revivalist, Billy Sunday (1862–1935), continued well into the twentieth century to denounce and ridicule "the bastard theory of evolution," winning wide approval from his audiences and even from several state legislatures. His near contemporary, Lyman Abbott (1835–1922), on the other hand, reached even wider audiences through his editorial labors and many books designed to reconcile the teachings of Christianity with those of Darwin. In evolutionary doctrine, we find support, Abbott wrote in 1915, for the view that "man is gradually emerging from an animal nature into a spiritual manhood." The Genesis account of creation was not the issue, Abbott asserted. "For the question whether God made the animal man by a mechanical process in an hour or by a process of growth continuing through centuries is quite immaterial to one who believes that into man God breathes a divine life." Just how and when such "breathing" occurred was a detail that Abbott was prepared to leave to others.

If biology provided the battleground for the late nineteenth and early twentieth century (and again later in the twentieth), psychology, sociology, and anthropology also kept the fires of intellectual and theological controversy burning. The theories of Sigmund Freud (1856–1939) challenged traditional doctrines of sin and salvation, guilt and repentance, innocence and depravity. For Freud religion was an illusion, for Karl Marx (1818–1833) an opiate, and for neither was religion a legitimate means for dealing with the ills of the individual or of society. Religion was, in fact, responsible for a good many of those ills, both men argued. In sociology, one found a positivism that dismissed all ideas not immediately derived from sense experience, with theology often being seen as a stage that humankind would inevitably outgrow—the sooner, the better. And in anthropology, one confronted a cultural relativism that seemed to destroy all hope of clear discrimination between good and evil, truth and error, to say nothing of heresy and orthodoxy. Religion was on the ropes.

Once again, those religious leaders who tried to keep a dialogue going between theologians on the one hand and scientists and social scientists on the other often appeared too ready to surrender the distinctiveness of their traditions or the fruits of their insights. On the other hand, those who like Billy Sunday declared that no reconciliation between science and religion was ever possible abandoned any claim to cultural authority or broad social impact. For much of the first half of the twentieth century, however, the issue was not who shaped the culture, but who owned the soul of revealed religion itself.

THEOLOGICAL BATTLE STATIONS

Modernists and fundamentalists quarrelled about more than who would run what agency, who would control what college, who would preach from what pulpit. They also argued about ideas. In one form or another the contest over ideas affected Catholicism and Judaism no less than Protestantism; and, in one form of another, that contest continues to the present day. In part, the issue was a hardy perennial of all human life: How much of the past does one hold on to and honor? How much of the future does one adapt to and welcome? But rarely did the partisan proposals or protests appear in such simplified form.

Within Protestantism, one debated both the future and the past: the future with respect to the Second Coming of Christ, the past with respect to biblical history and command. In the nineteenth century, as we have seen, large numbers of Protestants were from time to time caught up in heady expectations that the world would soon come to an end and that Christ would dramatically, visibly reappear to establish a Kingdom of God on earth in a new (or the old) Jerusalem. In the early twentieth century such views seemed outmoded to many who believed that the future was one of peace and progress, not of Armageddon (Revelation 16:16) and catastrophe. For these modernists, the Kingdom of God might indeed come, but if so it would come through the efforts of enlightened and energetic women and men working together for the greater good of the social whole. The Kingdom of God, on these terms, would come not because God had given up on an evil, warring world, but because God looked with pleasure and satisfaction upon what his sometimes erring children had managed to accomplish.

As many backed away from the notion of a visible Second Coming of Christ, other Protestants defended that proposition even more vigorously and in sometimes bewildering detail. After William Miller's "Great Disappointment" in 1843, few were willing to name a specific time or day for the Second Coming, but the notion that it would be soon, very soon, filled the air. Premillennialists (that is, those who believed the Christ's coming would precede the thousand years of peace and plenty foretold in the Book of Revelation) did not agree on all of the details. One of the more pervasive manifestations of this premillenial point of view, dispensationalism, was associated with the Plymouth Brethren in England and, in America, with the name of Cyrus I. Scofield (1843–1921) and his enormously popular Scofield Reference Bible which first appeared in 1909. Dispensationalism divided the world's history into seven ages or "dispensations," humankind now living in the sixth age known as "Man under Grace." This age will soon end with "the descent of the Lord from Heaven, when sleeping saints will be raised and, together with the believers then living, caught up 'to meet the Lord in the air' (1 Thessalonians 4:16,17)." Then the seventh and final dispensation will follow, "Man Under the Personal Reign of Christ," and this, said Scofield, "is the period commonly called the Millennium." Christ "will reign over restored Israel and over the earth for one thousand years. . . . The seat of his power," Scofield added, "will be Jerusalem."

Premillennialism, whether of the dispensationalist variety or some other, was enormously popular in much of American Protestantism. It was the particular emphasis of the Jehovah's Witnesses, the Seventh-Day Adventists, the International Church of the Foursquare Gospel (founded by Aimee Semple McPherson in 1927), Plymouth Brethren and many more. But it was also present in much of mainstream Protestantism, and this is where one found contests about the future most heated and most disruptive.

Shailer Mathews (1863–1941), Baptist professor at the University of Chicago and a leading modernist spokesman, confronted the issue directly and forcefully in 1917 in a brief tract entitled, "Will Christ Come Again?" His answer was No, in the sense that the premillennialists expected Jesus physically to return. Such a view, Mathews argued, misread history, misused the Bible, and misunderstood the spiritual nature of God. Premillennialists, said Mathews, deny "that God is capable of bringing about His victory by spiritual means." Though God is a spirit, he cannot in their view "save the world by spiritual means. In order to succeed He has to revert to physical brutality . . . [and] miraculous militarism." Nor did the premillennialists represent the essence of Christian orthodoxy. According to Mathews, nothing like their views could be found in the fathers of the early Church or the leaders of the Reformation. The premillennialist, said Mathews, demanded that the "Christian should give up intelligence and education in order to live the life of faith . . . [and] forces men to choose between the universally accepted results of modern culture and diagrams from the Book of Daniel." But in another and more significant sense, Mathews argued, Christ will come again as "a spiritual presence, leading us through the Holy Spirit into all truth, regenerating men and institutions." Here was the real Kingdom of God on earth and the true victory in spiritual battle: "the triumph of the ideals of Jesus will come when the spirit of Jesus comes into human hearts."

For many, Mathews' totally spiritualized millennium was wholly unacceptable. It was, said another Baptist, Isaac M. Haldeman (1845–1933) of New York City, a "burlesque." In a direct response to Mathews, Haldeman said that he read the professor's tract "with amazement, with pity and with indignation." Professor Mathews' view of the millennium was "nothing less than a burlesque, a grotesque and dishonoring caricature of one of the most sacred, immense and initial subjects of Holy Writ." Arguing carefully from the biblical text and sometimes returning to the original Greek, Haldeman declared that Mathews contradicted the plain sense of Scripture. He apparently regarded the New Testament, said Haldeman, as "nothing better today than a bundle of pre-Christian error." And in so far as "orthodoxy" was concerned, Haldeman replied that Christian history was full of testimony, especially in its earliest and "purest" years, of expectation regarding the Second Coming. For those so misguided as to believe that, without direct divine intervention, the world was getting better and the Kingdom of God was just around the corner, Haldeman had nothing but pity. Evil triumphs, not good; infidelity wins, not orthodoxy; spiritual and moral character deteriorates, not "evolves." So, Haldeman in the midst of World War I concluded, "I am hoping and intensely praying for the return of the Lord in my day and generation to put an end to this suicide of nations, this butchery and blasting, solace the hearts that are breaking, hush the lamentation, wipe away the tears of wives, of mothers and orphans."

Similarly among Presbyterians, Methodists, Disciples and others, one found stridently opposing views about the Second Coming. The visible return of Christ became for some a kind of "single issue theology": that is, a test of one's faithfulness as a Christian, one's loyalty as a churchmember. It became a leading "fundamental" within fundamentalism, a question to be pressed at the time for ordaining new clergy, a matter to be settled before calling a new pastor or hiring a new professor. And by no means was passionate dedication to the doctrine of the visible, imminent Second Coming a phenomenon associated chiefly with the period around World War I. In many circles, the concern has continued unabated, one measure of premillennial popularity being the issuing of a New Scofield Reference Bible by Oxford University Press in 1967. Copies sold numbered in the millions.

Underlying what might seem to be a rather narrow or specifically limited item of belief was a far broader concern: the authority of the Bible for this and all other matters of faith and morals. The Bible might even be a book of history, telling us when the world was created; or a book of science, telling us of the origins of man, and of races, and of supernatural suspensions of natural law. In the first century of Christian history, the test of orthodoxy was "What think ye of Christ?" In the twentieth century, the test was "What think ye of the Bible?"

This test clearly underlay the Mathews-Haldeman clash described above. Mathews said that premillennialists misused and misunderstood the Bible, regarding every recorded belief of early Christians "as the teaching of the Bible." Logically, this must mean, Mathews wrote, that contemporary Christians must believe "in a flat earth, the perpetuation of slavery, the submission to rulers like Nero." There was, however, another and better way to use the Bible, Mathews added, a way sometimes called "historical" but that "might better be called the common sense way." Christians utilizing their Bibles in this way know that "inspiration was progressive, accumulative, dependent upon and fitted to successive periods of human intelligence." Beliefs of the early Christians, for example, "can be understood only as they are studied in the light of the habits of thought prevalent in their times." That's just common sense.

Or was it nonsense? Haldeman opted strongly for the latter. "The truth is," Haldeman wrote, that "Professor Mathews and his school accept only that part of the Bible . . . which agrees with their theory of world progress, the march of humanity to higher and better things." Mathews' approach to the Bible was such as to deny that it was and is "the complete and perfect Word of God." And this, Haldeman clearly recognized, was the central issue. "Here is where Professor Mathews and premillennialists confront each other. This is the firing line. This is the 'front.' " Furthermore, this casual attitude toward biblical authority, this loving attitude toward modernity, has "given us a class of ministers who might as well preach in the name of Buddha or Confucius as Christ." It would be as impossible, Haldeman concluded, for premillennialists to question any statement in the Bible, no matter how insignificant, as it would be for Mathews to believe it.

Mathews and Haldeman, however, were only single protagonists. Each represented constituencies far broader than the University of Chicago on the one hand and premillennialists on the other. For Protestantism in the first half of the twentieth century (for Lutherans and Southern Baptists in the second half), "What think ye of the Bible?" was the question above all questions, the battle station which both drew and gave the greatest fire. In 1924 Harry Emerson Fosdick published a book entitled, *The Modern Use of the Bible*. Here he tried to summarize the results of modern biblical scholarship (linguistic, historical, archaeological) in a way that the average Protestant churchgoer could understand and perhaps even welcome. For Fosdick's point was that the Bible became even more meaningful, not less, more uplifting, not less, when one understood its different periods of development, its gradually arrived at insights. Now, as a result of all the new learning, "we can," Fosdick wrote, "trace the great ideas of Scripture in their development from their simple and elementary forms, when they first appear in the earliest writings, until they come to their full maturity in the latest books." We can follow any single idea, such as the idea of God, or any ethical precept such as honor or love, said Fosdick, from its rudimentary beginnings to rich fulfillment. Modern critics, Fosdick noted, are constantly accused of "tearing the Book to pieces, of cutting out this or that." But the precise opposite is true, he asserted. "The new approach to the Bible once more integrates the Scriptures, saves us from our piecemeal treatment of them, and restores to us the whole book seen as a unified development from early and simple beginnings to a great conclusion."

Fosdick had his admirers, but also his detractors who saw in this "modernity" just another sly attempt to evade clear biblical demands. These critics also saw the very foundation of Protestant Christianity being undermined in any questioning of the Bible's sufficiency and

62. Dr. Samuel McCrea Cavert, general secretary of the National Council of Churches, reads proof for the Revised Standard Version of the Bible that appeared in 1952. *National Council of Churches*

validity. The Bible, Charles Hodge of Princeton had long ago written, was the storehouse of all theology. Just as the biologist studied nature to gather his facts and arrive at truth, so the theologian studied the Bible in precisely the same way. Congregationalist Reuben A. Torrey (1856–1928) in a large book on *What the Bible Teaches* (1898) made thousands of biblical propositions perfectly plain, scientifically precise, authoritatively required. The modernists, said Torrey, set the Bible aside in order to substitute what they think is demanded "by the modern evolutionary method of thought." The modernist really does not believe in the Bible at all, Torrey declared, but he had neither the intellectual honesty nor the moral courage to say so. And as a successor to Hodge at Princeton, J. Gresham Machen (1881–1937) agreed that modernism was not a more sophisticated version of Christianity, but no Christianity at all. "In trying to remove from Christianity everything that could possibly be objected to in the name of science, in trying to bribe off the enemy by those concessions which the enemy most desires, the apologist has really abandoned what he started out to defend." The biblical critics and the modern liberal church were, for Machen, primarily interested in defending contemporary culture, doing so under the disguise of reforming and refining New Testament religion. But what they were really doing, Machen firmly believed, was undermining and destroying that "faith once delivered unto the saints."

Protestants felt strongly about ideas; they differed widely and sharply in their expectations for the future and in their understandings of the past. But Protestants were not alone in being torn by the tensions and novelties that modern scholarship had introduced into institutional religion. Roman Catholics, both European and American, confronted similar though not identical crises. Not as engaged in debate about the details of a Second Coming, Catholics were equally engaged about questions of progress, of history, of dogma, of the sacred authority of the Bible and the teaching authority of the Church. Not only were they engaged, but they were also besieged.

For a hundred years or more the Roman Catholic Church in Europe had been thrown on the defensive: attacked during the French Revolution, abused by Napoleon, forced to retreat wherever monarchy was dethroned or weakened, robbed of its Papal States, and reduced in its temporal power over and over again. Modernity was no great gift from heaven. Modernity, in fact, was a major mistake, as Pope Pius IX made clear in 1864 in his famous "Syllabus of Errors." By the time that the twentieth century arrived, the church was no more relaxed about the political sufferings that it had endured. Then, when to all these indignities, modern scholarship added its challenges to the dogmatic theology of the church, patience wore thin.

In 1907 Pope Pius X seized upon that dreaded word "modernism," turning it this way and that, and finding it from every perspective an object of ugliness and repugnance. In a long encyclical, *Pascendi Dominici Gregis* ("On the Modernists"), the pope saw these new thinkers prepared to elevate experience above tradition, inner feeling above external truth, evolution above revelation, and reason above faith. Modernists found the origin of religion in the subconscious which produces a kind of vague, ill-defined "religious sense." According to them, this "is the origin of all, even of supernatural religion." This would be hard enough to hear coming from the secular world, from agnostics or even atheists. But "there are Catholics, yea, and priests too, who say these things openly; and they boast that they are going to reform the Church by these ravings!" Even dogma is not exempt from their criticism, the pope affirmed, for they believe that dogma is not something given once and for all time, eternal and unchanging. No, they believe that "in a living religion everything is subject to change, and must in fact be changed. In this way they pass to what is practically their principal doctrine, namely, evolution." From the operation of that grand law of nature, nothing is exempt. The encyclical stated: "To the laws of evolution everything is subject under penalty of death—dogma, Church, worship, the Books we revere as sacred, even faith itself."

Nothing exempt—not even the Bible. For the modernists, the Bible was but a summary of experiences, special experiences to be sure, but nonetheless human experiences. "We may ask, what then becomes of inspiration? Inspiration, they reply, is in no wise distinguished from that impulse which stimulates the believer to reveal the faith that is in him by words or writings. . . . It is something like that which happens in poetical inspiration." And if the Bible was only a summary of experience, the Church (the modernists hold) was nothing more than "collective conscience." If, moreover, the Church's authority ultimately rested upon the individual conscience, then the Church must be subject to the conscience: that is, it must become more democratic. But the modernist is not through with scandalizing and horrifying. He even holds, said the pope, that the state must "be separated from the Church, and the Catholic from the citizen." The modernists in fact, the pope asserted, behave like liberal Protestants and can hardly be distinguished from them.

One difference between Catholics and Protestants, liberal or conservative, however, was the Vatican's powerful authority not only to scorn modernism but officially to condemn it and uproot it. This the pope did in language as stern as it was explicit: all bishops, all heads of religious orders, all directors of schools and seminaries were to exercise the greatest vigilance in seeing that modernism be blotted out. With respect to administrators and professors at Catholic universities, "anyone who in any way is found to be tainted with Modernism is to be excluded without compunction from these offices, whether of government or of teaching, and those who already occupy them are to be removed." Pius

X urged special caution concerning "those who show a love of novelty in history, archaeology, biblical exegisis," or a tendency to abandon or criticize the teachings of St. Thomas Aquinas, the "Angelic Doctor" of the thirteenth century. Every diocese, the pope added, shall have its "Council of Vigilance" with its appointed clergy to "watch most carefully for every trace and sign of Modernism both in publication and in teaching." Modernism for the Vatican was no innocent novelty to be tolerated with mild amusement; it was heresy to be fought against with every resource at the church's command.

In his encyclical, the pope had his eye more on Europe than America, for in the American church a full-fledged modernist was hardly to be found. What could be found, of course, were liberal Catholics arguing against conservative Catholics, Americanizing bishops contending with bishops who saw America as more the problem than the solution, world-affirming Catholics opposed to world-fleeing Catholics, Catholics who rejoiced in development and progress baffled by Catholics who rejoiced in neither. Such Catholic bishops in America as John Ireland (1838–1918) of St. Paul, Minnesota, and John Lancaster Spalding (1840–1916) of Peoria, Illinois, led the liberal forces, while such bishops as Michael A. Corrigan (1839–1902) of New York City, and Bernard J. McQuaid (1823–1909) of Rochester led the opposing conservative ranks. The effect of the 1907 encyclical, however, was to shift the odds for victory heavily to the side of the conservatives. In the words of one Catholic historian, "In one fatal blow the Pope destroyed the budding renewal of Catholic theology." As a consequence, Jay P. Dolan added, "the church paid a heavy price." The Protestant path of schism was avoided, but an artificial and enforced unity also extracted its cost.

Within Judaism, concerns were similar, but again not identical. No obsession with the Second Coming of Christ, of course, and no anxiety about the teaching authority of some central religious headquarters. But broader underlying questions about science, cultural evolution, revelation, tradition, and the uneasy relationship between sacred and secular disturbed or divided the religious community of Jews as it had that of Protestants and Catholics. The Torah or Laws of Moses occupied a unique place of honor, that uniqueness for a long time preventing a hearty embrace of biblical criticism by the observant Jew, especially among the Conservative and Orthodox branches. One argued instead about the interpretations of Mosaic law, the commentaries on that law—about the Talmud (Babylonian or Palestinian), about the Schools of Rabbi Shammai or Rabbi Hillel, about the Halakah (legal portions of Talmudic literature) and the Haggadah (non-legal portions, including the ritual readings for the Passover meal). But in all of this the biblical Torah itself stood largely untouched until the late twentieth century.

Under the auspices of the Jewish Publication Society, and after many years of intensive labor, a new translation of Hebrew Scriptures appeared in 1917. Long dependent upon Christian translations into English (except for the early work of Isaac Leeser), the American Jewish community now had its own "official" Bible, one that testified to the growing importance of the Jewish presence in the United States as well as to the maturing biblical scholarship of many of the nation's Jews. As the preface to this translation declared: "We have grown under providence both in numbers and in importance, so that we constitute now the greatest section of Israel living in a single country outside of Russia." It was only fitting, therefore, the translators added, that "we have applied ourselves to the sacred task of preparing a new translation of the Bible into the English language, which, unless all signs fail, is to become the current speech of the majority of the children of Israel."

The next several decades, representing a period of great biblical activity among both Protestants (the Revised Standard Version appeared

63. By 1974, Catholics, Protestants, and Greek Orthodox agreed on and approved a single translation of the Bible. *National Council of Churches*

in 1952) and Roman Catholics (the New American Bible appeared in 1970), saw Jewish scholars also busy with yet another translation that would take advantage of the newest manuscript discoveries and other developments in biblical scholarship. In 1962 a fresh translation of the Books of Moses was published under the title, *The Torah: A New Translation of the Holy Scriptures According to the Masoretic Text*. Twenty years later the whole of Hebrew Scriptures appeared in a precedent-setting translation that testified to the scholarly maturity of American Jewry who not only brought Reform, Conservative, and Orthodox together but who also worked closely with biblical scholars in Israel. Remarkably, biblical scholarship proved among America's Jews to be not so much an instance of division and bitter dispute as a matter of cooperation and a point of pride.

Of course, institutional divisions within Judaism persisted. Reform Judaism continued to be the group most comfortable with "modernity," though the Columbus Platform of 1937 was less optimistic about progress and more sympathetic to tradition than the 1885 Pittsburgh Platform had been. Conservative Judaism, stressing Zionism and the role of family worship, continued as a kind of middle ground between Reform and Orthodoxy, but was dismayed to discover that Orthodoxy did not gradually fade away. Orthodox Judaism, the official religion of the state of Israel, did not see itself so much as an "American religion" as it did the steady, uncompromising continuation of Jewish practice and belief across the centuries. To some degree, therefore, it isolated itself from the temptations of acculturation and the seductions of modernity. As a consequence, it also remained largely invisible outside such major centers of Jewish population as New York City and Los Angeles; however, the infusion of a strongly pietistic element known as Hasidism drew greater public notice to it, especially as portrayed in the popular writings of the novelist, Chaim Potok.

America in the twentieth century, moreover, introduced yet another stream into the Judaic landscape: namely, Reconstructionism. The work chiefly of Mordecai Kaplan (1881–1983), Reconstructionism argued that Judaism was more a religious civilization than it was a religion. The peoplehood of Israel, for example, was more important than the supernatural emphases of the Torah. The function of religion was more social than theological for Kaplan, more a matter of history than a matter of faith. And he hoped his school of thought would have particular appeal for the many Jews in America not affiliated with any temple or synagogue, yet who still found strength and support in their sense of belonging to an ancient tradition and to an identifiable people.

The peculiarly American character of Reconstructionism is evident in its very first platform issued in 1935, where this statement appears: "As American Jews we give first place in our lives to the American civilization which we share in common with our fellow Americans, and we seek to develop our Jewish heritage to the maximum degree consonant with the best in American life." If that sounded to some more like sociology than theology, Kaplan saw no reason for concern. The important issue, he argued, was "not what idea of God the individual Jew must hold," but to what common purpose "the Jews as a people are willing to be committed." Reconstructionism has few synagogues and few rabbis; yet, its embrace of reason and of American culture has its analogue in the "modernism" found among both Protestants and Catholics. The irony of Reconstructionism, however, is that its appeal has been to those Jews least interested in the synagogue, least devoted to the Torah. It is, to some degree, a kind of nonecclesiastical denomination.

The questions of faith and reason transcend any single religious group, any single century, any single country. As long as men and women do not live by bread alone, the questions will continue to press with some urgency. And as long as men and women do not surrender their freedom of thought, their answers will reveal a spectacular variety.

THEOLOGICAL AFTERMATH

One must keep in mind that the labels of "modernist" and "fundamentalist" represent special types more than they do the full-orbed reality that is American religion. At no time in the twentieth century has it been possible to classify the majority of church and synagogue members as belonging to either one or the other of these categories. Where does everyone else fit? Probably somewhere in the middle, attracted now to aspects of one position, then to aspects of another, but never wholly aligned with either "party." The two movements themselves, moreover, have not remained static, but have undergone shifting emphases and even internal divisions. After the bitterest battles in the first third of the century, it was possible to see modernists gradually lose their confidence in progress and their uncritical fondness for the surrounding culture. Similarly, it was possible to see fundamentalists lose their belligerence with respect to other Christians and their hostility to all forms of "applied Christianity."

Within Protestantism a broad coalition of conservatives, preferring to call themselves "evangelicals," joined together in 1942 to form the National Association of Evangelicals. As one of the leaders of the new coalition stated, we must "be wise and gracious enough to recognize that there are differences of doctrine among Bible-believing members of the Church of Jesus Christ upon which there is little hope that we will see eye to eye." Nonetheless, "profitless controversy over issues which are relatively unimportant" should not prevent a greater degree of cooperation and fellowship among the more than one million members entering into the association. In the following decade, an evangelical leader, Carl F. Henry (b. 1912), called for an abandonment of the old narrow legalism and, at the same time, for an embrace of the social implications of Christianity. The Christian religion, Henry pointed out in 1957, "is by no means the social gospel of modernism." But neither was it the mere "personal abstinence from dubious social externals" so dear to the hearts of earlier fundamentalists. "Christian ethics probes deeper," Henry observed, and the new evangelicals must apply "the gospel message" to "marriage and the home, labor and economics, politics and the state, culture and the arts, in fact, [to] every sphere of life."

On the liberal side, a man such as Reinhold Niebuhr (1892–1971) pulled sharply away from the naive optimism of an earlier generation. One cannot maintain, Niebuhr argued, that the progress of humankind is steadily upward or that, in the words of a popular cliché of the 1920s, "every day in every way we are getting better and better." One can hold such a position, Niebuhr declared, only by ignoring reality. The reality is that human nature is perverse and that society tends toward evil. Science, sanitation, and education cannot, will not, produce a

64. Reinhold Niebuhr, shown here in 1963, had by that time retired from Union Theological Seminary but not from the theological fray. *Religious News Service*

perfect world, Niebuhr asserted; neither will a sentimental Protestantism that refuses to confront the undeniable realities of war, greed, exploitation, prejudice, poverty, cruelty, injustice, and lust. We tell men to love and imitate Christ, assuring them (Niebuhr wrote) that all will be well. But Christ loved, and all was not well: he ended up on a cross. So a kind of "Christian realism" is called for, a realism that recognizes that the highest goal among nations is justice, not love; that the means to achieve justice sometimes requires force, even violence, even revolution. None of this language would the modernist have found acceptable or believable. Niebuhr preferred to speak of man's depravity, not his nobility; of society's folly, not its promise. By midcentury, neither modernism nor fundamentalism much resembled what each had been a generation before.

Niebuhr, a member of a small Protestant denomination called the Evangelical and Reformed Church (later merged into the United Church of Christ), transcended denominationalism, transcended Protestantism, transcended even the whole field of religion as he shaped the thinking of political scientists, statesmen, journalists, and a host of others. Similarly, a Jewish refugee from Germany and Poland, Abraham Heschel (1907–1973), moved beyond the confines of either Reform or Conservative Judaism to offer both comfort and rebuke to modern civilization as a whole. Arriving in the United States in 1940, Heschel before long found himself speaking to audiences all across the country as he contended that "The fate of mankind depends upon the realization that the distinction between good and evil, right and wrong, is superior to all other distinctions." Religion, particularly biblical religion, can assist humanity in making those critical distinctions. We move, wrote Heschel in 1951, like the heavenly bodies in ellipses, not circles. "We are attached to two centers: to the focus of our self and to the focus of God." The tragedy of modern civilization, said Heschel, is that "the vision of the sacred has all but died in the soul of man." No naive belief in progress there.

Heschel was himself an activist in the battle against evil: in Selma to identify with the cause of civil rights, in Washington to decry the folly of America's imperial ambitions. The soul of the individual as well as of the nation and of the world became Heschel's consuming concern. If we lose our sense of the sacred, he said, it is as though we have lost the light from the sun. The world stands or falls upon not its wealth or its power but its spiritual well-being. "All our life," he wrote, "hangs by a thread—the faithfulness of man to the concern of God." Moreover, everything worthwhile in what we are pleased to call "civilization" as opposed to barbarism and chaos "depends upon man's sense for the sacredness of life, upon reverence for this spark of light in the darkness of selfishness." Once "we permit this spark to be quenched, the darkness falls upon us like thunder." Heschel liked to tell the story of the blacksmith who learned everything there was to know about his trade, all the skills, all the tools, all the techniques of the true artisan. Only one thing he failed to learn: how to kindle a spark.

For Heschel and others, the role of religion was to teach humanity how to kindle a spark. Religion had lost too much time, too much respect, in fighting battles within the households of faith. Meanwhile, a bleeding, warring world needed help.

65. Rabbi Abraham J. Heschel addressed the problems of modern Judaism in particular and of modern civilization in general. *Jewish Theological Seminary of America*

CHAPTER 21

War, Peace, and Religious Renewal

From the 1940s through the 1960s, both the nation and its religious institutions endured many trials, confronted many unyielding realities, conquered many foes but fell victim to others. The nation found itself tested by war: in the forties, again in the fifties and the sixties and beyond. Churches and synagogues found themselves tested by brutal revelations of humanity's inhumanity, by awesome new technological powers, by temptations to become instruments or pawns in the Cold War. Amid the darkness, however, beacons of renewal and resurgence could be seen, especially for Roman Catholics in the 1960s.

WARS AROUND THE WORLD

Immediately following the surprise Japanese attack on Pearl Harbor on December 7, 1941, the United States entered into a war that had already engaged most of Europe since 1939 and much of Asia since the Japanese invasion of Manchuria in 1931. In the midst of America's involvement in the war, organized religion followed two broad approaches. In the first, ministries of faith offered consolation, guidance, inspiration, and a wide variety of war-related services. Bandages wrapped, food and medical supplies sent, entertainment and housing provided, Bibles dispatched, chaplains appointed, plaques honoring the dead dedicated—these and countless other activities characterized a good part of religion's wartime mission.

More than eight thousand ministers, rabbis, and priests served as chaplains in World War II. Confessions were heard within range of the noise of battle, hymns were sung above the roar of the battleship's throbbing engines, sermons were preached in artic snow and tropical heat, communion was offered in front-line hospitals and last rites within front-line "fox holes." Hasty services gave some dignity and limited solace to burials in often unmarked graves or in trackless seas. Chaplains lived in tents, trailers, troop ships, and open fields. Wherever combat soldiers and sailors moved, the uniformed clergy lived or died alongside. The four chaplains who stood arm in arm, Protestant

Catholic, Jew, on the decks of the *Dorchester* as that ship slowly sank into the Atlantic ocean symbolized for many the sacrifice of institutional religion in the conduct of the war.

A second approach threw religion's weight on the side of softening war's inevitable cruelties and severe dislocations. Even before the United States entered the conflict, Quakers and others engaged in humanitarian efforts abroad in an endeavor to clothe the needy, feed the hungry, and minister to the sick. Quaker representatives in France in 1940 reported that it was "heartbreaking to be charged with the responsibilities of deciding who shall eat and who shall go hungry, who shall have clothing and who shall have none. Dispensing charity in France today means exercising the power of life or death over one's fellows." How, a person on the scene anxiously asked, "does one do it and retain his sanity?" But Quakers and others working with the American Friends Service Committee did do it, before, during, and after the war. In 1947 the Nobel Peace Prize Committee agreed that the American Friends Service Committee itself should be honored for service rendered all over Europe and in China and India as well.

The refugee problem was more severe abroad than any had anticipated or than any would deal with satisfactorily. But the United States had its own "displaced persons" difficulties following Pearl Harbor. On grounds of national security but also on the unstated grounds of persisting racism, the nation decided that most of its West Coast Japanese population needed to be moved to "relocation centers" in Idaho, or Arizona, or elsewhere in the noncoastal West. More than one hundred thousand Japanese, the majority of whom were American citizens, sat out the war behind barbed wire and under armed guard, wondering about the merits of their citizenship in a country that continued to see so much through race-colored glasses. The churches could provide some help during this long indignity, but not much. Finally, over forty years later, the nation issued an official apology to all Japanese Americans for its wartime behavior, an apology that included financial reparation to those whose lives had been so abruptly interrupted, whose occupations and property had been so unnecessarily sacrificed.

Pacifism, too, had been sacrificed in the course of World War II. Although the 1930s had seen an unprecedented growth in pacifist agitation and sentiment among the churches (see above, pp. 227f), these views along with isolationist "Keep America Out of the War" campaigns quickly withered after 1941. Yet, many religious groups were determined not to be as uncritically supportive of this (or any) war as they had been of World War I. War was evil, though sometimes a necessary evil. And "just war" theories had to contend with unprecedented saturation bombings of heavily populated areas, with propaganda machines of larger magnitude than the world had ever known, with cruelties and tortures that could under no circumstances be justified. Many churchmen agreed that the war could be supported only on the grounds that it might thereby be brought more quickly to an end.

Pacifism, of course, did not wholly disappear. Mennonites, Church of the Brethren, and Quakers helped to run Civilian Public Service camps where conscientious objectors could render alternative service— especially in forestry, agriculture, and environmental protection. The privilege of claiming "CO" status was at this time still limited to young men who "by religious training and belief" objected to all warfare. For most draft boards, this meant a limitation to those who belonged to such historic "peace churches" as those named above. But even within these churches, the claims of conscience were by no means exercised uniformally. Though the majority of Brethren young men did seek alternative service, most Quaker and Mennonite youth did agree to serve in the armed forces. Seventh-Day Adventists provided a significant number of objectors during this war, as did even some mainline Protestant denominations. Jehovah's Witnesses fell into a special category, creating consternation among draft board members and confusion or resentment in the broader public. Technically not pacifists (since they would participate in Jehovah's War of Armageddon), the Witnesses nonetheless declined to participate in this war, since it was man's

66. Pictured here is an army chaplain serving at Fort Bragg, North Carolina, during World War II. *Library of Congress*

conflict, not God's. Many Witnesses ended up not in civilian camps, but in prisons.

The vast majority of Catholics, Protestants, and Jews, however, joined in the war even as, with steady vision, they joined in an effort to see that a just and durable peace followed the end of that war. While the allies spoke chiefly in terms only of "unconditional surrender," many religious and political leaders argued for a moral plane higher than that. Prominent Presbyterian layman, John Foster Dulles (1888–1959), later to become Secretary of State, led a group of churchmen in considering the proper grounds for an enduring peace. A World Council of Churches, organized in Amsterdam in 1948, gave most of its energies and monies to international relief for refugees and prisoners of war, along with assistance to European churches devastated by the bombings and military occupations. Church World Service, Catholic Relief Services, Lutheran World Relief, Jewish Joint Distribution Committee, Meals for Millions, and a host of other church-related entities worked tirelessly all around the world, trying to alleviate war's hurts as well as those conditions that made war more probable.

Sometimes the service rendered was personal and immediate: a cup

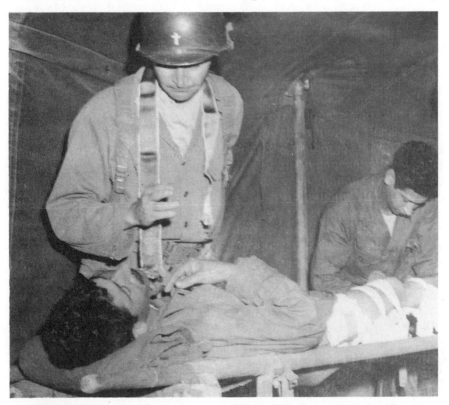

67. A Roman Catholic chaplain in Korea in 1951 ministers to a wounded soldier. *Department of Army*

of cold milk to a starving child at the edge of the Sahara Desert. Other times the service was more impersonal but more far-reaching: demonstrations to farmers in India of fertilizers that could increase food production by over three hundred percent. Smallpox inoculations were administered in North Africa and penicillin protection provided in the Middle East. The creation of the United Nations itself in 1945 soon led to other worldwide humanitarian efforts such as the UN World Health Organization, the UN Children's Emergency Fund, and the UN Relief and Rehabilitation Administration. All of these bodies, ecclesiastical and political alike, struggled to mitigate the effects of the modern world's deadliest plague.

Not all plagues, however, resulted from the military might of nations at war. The extermination in Germany of millions of Jews and others in such scenes of horror as Dachau and Auschwitz was the product of coldly calculated policies of state. Some warned during the war itself of Adolf Hitler's genocidal pogroms, Rabbi Stephen Wise in 1942 calling upon the United States and its allies "to serve notice upon the Nazi despots that the horror of Nazi mistreatment of civilians should cease, whether of Jews, Protestants, or Catholics, whether of Poles, Czechs or Greeks." Between 1936 and 1943, some 150,000 Jewish refugees were settled in the United States, a number whose significance pales in comparison with the millions who endured suffering, experimentation, torture, and death in the concentration camps.

Only when allied troops liberated those camps did the full horror of gas chambers and mass burials become evident. The Holocaust sickened the souls of modern men and women, Jew and Gentile alike, even as it challenged the traditional efforts of theology to account for evil: evil magnified, evil intensified, evil that mocked the very concept of civilization itself. Of those who wrote movingly or despairingly of the Holocaust and its message, none displayed greater sensitivity than Elie Wiesel (b. 1928), a native of Romania who came to the United States in 1956. Himself a childhood survivor of Auschwitz and other concentration camps, Wiesel saw dark implications for all humankind in what this tragic episode revealed to people about themselves, in what it revealed concerning "the silence of God." "Man's betrayal matches God's silence," Wiesel wrote in 1975. "If we are moved by the dehumanization of the victim," he added, "we must be shocked by the dehumanization of mankind." So is despair the answer? No, Wiesel responded, despair is the question: "It is the question, the question of questions. It is both man's way of questioning God and God's way of questioning man." And to this hardest of all questions, "there is no answer coming from either side."

Does this mean that all faith is lost? Again, Wiesel responded in the negative. One continued to believe in God, and at the same time will "go on questioning Him *through* such belief." The whole rabbinical tradition is one of questioning, Wiesel observed, quoting an earlier rabbi who noted that "no heart is as whole as a broken heart." To which Wiesel added that "no faith is as pure as a broken faith."

If the Holocaust strained one's faith to the breaking point, so Hiroshima and Nagasaki in 1945 tested faith and challenged humanity to somehow find a moral power equal to the awesome might of atomic power. In dropping a single bomb over Hiroshima on August 6, 1945, the United States wrought destruction on a scale hitherto beyond imagining: one hundred thousand Japanese killed instantly, and another hundred thousand mortally wounded. True, the unleashing of this power brought World War II quickly to an end, thereby saving an indeterminate number of lives. But it also put in the hands of fallible beings, and soon in the hands of many nations, a force that virtually took on a life of its own. Some saw religion as the only possible restraining counterforce, the only power capable of checking willful

68. U. S. Army chaplain leads in the observance of a Passover seder in Korea in 1953. *Department of Army*

pride, capable of instructing men and women in the art—now the necessity—of self-control.

Richard M. Fagley (b. 1910), a member in 1945 of the Federal Council of Churches' Commission on a Just and Durable Peace, wrote just two months after the bombs were dropped over Japan that the only alternative to total world disaster was "repentance and regeneration." Fear can take us only so far, he noted, for the "fear of destruction from atomic bombs in the present world of competing states would insure and hasten sudden, ruthless attacks" with those very bombs. "The fate of the world, therefore, in a literal sense," Farley concluded, "depends upon the ability of the moral and religious forces . . . to call men effectively to repentance, worship, service." The oneness of all humankind, rather than the competitiveness among all, must become the guiding principle by which a world is safeguarded and a civilization saved. Fagley's call for a religious solution came as the world entered the atomic age. Now, decades later, the questions of nuclear war, nuclear deterrence, nuclear disarmament, and nuclear proliferation continue to test the wills and the consciences of both individuals and nations.

The Holocaust and Hiroshima constituted turning points for both theological understanding and ecclesiastical leadership. Israel's Six Day War in 1967 also represented a turning point, especially for the American Jewish community. Differences among various Jewish groups such as Reform, Conservative, Orthodox, and Reconstructionist, now paled before a greater unity found in the support for the state of Israel and a joy in its survival since its founding in 1948. As Rabbi Arthur Hertzberg (b. 1921) observed, "the overarching religion of American Jews . . . is pride and glory in American Jewry's sharing in Israel." And sociologist Nathan Glazer (b. 1923) agreed that as a consequence of the Six Day War, "American Jews discovered that Israel meant much more to them than they realized." "If in the past it was possible for some Jews to separate their commitment to Judaism from their commitment to Israel," Glazer pointed out, "after 1967 this was no longer possible." The consequence of all this is that "Israel has become *the* Jewish religion for American Jews." This promised a greater unity among the nation's Jews, but, Glazer warned, it also raised a "potential conflict between loyalty to the United States and loyalty to Israel."

If the Six Day War brought unity, the long lasting Vietnam War (1964–1973) brought only bitterness and division. The longer the war continued and the greater the escalation of American military presence, the more uneasy or critical many segments of the American public, including the religious public, became. Rabbi Heschel observed that we were told that for America to leave Vietnam would be to lose face; to stay in Vietnam, however, the rabbi pointed out, would be for America to lose its soul. Heschel joined with Protestants and Catholics in calling for a stop to America's bombing of the Vietnam countryside, in urging that peace negotiations begin without waiting for total and unambiguous victory. In 1965 an organization called Clergy and Laymen Concerned About Vietnam was formed to give stronger voice to the religious protests. In 1966 the nation's Catholic bishops warned of the "grave danger that the circumstances of the present war in Vietnam may, in time, diminish our moral sensitivity to its evils." In 1967 the United Presbyterian Church affirmed that "there is no moral issue more urgently confronting our Church and nation than the war in Vietnam. The hour is late; the Church dare not remain silent. We must declare our conscience."

And so many did declare their consciences, marching in the streets, protesting on the malls in Washington, disrupting the campuses from coast to coast, and urging church as well as synagogue to even more forthright action. The Synagogue Council of America, the National Council of Churches, the World Council of Churches, and the papacy itself all raised their voices in behalf of military restraint before (in Heschel's words) "the rivers of tears and blood may turn into a flood of guilt." But the war did continue for years after all of these and other protests. Guilt did become a flood and restraint a phantom. By the time the war ended in 1973, the number of dead and wounded, American alone, soared to more than 200,000. The greater casualty, however, was to the nation itself: embarrassed by a war it could not win, impoverished in spirit by a war of uncertain purpose and unjust means. When at last a Vietnam War Memorial was erected in Washington, it was to honor the veterans of the conflict, not the war itself. Indeed, Vietnam may, by giving war a bad name, have offered some help to the world cause of peace.

WARRING FOR THE HEARTS AND MINDS

In the Eisenhower era (1953–1961) of the postwar world, a measure of peace and prosperity settled upon the land. In this period, Billy Graham (b. 1918) came to prominence as the leading revivalist in the second half of the twentieth century. Emphasizing a gospel of individual repentance and conversion, Graham saw himself as an evangelist above all else, a "proclaimer of the good news" that Christ died for all persons and was prepared to redeem or save those that believed. The evangelist was not, Graham acknowledged, primarily a theologian or a social reformer, and the evangelist's message was not the whole message of religion to a modern world. The task and the message were, nonetheless, excellent places to begin in promoting the power of the spiritual to a more prominent place. First, change the hearts of women and men, Graham argued (like Moody before him); then, one may proceed to transform the world.

Graham did over the years grow in his own understanding of how much responsibility the individual Christian bore for applying religion to the large social and political problems. In 1960 Graham reported that "my belief in the social implications of the gospel has deepened and broadened." Faith must express itself in action, he pointed out; otherwise, that faith was dead. "The evangelist must not hedge on social issues," Graham declared, and "the cost of discipleship must be made plain from the platform." The question for Graham was not whether religion was personal or social, for it was both; nevertheless, it was with the individual that all reform necessarily began. "Social sins, after all, are merely a large-scale projection of individual sins and need to be repented of by the offending segment of society." The experience of conversion, Graham argued, is not one that takes men or women out of society; rather, it enables them to work as partners with God, more powerfully than ever before, toward the reformation of all the social ills, the inequities and injustices, the corruptions and the crimes.

As an adviser to presidents, notably Dwight Eisenhower, Lyndon Johnson, and Richard Nixon, Graham enjoyed an unusual degree of public visibility. His many big-city "crusades," drawing thousands of people to football stadiums and civic auditoriums, also won great attention, particularly when radio and television carried the revival

69. Dr. Billy Graham joined with presidential candidate Richard M. Nixon in Pittsburgh, Pennsylvania, in the summer of 1968. *Religious News Service*

meetings themselves into millions of homes across the country. But Graham was more than a public figure who represented in some vague way the presence of religion in the affairs of the nation. He was, in addition, the leader of a new religious conservativism or neoevangelicalism that was to play an increasingly conspicuous role in national life. With Graham's strong backing and with members of his family directly involved, the conservative journal, *Christianity Today*, was launched in 1956, this magazine giving his movement not only visibility but respectability as well. Neoevangelicals were no longer perceived as being on the fringes of society, carping critics of a culture they could neither understand nor embrace, but now they were regarded as responsible defenders of the role of revivalism and indeed of religion itself in enhancing both personal and corporate life. Through a network of activities and agencies, Billy Graham (actually Dr. William F. Graham) helped created a real alternative between old time fundamental ism and old-time liberalism.

No other revivalist enjoyed the popularity that Graham did in the 1950s and 1960s. But some preachers, holding forth more privately in their own churches or in television studies, won audiences of enormous dimension. They did so by proclaiming not Graham's message of repentance and surrender, but a different message of awareness and victory. Norman Vincent Peale (b. 1898), Dutch Reformed pastor in New York City, astounded many, perhaps even himself, with the success of a book published in 1952: *The Power of Positive Thinking*. Breaking virtually all records in nonfiction sales, Peale's work opened with the simple but clearly winning advice to "believe in yourself!" One cannot succeed, Peale pointed out, without great self-confidence, "a humble but reasonable confidence." Self-confidence, once properly developed, "leads to self-realization and successful achievement," to health, wealth, and happiness. The goal of this book, Peale noted, was to "help you believe in yourself and release your inner powers."

Similarly, Monsignor Fulton J. Sheen (1895–1979) in a volume called *Peace of Soul* declared that the conversion experience "makes somebodies out of nobodies by giving them a service of Divine Sonship." It also improved one's health "by curing the ills that sprang from a disordered, unhappy, and restless mind." It cured depression and "enables the soul to live in constant consciousness of God's presence." In his exceptionally popular television programs, Sheen inspired confidence by his mere presence and steady assurance, promising a kind of spiritual tranquillity and calm that only faith could bestow. "The true peace that follows conversion is deepened, not disturbed, by the crosses, checks, and disquietudes of the world, for they are all welcomed as coming from the hands of the Loving Father." Look within for strength, not without. Claim those spiritual powers that are all around you (like radio waves), just waiting to be appropriated and put to use.

In a great deal of Peale's "positive thinking" and Sheen's "peace of soul" (as well as in much other analogous preaching and inspirational writing), the emphasis lay more on changing one's internal attitude than on changing the external world. Emphasis also often rested upon what religion can do for the individual: that is, religion was more useful for comfort and healing than for spiritual combat and struggle and service. On the other hand, some aspects of American religion in this same period approached religion much more in terms of political and social structures to be criticized and reshaped, much more in terms of dedication to "causes" that lay well beyond the limits of one's own body and mind and even beyond the limits of one's own community or country. And there lurked potential liabilities, potential vulnerabilities.

In the 1950s many liberal churchmen and women found themselves under attack as being communists or, at the very least, communist sympathizers or "dupes" of the communist conspiracy. Though some anticommunists sincerely feared the overthrow of the American system, other anticommunists used that fear in such a way as to weaken the forces of political and religious liberalism. Especially during the early 1950s when Joseph R. McCarthy (1908–1957), U. S. senator from Wisconsin, held much of the country captive to exaggerated anxieties about a "communist takeover," headlines and television time were

70. Monsignor Fulton J. Sheen speaking in White Plains, New York, in 1948; Francis Cardinal Spellman, archbishop of New York, is at the left. *Religious News Service*

guaranteed to any who pointed a finger at suspected subversives, whoever and wherever they might be.

When, therefore, a relatively obscure congressional aide charged that liberal Protestant clergymen led the ranks of traitors in America, he could be assured a national stage upon which to play his role and speak his piece. J. B. Matthews (b. 1894), chief investigator for the House of Representatives committee probing "un-American" activities, in 1953 publicly charged that since World War II "the Communist Party has enlisted the support of at least seven thousand Protestant clergymen" as either party members or "fellow-travelers, espionage agents, party-line adherents, and unwitting dupes." Without attempting to prove the validity of his figure of seven thousand, Matthews proceeded to ask how such wholesale defection could possibly happen. He found his answer in the "social gospel" that "infected the Protestant theological seminaries more than a generation ago." "Could it be," Matthews asked, "that these pro-Communist clergymen have allowed their zeal for social justice to run away with their better judgment and patriotism?" That question, so slyly put, suggested that one had best rein in his or her passion for social justice, that one had best be concerned about patriotism above all else. Otherwise, the finger-pointing and name-calling was almost certain to begin. (As a twentieth-century archbishop of Brazil commented, "When I fed the poor, they called me a saint. When I asked, 'Why are they poor?', they called me a Communist.")

One of those whose name was frequently called, Methodist Bishop G. Bromley Oxnam (1891–1963), was president of the Federal Council of Churches from 1944 to 1946 and president of the World Council of Churches for six years after that. Because he was so highly visible, a successful attack upon Oxnam could seriously weaken if not destroy the socially active wing of American Protestantism. The Un-American Activities Committee repeatedly implied that Oxnam was either a Communist or else, out of stupidity, he allowed the Communists to use him for their own causes. Such implications flowed out of the press releases over and over, with the bishop being given no opportunity to explain or defend or face his accusers. Finally, in July of 1953 Bishop Oxnam demanded to be heard, demanded to be given some semblance of American justice in those days of zealous Communist hunting.

After first stating his Christian faith to be unwavering and his rejection of both atheism and materialism to be complete, Oxnam severely rebuked the committee for its regular practice "of releasing unverified and unevaluated material" that the committee then accepted no responsibility for—and no responsibility for the untold damage that such material might do. Such action is irresponsible at best, deliberately malicious at worst, Oxnam charged. In either case, the result was the same: "to question loyalty, to pillory or to intimidate the individual, to damage reputation, and to turn attention from the communist conspirator who pursues his nefarious work in the shadows, while a patriotic citizen is disgraced in public." Then lecturing the committee sternly, the bishop affirmed that "the churches have done and are doing far more to destroy the Communist threat to faith and to freedom than all investigating committees put together."

When Senator McCarthy was formally censured by the U. S. Senate in 1954, his popularity and influence quickly waned, along with that of the many investigators, critics, and opportunists who rode along on his coattails. The net effect on American religion, however, and especially upon liberal Protestantism, was to weaken its moral leadership in those very "social justice" areas where such leadership was critically required. But in the Eisenhower era, peace and prosperity lulled many into a state of quiet disinterest so far as social injustices and inequities were concerned.

RELIGIOUS RENEWAL

For two decades following World War II, mainstream religion prospered. Church membership rose to nearly sixty-five percent of the national population, its highest proportion ever. Church attendance

71. G. Bromley Oxnam, Methodist churchman of considerable note, took on the House Un-American Activities Committee in 1953. *Methodist Information Services*

among Catholics rose to the point where their weekly attendance at worship reached about sixty percent. Contributions to church and synagogue, measured in the billions of dollars, steadily increased. And in 1957 the U. S. Bureau of the Census conducted a poll which discovered that an astounding ninety-six percent of the nation's citizens identified themselves with some religious tradition—whether or not they were members or contributors or attenders. With an adult population of about 120 million in 1957, the U. S. Census Bureau estimated about 70 million Americans thought of themselves as Protestant, about 30 million as Roman Catholic, and nearly 4 million as Jewish. Religious traditions other than the broad categories of Protestant, Catholic, or Jewish were also uncovered by the census, but only about four percent of the population indicated no religious identification at all.

The two decades following the Second World War were growth years for the major denominations and many of the minor ones as well. Religion also enjoyed a good deal of public confidence, as measured by the regular Gallup polls that asked about such things. So far as the American landscape was concerned, however, the most obvious sign of renewal was a burst of activity in ecclesiastical building that sought to take advantage of new technologies and new architectural forms. As Otto Spaeth, the founder of the Liturgical Arts Society, observed, "The first requirement of a church or temple today is that it be of today." The parishioner, Spaeth pointed out, "drives a streamlined car to work in an office or factory where everything has been designed for maximum efficiency and comfort." But then he "is asked to hurl himself back centuries to say his prayers in the pious gloom of a Gothic or Romanesque past." The obvious implication of all this, Spaeth concluded, is that "God does not exist today."

In the 1950s, therefore, one witnessed the designing and constructing of many sophisticated, tasteful, contemporary ecclesiastical edifices. In Portsmouth, Rhode Island, for example, under the direction of the liturgy-conscious Benedictines, the Priory of St. Gregory the Great was erected during the course of that decade. Utilizing sheet copper for the roofs, concrete slabs for the walls, redwood board for much of the interior, the resulting octagonal church created a stunning visual impact. The First Presbyterian Church of Cottage Grove, Oregon, on the other hand, avoided all traditional symbols of arch or steeple or stained glass. Dedicated in 1951, this church snuggled quietly into a residential neighborhood rather than rise majestically or pretentiously over all its surroundings. Built entirely of native fir, the church revealed the same severe simplicity in its interior design as it did externally. And between the two coasts, in Bloomington, Indiana, the First Baptist Church (dedicated in 1956) likewise intended its new structure to partake of modern materials and modern methods of construction. As a church committee declared, their building should provide a place of worship "so simple and meaningful and honest that no one will be made afraid by lavish appointments or pretensions of any kind." The committee also explicitly emphasized their desire to "provide in the stone and wood of the building a Christian symbol which will speak of man's search for God in the forms and with the materials of our time."

In this same period that American religion was enjoying an architectural renewal, it participated in a liturgical renewal as well. Liturgy, literally the "work of the people," gathers worshippers together in meaningful ritual that celebrates the collective past and enables the participant more effectively to prepare for the future. Through liturgy, Jews honor the exodus from Egypt, the law given on Mount Sinai, the temples dedicated before and after the Babylonian Exile, the deliverance of the oppressed Jews by Judas Maccabees, and many other events in the Jewish past. Similarly, Christian liturgy centers on remembrances of things past: notably, the birth, death, and resurrection of Christ. All of this is ancient, of course, but in the 1950s and beyond more conscious attention was given to the place of liturgy, even among groups that thought of themselves as largely "nonliturgical." And though denominational differences in liturgical expression could clearly be found, one could also find Presbyterians singing Lutheran hymns, Episcopalians offering Catholic prayers, Methodists and Baptists sharing in the congregational readings used on the occasion of the Lord's Supper. In this renewal as in many others, the Roman Catholic activity of the 1960s was particularly conspicuous.

72. Architectural renewal is evident in the Priory Church of St. Mary and St. Louis, in Creve Coeur, Missouri. *Hellmuth, Obata & Kassabaum, Architects*

In 1960, the voting public of the country for the first time elected a Roman Catholic as its president: John F. Kennedy (1917–1963). Religion was prominently under discussion in this presidential campaign, as it had been some thirty years before when another Catholic, Alfred K. Smith, ran for this high office (see above, p. 235). But some things had happened to the country and to religion in the intervening generation. Pluralism had become more acceptable or at the least more obvious; nativism and anti-Catholic bigotry had become less acceptable or at the least less blatant. Yet Kennedy found the "religious question" pressed upon him again and again during the course of the campaign. Clearly, it would not be enough to say that the U. S. Constitution prohibited the imposition of any religious test upon someone seeking federal office. Too many Americans were still unsure about papal claims in general, about papal influences in particular upon any Catholic presiding in the White House.

On three occasions, therefore, Kennedy dealt directly with the fact of his Catholicism: before the Society of American Newspaper Editors in Washington, D. C., in April of 1960; before the press in Los Angeles in July of that year after he had won the Democratic nomination; and, in September, before the Ministerial Association in Houston, two months

73. Pictured here is the chapel at Concordia Senior College in Fort Wayne, Indiana. *Concordia College*

prior to the election. To each audience, he made the point that he, like every other presidential candidate, was pledged to uphold and defend the U. S. Constitution, including its First Amendment guarantees regarding freedom of religion. He also argued, as had Alfred Smith before him, that he wished no votes cast for him just because he was a Catholic and no votes cast against him for that reason alone. And he noted that Roman Catholics had served in every other conceivable civil capacity without questions concerning their religion being raised. "Little or no attention was paid to my religion," Kennedy noted, "when I took the oath as senator in 1953—as a congressman in 1947—or as a

74. The modern interior of the chapel at Concordia Senior College. *Concordia College*

naval officer in 1941. Members of my faith abound in public office at every level except the White House."

In the United States the presidency, Kennedy observed, was not an instance of one-man rule. No president could ignore Congress, or the courts, or the voters. But despite this fact, sheer bigotry might prevail. "If that bigotry is too great to permit the fair consideration of a Catholic who has made clear his complete independence and his complete dedication to separation of church and state, then," said candidate Kennedy, "we ought to know it." While bigotry could certainly still be found, it had lessened sufficiently to permit the election in 1960 of the nation's first Roman Catholic president.

Two years before that election, another John was elevated to high office, a genial Italian churchman taking the papal title of John XXIII. His brief pontificate, from 1958 to 1963, was even more revolutionary than America's election of a Catholic president had been. In his late seventies when he was chosen as a presumably safe, compromise pope, John XXIII startled many, both in the church and beyond, by his own openness as well as by his intent to create a more open church. In sharp contrast to his austere and remote predecessor, Pius XII (whose long reign extended from 1939 to 1958), this short, round, smiling pope inspired affection and trust around the world. He escaped the Vatican "prison" as often as possible and labored during his four and one-half years to help his church escape the prison of the Vatican's long

75. Chief Justice Earl Warren administered the oath of office to the nation's first Roman Catholic president, John F. Kennedy, in 1961. *Religious News Service*

entrenched bureaucracy. Of humble origin in northern Italy (farming, the pope said, was his father's way of staying poor), this John kept the common touch, refusing to allow himself to be isolated or arbitrarily elevated.

Two major encyclicals demonstrated the spirit of the man and of a pontificate that would embrace the modern world rather than fear or condemn it. In 1961, the letter *Mater et Magistra* ("Mother and Teacher") addressed itself to social, economic, and political questions in terms drawn not from medieval conditions and language but from twentieth-century concerns and demands. Pope John probed the standards for justice and equity in an industrialized world; he searched for ways to assure a family life that would be "decent and humane"; he defended social insurance and social security as appropriate means "whereby imbalances among various classes of citizens are reduced"; and he spoke in behalf of an improved rural life through governmental provision for such essentials as "pure drinking water," good housing, decent roads, and appropriate education. Even before the phrase "third world countries" had been coined, John XXIII noted that "perhaps the most pressing question of our day concerns the relationship between economically advantaged commonwealths and those that are in process of development." The Church had a message for and a responsibility to those, above all others, to whom all human dignity and hope had been denied.

Attracting even more attention was the second encyclical, *Pacem in Terris* ("Peace on Earth"), issued in 1963. That attention came in part, of course, from the topic itself, but also in part because this pope went out of his way to address his letter to those beyond the Roman Catholic community, indeed to "all men of good will." Beginning with a recognition of basic human rights, including the right of all persons "to honor God according to the sincere dictates" of their own consciences, John XXIII proceeded to urge that all governments provide a "charter of fundamental human rights . . . drawn up in clear and precise terms and that it be incorporated in its entirety in the constitution" of that nation. Only if there was justice at home could one begin to speak meaningfully of justice abroad. Only as "an equal natural dignity" was recognized as the fundamental right of all persons could powerful nations begin to treat other nations in terms of their "equal natural dignity as well." When that happens, peace becomes a genuine option.

The pope urged a cessation to the arms race, an obliteration of all lingering traces of racism, a limitation on the burgeoning power of individual nations. Problems that are worldwide required worldwide authority, he argued, perhaps even a world government or at least a greatly strengthened United Nations. "The moral order itself," the pope declared, "demands that such a form of public authority be established." An authority of this magnitude can then "tackle and solve problems of an economic, social, political, or cultural character which are posed by the universal common good." Years later, "men of good will"—Protestant, Catholic, Jewish, Moslem, Buddhist, and so on—were still studying and evaluating this important encyclical and its vital subject of concern. "In no religious document of our time," Norman Cousins wrote in 1965, "is there a more profound awareness that peace is the one overriding issue and challenge of our age than in *Pacem in Terris*." And in no document was there a more determined effort to move nations beyond their nationalism, races beyond their racism, and churches beyond their ecclesiastical parochialism.

Even more than for these two major letters, however, John XXIII was remembered for his calling of the modern world's most important church council: Vatican II, which met from 1962 to 1965. Not since the Council of Trent in the sixteenth century had so much been undertaken, had so much been at stake, as in this herculean effort of the Roman Catholic Church to come to terms with the non-Catholic world, with the non Christian world, with the complex, secular, pluralistic modern world. John XXIII did not live to see the council complete its work; he did live long enough to open that window in the Vatican that would, as he said, let in some fresh air. To some bureaucrats, it must have seemed as though a wind of hurricane force blew through that single window. Before Vatican II was through, sixteen official documents had been drawn up, argued over, revised, debated and finally voted upon by bishops assembled from all over the world. And before Vatican II was through, the Roman Catholic church would be a much altered, much shaken institution.

Still another John now enters the story, namely the Jesuit theologian and professor, John Courtney Murray (1904–1967). Introducing into Vatican II what was generally called the "American document," the "Declaration on Religious Liberty," Murray watched over the precarious movement of this document through all the hazards of debate and dedicated resistance. Like a mother hovering over a sick child, Murray would not let his attention wander or his guard fall as he defended, pleaded, cajoled, and persuaded a majority that the time had at last come for the Catholic Church to recognize the reality of, indeed the desirability of, a full religious freedom. This document was, Murray wrote, clearly "the most controversial document of the whole Council," primarily because it implicitly recognized what had long been denied: namely, that doctrine does develop, that dogma does change. "The notion of development, not the notion of religious freedom, was the real sticking-point," Murray commented, with the sharp differences between the "Syllabus of Errors" in 1864 and this document of a century later still waiting "to be explained by theologians." The declaration on religious freedom represented a tremendous breakthrough, Murray explained, as it brought "the Church at long last abreast of the consciousness of civilized mankind." It represented a "transition from the sacral society to the secular society" and, at the same time, it symbolized the church's acceptance of "historical consciousness."

If the document was symbolically important, its substantive value is not to be dismissed. For the church now recognized the utter inappropriateness of coercion in matters of conscience. "Truth cannot impose itself except by virtue of its own truth, as it makes its entrance into the mind at once quietly and with power." Sounding very much like Roger Williams or William Penn, the council agreed that "the exercise of religion, of its very nature, consists before all else in those internal, voluntary and free acts whereby man set the course of his life directly toward God. No merely human power can either command or prohibit acts of this kind." And sounding somewhat like the First Amendment, the council acknowledged that both the nature of man and the nature

76. John Courtney Murray, S. J., was the architect of the Declaration on Religious Liberty adopted by Vatican II in 1965. *Woodstock College*

of religion require the right of free assembly and freedom of worship as conscience does direct. Somehow Murray also persuaded the authorities voting in Rome at the end of 1965 to concede that the church at times has acted in a manner "hardly in accord with the spirit of the Gospel or even opposed to it." The church at this point demands no special privilege, only "that full measure of freedom which her care for the salvation of men requires." John Courtney Murray could and did take as much pride in his authorship of this document as Thomas Jefferson had taken in his authorship of Virginia's Statute for Religious Freedom. Both men served their nation and their age well.

Vatican II, of course, did much more than issue a pronouncement in favor of religious freedom. It revised the liturgy so that a far wider use of the language of the people replaced the mandatory Latin. The order of the Mass itself should also be revised, the council declared, "in such a way that the intrinsic nature and purpose of its several parts, as also the connection between them, can be more clearly manifested." In addition, the council extended its hand to other Christians, now seen not as "erring schismatics" but as truly brothers and sisters in Christ. Special efforts were made to soften the antagonism between the Western and the Eastern Churches, the pertinent document observing that "History, tradition, and numerous institutions manifest luminously how much the universal Church is indebted to the Eastern Churches." And on behalf of Jews, the council endeavored to lift the centuries-old burden of Jews, all Jews past and present, being collectively responsible for the crucifixion of Christ. That event cannot be blamed "upon all the Jews then living, without distinction, nor upon the Jews of today." Jews should not be regarded as under some special curse; on the contrary, "God's all-embracing love" extends to them as to all men. The church, moreover, "deplores the hatred, persecutions, and displays of anti-Semitism directed against the Jews at any time and from any source."

Vatican II could not, even in three years, address every issue that pressed hard upon the Roman Catholic Church or upon the Church universal. It could, however, reveal a new spirit of dialogue and mutual respect, a new freshness in perspective and interpretation, a new courage in confronting the problems of its own history and of the world's history. When Vatican II was underway, the key word heard nearly everywhere was *aggiornamento*: that is, a bringing up-to-date, a modernizing of the Church, a making religion relevant to this day, this time. Vatican II set a model for religious renewal, its pattern being imitated by some and scorned by others. A few Roman Catholics even broke away, preferring to keep the Latin rite unchanged, the traditions unmodified. Most churchpeople in America, however, as elsewhere, found that fresh air coming in through the Vatican window to be both invigorating and challenging. For a great many Americans, three Johns of the 1960s signalled the beginning of a new epoch.

Suggested Reading for
Part Four

For source material pertinent to the discussion in this section of the book, see Gaustad, *Documentary*, Vol. 2, Chaps. 9–11. Also see the second volume of the important reference work edited by H. Shelton Smith et al., *American Christianity: An Historical Interpretation with Representative Documents* (New York, 1963).

America's entry onto the world stage of nations is neatly outlined in the older work by Julius W. Pratt, *Expansionists of 1898: Acquisition of Hawaii and the Spanish Islands* (New York, 1936). R. H. Abrams draws, sometimes overdraws, the picture of institutional religion lining up in support of the war effort in 1917: *Preachers Present Arms* (New York, 1933), while the pacifist stance is described in Charles Chatfield's study, *For Peace and Justice* (Knoxville, Tenn., 1971).

On the missionary effort broadly within Christian history, one should consult the many detailed volumes of Kenneth Scott Latourette, especially his five-volume work on *Christianity in a Revolutionary Age* (New York, 1958–1962), along with the briefer survey by Stephen Neill, *A History of Christian Missions* (Baltimore, Md. 1964). For America's Protestant labors, the best treatment is that of William R. Hutchison, *Errand into the World* (Chicago, 1987); on the Roman Catholic side, one may turn to R. B. Considine, *The Maryknoll Story* (New York, 1950). The frequent and often surprising overlap between missionary activity and U. S. foreign policy receives careful examination in J. Bruce Nichols, *The Uneasy Alliance* (New York, 1988).

The unhappy story of bigotry in the nation is authoritatively treated in John Higham's *Strangers in the Land: Patterns of American Nativism, 1860–1925* (New Brunswick, N.J., 1955). More narrowly focussed studies include D. M. Chalmers, *Hooded Americanism: The History of the Ku Klux Klan* (Garden City, N.Y., 1965); and, Donald L. Kinzer, *Episode in Anti-Catholicism: The American Protective Association* (Seattle, 1964). The 1928 presidential campaign receives monographic treatment in E. A. Moore, *A Catholic Runs for President* (New York, 1956). Also see Alan Brinkley, *Voices of Protest: Huey Long, Father Coughlin, and the Great*

Depression (New York, 1982). The story of prohibition is engagingly told by Andrew Sinclair in *Prohibition: Era of Excess* (Boston, 1962).

On the growth and expansion of mainstream religion, see E. S. Gaustad, *Historical Atlas of Religion in America* (rev. ed, New York, 1976) as well as annual compilation now called *Yearbook of American and Canadian Churches* and distributed by Abingdon Press. For others not generally included in the "mainstream" category, see R. Laurence Moore, *Religious Outsiders and the Making of Americans* (New York, 1986); also, Irving I. Zaretsky and Mark P. Leone, *Religious Movements in Contemporary America* (Princeton, N.J., 1974).

The Protestant struggles early in this century may best be followed through the analytical efforts of two authors: William R. Hutchison, *The Modernist Impulse in American Protestantism* (Cambridge, 1976); and, George M. Marsden, *Fundamentalism and American Culture: The Shaping of Twentieth-Century Evangelicalism, 1870–1925* (New York, 1980). Also see the volume edited by Marsden, *Evangelicalism and Modern America* (Grand Rapids, 1984). Catholic tensions in the same period are explicated by Robert Cross in *The Emergence of Liberal Catholicism in America* (Cambridge, Mass., 1958); also, in Aaron I. Abell, *American Catholicism and Social Action* (New York, 1960); and, in Philip Gleason, ed., *Catholicism in America* (New York, 1970). The development as well as the character of Judaism's principal divisions in America can be traced in Jacob Neusner, ed., *Understanding American Judaism: Toward the Description of a Modern Religion*, Vol. 2 (New York, 1975), as well as in Marc Lee Raphael, *Profiles in American Judaism: The Reform, Conservative, Orthodox, and Reconstructionist Traditions in Historical Perspective* (San Francisco, 1984).

The intellectual and theological climate responsible for "modernity" in its many manifestations have understandably received exhaustive attention. On the philosophical side, useful surveys include these studies: Bruce Kuklick, *The Rise of American Philosophy* (New Haven, Conn., 1977) as well as his later book, *Churchmen and Philosophers* (New Haven, Conn., 1985); John Edwin Smith, *The Spirit of American Philosophy* (New York, 1963); and, Morton White, *Science and Sentiment in America: Philosophical Thought from Jonathan Edwards to John Dewey* (New York, 1972). With respect to Whitehead's influence in particular, see Delwin Brown et al., eds., *Process Philosophy and Christian Thought* (Indianapolis, 1971).

The struggles between science and religion attracted much attention in the nineteenth century, but in the twentieth as well. Recent examinations include James R. Moore, *The Post-Darwinian Controversies* (Cambridge, England, 1979) and Ronald L. Numbers, *God and Nature* (Berkeley, Calif., 1987). For specific figures caught in the contest, see Donald Fleming, *John William Draper and the Religion of Science* (Philadelphia, 1950); Lester Stephens, *Joseph Le Conte, Gentle Prophet of Evolution* (Baton Rouge, La., 1982); Ira V. Brown, *Lyman Abbott: The*

Christian Evolutionist (Cambridge, Mass., 1953); and, Lawrence W. Levine's biography of William Jennings Bryan, *Defender of the Faith* (New York, 1965).

In the warring world of the 1940s and beyond, special attention to religion is given in J. T. Addison, *War, Peace, and the Christian Mind* (Greenwich, Conn., 1953); and in R. L. Moellering, *Modern War and the American Churches* (New York, 1956). With respect to the nuclear age, see Edward L. Long, *The Christian Response to the Atomic Crisis* (Philadelphia, 1950). Of the vast literature regarding the Holocaust, two books may be cited: Arthur Cohen, *The Tremendum: A Theological Interpretation of the Holocaust* (New York, 1981); and Irving Abrahamson, *Against Silence: The Voice and Vision of Elie Wiesel* (New York, 1985). And on the agonies of conscience created by Vietnam, one may consult M. P. Hamilton, ed., *The Vietnam War: Christian Perspectives* (Grand Rapids, Mich., 1967); and, T. E. Quigley, ed., *American Catholics and Vietnam* (Grand Rapids, Mich., 1968).

The revivalism of Billy Graham has been evaluated by Stanley High in 1956, *Billy Graham* (New York), and more critically in 1972 by J. E. Barnhart, *The Billy Graham Religion* (Philadelphia). William G. McLoughlin has put revivalism into helpful perspective in his provocative interpretation, *Revivals, Awakenings, and Reform* (Chicago, 1978). Donald B. Meyer surveys the peace of mind or soul phenomena in his *Positive Thinkers* (Garden City, N.Y., 1965), but one should also turn to the readily available writings of Norman Vincent Peale, Fulton J. Sheen, Joshua Loth Liebman, Robert Schuller, and others.

On the liturgical and architectural renewal in recent decades, these guides have proved helpful: E. B. Koenker, *The Liturgical Renaissance in the Roman Catholic Church* (Chicago, 1954); M. J. Taylor, S. J., *The Protestant Liturgical Renewal: A Catholic Viewpoint* (Westminster, Md., 1963); Albert Christ-Janer and Mary Mix Foley, *Modern Church Architecture* (New York, 1962); and, Rachel Wischnitzer, *Synagogue Architecture in the United States* (Philadelphia, 1955). For Kennedy's religious statements, see N. A. Schneider, *Religious Views of President John F. Kennedy* (St. Louis, 1965). The Second Vatican Council enjoyed excellent reporting at the time of its meeting, as well as careful evaluation thereafter; see, for example, David J. O'Brien, *The Renewal of American Catholicism* (New York, 1972). John Courtney Murray's important contribution is evaluated in these two studies: Thomas T. Love, *John Courtney Murray: Contemporary Church-State Theory* (Garden City, N.Y., 1965); and, Donald E. Pelotte, S. S. S., *John Courtney Murray: Theologian in Conflict* (New York, 1976).

Part 5

RELIGION IN AN AGE OF LIMITS

CHAPTER 22

The Courts, The Schools, The Streets

In the years following World War II, even the most secular of Americans could not help but notice the powerful presence of religion in the nation. For that presence made itself felt in a host of public places: the daily press, the political campaigns, the placard-waving protests, the call for constitutional amendments, and the courts. Above all else, the courts—municipal, state, and federal—found their dockets crowded and their seating capacity strained as contentious religious partisans cried out for justice and fair play. In an age of limits, no longer did traditional habitual behavior go unchallenged. No longer did the sentiment of the majority or the consensus of an elite predict the outcome of any given religious controversy. From the perspective of litigation, at least, the nation with its patterns of religious behavior and belief had unmistakably entered upon a new era.

For the first century and a half of national existence, religious issues rarely reached the U. S. Supreme Court, even more rarely did they arouse passionate public response. Beginning in the 1940s, however, that high Court found religion cases to be part of an almost daily diet, with those cases increasing in both frequency and difficulty in succeeding decades. The public divided sharply over judicial outcomes, even as justices repeatedly divided sharply with each other. More and more it appeared that religion in America was something that one took to court.

The reasons for this dramatic burst in confrontation and litigation are several. First, the Supreme Court in a 1940 case decided that the First Amendment was applicable to the states: that is, states no less than the federal government itself were bound to respect the free exercise of religion and to avoid any establishment of religion. Second, the ever-growing pluralism of the country had, by World War II, become so palpably evident that one could not pretend or suppose or act as though all citizens believed and behaved alike. Third, specific organizations such as Americans United, the American Jewish Congress, the American Civil Liberties Union, and others, helped bring religion cases to the highest court in order to test the protections and the limits of the

First Amendment with respect to religion. Fourth, a growing federalism meant that national government and religious institutions were bumping into each other more and more frequently. And fifth, the Constitution itself became increasingly the sole symbol of unity as well as the source of both goodness and truth; one must therefore turn often to that sacred charter and to its official interpreters in order to find one's way in a bewildering, morally complex world.

77. Shown here is the United States Supreme Court in the foreground, with the Library of Congress in the background. *Baptist Joint Committee on Public Affairs*

Whatever the combination of factors at work, the Supreme Court in a single decade such as the 1970s or 1980s heard more church-state cases than it had in the years from 1790 to 1940 added together. Issues heard today, moreover, could reappear tomorrow in a slightly altered form; or, issues heard today were heard again later with surprisingly different results. Even as the Court was feeling its way through an ever darkening thicket, so American society was groping for some clear path into a brighter light.

CASES OF CONSCIENCE

The "free exercise" clause of the First Amendment has been called upon many times to protect behavior guided by conscience, shaped or determined by religion. No group in America's history has done more to enlarge the understanding of what free exercise really means than the Jehovah's Witnesses who, time and time again, have pressed their claims all the way through the legal system. Preaching in public parks, distributing religious literature, violating Sunday "blue laws," trespassing and failing to obtain a municipal license—these and a host of other issues led to confrontations between the Witnesses and the law enforcement or judicial agencies. But nothing attracted as much attention as the two cases concerning the requirement that the salute and Pledge of Allegiance to the American flag be offered as a daily exercise in the public school.

In 1940 the U. S. Supreme Court heard a case (*Minersville School District v. Gobitis*) that arose from the refusal of two Jehovah's Witnesses children, William and Lilian Gobitis (ages ten and twelve, respectively), to salute the flag and join in the Pledge of Allegiance each school day. Their refusal was based upon the teaching of their denomination that such action constituted idolatry, for it violated the commandment in the Book of Exodus to have no other gods before Jehovah: "You shall not make yourself a graven image. . . . You shall not bow down to them or serve them" (Exodus 20:3–5). Witnesses had gradually come to this position during the 1930s when they were being persecuted in Adolph Hitler's Germany, especially when they decided that the arm raised in a "Heil Hitler" salute was itself idolatry. State courts in America who had heard cases based on the refusal of Witnesses' children to salute the flag regularly found against them or else threw the case out of court on the ground that no substantial question of freedom of religion was involved.

So also in 1940 the Supreme Court, by a vote of eight to one, ruled that the requirement imposed by the small school district in Pennsylvania was a constitutional one. Justice Felix Frankfurter (1882–1965), speaking for the Court, acknowledged that the dilemma long ago posed by Abraham Lincoln spoke to the issue then before the justices: "Must a government of necessity be too strong for the liberties of its people, or too weak to maintain its own existence?" Recognizing that the failure of the Gobitis children to salute the flag was indeed based upon religious scruple, Frankfurter nonetheless argued for the critical importance of the flag as "the symbol of our national unity." He also declared that "The ultimate foundation of a free society is the binding tie of cohesive sentiment," adding that the flag was important for the creation and maintenance of "that unifying sentiment without which there can ultimately be no liberties, civil or religious." On the other hand, Justice Harlan Stone (1872–1946) dissented from the majority view, declaring that the very essence of civil and religious liberty was "the freedom of the individual from compulsion as to what he shall think and what he shall say, at least where the compulsion is to bear false witness to his religion." But in 1940, Frankfurter prevailed.

Two results of that decision against the Witnesses quickly surfaced. First, popular resentment against the Witnesses mounted as war-time patriotism increased in fervor. Witnesses were victims of mob violence all across the country, from Maine to Oregon; also, many communities that had no formal requirement for all schoolchildren to salute the flag now added such, making public school attendance increasingly problematic for all Jehovah's Witnesses. Second, legal scholars, religious leaders, editorial writers, and others joined in a chorus of general condemnation of the 1940 decision as being undemocratic in tone and in effect, especially as the burden of the adverse decision fell upon a hapless and widely persecuted minority. It also soon became clear that several members of the Court itself were having second thoughts.

In 1943, therefore, the Court agreed to hear a very similar case arising in this instance from West Virginia. But if the case was similar, the results were vastly different. Now (in *West Virginia State Board of Education v. Barnette*) the Court reversed its earlier finding and did so in ringing, stirring language. Speaking for the Court, Justice Robert

78. Church of the Brethren conscientious objectors render alternative civilian service during World War II at Camp Stronach in Michigan. *Brethren Historical Library & Archives*

Jackson (1892–1954) agreed that national unity was vital and such unity, fostered "by persuasion and example," was not questioned. "The problem," Jackson added, "is whether under our Constitution compulsion as here employed is a permissible means for its achievement." Then Jackson affirmed: "If there is any fixed star in our constitutional constellation, it is that no official, high or petty, can prescribe what shall be orthodox in politics, nationalism, religion, or other matters of opinion, or force citizens to confess by word or act their faith therein." If there were any exceptions at all to that fundamental and inalienable right of all Americans, Justice Jackson confessed that he could not think of them. As might be expected, Justice Frankfurter wrote a long and passionate dissent, but in 1943 he did not carry the day.

Religious minorities also helped broaden the understanding of "free exercise" with respect to the many Sunday laws on the books of nearly every village and town east of the Mississippi River. But in this instance, Orthodox Jews and Seventh-Day Adventists rather than Jehovah's Witnesses led the judicial battles. For the two former groups, the Sabbath began at sundown on Friday evening, not at sunrise on Sunday morning. If an Orthodox Jew kept his shop closed on Saturday as a religious requirement, he found that he must also close his shop on Sunday as a legal requirement. As a consequence, he suffered economic penalties not imposed upon the majority who already accepted Sunday as the appointed day of rest and worship. In 1961 the Court heard two cases, one from Pennsylvania and one from Maryland, challenging the validity of the Sunday closing laws. Chief Justice Earl Warren (1891–1971) in both cases argued that the laws were more part of general welfare regulation than they were a sign of sectarian favoritism. He also stated that such laws, imposing "only an indirect burden upon the free exercise of religion," met the tests of constitutionality.

In the first case (McGowan v. Maryland), Justice William O. Douglas (1898–1980) dissented sharply, pointing out that the state had no right to "make protesting citizens refrain from doing innocent acts on Sunday because the doing of those acts offends sentiments of their Christian neighbors." Imagine a situation, Douglas suggested, where you have a state legislature composed chiefly of Orthodox Jews and Seventh-Day Adventists. They pass a law, let us suppose, making it a crime to keep a business open on Saturday. "Would a Baptist, Catholic, Methodist, or Presbyterian," Douglas asked, "be compelled to obey that law or go to jail or pay a fine?" Constitutional rights were not to be decided by numerical dominance. And in the second case of 1961 (Brownfield v. Brown) Justice Potter Stewart (1915–1985) dissented in these succinct words: "Pennsylvania has passed a law which compels an Orthodox Jew to choose between his religious faith and his economic survival. This is a cruel choice." Moreover, Stewart added, "It is a choice which I think no State can constitutionally demand." What, after all, were the rights of the religious conscience?

This question had its clearest answer two years later in the case of *Sherbert* v. *Verner*. There, the Court decided that a Seventh-Day Adventists who had been denied unemployment benefits because she would not work on Saturday was, in fact, entitled to such benefits. For to hold otherwise, said Justice William Brennan (b. 1906), was to force this person "to choose between following the precepts of her religion and forfeiting benefits on the one hand, and abandoning one of the precepts of her religion in order to accept work on the other hand." This was equivalent, Brennan added, to imposing a special fine on anyone who chose to worship on Saturday rather than Sunday. Justice Stewart agreed with the Court's opinion in this instance, believing the crux of the matter to be that the Constitution "commands the positive protection by government of religious freedom—not only for a minority, however small—not only for the majority, however large, but for each of us." Brennan in an earlier dissent had also found what he believed to be the central issue in the remark of one of those debating the passage of the First Amendment in 1789: "The rights of conscience are, in their nature, of peculiar delicacy, and will little bear the gentlest touch of governmental hand."

In America's history, that delicacy of conscience has been most apparent in the many cases relating to military conscription and service. For as long as the nation has been involved in war, it has wrestled with the issue of conscientious objection to war and sometimes to any involvement, however indirect, in a war effort. In the 1960s, however, the problem was greatly aggravated by the duration and unpopularity of the Vietnam War, by the widespread refusal of young men either to register for the draft or to accept conscription into the armed forces. No longer was it enough to ask whether one were a Mennonite or a Moravian. Nor was it enough to ask what the First Amendment required. The Court now had the additional task of trying to interpret the language of Congress in its Universal Military Training and Service Act of 1948 or its Selective Service Act of 1967. And in all of this debate about legislative language and legislative intent, conscience itself was put on trial.

In the 1965 case of *United States* v. *Seeger*, the Court explored the breadth of the word "religion," for Congress had specified exemption from the military draft would be granted only to "those persons who by reason of their religious training and belief are conscientiously opposed to participation in war in any form." By 1965 the nation was manifestly pluralistic in its forms of "religious training and belief," a fact that the Court explicitly recognized. And though Congress had even in its provision for exemption used the term "Supreme Being," the Court decided to take that not to mean any specific theistic system of belief. Rather, as Justice Douglas said in his concurring opinion, "any person opposed to war on the basis of a sincere belief, which in his life fills the same place as a belief in God fills in the life of an orthodox religionist, is entitled to exemption under the statute." To this remarkably liberalized interpretation, there were no dissents in 1965.

Five years later, however, the Court (in *Welsh v. United States*) began to pull back, as the justices divided five to three on the question of how broadly this whole matter of conscience could be interpreted. First, did "conscientious" always and necessarily have a religious base? Second, could one object not to war in general but only to a particular war, doing so on "conscientious" grounds, not political ones? Third, and always the hardest question of all, how does one draw the line between the requirements of national interest on the one hand and the protections of "free exercise of religion" on the other? A majority of the Court decided that persons should be exempted from military service if their "consciences, spurred by deeply held moral, ethical, or religious beliefs, would give them no rest or peace if they allowed themselves to become a part of an instrument of war."

For the minority of the Court, however, this was stretching both the language of Congress and the Constitution much too far. Religion has been given a privileged position by both, the dissenters argued, and the Court should not so dilute the meaning of the word as to have it cover every conceivable "sincere belief." A year later, the Court pulled back even farther, holding that not all dissent and disagreement about war, especially about a particular war (in this instance, Vietnam), was the equivalent of a truly conscientious objection. The nation must be careful, the Court stated, to see that those drafted for military service are not chosen "unfairly or capriciously"; otherwise, "a mood of bitterness and cynicism might corrode the spirit of public service."

The matter of national unity can never be taken lightly, whether the issue is one of saluting the flag, protecting a minority, or exempting some citizen from obligations that fall upon all others. On the other hand, perhaps the most jealously guarded American right over the past two hundred years has been not merely to believe, but to *exercise*, to work out the implications of those religious convictions in both public and private life.

THE SCHOOLS, PUBLIC AND PRIVATE

In public schools the issue with respect to religion has been primarily curricular: what can be taught or recited in the classroom. In private schools the issue with respect to religion has been primarily financial: what can be paid for in the sectarian or parochial school by the tax monies of all citizens. Both issues have proved troublesome not only to the courts, but they have also aroused widespread public passion and involvement in a way that few other policy questions have managed to do in times of peace.

In the public schools, controversy in the last two decades has swirled most intensely around two concerns: (1) prayer and Bible reading; and, (2) creationism or "creation science." The first of these has a long history since, as has been previously noted, public schools grew up in the midst of a Protestant ethos that not only allowed but encouraged Bible reading, praying, and hymn singing as a routine part of the school day. Not until the 1960s, however, did the U. S. Supreme Court deal directly with these issues, though they had earlier reviewed such matters as "released time" (sectarian instruction offered on school property) and "dismissed time" (sectarian instruction offered elsewhere than on school property).

In 1962 the case of *Engel* v. *Vitale*, making its way up the judicial ladder from the state of New York to the U. S. Supreme Court, concerned the recital of a prescribed prayer, written by the Regents of the state, that was required in every public school classroom in New York. Two facets of this case were most striking: one, the decision that such a practice was unconstitutional and must therefore cease was virtually unanimous (a single dissent only); and two, the public outcry in condemnation of the decision was enormous and unrelenting. A quarter of a century later, citizens' groups of one type or another still searched for ways to circumvent the Court's opinion either by passing a constitutional amendment or by removing such matters from the Court's jurisdiction.

The majority opinion itself, delivered by Justice Hugo Black, found the New York practice a violation of that other prohibition of the First Amendment, the Establishment Clause: "Congress shall make no law respecting the establishment of religion." The New York practice, Black wrote, was "wholly inconsistent" with this constitutional clause since the state was engaged in promoting "a solemn avowal of divine faith and supplication for the blessings of the Almighty." If the constitutional language has any meaning at all, Black declared, it "must at least mean that in this country it is no part of the business of government to compose official prayers for any group of the American people to recite as a part of a religious program carried on by government." After reviewing the history of religious freedom in America, Black acknowledged that the nation's religious heritage was a rich and vital one. But the Court's decision, he emphasized, showed no hostility toward either religion or prayer. On the contrary, the aim of both the First Amendment and of the Court in this case was "to put an end to governmental control of religion and of prayer" and not "to destroy either." "It is neither sacrilegious nor antireligious," Black concluded, "to say that each separate government in this country should stay out of the business of writing or sanctioning official prayers," leaving "that purely religious function to the people themselves and to those the people choose to look to for religious guidance."

Protestations to the contrary notwithstanding, large segments of the public cried out that the decision was indeed antireligious, sacrilegious, atheistic, and perhaps even Communist-inspired. Political figures generally condemned the decision, though President Kennedy was a conspicuous exception. Religious leaders of many stripes gave vent to their outrage. "I am shocked and frightened," Francis Cardinal Spellman (1889–1967) declared, "that the Supreme Court has declared

"WHAT DO THEY EXPECT US TO DO— LISTEN TO THE KIDS PRAY AT *HOME?*"

79. Passions ran high in the Supreme Court rulings on prayer, as this 1963 cartoon suggests. From *Straight Herblock* (Simon & Schuster, 1964). Reprinted with permission of the Washington Post.

unconstitutional a simple and voluntary declaration of belief in God by public school children." "God pity our country," said Billy Graham, "when we can no longer appeal to God for help." The Supreme Court, said Episcopal Bishop James A. Pike (1913–1969), "has just deconsecrated the nation." All of the Hearst newspapers expressed their strong disapproval, along with such major dailies as the *Boston Globe*, the *Chicago Tribune*, and the *Los Angeles Times*. Headlines, editorials, sermons, and syndicated columns flowed like water in their chorus of condemnation.

"To whom it may concern: Our something-or-other, who art in somewhere-or-other, hallowed be thy what-cha-ma-call-it . . . "

80. Passions continued to run high for years after the United States Supreme Court heard its first "prayer case"; this Paul Conrad cartoon appeared in 1971. © *1971. Reprinted with permission of Los Angeles Times Syndicate*

To be sure, other voices were heard, a bit more quietly at first. Several Protestant theologians praised the opinion as one protecting "the integrity of the religious conscience and the proper function of religious and governmental institutions." Baptist spokesmen, both north and south, approved of the decision, though they acknowledged that at the grass roots level much grumbling would be heard. The American Jewish Committee joined with the Synagogue Council of America and many other Jewish organizations, both local and national, in filing a "friend-of-the-court" brief in opposition to the use of the Regents Prayer. Martin Luther King, Jr., pronounced the decision to be "sound and good, reaffirming something basic in the nation: separation of church and state." Many major newspapers editorially backed the court, including the *New York Times*, the *Washington Post*, and the *St. Louis Post-Dispatch*. The *Christian Science Monitor* wrote that "both religion and government are stronger when each stands on its own feet." The Court had announced its decision on June 25, 1962, as its regular term came to a close; in that way, the country would have the whole summer to adjust to the new reality. It turned out to take much longer than that.

The following year the Court did little to heal the wounds or settle the dust when in *Abingdon v. Schempp* it went on to say that ritual Bible reading and recitation of the Lord's Prayer in the public schools were likewise unconstitutional. There the Court made clear a distinction between the practice of religion on the one hand and the study of religion on the other; the former was clearly unconstitutional so far as governmental agencies or offices or schools were concerned, but the latter was not only appropriate, it should even be encouraged. The Bible could be studied, religion could be studied, the role of religion in American life could be studied, but "the exercises here do not fall into those categories. They are religious exercises, required by the states [Maryland and Pennsylvania] in violation of the command of the First Amendment." Those opposed to the 1962 decision were not soothed by the 1963 one; those supporting the 1962 decision were not stimulated in 1963 to do much about instituting a genuine program of study about religion in the public schools.

Reactions to these two major Supreme Court judgments took a variety of forms. One reaction indicated that the law of inertia was more powerful than the law of the land: that is, many school districts continued, as before, with daily prayers and reading of the Bible. Another reaction was, of course, to comply with the rulings. Still another was to try in some way to clip the wings or restrict the power of the Court, one congressman from Texas even introducing a bill that would empower Congress to override (by a two-third vote) any ruling of the Court with which it disagreed. But the most sustained reaction of all, continuing for decades, was to propose an amendment to the Constitution that would have the effect of negating the 1962 and 1963 decisions. Wordings would vary and political alignments would shift, but the campaign continued.

Soon after the 1962 decision, about 150 different amendment proposals were put forward in Congress. This does not count, of course, the many suggestions offered outside those legislative halls. Congressman Frank Becker of New York gathered much support for what came to be called the "Becker amendment" that would make prayer and Bible reading constitutional, "if participation therein is on a voluntary basis, in any governmental or public school institution, or place." Such an amendment was necessary, Becker explained, "if we are to prevent the advocates of a godless society to accomplish in the United States that which the Communists have accomplished in Soviet Russia." But another New York congressman, Emmanuel Celler, held hearings before his House Judiciary Committee that succeeded in showing much public resistance, including that of major religious bodies, to such an amendment. The Becker amendment never came to a vote.

In the Senate a few years later, Senator Everett Dirksen of Illinois introduced a similar amendment that did come to a vote in September of 1966. There it was narrowly defeated, but the cause did not die. Other amendments were proposed in the 1970s and in the 1980s when no less a figure than President Ronald Reagan himself introduced an amendment, the wording of which had over the years been refined and clarified. "Nothing in this Constitution," it read, "shall be construed to prohibit individual or group prayers in public schools or other public institutions." At the same time, however, "No person shall be required by the United States or by any state to participate in prayer." After weeks of debate and rapt public attention, the Senate in March of 1984 voted: fifty-six for, and forty-four against the Reagan amendment. But since a two-thirds vote is required for a constitutional amendment, the measure lost. One indication of the intense interest, however, was the fact that all one hundred U. S. senators were present for this crucial count. That intense interest continues to the present moment, to be sure, sometimes more evident at the state level, sometimes at the federal level as the Supreme Court is required to judge still other prayer proposals, or moments of silence and meditation. (See, for example, the 1985 case arising from the state of Alabama, *Wallace* v. *Jaffree*).

The other religious contest in which public schools have been engaged concerns the curriculum itself: what books are required or recommended, what philosophies are espoused or rejected, what course of study are all students obliged to pursue? Some school districts have engaged in censorship on religious grounds, arguing that certain books (*Cinderella*, for instance) may deal in "occultism, secular humanism, evolution, disobedience to parents, pacifism, and feminism." Other districts have been presented with parental petitions to excuse their children from certain required courses, permitting home instruction or creating a separate curriculum. The most heated debates, however, have centered specifically on the science courses with reference to Darwinism taught not as theory but as fact, with no alternative explanations for the origins of life being offered.

The alternative most frequently proposed has been a religious explanation of those origins, an explanation based to a large degree on the Book of Genesis and bearing the name of "creationism." In 1981 the U. S. district judge in the state of Arkansas reviewed a law entitled, Balanced Treatment for Creation-Science and Evolution-Science Act. The court found this law to be unconstitutional since it amounted to government sponsorship and support for a particular sectarian point of view. The creationists, said the judge, "take the literal wording of the Book of Genesis and attempt to find scientific support for it." Since this law has the effect of advancing religion, he argued, it cannot be found constitutional. Interestingly, most recognized religious groups in Arkansas (Catholics, Methodists, Presbyterians, Union of American Hebrew Congregations, and so on) joined in the legal action to have this law overturned. But as the judge pointed out in his conclusion, whether the supporters of the Act constituted a minority or a majority was irrelevant to his finding. "No group, no matter how large or small, may use the organs of government, of which the public schools are the most conspicuous and influential, to foist its religious beliefs on others."

Seven years later, in 1968, the U. S. Supreme Court was asked to consider an even older Arkansas law that prohibited teachers in the public schools and the public universities from teaching any theory suggesting that man evolved from some other form of life. The Court agreed unanimously that the 1928 Law was as defective as the 1961 "balanced treatment" act, for it too advanced the narrow religious interest that "the Book of Genesis must be the exclusive source of doctrine as to the origin of man." This was not religious neutrality, the Court pointed out, but religious favoritism. "Plainly, the law is contrary to the mandate of the First, and in violation of the Fourteenth, Amendment to the Constitution."

Then in 1987 the state of Louisiana was the subject of Supreme Court action as another "balanced treatment" law came up for review. In Edwards v. Aguillard the Court said—but not unanimously—that the history of legislative action in Louisiana clearly demonstrated that its purpose was "to provide persuasive advantage to a particular religious doctrine that rejects the factual basis of evolution in its entirety." In that advancing of a specific religious doctrine, its constitutional defectiveness lay. Two dissenters, however, argued that the law had a secular basis as well as a religious one, and that this purpose must be recognized. "The people of Louisiana, including those who are Christian fundamentalists," the dissenters noted, "are quite entitled, as a secular matter, to have whatever scientific evidence there may be against evolution presented in their schools." If there is no such scientific evidence, that (said Chief Justice William Rehnquist [b. 1924] and Associate Justice Anthony Scalia [b. 1936]) was another question, but one which the Supreme Court did not have before it the evidence to decide.

Votes have gone against creationism repeatedly, but not with perfect unanimity. One consequence of the public discussion has been a new awareness that Darwinism is indeed only a hypothesis or theory, though admittedly the highly favored theory of the entire scientific community in the late twentieth century. Another consequence, of course, has been to arouse in certain circles still more resentment against the public schools, with some parents, on curricular grounds, turning to private education. But private education, no less than public, managed to inspire much litigation and much discussion about that metaphoric "wall" of separation.

As noted above, within the realm of private education, the issues were not so much curricular as they were financial. And these money questions could and did take a bewildering variety of forms. Though historically the public versus private education issue, has been seen as largely a Protestant versus Roman Catholic issue, in recent decades the contest has become considerably more complex than that. The Supreme Court, moreover, has felt the necessity of inventing a whole new set of guidelines in an effort to determine whether or not the Establishment Clause of the First Amendment is being violated. The simple phrase that "Congress shall make no law respecting an establishment of religion" has proved inadequate for the many contemporary queries regarding textbook purchases, salary subsidies, construction loans, tax credits, voucher plans, financial help in buying maps or projectors or standardized tests, or whatever. To get through this maze, the Court needed a compass or at least a clear grid with coordinates sharply delineated.

So the Court asked itself, as case after case fell into its lap, a series of questions: Does this particular law benefit mainly the child or the church school? Does this law have a prevailingly secular purpose? Whatever the purpose of a given law, is the effect of that law such as to advance or inhibit religion? Or is it neutral with regard to religion? Further, does the administration of the law require government (federal or state or local) to become "excessively entangled" with religion? And finally, is such a law likely to unify the body social, or to divide it by fanning the flames of religious passion? With such an array of questions and with such an array of cases, it will probably come as no surprise that the Court had difficulty making up its mind or reaching any degree of unanimity in its decisions. (In one 1977 case arising from Ohio, the justices issued seven separate dissents to one or more parts of the decision!)

The modern story begins with the famous case of *Everson* v. *Board of Education* that the Court heard in 1947. The case is famous for several reasons: one, it explicitly applied the Establishment Clause (by way of the Fourteenth Amendment) to the states; two, it began, with its five-to-four decision, a tradition of a much divided court in cases related to religious schools; and three, it used the strongest separationist language one could readily imagine, yet decided in favor (by the slimmest majority, to be sure) of a practice that to the dissenters seemed the opposite of separation in matters of church and state. The facts of the case can be briefly stated. A New Jersey law authorized school districts to use public transportation (instead of their own school buses), reimbursing the children for the bus fares. In one township in the state, children riding the public buses to parochial schools were also reimbursed. The question: was this latter practice constitutional?

Justice Hugo Black, speaking for the majority of five, concluded the Court's opinion in these words: "The First Amendment has erected a wall between church and state. That wall must be kept high and impregnable. We could not approve the slightest breach." Then, the surprise: "New Jersey has not breached it here." The dissenters, shaking their heads in disbelief, declared that the majority's advocacy of "complete and uncompromising separation of Church from State" seemed "utterly discordant with its conclusion." The long dissenting opinion, reviewing the history of church-state separation, and especially of

81. Sixth graders in a Roman Catholic parochial school on Staten Island, New York, in the early 1960s. *National Catholic Educational Association*

James Madison's "Memorial and Remonstrance" (see above, p. 118), concluded that the issue was not one of how much money was being spent to transport children to parochial schools, how modest the accommodation here offered really was. "Now as in Madison's day it is one of principle, to keep separate the separate spheres as the First Amendment drew them; to prevent the first experiment upon our liberties; and to keep the question from being entangled in corrosive precedents." Anyone reading the full text of both majority and dissenting opinions could only conclude that a rough road lay ahead.

And so it did. As the cases tumbled in during the sixties, seventies, and eighties, the Court divided again and again; state legislatures tried again and again to find other avenues for financial assistance to parochial schools. In a New York case in 1968 a majority of six justices agreed that a state law that would lend textbooks free of charge to all students in grades seven through twelve, including parochial school students, was in fact constitutional. Dissenters, mincing no words, pronounced the New York State law "a flat, flagrant, open violation of the First and Fourteenth Amendments." That law called "for furnishing special, separate, and particular books, specially, separately, and particularly chosen by religious sects or their representatives for use in their sectarian schools." Under those circumstances, the dissenters said, the New York law must be declared unconstitutional. Not so, said six; 'tis so, said three.

In a case from Pennsylvania heard in 1974 (*Meek* v. *Pittenger*), the Court divided once again, six to three, but this time the majority of six moved in the direction of restricting the use of public monies for parochial schools. Helping with textbooks was ruled acceptable, but helping

82. A program of religious instruction was offered just off the campus of the public schools in Fort Wayne, Indiana, in 1964. *Religious News Service*

with many other "auxiliary services"—counseling, remedial classes, testing—was not acceptable. But the complexity of the case began to resemble a theatre of the absurd as "Mr. Justice Brennan concurred in part and dissented in part" and filed an opinion in which two other justices joined. "Mr. Chief Justice Burger concurred in the judgment in part and dissented in part and filed opinion. Mr. Justice Rehnquist concurred in the judgment in part and dissented in part and filed opinion" in which another justice joined. Did anybody know which way the compass pointed, or did magnetic north just keep jumping around?

Of course, when the Court is so badly divided, it is a fairly good sign that society is divided as well. Public schools in the 1960s and beyond came under increasing criticism from many segments of society. Private schools, meanwhile, ceased to be the preserve mainly of Roman Catholics, as many traditional supporters of public schools now—for a variety of reasons—began to develop schools of their own. Sometimes the issue was religion, sometimes morals or safety, sometimes quality of education and curricular content, sometimes ethnicity or race or social class. By the 1980s the issues had become much more complex than those relating just to separation of church and state, though that surely remained. Also by the 1980s the efforts to find more suitable or judicially acceptable means for publicly supporting private education had won some significant victories.

One notable and surprising victory pertained to a Minnesota case that the Court decided in 1983. In *Mueller v. Allen* the Court examined a state law that permitted all parents to deduct from their taxes between five and seven hundred dollars per child for tuition, textbooks, and transportation to any school, public or private. Perhaps the only thing predictable about this case was that the justices would be divided and so they were, five to four, with the majority finding the Minnesota law to be permissible, since whatever aid reaching the parochial schools did so as a result of individual parental decision and not as an "imprimatur of state approval." Dissenters pointed out that ninety percent of all students attending private schools went to schools permeated with religious instruction, and that no effort had been made to restrict the public monies to secular rather than religious uses. Also, it was noted that the decision in this case contradicted earlier judgments of the Court.

If the dissenters were correct in that last point, it would not be surprising. For the justices recognized, more than once, that whether voting with the majority or with the minority, they followed no crystal-clear or steady direction. One justice confessed in 1977 that the Court's decision in the whole arena of parochial education "often must seem arbitrary." But another justice, trying to put the best face on the situation, said in 1980 that the Court "sacrifices clarity and predictability for flexibility." Flexibility might by others be called inconsistency, for the patterns were admittedly often difficult to discern. The appointment of each new justice, the election of each new president, the make-up of each new Congress aggravated the difficulties and sometimes confounded the nation.

MATTERS OF LIFE AND DEATH

As strongly as citizens have felt about such issues as saluting the flag or praying in the public school or funneling tax monies to the private school, one encountered controversies even more inflammatory, even more divisive. These controversies, moreover, by their nature tended to be more personal and private; yet, their resolution was repeatedly sought in very public ways. Not just in the churches or the courts or the schools have contending parties argued their respective points of view, but in the streets as well where sometimes violence has replaced debate.

State and federal courts have been required to deal with laws concerning contraceptive devices or birth control instruction. They have had to adjudicate cases of euthanasia or "mercy-killing," cases made more complex by the modern technical ability to sustain biological life long after life of any discernible quality has ceased. In the case particularly of Jehovah's Witnesses, the courts have had to remove a child temporarily from the custody of the parents so that a life-saving blood transfusion might be administered. In the case of spiritual or faith healing, and especially if a person died without having medical assistance made available, questions of criminal neglect demanded legal resolution. Cities have been restrained by religious pressure groups from flouridating their water systems. Vaccination against smallpox or polio have become church-state controversies. The morality of suicide and of capital punishment has repeatedly emerged as a subject for theologians, politicians, ethicists, and others to debate; here too sometimes the theoretical discussions have spilled over into passionate demonstrations.

One subject, however, has outbid all the others in the degree of public attention that it received and in the vigor on the opposing sides that it aroused. Abortion, like many of those issues noted above, is not a church-state question in the sense that the First Amendment always provided the grounds for judicial opinion. But abortion, like those other matters, was a religious question in the sense that churches and voluntary religious associations repeatedly appeared as chief antagonists or litigants or lobbyists. And with respect to the abortion controversy in particular, some observers have gone so far as to refer to it as a "religious war." While this may be an overstatement, it is not an exaggeration to say that religion has been thoroughly caught up in this one pivotal "matter of life and death."

In the 1960s and 1970s the move to remove abortion from the criminal code gained much religious support, particularly Protestant and Jewish. A professor at the Episcopal Theological School in Cambridge in his capacity as director of the Association for the Study of Abortion led much of the "pro-choice" reform, aided by the official statements of such denominations as the United Church of Christ in 1971 and the United Methodist Church in 1972. On the other hand, many evangelical and fundamentalist Protestants joined the ranks of the "pro-life" forces, as did the Church of Jesus Christ of Latter-day Saints. But through much of the continuing controversy, the Roman Catholic Church has been seen as the most consistent and powerful foe of abortion.

In 1973 the Supreme Court at last agreed to hear an abortion case, the result in *Roe v. Wade* doing little to mend the social and religious divisions. Indeed, that 1973 case has become a kind of rallying point for the critics and the supporters of the Court's decision. The Court began with a recognition that this was an issue of utmost tenderness and deepest conviction. "One's philosophy, one's experiences, one's exposure to the raw edges of human existence, one's religious training, one's attitude toward life and family and their values, and the moral standards one establishes and seeks to observe, are all likely to influence and to color one's thinking and conclusions about abortion." The Court then reviewed at great length historical attitudes regarding abortion from the ancient world up through English Common Law and early American law. The Court also evaluated the official pronouncements of such agencies as the American Medical Association, the American Public Health Association, the American Bar Association, the Roman Catholic Church, the National Council of Churches, and others. As a result of this extensive review, the Court decided that in the first trimester of pregnancy the decision about abortion "must be left to the medical judgment of the pregnant woman's attending physician." In the second trimester, the state may, if it so chooses, "regulate the abortion procedure in ways that are reasonably related to maternal health." And in the final trimester, the state may, if it chooses, regulate or even prohibit abortion except where it is judged necessary "for the preservation of the life and health of the mother."

One of the two dissenters in this case, Justice William Rehnquist (now Chief Justice) argued that this entire issue should be left in the hands of the states rather than in those of the federal government. As the 1980s drew to a close, that sentiment steadily increased. Similarly, the sentiment to get the federal government out of the business of subsidizing or funding abortions also grew, sentiment in this case taking the form of both legislative action (along with constitutional amendment proposals) and popular demonstration—including the bombing of abortion clinics. During his eight years in office President Reagan identified closely with the "pro-life" forces, declaring January 22 (the anniversary of *Roe v. Wade*) as National Sanctity of Human Life Day. When demonstrations opposing abortion were held on that day, counter-demonstrations (sponsored, for example, by the National Organization for Women) contended for a woman's right to seek an abortion.

In the presidential campaigns of 1984 and again in 1988, abortion emerged as a major issue, for some the single issue upon which to base one's vote. In appointments to the Supreme Court as well as to all lower federal courts, the prospective jurist's views on abortion often overshadowed everything else. However political and public the arguments have become, many agree that this issue is, at bottom, a moral and religious and profoundly personal concern. American religion will not cease to be deeply involved. The hope is that American society will, somehow, cease to be deeply divided.

CHAPTER 23

Alienation, Liberation, Union

When thirteen quarreling colonies managed to agree on the cause of independence from Britain and when, a few years later, thirteen jealous states managed to agree on a Constitution, the question of national unity might appear to have been settled. Two hundred years later, however, most observers would admit that a genuine unity of a society and a people still proved elusive. The American pledge of "one nation, under God, with liberty and justice for all" seemed more an article of faith than an empirical fact. Some even questioned whether it was still an article of faith. Particularly in matters of race and of gender, unity yielded to separation and recrimination. And while some churches overcame long-standing divisions, that mending did not produce immediate reconciliations in society at large.

CIVIL RIGHTS AND THE CHURCHES

The most conspicuous religious crusades of the 1950s and 1960s concerned civil rights, initially and dramatically aimed at improving the status of the nation's black citizens. The most conspicuous leader of this crusade was a black Baptist minister, Martin Luther King, Jr. (1929–1968). But his crusading army included far more than Baptists, far more than blacks, as Protestant clergymen of many communions, Catholic priests and Catholic nuns, Jewish theologians and rabbis, Orthodox bishops and laity, joined in marching and in praying in the interest of "liberty and justice for all." In unity they also endured abuse, arrest, imprisonment, pain, suffering, and death.

A native of Atlanta, Georgia, King attended Morehouse College in his hometown, then went north for graduate education in Pennsylvania and in Massachusetts. Returning to the South in 1954, King accepted the position of pastor of the Dexter Avenue Baptist Church in Montgomery, Alabama. There, almost by accident, he found himself in the eye of a gathering storm. Toward the end of 1955 one black citizen of the city refused to accept the pattern of blacks sitting only in the rear of the public buses. When, after a long and tiring day, Rosa Parks (b.

1913) boarded the bus to find all seats in the rear already taken, she simply sat in the first available seat toward the front. She declined to move. But by not moving that day, she moved a whole people as the Montgomery "bus boycott" was born.

Blacks, the major patrons of the city's public transportation system, under King's leadership agreed not to ride the buses again until this pattern of segregated seating was abolished. The black community gradually came to recognize, King noted, "that it was ultimately more honorable to walk the streets in dignity than to ride the buses in humiliation." The nonviolent protest, lasting more a year, resulted in victory on that small point, but it also thrust King to a crusading leadership that would last for the remaining years of his life.

Marchers moved from Montgomery to Selma; from Meridian, Mississippi, to Jackson; from St. Augustine, Florida, to Atlanta, Georgia; then to the black ghettos of northern cities as well. In Birmingham, King was arrested in the spring of 1963 and jailed along with other religious leaders who had joined him in public protest. From that jail, King wrote a letter to some Atlanta clergymen who had complained about King's activities that took him far from his own church in Montgomery and his pastoral responsibilities there. Why was King in Birmingham?, they had asked. He was there, King replied, because that

83. With respect to civil rights, both the nation and its churches turned a corner in the 1960s. This march on Selma, Alabama, in 1965 brought together priests, rabbis, nuns, and ministers in their support of Martin Luther King, Jr. *Religious News Service*

was where injustice could be found, and "injustice anywhere is a threat to justice everywhere." Comparing himself to ancient prophets who took their message everywhere God led them to go, and to the early Christian Apostle Paul (who also ended up in jail), King declared: "so am I compelled to carry the gospel of freedom beyond my own hometown."

King carried that gospel most powerfully to Washington, D. C., when in August of 1963 he led a march of tens of thousands to the mall near the monument erected in honor of the nation's first president. There King spoke not only to the thousands assembled, but also by way of television to the millions far from the Capitol. And he spoke to the national soul, reminding them of his dream that had at one point also been the American dream. It was a dream of that day when the "jangling discords of our nation" shall be transformed "into a beautiful symphony of brotherhood." It was a dream of that day when "all of God's children will be able to sing with new meaning, 'My country 'tis of thee, sweet land of liberty, of thee I sing.' " On that grand day, it will at last be possible, King proclaimed, for "all of God's children, black men and white men, Jews and Gentiles, Protestants and Catholics . . . to join hands and sing in the words of the old Negro spiritual, 'Free at last! free at last! thank God almighty, we are free at last.' "

The next year, following the assassination of President John F. Kennedy, a civil rights bill was passed by the U. S. Congress, the rhetoric of Martin Luther King making a powerful difference. So had the visible presence of so wide a spectrum of religious leadership in the movement made a difference. So had the increased lobbying by such agencies as the National Catholic Welfare Conference, the National Council of Churches, and B'nai B'rith along with its twentieth-century offspring, the Anti-Defamation League. Then in Memphis, Tennessee, three days before Palm Sunday of 1968 King himself fell before an assassin's rifle shot. And though his life ended, his crusade did not.

In 1969 Father Theodore Hesburg (b. 1917) of Notre Dame University agreed to serve as chairman of the federal government's Civil Rights Commission; it was more than an honorary position as Hesburg became a most courageous spokesman for civil rights. In that same year, James Forman (b. 1928) issued a "Black Manifesto" that specifically challenged the nation's religious institutions to cleanse themselves of all institutional racism and begin to repair the damage done to millions of their fellow citizens. King's own organization, the Southern Christian Leadership Conference, was joined by a National Conference of Black Churchmen in making "black power," and notably black religious power, a social and political reality. In the 1970s a young black theologian, James Cone (b. 1938), spoke and wrote in behalf of a new kind of religious thinking, a black theology necessarily called forth by "the failure of white religionists to relate the gospel of Jesus Christ to the pain of being black in a white racist society." And in the 1980s, the preacher-politician, Jesse Jackson (b. 1941), kept the crusade very much alive.

By that point in the late twentieth century, other minorities found their voice and sought their place in both the society and the ecclesiastical marketplace. Hispanics, long shut out from the hierarchy of the Roman Catholic church despite the fact that they comprise about one-fourth of all America's Catholics, began to emerge in roles of leadership there. Similarly, in the wider society, Chicanos in the American West and Southwest gained in both economic and political prominence. The nation's second largest, but for so long largely invisible, minority had also rejected the back of the bus as their only rightful place.

A Roman Catholic layman, Caesar Chavez (b. 1927), organized the migrant Mexican-American laboring force in California with sufficient effectiveness as to win wide attention and support well beyond the laboring ranks themselves. In 1973 Chavez accepted the annual Reinhold Niebuhr Award in honor of his successful efforts (and that of his National Farm Workers' Union) in joining social passion to political realism in a way that Niebuhr himself had so often done. Three years

84. In a unique meeting Martin Luther King, Jr. and Malcolm X greeted each other in Washington, D. C., in 1964. A potential coalition became impossible when Malcolm X was assassinated a year later with King's assassination following three years after that. *Religious News Service*

before that Chavez had been invited to San Antonio, Texas, to witness the elevation of the first Hispanic to the office of bishop in the Catholic church. Out of 225 bishops in the Catholic church at that time, one was Hispanic—hardly a tidal wave or even a case of proportional representation, but at least one small step had been taken on behalf of the invisible minority.

Other steps, some not so small, indicated that the decades of the seventies and eighties belonged, so far as Roman Catholicism in America was concerned, to the Hispanics, a population of around twenty million by the end of the eighties. National Hispanic Pastoral Conferences (*Encuentros*) began to be held in 1972. At the second such conference (*Segundo Encuentro Nacional Hispano de Pastoral*) in 1977 the Pope sent his greetings and the president of the National Conference of Catholic Bishops convened the group with the assurance that the church would do all that it could, "as a matter of strict justice, to help people in their struggle to overcome everything which condemns them to a marginal existence." Archbishop Joseph L. Bernardin (b. 1928) of Cincinnati also spoke in positive terms of the Hispanic culture "which is so interwoven with your Catholic faith." "In our highly secularized society," the archbishop added, "we need your witness to the faith and the many other gifts you offer." By that time, the number of Hispanic bishops had grown from one to eight, and a Secretariat for Hispanic Affairs had become a regular part of the United States Catholic Conference.

In 1983 the nation's bishops issued a Pastoral Letter on "The Hispanic Presence: Challenge and Commitment" that revealed a new level of consciousness within the entire Catholic community. No longer should Spanish-speaking parishes have priests who spoke English only. No longer should liturgy fail to reflect and incorporate the contributions of Hispanics artists and musicians. No longer should the priesthood be seen as the privilege of a very few. "We call upon Hispanic parents," the bishops said, "to present the life and work of a priest or religious as a highly desirable vocation for their children, and to take rightful pride in having a son or daughter serve the church in this way." And no longer should justice be denied to the Hispanic population at large. The bishops spoke specifically in 1983 of "those social concerns which most directly affect the Hispanic community, among them voting rights, discrimination, immigration rights, the status of farmworkers, bilingualism and pluralism." These, said the hierarchy, "are social justice issues of paramount importance to ministry with Hispanics and to the entire Church."

By the mid-eighties the Church was ready to recognize the special flavor of Hispanic Catholicism, of its traditional feasts and special holidays, of its popular piety that "in the course of almost five hundred years in the Americas" had taken such deep cultural roots. "Hispanic spirituality," the bishops noted, "places strong emphasis on the humanity of Jesus, especially when he appears weak and suffering, as in the crib and in his passion and death." The symbolic richness of this piety, in statues, images, processions, holy places, festivals, is today perhaps no where more dramatically expressed than in Santa Fe, New Mexico, once the political capital of Spanish North America and now in many respects the spiritual capital. In that city, history and religion and culture are so thoroughly intertwined that they cannot be separated. Our Lady of Guadalupe, the patron saint of Mexico, enjoys special prominence in the homes, the sanctuaries, and the affections of those who live in a city whose very name means "holy faith." There and throughout the country, Hispanic Catholicism was more than the memory of a proud past: it was a confident march toward a future in which participation would be rewarding and full.

Native Americans in the 1960s and 1970s also won wider recognition of their freedoms, especially of their religious freedoms. During much of U. S. history, the Indians did not enjoy the relative luxury of being an invisible minority; on the contrary, they were highly visible and fiercely resisted. That resistance, even in relatively modern times, took the form of discouraging if not forbidding many religious practices endemic in Indian cultures. Sometimes a kind of accommodation took place: Apaches singing Christian hymns, but retaining the Apache language; Zuni religious figures painted on the walls of the Catholic mission church; celebrations of the mass in the Pueblo with many tribal dances as part of the ritual.

Another sort of accommodation occurred with the creation of the Native American Church that by 1960 had been chartered in a dozen states. This church stood within the Christian tradition but at the same time stood firmly within the Indian tradition as well. Since the American Indian had been denied political freedom, perhaps in such a church a measure of religious freedom could be found. The ritual use of peyote could be compared to the ritual use of wine in the service of communion: in both cases carefully controlled by the group, in both cases accompanied by spiritual self-examination and high moral purpose. Such use, it was generally agreed, could be allowed as long as the surrounding culture was in no way damaged thereby.

In the 1960s, however, many of the young people in that surrounding culture turned more and more to drugs of one kind or another. As law enforcement authorities grew more nervous, three Navajo Indians were arrested in 1962 near Needles, California, for using peyote as part of their religious ritual. Found guilty of violating state law, they appealed to the California Supreme Court. That court in 1964 found in favor of the Navajos and their religious freedom, the Court noting that the theology of the Native American church "combines certain Christian teachings with the belief that peyote embodies the Holy Spirit and that those who partake of peyote enter into direct communion with

God." This was not traditional Christianity, to be sure, but then in a mass society such as ours, said the Court, pressures for total conformity must be resisted. "The varying currents of the cultures that flow into the mainstream of our national life give it depth and beauty." The state has an "interest" in enforcing its laws against narcotics, but the state has an even weightier interest, the Court concluded, in permitting a ritual that involves "the very essence of religious expression."

If this 1964 case represented a small step in the direction of greater religious freedom for the Indians, another step was taken in 1970 when the sacred Blue Lake and surrounding lands of the Taos Pueblo in New Mexico were returned to the Indians. In signing the bill, President Richard Nixon (b. 1913) indicated that the basic issue was religious freedom for this tribe. For seven hundred years before European religion came to America's shores, he noted, "the Taos Pueblo Indians worshipped in this place. We restore this place of worship to them for all the years to come."

Then in 1978 the U. S. Congress took a still larger step when it passed the American Indian Religious Freedom Act. That such an act was necessary almost two hundred years after all other Americans had been guaranteed their religious freedom is the most eloquent commentary on what the Indian had long endured. At last, native religions (with emphasis on the plural) could spring forth in bountiful variety: in

85. Father Ksistaki-Poka, the first Blackfoot Indian to be ordained as a Roman Catholic Priest, blesses his fellow tribesmen. *Religious News Service*

the rites of passage for birth, puberty, marriage, and death; in the shaman's power as healer and teacher; in the agricultural and communal celebrations; in the attention given to sacred places and sacred times; in the broad reverence for land, for nature, for life. In 1924 citizenship had been granted to the Native Americans. In 1978 that citizenship began to be taken more seriously, as Congress declared official U. S. policy now to be "to protect and preserve for American Indians their inherent right of freedom to believe, express, and exercise the traditional religions of the American Indian, Eskimo, Aleut, and native Hawaiian, including but not limited to access to sites, use and possession of sacred objects, and the freedom to worship through ceremonials and traditional rites." Under this protective umbrella, Indians and others have reclaimed burial sites and sacred relics, have again been guaranteed access to ancestral sacred places, and have with new assurance celebrated the faith of their fathers and mothers.

GENDER EQUITY AND RELIGION

The drive for women's rights in America has been a long one, filled with frustration, disappointment, and defeat. Religion in America has not always been in the vanguard of that battle. To speak more bluntly, religion has more often been the restraining anchor, the unyielding institution, the bastion of male domination that had behind it the force of centuries-old traditions usually reinforced by a "thus saith the Lord." Despite all that, however, women have led religious movements of their own, have dominated church membership rolls for decades, have exercised leadership in such disparate areas as foreign missions, religious education, social reform, health care, and family services. Yet, most doors to their wider participation have not opened easily and some have not opened at all.

Much attention has been given to what has been called the "rhetoric of sexuality." Language, especially that found in the standard liturgies and in the traditional hymns, regularly used the male pronoun not only for God but for all the people of God. Women could understandably feel slighted if not actually excluded by scriptures, prayers, and songs that apparently made no place for them. The hymn, "Rise Up, O Men of God," proved less than stirring to those who saw in such words only continued patriarchal domination and sexist exclusion. As Rosemary Ruether (b. 1936) has pointed out, the ruling group uses language to define reality in its own terms, reducing the subordinate group to a point of near invisibility. "Women," said Ruether, "more than any other group, are overwhelmed by a linguistic form that excludes them from visible existence." In speaking only of the "fatherhood of God" and the "brotherhood of Man," language forsakes all pretense of neutrality, of even-handedness. It is time, wrote one author, to move

Beyond God the Father; wrote another, it is a time for a *Changing of the Gods*; and still others spoke of *Womanspirit Rising*.

Elaine Pagels (b. 1943), noted professor at Princeton University, observed that the problem of language is most acute in Judaism, Christianity, and Islam where, in contrast to most other religions, there is no feminine symbolism for God. While theologians of these monotheistic religions contend that the masculine terms are not really gender terms at all, the actual language used "conveys a different message and gives" a different impression. In Catholicism, Pagels wrote, one does find a special reverence for Mary, but it is Mary as "mother of God," not as God the Mother on a par with God the Father. In Judaism too, as another author argued, it was time to move beyond God the Father with a complementing image of God as female; otherwise, the rhetoric of sexuality served as "both a mirror and a legitimation of the oppressing and eclipsing of women." Language deals mainly with symbols, to be sure, and when men or women speak of God, they speak only of images, but both symbols and images, to be most useful, require universality, not particularity; inclusiveness, not segregation or subordination.

The gender problem, however, is even more acute when one deals not with symbols, but with the realities of authority, of office, of power: How many women on governing boards of denominations and seminaries, of local churches and synagogues? How many women in positions of genuine religious responsibility beyond the home? But most of

86. Amid much controversy and some schism, the Episcopal church in the 1970s began ordaining women to the priesthood; here three such recently ordained priests join in celebrating the Lord's Supper (or Eucharist) in New York City in 1974. *Religious News Service*

all, of course, how many women accepted as equals in the professional ministry of the several denominations themselves? The issue of ordination dominated all others in the 1970s and 1980s as each churchly tradition considered its options and reexamined its historic positions. No uniformity of response was forthcoming.

Some Protestant groups, for example the Pentecostal and Holiness bodies, had a long tradition of female preaching. Quakers with their tradition of no professional clergy listened to male and female alike, as the Spirit moved. In Christian Science the number of female practitioners greatly outnumbered the male, and in other smaller bodies gender equity was freely and casually pursued. But in the majority of mainstream Protestant groups, ordination of women did not come easily and steps taken in that direction were anything but casual.

When, for example, the Episcopal Church in 1976 ruled that women could be ordained priests, a dozen or more churches soon broke away from the parent body, forming a separate diocese for those who "wish to remain faithful to the traditional Church." "Most of the reasons the church gave for ordaining women," the dissenters explained, "are on a sociological plane, not a theological plane." Equality between the sexes, they also argued, did not imply identify of function for the sexes. Meanwhile, the Episcopal Church itself continued with the ordination of women priests and then, in 1989, confirmed the election of the first female bishop in the church, Barbara C. Harris (b. 1935). Here, too, the action was accomplished only amid resistance and many expressions of displeasure; yet, the Church as a whole appears steady in its course of extending more and more opportunities for women to enter the professional ministry at all levels.

Within Lutheranism the progress has been uneven as separate segments have moved toward the ordination of women at varying speeds. The Lutheran Church in America in 1966 called for a "reexamination of all stereotyped cultural and social differences between man and woman, to determine those that are relative and outmoded and consequently irrelevant and even harmful to the church's ministry." In the late 1960s, three large Lutheran groups held an Inter-Lutheran Consultation on the Ordination of Women. Two of the three groups had approved such ordination by 1970, but the third, the more conservative Lutheran Church-Missouri Synod, did not. That group preferred to debate not whether women could become ministers but whether they could attend business meetings of the church and, if they could attend, whether they could be granted the right to vote. In 1969 this synod agreed that the oft-quoted scriptural injunction for women to "keep silent" in church did not necessarily apply to congregational meetings, but it did apply to holding the pastoral office.

Some denominations, rather than taking tentative steps in the direction of female ordination, took steps backward. The Southern

Baptist Convention had ordained women as early as 1964 and by the mid-1980s had ordained over four hundred women. By that latter date, however, ordaining women to the ministry had become highly controversial, with an increasingly conservative or fundamentalist leadership becoming ever more outspoken in opposition to such action. In its 1984 annual meeting the convention declared that women should not assume a role of authority over men; women were excluded from the pastoral ministry to "preserve a submission God requires because the man was first in creation and the woman was first in the Edenic fall." One response to that was to argue that if women were the first to discover sin, they could better recognize it and more effectively cast it out. Neither that reply nor a series of other confrontations, however, resolved an issue that became more controversial, not less. In 1986 the convention's Home Mission Board voted not to grant funds to any church that employed a woman pastor. But in 1988 an ordained Southern Baptist woman called upon her denomination to be more prophetic on the question of gender equality than it had managed to be on the matter of racial equality. "The pressing spiritual, emotional, and physical needs in our world," she wrote, "demand that Southern Baptists cease to limit the ministry of over half our members."

In Roman Catholicism the question of the ordination of women has been highly visible and the resistance, to this point, highly successful. Nonetheless, slow tidal changes are underway. In 1972 the Leadership Conference of Women Religious was organized in the United States, a body that represented about ninety percent of all sisters and nuns in this country. Two years after its organization, the conference supported "the principle that all ministries in the Church be open to women and men as the Spirit calls them." In 1976 hundreds of Catholic women organized a Women's Ordination Conference to protest against "a priesthood that is elitist, hierarchical, racist, classist." Taking a strong stand on behalf of equal *rites* for Catholic women, this group and others associated with it contended that "what is central to the historical Jesus is his humanity and not his maleness." Woman, no less than man, was created in the image of God, they argued in 1976, and the movement seemed well on the road.

The following year, however, the road became bumpy when the Vatican released its "Declaration on the Question of the Admission of Women to the Ministerial Priesthood." Christ was a male, the report solemnly explained, and he called as apostles only males. Moreover, one can find no evidence of an intent to widen the ministry to include females, the declaration affirming (in the words of Rosemary Ruether) "some mysterious sacramental bond between Christ, maleness, and priesthood." But as Ruether also pointed out, the Vatican statement was met with a mixture of incredulity and ridicule, the end result being that Catholic opinion in this country that favored the ordination of women actually went up, not down. Opinion grew particularly strong in ecclesiastical circles for admitting women to the lowest order of the ministry, the diaconate (deacons), an order that in New Testament times stressed the role of charity and service.

Meanwhile, the Roman Catholic Church confronted special problems with respect to the thousands of nuns that served in one capacity or another in America. Two problems stood out. The first was that the general trend toward gender equality and female liberation has caused many nuns to chafe under the severe restrictions of dress, behavior, and male authority. Some small orders disbanded as entities under church discipline, and thousands of individual nuns left the cloister to serve as church administrators, prison chaplains, social workers, and even on occasion holders of public office. The second problem was the declining attractiveness of the convent as a religious vocation for Catholic young women. The number entering any order declined sharply from a high of over thirty thousand in the years from 1958 to 1962 to a low of less than three thousand in the years between 1976 and 1981. In 1960, the total number of sisters in America was about 170,000; by the late 1980s that number had fallen to a little over 100,000.

Like Lutheranism, Judaism found itself moving with uneven step toward a full clerical equality for women. Reform Judaism made the initial breakthrough when it ordained its first female rabbi in 1972. Rabbi Sally Priesand (b. 1946) spent eight years preparing for that moment, preparing (as she wrote) "for a profession that no woman had yet entered." The happiness of the event in 1972 was somewhat diminished by the resistance of many congregations to hire or even interview her. But then the Stephen Wise Free Synagogue in New York City offered her the position of assistant rabbi and that was "a blessing in the true sense of the word." She committed herself, she noted, to the survival of the Jewish tradition, "knowing that Judaism had traditionally discriminated against women [and] that it had not always been sensitive to the problems of total equality." But, said Rabbi Priesand, Judaism has "tremendous flexibility," this enabling the tradition to survive for so many centuries and likewise enabling her to work toward "the necessary changes which will grant women total equality within the Jewish community."

At the leading institution of Conservative Judaism, the Jewish Theological Seminary of New York City, the faculty in 1979 voted to postpone "indefinitely" the question of ordaining female rabbis. Indefinitely turned out to last only four years as that same faculty in 1983 voted thirty-four to eight to open the doors for such ordination. By that time, Reform Judaism had ordained over sixty young women and the small Reconstructionist branch over a dozen. Resistance among Conservative rabbis to the 1983 decision took the form of vocal reproof rather than schism, one rabbi pleading for "a great deal of compassion lest we fall into the kind of polarization that exists among our friends in the Orthodox world."

That "Orthodox world," both in Israel and in America, did present problems so far as women were concerned, and not just in the matter of ordination. Orthodoxy in America stood firm against ordination, but that did not mean that no winds of feminism blew there. Blu Greenberg (b. 1926), wife of an Orthodox rabbi and mother of children being raised in the Orthodox tradition, wrote in 1981 of her gradual realization of how total the male domination in that branch of Judaism had been. Under the stimulus of the feminist movement of the 1960s, she reported, "I became sensitized to issues and situations that previously had made no impression upon me." She did not find the tradition of Orthodoxy in past centuries to be bad; what she did find was that, even within Orthodoxy, the tradition could be made better.

In that other orthodoxy present on the American scene, namely Eastern Orthodoxy, the breezes of feminism blew even more softly. With many ethnic and national divisions, each segment of Orthodoxy was reluctant to reveal itself as somehow less traditional, less bound by history and doctrine, than another. This Orthodoxy, moreover, has been less susceptible than most other religious bodies in America to the underlying cultural shifts. Having not been part of the West's Renaissance or Reformation or Enlightenment, the Eastern Churches remain

87. In 1972 Reform Judaism ordained its first female rabbi: Sally Priesand standing in the center. *Religious News Service*

largely insulated from such populist waves as the feminist movement. Maleness there stands firm.

Such male domination maintained in much of Judaism and Christianity, or relinquished only with exquisite reluctance, provoked some feminists to move away from these traditional religions altogether toward a kind of neopaganism that saw itself as a revival of ancient nature religions. Women write of the Mother Goddess, of witches and druids, of priestesses and mystic presences. Women's experience becomes a uniquely significant source for insight about the divine, not equal to that of the male, but above it. For these women, patriarchy is so deeply rooted in biblical religion that it can never be completely removed. One must turn, then, from man-centered, man-dominated, man-infected traditions to others where women spoke and taught and governed. In such new—or old—forms of religious expression, women (it was argued) represent authentic humanity, with males representing the oppressive, rapacious, and destructive. The danger in much of this radical paganism was, as Rosemary Ruether has noted, that women "will do unto males very much what feminists have accused males of doing to women in patriarchal religion."

In one form or another institutional religion in America confronted in the closing years of the twentieth century the issue of gender equity. The problem was posed in the story of the Garden of Eden; it was addressed in the New Testament's assurance that "in Christ there is neither male nor female" (Galatians 3:28); if solved, however, it will only be in the contingencies and flux of history, not in the citing of ancient authority on in pursuing the precedents of denominational hierarchy.

LIBERATION THEOLOGY

Many of the groups discussed above, along with others not singled out, found support and reassurance in the recent intellectual development known as liberation theology. Such theology spoke to the oppressed, to the outsider, to the outcast. Poverty, hunger, injustice, and oppression were seen as theological problems, not simply political or social inequities; the theology that failed to address such problems, that failed to concern itself with discrimination and domination, was a theology irrelevant at best, wicked and exploitive at worst. For many who advanced this new point of view, a major question was whether Christianity could recapture its initial identification with those on the margins of life.

In his book, _A Black Theology of Liberation_, James Cone argued that "there can be no Christian theology which is not identified unreservedly with those who are humiliated and abused." Since Cone felt this description to apply most closely to the black community in America, he believed that from that community alone could come a revived New Testament Christianity that identified not with the rich and powerful but with the poor and weak. The dominant theology in America, Cone wrote, has been "a theology of the white oppressor, giving religious sanction to the genocide of Indians and the enslavement of black people." That was why blacks must seize upon a new kind of theology, a liberating theology, that will see the Christian gospel "as inseparable from the necessary power to break the chains of oppression." The Exodus from Egypt under Moses stands, Cone explained, as God's first liberating event, freeing men and women from a cruel bondage. The resurrection of Jesus was another kind of liberating event, freeing all from the fear and sting of death. As the National Committee of Black Churchmen declared in 1969, "Jesus is the Liberator!" "The demands that Christ the Liberator imposes upon all men requires all blacks to affirm their full dignity as persons and all whites to surrender their presumptions of superiority and abuses of power."

Similarly, Hispanics could lay claim to the authority and power of this new theology, especially since many of the leading voices raised on behalf of liberation theology came from Latin America. Gustavo Gutiérrez (b. 1928), for example, wrote that liberation theology involved the commitment "to abolish injustice and build a new society." The verification for a theology of this kind, Gutiérrez added, lay in the practice of this commitment, in an "effective participation in the struggle which exploited classes have undertaken against their oppressors." Despite clear Vatican reservations and hesitations, bishops in the United States in 1983 could describe the conditions in Latin America, "the home of 350 million Catholics," in language as strong as that employed by any exponent of liberation theology. Conditions of life in Latin America, the bishops wrote, "are oppressive and dehumanizing; they foster violence, poverty, hatred, and deep divisions in the social fabric; they are fundamentally at variance with Gospel values." The bishops even praised the Catholic poor for being "vibrant witnesses to the liberating quality of the Gospel."

Women, too, found inspiration in this new theology, seeing it as rendering critical assistance in not only freeing women from oppression but also in freeing them for "new ways of living and new views of ourselves as persons." A caucus of Protestant women gathered in Detroit in 1969 identified the struggle for female liberation with that "of blacks, brown, youth, and others." They also indicated that when "we talk about woman's liberation in the life of the church we are thinking about what is going on in the Roman Catholic Church as well as in the Protestant and Orthodox churches," and among black women as well as white.

Black women felt a double oppression: first, as blacks and second, as women. As one black woman noted, even in so progressive and radical a movement as Black Theology, women had no place. "Black males have gradually increased their power and participation in the male-dominated society, while Black females have continued to endure the stereotypes and oppressions of an earlier period." It will be true among blacks as among whites, this author asserted, that theology done by men only "served to undergird patriarchal structures in society." Liberation theology must apply to all oppressed classes, must demonstrate a sensitivity that is universally compassionate and inclusive.

But liberation theology was acclaimed not only by those classes who had special reason to seek it succor. John C. Bennett (b. 1902), former president of Union Theological Seminary in New York City, saw this theology, especially as initially and powerfully expressed in Latin America, as a stimulus for North America—even though "North Americans have never in the past taken Latin American thought seriously," and even though the North American situation differs sharply from that found farther to the south. But many problems were still unsolved in the United States, and to these problems liberation theology had something to say. For example, said Bennett, this theology spoke with great force to "the misery of most of the human race that is the result of injustice and oppression, of poverty and hunger." We have known of this, of course, Bennett readily admitted, but we have not dealt with the problem *theologically*. Such theology was especially important for the United States to take seriously since we are "the dominating power in the Western hemisphere" and that fact alone has been responsible for much of the oppression, notably south of our borders. And finally, Bennett wrote, liberation theology held the best promise for great and essential change in the character of Catholicism in this hemisphere. A church that had generally been viewed as socially reactionary and politically repressive in Latin America, Bennett wrote, has now in some countries already become the primary "defender of the human rights of all peoples."

The Roman Catholic Church worldwide has indeed struggled with its image in Latin America even as it has struggled with the whole idea of liberation theology. Theologians Gustavo Gutiérrez of Peru and Leonardo Boff (b. 1938) of Brazil both drew much suspicion, the latter even being ordered to observe a period of public silence for a year or more. In 1984 the Vatican issued an "Instruction on Certain Aspects of the 'Theology of Liberation'" that severely criticized the movement, especially for its Marxist cast. Promising at that time a more "positive" statement later, the Vatican in 1986 issued an "Instruction on Christian Freedom and Liberation." This second document honored such principles as human dignity and freedom that made possible "judgments on social situations, structures, and systems." Spiritual questions were prior, of course, but "the conversion of heart in no way eliminates the need for unjust structures to be changed." While pastors were not "to intervene directly in the political construction and organization of social life," it nonetheless remained true that profound reflection upon the Christian law of love can "set in motion ambitious programs aimed at the socio-economic liberation of millions of men and women caught in an intolerable situation of economic, social, and political oppression." North American bishops, along with North American blacks, Hispanics, and women, could not ask for much more.

UNIONS AND REUNIONS

With all the evidence of alienation or separations based on race or gender or class, one finds also, of course, divisions based on religion. The scandal of schism and separation appears, decade by decade, to grow only more scandalous, more flagrant, more irreversible. Denominations, amounting to countless divisions in themselves, further divide as the bewildered observer searches for a pattern in that multicolored quilt known as "religion in America." But there is another side to that story, especially in the latter decades of the twentieth century, and that side also deserves some recognition.

Aside from such broadly cooperative groups as the National Association of Evangelicals formed in 1942, the World Council of Churches founded in 1948, and the National Council of Churches whose old federated structure was revised in 1950, many denominations have taken steps that led to actual merger. The Congregational Christian Churches (the result of an earlier union in 1931) in 1957 merged with the largely German Evangelical and Reformed Church to form what is now called the United Church of Christ. The Methodists, having brought their southern and northern sections together in 1939, joined with a German Methodist group in 1968 to form the United Methodist Church. Both Congregationalism and Methodism, strengthened by mergers, nonetheless found themselves weakened by a slow but steady decline in membership.

Presbyterianism in America, divided earlier by questions regarding revivalism, education, slavery, and ordination, managed in 1983 to bring together the northern and southern halves of a denomination that split just prior to the Civil War. The resulting body, taking the name of the Presbyterian Church (U.S.A.) built upon an earlier union (1958) between northern Presbyterians and a Scottish communion called the United Presbyterian Church of North America. One-quarter century after that merger, the even larger and more significant one took place, creating a church of over three million members, by far the largest representative of that ecclesiastical family in America. Not all Presbyterians joined in the new Church, to be sure, the Presbyterian Church in America, for example, holding its membership of less than one-quarter million to a more conservative stance, both theologically and socially.

Lutheranism had been divided not so much by such issues as slavery and revivalism as by its countries of origin and its periods of immigration. But modern mergers have overcome many of those historic separations. In 1960 the American Lutheran Church (ALC) gathered together midwesterners of German, Norwegian, and Danish extraction; then, two years later the Lutheran Church in America (LCA) represented a union of German, Danish, Finnish, and Swedish elements. The former with a membership of over two million and the latter with a membership of just under three million then pulled off still another merger in 1988 to create the Evangelical Lutheran Church in America. Also joining in this splash of ecumenicity was a smaller group that had in the turmoil of the 1970s separated from the more conservative Lutheran Church-Missouri Synod. Martin E. Marty (b. 1928), a member of that smaller group and a leader in the complex negotiations for merger, described the final vote of approval as the "most decisive day" for Lutheranism in North America. Mergers in and of themselves are not destiny, to be sure, but they increase the possibility that an emboldened, unified, historic tradition might help shape a destiny.

The most ambitious effort to shape the destiny of institutional religion in America, launched with much fanfare in 1960, first took the name of the Consultation on Church Union (COCU) then, keeping the same anagram, the Church of Christ Uniting. For more than a quarter of a century, earnest and sometimes tense negotiations have taken place among Methodists (both black and white), Presbyterian, Episcopalians, Disciples, Congregationalists (under the name of United Church of Christ), and from time to time other denominations as well. All large Protestant groups were involved except for Lutherans and Southern Baptists, and all those involved began with considerable enthusiasm and high optimism that an actual merger of twenty million or more American Protestants might take place sometime in the 1970s.

By the 1980s, however, both optimism and enthusiasm waned as delegates to the successive plenary sessions solved one problem only to find several others immediately taking its place. Some theological agreement was reached in 1984, but ecclesiastical hurdles (the power of bishops, the relationship with worldwide denominational fellowships, and the like) remained. In the late 1980s, COCU pulled back from the idea of full merger to what was called "Covenant Communion." Under the terms of this proposed agreement, the several member denominations would ordain clergy jointly, hold baptismal services in common, cooperate in such areas as foreign missions and domestic social agenda. Each church would continue, however, to govern its internal affairs and to maintain close ties with such transnational bodies as the Anglican Communion and the World Alliance of Reformed Churches. The Church of Christ Uniting still retains its earlier vision, but may have lost some of its earlier fire.

Perhaps the most dramatic strides in the last quarter-century or so have come from a source that in many respects was the least expected: the Roman Catholic Church. Part of the turn-around was no doubt due to the personality and charm of Pope John XXIII himself, but changes were institutional no less than personal. Beginning with John's creation of a Secretariat for Promoting Christian Unity in 1960, the Catholic church has repeatedly demonstrated a desire for dialogue as well as an openness to mutual instruction. Vatican II issued its decree on ecumenism in 1964, this important document signalling—in the words of one Protestant observer—"the beginning of a new era in the relation of the Churches to one another." That it was a new era quickly became

88. The official emblem of the National Council of Churches was adopted five years after the creation of this ecumenical body. *National Council of Churches*

evident as steps were taken to enlarge Catholic participation in the World Council of Churches, as Pope Paul VI received the Archbishop of Canterbury in 1966 and, in 1967, journeyed to Istanbul to pay an official visit to Patriarch Athenagoras I. In 1975 Paul canonized the first American-born saint, Elizabeth Seton (1774–1821), paying respectful tribute to her upbringing in New York City as an Episcopalian. In that same year he addressed a committee charged with special responsibility for improved Christian-Jewish relations, urging that "a true dialogue may be established between Judaism and Christianity." What Vatican II delivered in 1964 set the tone for decades to come; much was done, even if much remained to be done.

John Paul II who ascended to the papal office in 1978, through his extensive travels and countless meetings, continued the ecumenical efforts among the Orthodox, the Protestants, and the non-Christians as well. In 1979 he, too, made the pilgrimage to Istanbul, assuring Patriarch Dimitrios I that the thousand years of common history between East and West (before the final schism in 1054 A.D.) should be sufficient basis for greater unity "between our sister-Churches." Dimitrios responded that "Your coming here, full of Christian charity and simplicity, means more than a mere meeting between two local bishops." East

89. One symbol of ecumenicity, the annual Alfred E. Smith Dinner in New York City, brought these diverse figures together in 1968: Vice-President Hubert H. Humphrey (Congregationalist), Archbishop Terence J. Cooke (Roman Catholic), President Lyndon B. Johnson (Disciples of Christ), and Richard M. Nixon (Quaker). *Religious News Service*

and West might perhaps be one again: "We believe that at this moment the Lord is present among us here." In that same year, John Paul II addressed ecumenical leaders gathered in Washington, D.C., welcoming "the opportunity to embrace you, in the charity of Christ, as beloved Christian brethren and fellow disciples of the Lord Jesus." The language was new; so indeed was the spirit.

But apart from these highly visible papal visits and papal words, dialogues were more quietly begun between Roman Catholics and the Lutheran World Federation in 1965; with the Anglican Communion and the World Methodist Council in 1966; with the World Alliance of Reformed Churches in 1968; with Pentecostals in 1972; and with Disciples of Christ in 1978. Meanwhile, Protestants were themselves carrying on quieter dialogues away from the public spotlight: Lutherans with Anglicans; Episcoplians with the Orthodox; the United Church of Christ with the Disciples of Christ; the Methodists with the Episcopalians—and so on. In 1973 the Orthodox Church in America issued its own decree on "Christian Unity and Ecumenism." Thus the tempo was maintained, not just in the United States but around the world.

That tempo increased sharply when in late 1989 Mikhail Gorbachev met with John Paul II to begin a long-awaited rapprochement between communism and Catholicism. This worldwide dimension was perhaps the most significant aspect of ecumenicity as the year 2000 approached. For it was a world grown increasingly secular, divided, threatened, perplexed. If a thousand religious voices could not be heard beyond their own quarreling households, possibly a few voices speaking in greater unity and with greater charity could rise above all fratricidal strife.

CHAPTER 24

The Era of Limits

By the end of the nineteenth century, the United States had marched across a continent and giant-stepped across the Pacific to the Hawaiian Islands and the Philippines. Also, by the end of that century, religion in America had taken on a confidence and ebullience typified in the phrase, "evangelization of the world in this generation." No barriers arose that could limit the conquest of either land or souls. Toward the end of the following century, however, limits of many kinds did appear: limits on the power of both the nation and its religious institutions. Nationally, those limits presented themselves most clearly in Southeast Asia and in Central and South America, in the struggle for total security in a nuclear world, in the contest for economic superiority, and in the new sense of an exploited, exhausted environment. In religion as well, many limits appeared.

ECCLESIASTICAL LIMITS

The Roman Catholic church, an institution whose authority seemed least vulnerable to limits, found itself repeatedly challenged on the American scene in the 1960s and beyond. In the growing anxiety about nuclear war, the Trappist monk Thomas Merton (1915–1968) took an early stand on behalf of nonviolence and against all war, asserting pacifist views for which a majority of the church was not yet ready. Merton's popular autobiography of the late 1940s, *Seven Storey Mountain*, insured that his leadership in the peace movement would win wide attention. Even wider attention came to a Jesuit father, Daniel Berrigan (b. 1921), and his brother in the Josephite order, Philip (b. 1923), when they encouraged resistance to the military draft and especially when in 1968 they burned draft board records in Catonsville, Maryland. Both men, arrested and jailed by the government and censured by ecclesiastical superiors, proved an embarrassment to church authorities and to much of the Catholic constituency. Catholics, long accused in American history of not being sufficiently pro-American and patriotic, found these radical actions of the Catholic Left unacceptable. Could the Church do nothing to silence such voices?

America's bishops initially held aloof from all the protests against

Vietnam, though in 1968 they did support the right of Catholics to declare themselves conscientious objectors—a new experience for Catholics in America. Many years later, in 1983, the nation's bishops disturbed many with their pastoral letter, "The Challenge of Peace: God's Promise and Our Response." The letter adopted a critical tone, critical even of the United States, that disturbed conservative Catholics who thought their bishops were meddling in politics and matters beyond their ken. "We fear," wrote the bishops, "that our world and nation are headed in the wrong direction." What was called for was not larger stockpiles of atomic weapons, but a "moral about-face." Somehow the nation and the world "must summon the moral courage to say No to nuclear conflict," the bishops concluded, "No to weapons of mass destruction; No to an arms race which robs the poor and the vulnerable; and No to the moral danger of a nuclear age which places before humankind indefensible choices of constant terror or surrender." The time had come for peacemaking, not as mere political policy, but as "a requirement of our faith." The bishops had not disciplined the Mertons and the Berrigans: they had joined them.

Beyond America's bishops, of course, stood the Vatican and the authority of the pope. That authority came in for its sharpest criticism and resistance when in 1968 Pope Paul VI issued an encyclical entitled, *Humane Vitae* ("On Human Life"). Contrary to wide expectation, this encyclical did not moderate or modify the church's historic position with respect to contraception, but strongly reaffirmed the long-standing prohibitions against any artificial form of birth control. "Each and every marriage act," the papal letter declared, "must remain open to the transmission of life." Repeated surveys in the United States revealed that Catholics practiced birth control at about the same rate as non-Catholics in similar economic or social classes. Not too surprisingly, then, criticism of *Humane Vitae* abounded; and where it was not criticized, its prohibitions were simply ignored. But as priest, sociologist and novelist Andrew Greeley (b. 1928) noted, the effect on the church was almost wholly negative. Vatican II, it now appeared, had been reversed by an action that, said Greeley, "sent the whole church into sudden and dramatic decline." Theologians at the Catholic University of America were quick to point out that the encyclical was not "an infallible teaching" and, that like many other positions taken by the church in the past, this one too could prove to be "inadequate or even erroneous." The Catholic theologians concluded, against the Pope, "that spouses may responsibly decide according to their conscience that artificial contraception in some circumstances is permissible and indeed necessary to preserve and foster the values and sacredness of marriage."

If that sounded as though the Vatican and some Catholic thinkers in this country were on a collision course, that turned out to be clearly the case when in 1986 Father Charles Curran (b. 1934), member of the theological faculty at the Catholic University of America, was censured and suspended from his teaching duties. The Vatican informed Curran that he was neither "suitable nor eligible" to continue as a member of the faculty because his instruction in such matters as birth control, homosexuality, abortion, divorce, and premarital sex took positions not approved by the church. Curran countered that he would fight his suspension and that, even more, he would fight the tendency in his church to confuse what was essential to the faith with what was peripheral. "Authoritarianism," he stated, "makes everything of the same importance, whether it's central to the faith or not—it makes belief in Jesus Christ of the same importance as 'no meat on Friday.'" The purpose of theology, Curran argued, was always to be "pushing and probing . . . always on the cutting edge." Clearly, Curran had pushed; just as clearly, he was being pushed back, with questions of orthodoxy and infallibility being mixed with questions of academic freedom and tenure.

90. Father Charles Curran in a 1986 press conference defended his position as a professor of Moral Theology at Catholic University of America. *Religious News Service*

A poll taken in 1986 revealed that eighty-three percent of America's Catholics between the ages of eighteen and thirty-nine favored artificial birth control. That pervasive sentiment coupled with Father Curran's specific objections demonstrated clearly the limits of ecclesiastical authority. That authority, nonetheless, continued to be wielded against others. Later in 1986 a long-time member of the Society of Jesus was ordered to resign from that society because of a survey of the nation's bishops where he asked their views on such sensitive matters as celibacy and women priests. Then a professor of Canon Law at Catholic University was denied tenure because he questioned the exclusion of divorced Catholics from the sacraments. Still later, two nuns in West Virginia were disciplined because they had suggested in an open letter that some Catholic teaching on abortion was still subject to discussion and debate. And at the end of 1988 Father Matthew Fox, O. P. (b. 1940), was ordered to a year of silence because his theology seemed too daring, his identification with spiritual visions that were "people-oriented, politically conscious, and earthy" too risky. All of this heavy-handed exercise of authority, warned the Archbishop of Milwaukee, may drive people from the church more than it draws them to it. The pope as bishop of Rome, moreover, several American bishops argued, must take more seriously than he yet has the necessity to work with other bishops on a "collegial" basis rather than in a wholly unilateral fashion. Vatican II had called for just such collegiality in the governance of the Roman Catholic Church; twenty-five years after that call, it had not yet become a reality.

The Catholic Church, however, was not the only religious institution in America to find its authority challenged or defied. The Lutheran Church-Missouri Synod in the 1970s tried to rein in the president and faculty of its very own institution, the Concordia Seminary located in St. Louis. But the majority would not be reined in, preferring to separate themselves from that synod in which they had been nurtured so that they might create their own church. Here the issue was not about sexual teaching, but about churchly authority. As the president of the denominational seminary indicated in 1975, the question was whether new doctrinal statements could be imposed upon all members of the synod. Such imposition, said John Tietjen (b. 1928), "strikes at the heart of what it means to be a Lutheran church." Rather than assuring a conformity, it provokes a resentment of and resistance to authority arbitrarily imposed. The Missouri Synod in the 1970s discovered its ecclesiastical limits.

In the 1980s the Southern Baptist Convention also confronted such limits. Long the prime example of growth without wearying, of zealous evangelism without weakening, this large convention of some fifteen million members had by the end of the eighties elected leadership that was evermore determined to exercise a strict doctrinal control.

Seminary faculty were fired, missionaries were recalled, denominational colleges and universities were subjected to paralyzing attack. A fundamentalist takeover of denominational agencies and boards, planned to take place over a ten-year period, was largely completed as the final decade of the twentieth century got underway. Doctrinal conservatism was linked to political and social conservatism as the new leadership turned against women in the ministry, against many of the racial strides that had been taken, even against the historic Baptist stand for separation of church and state.

Resistance took many forms: reasserting the traditional power of the laity in Baptist churches, withholding voluntary payment to agencies deemed to be in the wrong hands, abandonment of the denominational seminaries, flight of Southern Baptist ministers from that convention's authority to other Baptist bodies or even to other denominations altogether. The "brain drain" of younger men and women would prove particularly costly. Organized resistance, meanwhile, resulted in the creation of a Southern Baptist Alliance in the late 1980s, this coalition of about forty thousand "moderates" or liberals emphasizing the freedom of conscience and the priesthood of every believer. Especially since World War II, "success" and "triumph" had been the watchwords of the Southern Baptist Convention: membership rising, contributions mounting, missions flourishing, good will abounding. By the end of the eighties, however, the watchwords had become "caution" and "contention."

If in recent years, any aspect of American religion might have appeared more successful than even the Southern Baptist Convention, it was the electronic church and its highly visible, highly personable evangelists. By the 1980s the financial contributions to this entire enterprise totalled about one billion dollars, with the leading money-raisers being such household names as Oral Roberts, Pat Robertson, Jerry Falwell, Jim and Tammy Bakker, and Jimmy Swaggert. So rapidly had this phenomenon grown, so wealthy had it become, that the average parish church felt threatened if not deserted. Whole networks were bought, whole universities were built, hotels and theme parks and powerful lobbies sprang into being. Were there no limits to the power, the influence, the political and social clout of this exploding electronic church?

In the late 1980s, the answer to that question turned out to be a resounding Yes. Oral Roberts felt the sting of ridicule for his vision of a ninety-foot Jesus and his pledge to fast unto death if contributions did not increase; his hospital beds in Tulsa, Oklahoma, stood empty and his medical school suffered both financially and professionally. Pat Robertson felt the sting of defeat in his 1988 bid for the Republican presidential nomination; he too had known ridicule for his theological views as well as his claims of spiritual healing. Jerry Falwell, organizer of the Moral Majority in 1979, rode high for a time, but an overidentification with right-wing political causes compromised his moral and religious agenda. But when Jim Bakker in 1987 confessed to sexual indiscretions and when Jimmy Swaggert the following year was obliged to do the same, the house of televangelism began to crumble. Contributions declined sharply—not just for Bakker and Swaggert—and financial empires began to fall apart. Budgets had to be cut back, employees had to be let go, and the number of television hours had to be greatly reduced. Between 1980 and 1987, Gallup pollsters found that the number of people who regarded television evangelists as untrustworthy in financial matters almost doubled. Problems multiplied in the secular courts as well as in several denominational headquarters, as the electronic church struggled for respectability once again. But for the moment, it has reached its limit of influence and affluence.

Declining fortunes in one segment of American religion did not lead automatically to rising fortunes elsewhere. Membership in mainstream denominations actually fell in the 1960s and 1970s, in some cases

91. The Southern Baptist Convention gathered in Las Vegas in 1989 where, once again, the fundamentalist faction prevailed over the moderate group. *Religious News Service*

sharply so. Some found the reasons for this decline in liberal theology or relaxed discipline; some found the reasons in demographic changes or social factors; some found no convincing reasons at all why American religion, steadily on the rise for two hundred years, should suddenly reach a plateau or enter into a valley. The shortage of nuns in the Roman Catholic church grew acute, and the number of men entering the Catholic priesthood began to fall. Presbyterians, Episcopalians, and Disciples suffered severe losses in membership, while others struggled just to keep up with the general population growth of the nation. Most revealing of all, the mainstream's National Council of Churches found itself rent by controversy, impoverished by declining contributions, and mired in its own bureaucracy. Institutional religion ceased to be the "growth stock" that it had been for so long, the limits of authority, of power, and of numbers becoming all too evident by 1990.

THEOLOGICAL LIMITS

Once the "queen of the sciences," theology found itself gradually shoved aside in favor of other sciences and by the growing specializations in a technological world. When Paul Tillich (1886–1965) published his three-volume *Systematic Theology* over a twelve-year period from 1951 to 1963, this impressive work represented the last great American effort to explicate the whole of Christian thought for the modern world. Explaining that theology "moves back and forth between two poles, the eternal truth of its foundation and the temporal situation in which the eternal truth must be received," he acknowledged that "not many theological systems have been able to balance these two demands perfectly." What is perhaps more relevant is that, since those words were written, few have tried.

On the contrary, most theologians retreated from comprehensiveness, many from certitude, and a few from any consideration of transcendence at all. In seminary instruction, theology often receded before such new curricular demands as pastoral counseling, parish management, and pulpit technique. Just as philosophers grew more hesitant about metaphysical inquiry and system building, so theologians saw their discipline become part of biblical study or reduced to what was often called "practical theology." It was easier to study theologies of the past than it was to create theologies for the future.

Besides, one might argue that traditional theology had become a way of avoiding the tasks at hand rather than undertaking them. In 1965 a young theologian published a surprisingly popular book called *The Secular City*. Here Harvey Cox (b. 1929) explained that modern men and women found meaning not in the world beyond, but in the world that was before and all around them. They did not discover meaning, they created it. The world, Cox wrote, "does not come to man already finished and ordered. It comes in part confused and formless and receives its significance from man." Theology must come down from its high table to dwell with and speak to the pressing problems of modern women and men.

Cox would distinguish clearly between secularity on the one hand and secularism on the other. The former was good, it was liberating; "it dislodges ancient oppressions and overcomes stultifying conventions." The latter was bad, substituting another rigid orthodoxy for the one outgrown. It "short-circuits the secular revolution by freezing it into a new world-view." But secularity signified "the point where man takes responsibility for directing the tumultuous tendencies of his time." God is not revealed out of time, out of history; nor is he the special gift of the churches to their members. "Jesus Christ comes to his people," Cox wrote, "not primarily through ecclesiastical traditions, but through social change." Christ "is always ahead of the church, beckoning it to get up to date." The enormous popularity of Cox's small book (and within a year there was even a book about the book) suggested that many were prepared to examine a theology that did not "look like theology," did not appear in a distinctive ecclesiastical garb, did not require its own in-house vocabulary.

One question that Cox posed, quoting a young German theologian, was this: "How do we speak in a secular fashion of God?" To traditional theologians, the question made little sense; to the extent that they understood it, their answer would be, "We don't." And so they continued to speak of God in a religious fashion. To some radical theologians, on the other hand, the answer was also, "We don't." And so they began to speak in a secular fashion, but not of God. The "death of God" theologians, also a phenomenon of the 1960s, argued that though it was once appropriate to have a belief in God (as in biblical

92. The Reverend Jerry Falwell addressed huge congregations in his Baptist Church in Lynchburg, Virginia; his television audience was estimated to be as high as four million at the peak of his popularity. *Religious News Service*

times, or in the sixteenth century), it was not appropriate now. The theologian today, as one of this persuasion argued in 1966, was "a man without faith, without hope, with only the present, with only love to guide him." In the death of God theology, one saw only the nearest limits, not the distant horizons.

Religious humanism likewise found the transcendent outmoded and irrelevant. Religion should be retained, because it has brought to humankind those values that might possibly prevent such gross cruelties as "the gas chambers at Dachau" or "the mass removal of dissidents to Siberian work camps." Man created God, not the other way around, as one Unitarian-Universalist spokesman explained in 1967. But if we grant that God has died, we must see that religion does not. For we must hold on "to the values that man has built, not received as a gift of divine revelation, but built painstakingly over the ages of mistakes." Within a perspective such as this, theology reached not for the stars but for the Commandments.

More traditional theologians, meanwhile, wrestled with their own specialized burdens that prevented soaring theological flights. Some were confined by respected confessions, some by biblical modes of interpretation, some by external ecclesiastical authority, and some by the limits of their own education. Catholics in America, long aware of their modest contribution to the intellectual grandeur of the Church Universal, found their greatest theological stimulation in the universities and among the laity. Liberal Protestants, disabused of the notion that modernity brought inevitable blessing, found their inspiration first in an older orthodoxy, then in an aesthetics or poetics of religion. Conservative Protestants, weary of waging the same old wars in the same old terms, took on the responsibility of first-class scholarship in both biblical studies and history. Fundamentalists lost their certitude, or at least with certainty lost the ability to hold themselves together on the basis of fixed and unchanging absolutes. And Jewish religious leaders, long convinced that the Torah must be beyond criticism or revision, saw in 1981 the publication of "a modern commentary" on the Books of Moses themselves.

Theology, the crowning peak of all knowledge in pre-modern times, had been rudely pushed from its privileged position atop the mountain. But all around the base of that mountain, climbers in the 1980s resumed their slow ascent.

RELIGION AND POLITICS

If from one point of view, religion in the final quarter of the twentieth century seemed boxed in and restrained, from another perspective, religion seemed boundless and aggressive. The rise of the "new Christian Right" in the 1970s and 1980s frightened some even as it surprised nearly all. For most fundamentalists in the era after the Scopes trial, the world was something to scorn, to flee from, to keep oneself uncontaminated by. "Worldly" was a synonym for sinfulness and corruption, for straying from the approved paths of piety and purity. Let the liberals have the "best seats in the house." It mattered not, for soon that house would be destroyed.

In recent years, however, all that changed as a myriad of organizations sprang into existence designed to give conservative religionists a powerful voice in public affairs. Not only would they rejoin the world, they would control it and shape it. In 1979 one saw in rapid succession the creation of these entities: the Moral Majority, led by a Baptist minister of Lynchburg, Virginia; the Christian Voice, with headquarters in Pasadena, California, and with strong congressional representation in Washington, D. C.; the Religious Roundtable of Arlington, Virginia, directed by a Texas evangelist, James Robison. These groups shared similar if not identical agendas, they also shared ties with the political Right, both nationally and at the local levels. They united in promoting prayer in the public school, in opposing abortion, in condemning pornography, in despairing over the growth of "secular humanism," and in promoting in whatever way possible a "return" to a Christian America. They also united in such media events as a "Washington for Jesus Day" held in 1980 on the Washington Mall, with the speakers reflecting both political and religious conservative ranks.

Items around which Christian Right forces rallied sometimes appeared more obviously "Right" than "Christian." For example, these forces opposed nuclear test ban treaties; supported the defense of Taiwan; opposed the Panama Canal treaty; supported the increases in national defense; and opposed all of the following: the Equal Rights Amendment, sexual or racial quotas in education and employment, the creation of a Department of Education, and forced school busing. Few argued the legality of the radical Right's participation in politics, though many argued the morality or propriety of the positions taken. One could question, moreover, the campaign to return to a "Christian America" that had never been, as well as the effort to promote in the future a "Christian America" that, constitutionally, could never be.

Such lobbying groups wielded significant power in the 1970s and 1980s, claiming credit for victories in certain elections, for successes in unseating members of Congress who had not voted "Right" on a host of issues, for raising large sums of money and for reaching millions through mass mailing lists of impressive scope. In the nation's capital as well as in state capitals and in city halls and county offices, the Christian Right was clearly a force to be reckoned with. But even that power had limits. The nation's religious broadcasters, controlling over three hundred television stations and nearly fifteen hundred radio stations in the late eighties, found that audiences were turning away and that income was falling. From 1986 to 1988 the viewing audience of the five largest television ministries fell from nearly seven million to about three million. Falwell's "Old Time Gospel Hour" in a year's time lost over thirty radio stations, even as revenue dropped by about ten million dollars in that two-year period. The Bakkers' much besieged PTL ("Praise the Lord") network lost more than half its stations in 1988, with its financial difficulties rising to such heights as to require supervision by the civil courts.

The power of the Christian Right as well as the limits of its power can perhaps be best seen in the presidential elections and aspirations of recent years. The 1976 campaign pitted the Georgian Jimmy Carter (b. 1924) against the Nebraska-born but Michigan-raised Gerald Ford (b. 1913). Ford, the incumbent president, had come into the White House not by direct election of the people, but by virtue of the resignation of Richard Nixon in 1974 from the presidency. That resignation, amid the scandals associated with Watergate, had raised ethical questions of the highest order and religious questions as well in what had been called a "breach of faith." Both Ford and Carter were conservative Protestants, the former an Episcopalian (but with a son studying for the ministry in a conservative seminary in Massachusetts), the latter a Southern Baptist who had no difficulty associating himself with "born-again religion."

Curiously, however, the Southern Baptist was more liberal than the northern Episcopalian. A faithful deacon in the local Baptist church in Plains, Georgia, a dedicated Sunday school teacher and Bible reader, Jimmy Carter surprised many by his theological sophistication (Reinhold Niebuhr was a favorite), his strong dedication to separation of church and state (thus losing him the support of the Christian Right), and his passionate commitment to human rights, not only within the borders of the United States but all around the world. The *New York Times* commented, regarding the 1976 campaign, that "Jimmy Carter's open espousal of his Christian beliefs . . . has raised the issue of religion's place in politics more arrestingly than in any Presidential race since John F. Kennedy's in 1960." Early in the campaign, many liberals were nervous about a candidate that apparently took his religion seriously; late in the campaign, however, many conservatives found Carter much too liberal for their taste. Conservative evangelical forces officially backed many "Christian" candidates in 1976; Jimmy Carter, who won, was not among them.

In 1980 a new political figure, so far as national politics was concerned, emerged: Ronald Reagan (b. 1911), by profession an actor but most recently a two-term governor of California. In the race between the Southern Baptist churchman, Carter, and the Southern California communicator, Reagan, one might suppose that the mantle of religion would be wrapped more tightly around the former. It was Reagan, however, who claimed the attention and the affection of the Christian

Right as he called for a moment of silent prayer at the 1980 Republican National Convention, as he repeatedly urged a spiritual revival upon the nation, as he criticized the Supreme Court's "misinterpretation" of the First Amendment. By the time that the election was held, Carter was no longer honored as the Bible-believing, church-attending, born-again conservative Christian. That role had been assigned to another.

In his first term as president, Ronald Reagan and the Christian Right drew even closer together. The president presided at National Prayer Breakfasts, addressed the National Religious Broadcasters Conventions, spoke to conventions of the National Association of Evangelicals, and gave a religious spin to his remarks before the Conservative Political Action Conference. In 1982 he proposed a constitutional amendment that would, in his words, "restore the simple freedom of our citizens to offer prayer in our public schools and institutions." "I am confident," the president added, "that such an amendment will be quickly adopted, for the vast majority of our people believe there is a

93. Pope John Paul II, the first Roman Catholic pontiff to visit the U. S. Capitol, is shown here with President Jimmy Carter in 1979. *Religious News Service*

need for prayer in our public schools and institutions." Early in 1983 Reagan spoke to the National Religious Broadcasters of his respect for and confidence in the Bible. "Within the covers of that single book," he said, "are all the answers to all the problems that face us today." In that year he agreed to serve as honorary chairman for what was proclaimed as the "Year of the Bible." In 1984, on the anniversary of the Supreme Court decision with respect to abortion, President Reagan proclaimed the National Sanctity of Human Life Day, affirming that abortion had denied to the unborn "the first and most basic of human rights, and we are infinitely poorer for their loss."

In the campaign later that year between the incumbent president and Walter Mondale (b. 1928), two Protestants again headed their respective party's tickets. So thoroughly had the Reagan cause become identified with the cause of the Christian Right that an irritated Walter Mondale observed that "most Americans would be surprised to learn that God is a Republican." Mondale also warned that the Reagan-Right alliance threatened to "corrupt our faith and divide our nation." The son of a minister and son-in-law of another, Mondale was no stranger to religion in general or to the nation's Protestant heritage in particular, but he did not believe that political campaigns should become the equivalent of religious crusades. "Policy debates," he told a B'nai B'rith gathering in the fall of 1984, should not be transformed into "theological disputes." And Jesuit Father O'Hare commented that religious leaders could well "enunciate the values and clarify the moral principles involved in public policy issues." But, he added, when it came to endorsing specific candidates or particular legislation, then "our religious leaders would do well—as certain of our Catholic bishops are doing," to refrain from further political action.

In 1984 not all attention was given to the top of the ticket. For the first time a major party (the Democrats) had nominated a woman for the office of vice president; she was a Roman Catholic; she had an opinion on abortion. When Geraldine Ferraro (b. 1935) indicated that, though personally opposed to abortion, she supported the 1973 Supreme Court decision as a matter of public law, she became the object of both noisy demonstrations in the streets and official rebuke in the quieter corridors of the Church. The Archbishop of New York, John J. O'Connor (b. 1920), did not rebuke the vice presidential candidate directly, but noted that "some needs are so crucial that they require the best leadership this country can provide." For himself, he said, "I am passionately convinced that no need is more crucial than to protect the rights of the unborn." On that issue, the Democratic Catholic compared ill with the Republican Protestant, costing the former votes despite the effort of New York's Governor Mario Cuomo (b. 1932), also a Roman Catholic, to come to Ferraro's rescue. In a major address at Notre Dame University he declared that "although we believe abortion is wrong, we may and do honorably disagree among ourselves on specific legal and political remedies." On many grounds other than religion, of course, the Democratic ticket lost in favor of the Republican one in 1984.

In his second term, President Reagan continued to champion many of the causes promoted by the Christian Right. After eight years in office, however, he left most items on the latter's agenda uncompleted: no constitutional amendment on prayer in the public schools; no constitutional amendment with respect to abortion; no overthrow of Darwinism by Creationism in the curriculum; no fundamental shift in public law regarding pornography or morality. Upon leaving the presidency in January of 1989, Mr. Reagan pledged to continue to lobby and labor on behalf of the unfinished agenda. Clearly, however, the ability of religious leaders to translate sectarian concern into public policy had its limits—more so, no doubt, in the 1980s than in the much earlier year of the Eighteenth Amendment's ratification in 1919.

The campaign of 1988 kept religion in the forefront of the news. Two ordained clergyman ran for the presidential office, Jesse Jackson on the Democratic side, and Marion G. (Pat) Robertson (b. 1930) on the Republican side. The liberalism of the former disquieted a great many voters, as did the conservatism of the latter. Both were Baptists, but there the similarities ended. Jackson's concerns were heavily economic and social, while Robertson's were predominantly moral and

94. The Reverend Pat Robertson filed his candidacy for the presidency in Columbia, South Carolina, in 1988. *Religious News Service*

theological. Robertson had earlier dismissed the whole idea of separation of church and state as a Soviet invention, also arguing that only Christians and those Jews who "trust the God of Abraham, Isaac, and Jacob" were qualified to rule, "to take dominion" and institute a reign of the righteous. But neither clergyman (Robertson resigned his ordination when he announced his plans to run for the presidency) received the nomination of his party in the summer of 1988.

The fall presidential campaign instead involved an Episcopalian against one reared in the tradition of Greek Orthodoxy. Episcopalianism would be no novelty for the White House, but Eastern Orthodoxy—for so long hardly visible on the political stage in this country—would surely have been. However, the long-time Episcopalian, George Bush (b. 1924), triumphed over the Massachusetts governor, Michael Dukakis (b. 1933), in an election that, like the one in 1984, was not very close. Bush, who had shored up his alliances with the religious Right and who had early won the hearty endorsement of Jerry Falwell, helped his cause by selecting as his running mate, Dan Quayle (b. 1947) whose family and whose wife's family were identified with

95. The Reverend Jesse Jackson campaigned for the presidency, often from church pulpits, in 1988. *Religious News Service*

the conservative religious agenda. President Bush's religious roots went deep, as a vestryman of St. Anne's Episcopal Church in Kennebunkport, Maine, and as a regular communicant in St. Martin's Episcopal Church in Houston, Texas. From a traditionally mainstream religious heritage, Bush's stance might prove to be more "centrist" with respect to many issues on the agenda of the Christian Right.

At his inauguration in 1979, President Bush chose to abandon the practice of inviting representatives of Protestant, Catholic, Jewish, and Eastern Orthodox faiths to pray. Instead, he chose an old family friend, Dr. Billy Graham, who at the age of seventy had become a kind of patriarch of what Benjamin Franklin had called "public religion." Graham kept his prayer broadly in the Judeo-Christian tradition, concluding with the ancient Hebrew blessing: "May the Lord bless thee and keep thee: the Lord make his face shine upon thee, and be gracious unto thee: the Lord lift up his countenance upon thee and give thee peace." No agenda peculiar to either the religious Left or Right could be discerned there.

PLURALISM AND ITS LIMITS

On November 18, 1978, the American public learned that religious pluralism had its limits. That was the day when in Jonestown, Guyana, over nine hundred followers of James (Jim) Warren Jones joined their spiritual leader in the mass suicide: men, women, and children who had been part of a religious commune that began in rural northern California, then moved to San Francisco, then fatefully to the steamy jungles of South America. The public had long complained about "brainwashing cults," about children or young people kept in isolation from their parents; about the Children of God or the Meher Baba movement; or the counterculture turning on, tuning in, dropping out associated with Timothy Leary; or the high school indoctrinations instigated by Maharishi Mahesh Yogi. Parents sometimes forcibly removed their young from the grip of a religious group; courts sometimes granted the right of conservatorship to prevent a return to a commune or cult; "deprogramming" sometimes became a full-time profession for specially trained abductors. Tensions and tears abounded, but all this was as nothing compared to Jonestown.

In Jonestown all arguments about toleration and freedom of religion collapsed, all patience snapped. In Jonestown the theoretical merits of pluralism had no defenders, as parents and relatives and concerned religious leaders tried to determine how and why everything went so tragically wrong. Perhaps the U.S. government should have done more to prevent this sort of thing, some argued. Perhaps private groups needed to fight the strange or novel in religion while it was still small and weak, others argued. Perhaps society needed a clearer understanding of what qualified as "religion," of what was worthy of protection under the First Amendment, still others maintained. Ten years after the Guyana horror, Jonestown remained a line of demarcation, a kind of public announcement that pluralism had its limits.

This idea had been coming for some time, as the claims for protection under the First Amendment grew increasingly absurd. Prisoners professed a religion whose ritual required the consumption of Scotch whiskey and steak every night. For five dollars or more the Universal Life Church would provide certificates of ordination to anyone who applied. In 1965 the Neo-American Church won incorporation under the laws of California, but when that "church" tried to claim a right to use hallucinogenic substances on the grounds that this was essential to its ritual, a U. S. district Court declined to allow the exemption. (This church's case was not helped by the fact its leader was known as Chief Boo Hoo, its symbol was a three-eyed toad, its sacred songs were "Puff, the Magic Dragon" and "Row, Row, Row your Boat," and its slogan was "Victory over Horseshit.") The Internal Revenue Service, moreover, had long been watchful over groups claiming tax exemption on religious grounds, and even watchful of well-known groups that claimed exemption for businesses that had no direct connection with religious practice or belief.

After Jonestown, everyone in government or out became more watchful. In 1981 Bhagwan Shree Rajneesh and his followers paid six million dollars for a huge ranch in central Oregon. Within two years the six hundred or so followers had managed to take over the tiny town of Antelope, elect their own city council, buy more property in Portland, and attract a disproportionate amount of media attention. They had also managed to infuriate most of their Oregon neighbors, achieving this through a combination of ostentatious living, practicing a therapy of group sex, threatening the water supply of the region, and engaging in questionable financial practices. By 1985 internal conflicts and disorder, together with external hostilities and reactions (including an indictment from a federal grand jury for immigration fraud), led to swift decline and then collapse of Rajneeshpuram and the return of its leader to India. But in Oregon as well as in West Virginia, where a Hare Krishna commune called New Vrindaban enraged its neighbors by mayhem, child abuse, and murder, it was clear that the claims to religious freedom could not, and did not wipe away all sins. No mass suicides occurred in either Oregon or West Virginia, but mass indignation defined the limits.

The Unification Church, under the leadership of Sun Myung Moon, ran afoul of the courts, the communities, and public opinion in the 1970s and 1980s. Never a large group, it amassed considerable wealth that could not be clearly identified as belonging to the church or to

Moon himself. This led in 1982 to a tax fraud conviction against its Korean leader, the conviction followed by a term in prison. Efforts to buy up most of the property in Gloucester, Massachusetts, in the mid-1980s met with vigorous community resistance, just as Moon's presiding over mass marriages of his followers galvanized public opinion against him. The Unification Church engaged in an effort, far more systematic than most, to win a respected place in the pantheon of American religion, inviting scholars and theologians to international gatherings where all expenses were paid and where a sophisticated defense of Unification doctrine was presented. For much of the public, however, in a post-Jonestown phase, this church remained another example of the kind of personality cult that weakened or destroyed individual responsibility and integrity. The fear, of course, was that it might end up by destroying even more than that.

Quite apart from the concern about marginal groups pejoratively identified as "cults," American religion by the end of the 1980s could no longer be thought of exclusively in terms of a Judeo-Christian heritage. The Orient had arrived in some force, and the Orient showed no signs of withering away. Buddhism by 1987 had acquired sufficient strength and permanence to win a place in the chaplaincy corps of the U. S. Armed Forces. With more than two thousand Buddhists serving in the military (one, with the rank of colonel, died in the *Challenger* explosion in 1986) and with 150,000 members of the Buddhist Churches of America, the time had come to broaden a chaplaincy that had up to this point been exclusively Christian and Jewish.

Buddhist chaplains, like Christian chaplains, are required to serve many others besides those of a single sect such as the one which first won recognition: the "True Pure Land" tradition of Japanese Buddhist

96. California's newest Buddhist temple, Hsi Lai Temple in Hacienda Heights, was formally inaugurated in November, 1988, with the hosting of the first World Fellowship of Buddhists to be held in the West. *International Buddhist Progress Society*

that adopted the name of Buddhist Churches of America. Nichiren Shoshu, with even a larger membership, aggressively recruits members in the United States, promising peace within the individual as well as throughout the world. The meditative style of Zen Buddhism exists in many forms and attracts members at several levels of commitment, most of its converts being Western rather than Asian. By the 1980s American interest in and knowledge of Zen had moved far beyond that made available in the popular novel of Jack Kerouac, *The Dharma Bums,* published in 1958. Buddhism arrived also from Tibet, from Sri Lanka, and from China by way of Taiwan. In 1988 a major Chinese Buddhist temple was dedicated near Los Angeles, that dedication providing an appropriate moment for the World Fellowship of Buddhists to gather in, of all places, southern California.

Hinduism first appeared in the United States in the form of elite missionary movements such as the Vedanta Society and the Self-Realization Fellowship. Almost invisible to the wider society, these groups had a chiefly intellectual rather than broadly popular appeal. By the 1960s, however, Hinduism in various organizational manifestations had begun to make converts among young middle-class Americans, and by the 1970s this ancient religion of India also had a major Asian population to minister to in America. With a growing number of emigrants from India in this country (over one-half million by 1985), Hinduism will continue to be the principal vehicle by which an entire cultural tradition is transmitted to the Western Hemisphere. But other religious traditions derived from India, namely Jainism (which is ancient) and Sikhism (which is relatively recent) also transport the culture of the mother country to the adopted one. It may take centuries,

97. This lovely mosque in Plainfield, Indiana, serves as host to the Muslim Student Association of the United States and Canada. *Islamic Society of North America*

however, before either Buddhism or Hinduism is truly acculturated in a land whose religious heritage is so markedly different.

Less "foreign" in a religious sense, Islam may be able to adjust more quickly. This Near Eastern religion, arising from the same soil as Judaism and Christianity, honors many of the same prophets, is a "religion of the book" in a manner similar to that of its better known predecessors. Though a vigorously missionary religion in its speedy conquests from the seventh century onward, Islam has not been notably "evangelical" in North America, except for the special case of the Black Muslims. The latter group, not wholly orthodox from the Islamic point of view, may perhaps be best thought of as more anti-Christian than pro-Moslem. Among white Americans, conversion has come about chiefly through intermarriage. Again it was immigration that gave this religion a significant and enduring presence in North America, with the number of adherents by the end of the 1980s being somewhere between two and three million. A beautiful Islamic center was erected in Washington, D. C., in 1952, with thirty more such centers being created by 1990. An Islamic Society of North America, formed in 1982, served especially the students and former students living in the United States. And an American Islamic College, established in Chicago in 1983, offered for the first time in this country the opportunity for systematic study of Islamic thought and culture. Such was vital if for no other reason than not permitting the Ayatollah Khomeini of Iran to represent the whole of a religious tradition that stretches all the way from Indonesia in the east to Morocco in the west.

Once this was a land of tribal religions whose origins are hidden from history. Then, it became noticeably Protestant, then Protestant and Catholic, then Protestant and Catholic and Jewish and Eastern Orthodox. Then Christianity and Judaism found themselves joined by emissaries from the ancient East, most conspicuously Buddhism and Hinduism—each with a sectarian variety that could match almost anything that Protestantism had ever been able to offer. Then the religion of Muhammed, "the last of the prophets," made its way as well to American shores. Pluralism had become the hardy perennial of the American garden.

If alive today, Peter Stuyvesant of old New York would probably resist that overly lush garden growth. William Penn of his own colony would probably accept it. John Humphrey Noyes of Vermont would probably rejoice in it. Lyman Beecher of Connecticut would probably be horrified by it. Thomas Jefferson of Virginia would probably try to reform it. Alexis De Tocqueville of France would probably try to explain it, and Philip Schaff of Germany would probably try to unify it. All those options—and more—still remain.

Suggested Reading for Part Five

For primary sources relevant to the material covered in Chapters Twenty-Two through Twenty-Four, see the Gaustad *Documentary*, Vol. 2, Chaps. 11–12. For appropriate primary material related to the Supreme Court, one may turn to the relevant volumes of the *U. S. Reports* themselves (published by the U. S. Government Printing Office) as well as to the valuable *Landmark Briefs* (Frederick, Md.), an ongoing series edited by Gerhard Casper and Philip Kurland and found in most major libraries. Supreme Court decisions are generally written in an effort to educate and persuade; therefore they avoid highly technical or forbidding language, and the student should not hesitate to turn to them directly. Authoritative guidance through this maze is provided by John T. Noonan, Jr., in his remarkable study, *The Believer and the Powers that Are* (New York, 1987).

On "free exercise" issues generally, see Dean Kelley, ed., *Government Intervention in Religious Affairs* (New York, 1982); and, Milton R. Konvitz, *Religious Liberty and Conscience* (New York, 1968). The 1940s episode involving Jehovah's Witnesses and the American flag is covered in illuminating detail by David R. Manwaring in his *Render Unto Caesar: The Flag Salute Controversy* (Chicago, 1962). Sunday laws and Sunday cases may be examined in, among other places, the many books by Leo Pfeffer: for example, *Church, State, and Freedom* (2d ed., Boston, 1967); *God, Caesar, and the Constitution* (Boston, 1975); and, *Religion, State and the Burger Court* (Buffalo, 1985). Excellent background for the conscientious objection issue that became so heated in the early 1970s may be found in Peter Brock's *Pacifism in the United States* (Princeton, N.J., 1968), but the specific cases mentioned in Chapter Twenty-Two remain the very best sources for the student.

Issues raised in the general area of religion and the public schools are explored from a variety of perspectives in the volume edited by Theodore R. Sizer, *Religion and Public Education* (Boston, 1967). The best historical background is provided by Robert S. Michaelsen, *Piety in the Public School* (New York, 1970). With respect specifically to the matter of prayer and Bible reading, see these informative studies: David L. Barr and Nicholas Piediscalzi, eds., *The Bible in American Education* (Chico, Calif., 1982); Donald E. Boles, *The Bible, Religion and the Public Schools* (Ames, Iowa, 1965); and, John H. Laubach, *School Prayers: Congress, the Courts, and the Public* (Washington, D.C., 1969). Creationism has received much recent attention; see, for example, Marcel C. LaFollette, ed., *Creationism, Science, and the Law* (Cambridge, Mass., 1983); and, Dorothy Nelkin, *The Creation Controversy: Science or Scripture in the Schools* (Boston, 1984).

With respect to the parochial schools where the concerns are chiefly monetary ones, see Donald A. Erickson, ed., *Public Controls for Nonpublic Schools* (Chicago, 1969); George R. La Noue, *Educational Vouchers: Concepts and Controversies* (New York, 1972); Marvin Schick, ed., *Governmental Aid to Parochial Schools—How Far?* (New York, 1968); and, Daniel J. Sullivan, *Public Aid to Nonpublic Schools* (Lexington, Mass., 1974). Since the Roman Catholic church has by far the largest system of parochial education in the United States, the literature with respect to that one institution is voluminous. The following titles are representative: Virgil C. Blum, *Catholic Education: Survival or Demise?* (Chicago, 1969); Daniel J. Callahan, ed., *Federal Aid and Catholic Schools* (Baltimore, Md., 1964); George A. Kelly, ed., *Government Aid to Nonpublic Schools: Yes or No?* (New York, 1972); and a valuable documentary history edited by Neil G. McCluskey, *Catholic Education in America* (New York, 1964).

On those most sensitive matters of life and death, one may turn to such recent works as these: John T. Noonan, *A Private Choice: Abortion in America in the Seventies* (New York, 1979); Daniel Callahan, *Abortion: Law, Choice and Morality* (New York, 1972); David M. Feldman, *Birth Control in Jewish Law* (New York, 1968); Beverly W. Harrison, *Our Right to Choose: Toward a New Ethic of Abortion* (Boston, 1985); Kristin Luker, *Abortion and the Politics of Motherhood* (Berkeley, Calif., 1984); Norman St. John-Stevas, *The Agonizing Choice: Birth Control, Religion and the Law* (Bloomington, Ill., 1971); and, Daniel C. Maguire, *Death by Choice* (New York, 1974).

The civil rights movement, along with religion's involvement at several levels, may be explored through biographical studies of key figures as well as in a topical fashion. Martin Luther King, Jr., is the subject of these recent books: Stephen B. Oates, *Let the Trumpet Sound* (New York, 1982); David L. Lewis, *King: A Critical Biography* (New York, 1970); and a useful compilation of King's major writings, edited by James M. Washington, *A Testament of Hope* (San Francisco, 1986). On the Hispanic emergence within Roman Catholicism, see the July/August 1980 issue of the *New Catholic World* as well as the National Catholic Documentary Series, September 11, 1980, "The U. S. Church's Hispanic Catholics." The latest treatment of the Indians and their encounters with the law is David F. Aberle, *Peyote Religion Among the Navaho* (Chicago, 1982).

The many new developments with respect to women and religion should be explored first on the level of language: Phyllis Trible, *God and the Rhetoric of Sexuality* (Philadelphia, 1978). Then one may move on to the even more troublesome questions of authority and ordination. In that regard, the broadest coverage is given in Rosemary Radford Ruether and Eleanor McLaughlin, eds., *Women of Spirit: Female Leadership in the Jewish and Christian Traditions* (New York, 1979). But also see these treatments from within a more restricted denominational frame: Richard L. Greaves, ed., *Triumph Over Silence: Women in Protestant History* (Westport, Conn., 1985); Sally Priesand, *Judaism and the New Woman* (New York, 1975); Blu Greenberg, *On Women and Judaism* (Philadelphia, 1981); Sarah Bentley Doely, *Women's Liberation and the Church* (New York, 1970); and Sonia Johnson, *From Housewife to Heretic* (New York, 1981).

For the far-reaching implications of liberation theology, one may begin with the two best known Latin American exponents thereof: Gustavo Gutiérrez, *A Theology of Liberation* (Maryknoll, N.Y., 1973), and Leonardo Boff, *Liberation Theology: From Dialogue to Confrontation* (San Francisco, 1986). A broad survey edited by L. Dale Richesin and Brian Mahan will prove useful: *The Challenge of Liberation Theology* (Maryknoll, N.Y., 1981); also, Robert M. Brown, *Theology in a New Key: Responding to Themes of Liberation* (New York, 1978). With specific reference to the adaptation of this perspective by blacks, see Gayraud S. Wilmore and James H. Cone, eds., *Black Theology: A Documentary History, 1966–1979* (Maryknoll, N.Y., 1979).

The ecumenical movement has been briefly but helpfully surveyed in William G. Rusch, *Ecumenism—A Movement Toward Church Unity* (Philadelphia, 1985). Many valuable documents on the Roman Catholic side may be consulted in Thomas F. Stransky, C. S. P., and John B. Sheerin, C. S. P., eds., *Doing the Truth in Charity* (New York, 1982). Also see Harding Meyer and Lukas Vischer, eds., *Growth in Agreement: Reports and Agreed Statements of Ecumenical Conversations on a World Level* (New York, 1984); Ernst Lange, *And Yet It Moves: Dream and Reality of the Ecumenical Movement* (Grand Rapids, Mich., 1979); Paul A. Crow, Jr., *Christian Unity: A Matrix for Mission* (New York, 1982); and, Peter von der Osten-Sacken, *Christian-Jewish Dialogue: Theological Foundations* (Philadelphia, 1986).

Catholic difficulties with or challenges to authority can be followed in such books as these: Daniel Berrigan, *The Trial of the Catonsville Nine* (Boston, 1970); William H. Shannon, *The Lively Debate: Response to Humane Vitae* (New York, 1970); and, William W. May, ed., *Vatican Authority and American Catholic Dissent: The Curran Case and Its Consequences* (New York, 1987). The Lutheran Church-Missouri Synod tribulations receive careful explication in James E. Adams, *Preus of Missouri and the Great Lutheran Civil War* (New York, 1977); for the somewhat similar struggles within the Southern Baptist Convention, see Joe E. Barnhart, *The Southern Baptist Holy War* (Austin, Tex., 1986). On the major evangelists of the 1980s, see among many other possibilities these books: Jeffrey Hadden and Charles E. Swann, *Prime-Time Preachers: The Rising Power of Televangelism* (Reading, Mass., 1981); Jerry Sholes, *Give Me That Prime Time Religion* (New York, 1979); David E. Harrell, Jr., *Pat Robertson* (San Francisco, 1988); Joe E. Barnhart, *Jim and Tammy: Charismatic Intrigue Inside PTL* (Buffalo, 1988); and, a much more sympathetic treatment of the whole enterprise before the major scandals broke, Ben Armstrong, *The Electronic Church* (Nashville, 1979).

For Paul Tillich's theology and its facets, great assistance is provided in C. W. Kegley and R. W. Bretall, eds., *The Theology of Paul Tillich* (New York, 1952). On Harvey Cox's enormously popular book, see Daniel Callahan, ed., *The Secular City Debate* (New York, 1966). For the death of God group, J. L. Ice and J. J. Carey have edited the principal reactions in *The Death of God Debate* (Philadelphia, 1967). One way of seeing how far old fundamentalism has come in moving toward new evangelicalism is to follow the story of Fuller Theological Seminary (Pasadena, California) as told by George M. Marsden, *Reforming Fundamentalism* (Grand Rapids, Mich., 1987); in this same connection, see the fine book by Mark Noll, *Between Faith and Criticism* (San Francisco, 1986).

On the new Christian Right and American politics, the options are many. Richard Pierard in *The Unequal Yoke* (Philadelphia, 1970) argues that political leaders have had more influence on religious leaders than vice-versa. Two books suggest that the impact of this new alliance may have been exaggerated: Anson D. Shupe and William A. Stacey, *Born Again Politics and the Moral Majority* (New York, 1982); and, Samuel S. Hill and Dennis E. Owen, *The New Religious-Political Right in America* (Nashville, 1982). Also see Erling Jorstad, *The Politics of Moralism: The New Christian Right in America* (Minneapolis, 1981) along with Peggy L. Shriver, *The Bible Vote: Religion and the New Right* (New York, 1981). The most recent volume (and a valuable one) treating this tangled thicket is that edited by Mark Noll, *Religion and American Politics* (New York, 1989).

The Jonestown tragedy has been examined from a variety of viewpoints. The following accounts should be noted: George Klineman et al., *The Cult that Died* (New York, 1980); M. S. Yee et al., *In My Father's House* (New York, 1981); and, James Reston, Jr., *Our Father Who Art in Hell* (New York, 1981). The Unification Church has received so much comment that we now have an entire bibliography on that subject alone: namely, Michael L. Mickler, *The Unification Church: A Bibliography and Research Guide* (New York, 1987). (Under the general editorship of J. Gordon Melton, the Garland Publishing Company is issuing other "Bibliographies on Sects and Cults in America.") Background on "early

Rajneesh" is available in Bernard Gunther, *Dying for Enlightenment: Living with Bhagwan Shree Rajneesh* (San Francisco, 1979), but for later developments see the two excellent articles in *The New Yorker* by Frances FitzGerald, September 22 and 29, 1986; as well as *Golden Guru* (Lexington, Mass., 1988) by James S. Gordon.

On the mood of the early 1980s, a more general study by G. Bromley and A. D. Shupe, Jr., is most revealing: *Strange Gods: The Great American Cult Scare* (Boston, 1982). On Buddhism in America, see Rick Fields, *How the Swans Came to the Lake: A Narrative History of Buddhism in America* (Boulder, Colo., 1981). For Hinduism and other religions of India, two more general books will be useful: Robert S. Ellwood, Jr., *Alternative Altars: Unconventional and Eastern Spirituality in America* (Chicago, 1979); and, Thomas Robbins and Dick Anthony, eds., *In Gods We Trust: New Patterns of Religious Pluralism in America* (New Brunswick, N.J., 1980). For Islam, the edited work by Earle H. Waugh and others is the best source: *The Muslim Community in North America* (Lincoln, Nebr., 1983). And for learning how to cope with if not rejoice in pluralism's lush growth, one can do no better than turn to Martin E. Marty's *Religion and the Republic: The American Circumstance* (Boston, 1987).

BIBLIOGRAPHY

Since most relevant titles have been listed in the five Suggested Reading sections, this general bibliography will be limited to only the most significant works of reference. For bibliographical assistance, the two-volume compilation of Nelson R. Burr, *A Critical Bibliography of Religion in America* (Princeton, N.J., 1961) remains indispensable, even if now somewhat dated. Ernest R. Sandeen and Frederick Hale provided an update in their *American Religion and Philosophy* (Detroit, 1978) that also has the distinct advantage of three separate indexes: by author, title, and subject. Even more recent is the two-volume work edited by John F. Wilson, *Church and State in America: A Bibliographical Guide* (Greenwood, Conn., 1986, 1987); despite the limitation implied by the title, the church-state dimension is interpreted with such breadth as to encompass much of American religion in general. The resources in this field have been most recently described in Anne T. Fraker, ed. *Religion and American Life* (Urbana, Ill., 1989).

Charles H. Lippy and Peter W. Williams edited an enormously valuable three-volume *Encyclopedia of the American Religious Experience* (New York, 1988) that brings the expertise of many contributors to bear upon the subject. This invaluable reference work is made far more useful by a 113-page index that, unlike many indexes, is easy to read and a model of clarity. On religious groups in America, one may consult J. Gordon Melton, *Encyclopedia of American Religions* (2d ed., Detroit, 1987).

For geographical assistance in examining religion in America, see Edwin S. Gaustad, *Historical Atlas of Religion in America* (rev. ed., New York, 1976) as well as an atlas of the modern period only, Jackson W. Carroll et al., *Religion in America, 1950 to the Present* (San Francisco, 1979). Biographical guidance may be found in Henry W. Bowden, *Dictionary of American Religious Biography* (Greenwood, Conn., 1977).

One is never fully abreast of American religion, of course, since the changes never stop, but only intensify in pace. To help in keeping current, one may turn to the annual Gallup Reports on "Religion in America," these reports being issued by the American Institute of Public Opinion in Princeton, New Jersey. A *Yearbook of American and Canadian Churches*, published and distributed by Abingdon Press of Nashville, Tennessee, also assists in keeping up to date. Beyond that, for the latest books in the field, one should consult such quarterly periodicals as these: *Religious Studies Review, Church History, Catholic Historical Review*, and *American Jewish History*. Beginning in 1988, the American Academy of Religion together with the Society of Biblical Literature have issued an annual *Critical Review of Books in Religion* that will also prove invaluable.

Index